THE MORAL QUEST

FOUNDATIONS OF CHRISTIAN ETHICS

STANLEY J. GRENZ

InterVarsity Press
Downers Grove, Illinois

InterVarsity Press
P.O. Box 1400, Downers Grove, IL 60515-1426
World Wide Web: www.ivpress.com
E-mail: mail@ivpress.com

InterVarsity Press® is the book-publishing division of InterVarsity Christian Fellowship/USA®, a student movement active on campus at hundreds of universities, colleges and schools of nursing in the United States of America, and a member movement of the International Fellowship of Evangelical Students. For information about local and regional activities, write Public Relations Dept., InterVarsity Christian Fellowship/USA, 6400 Schroeder Rd., P.O. Box 7895, Madison, WI 53707-7895.

ISBN 0-8308-1568-6

Printed in the United States of America ∞

Library of Congress Cataloging-in-Publication Data

Grenz, Stanley, 1950-
The moral quest: foundations of Christian ethics/Stanley J. Grenz.
p. cm.
Includes bibliographical references.
ISBN 0-8308-1568-6 (pbk.: alk. paper)
1. Christian ethics. I. Title.
BJ1251.G75 1997
241—dc21 *97-28853*

20 19 18 17 16 15 14 13 12 11 10 9 8 7 6 5 4 3 2 1
16 15 14 13 12 11 10 09 08 07 06 05 04 03 02 01 00

To Dr. Vernon C. Grounds
pilgrim on the moral quest
stalwart example of Christian integrity

Preface

In him we were also chosen . . . in order that we . . .
might be for the praise of his glory.
(EPHESIANS 1:11-12)

When I entered the fifth grade in the fall of 1960, I encountered a major ethical problem: gym class included a unit on square dancing. The dilemma was quickly resolved when my father (who was also my pastor) sent a note to my teacher requesting that I be exempted on the basis that such worldly practices were "against our religion." Being privileged to watch comfortably from the sidelines as the other children awkwardly learned how to "swing yer partner" made me the envy of all the boys in my class.

In high school, however, I was the one doing the envying. The religious ban meant that I couldn't accompany my friends to the school dances. And even if I had, I wouldn't have known what to do when I got there. Fortunately for my social life, the prohibitions did get lifted in another area. Unlike my older brother, who'd had to content himself with the television set, I could go to movies.

Maybe it was that early quandary over dancing that did it; in any case, from childhood on I have engaged in ethical reflection. Even before I knew what the word *ethics* meant, I was asking the central ethical questions: What does it mean to live as Jesus' disciple? Are Christians to be known by what we *don't* do? For as long as I can remember, I have always thought about, and talked about, the moral issues of the day. Yet it wasn't until I was in my twenties that a more conscious interest in the subject itself was sparked. My philosophy major included a course in the history of ethics. And the M.Div. program at Denver Seminary contained a similar requirement in Christian ethics.

Five years after graduating from seminary, I joined the faculty at the

North American Baptist Seminary in Sioux Falls, South Dakota (1981). Just before I arrived, the school voted a new requirement: all M.Div. students were to take an ethics course. But no one on the faculty was academically qualified to teach the subject. Because I had at least a limited background in the field—"and after all, your doctorate was in systematic theology," the dean added—the task fell to me. Now for the first time I began to take ethics seriously as a discipline within the theological curriculum. *The Moral Quest* is the result of the subsequent fifteen-plus years of teaching ethics.

So this book is an ethics text. More specifically, it is a statement of *theological* ethics. As such, it attempts to lay a foundation for Christian ethical living.

At first glance, exploring the realm of ethics may appear daunting. In a sense, however, the subject of the volume is as much of an "old friend" to you as it is to me. To live here below is to face questions of ethics continually. And to be human entails engaging in the moral quest. But more important, as those who participate in the Christian community, we are concerned to be a holy people, those whose lives are pleasing to our God and Savior. This concern lies behind the writing of *The Moral Quest* and, I hope, your interest in reading it as well.

The embeddedness of this book in the Christian community explains the unabashedly Christian focus found in its pages. My overarching goal is to develop a foundation for the specifically Christian vision of the moral life, but to do so conscious of the traditional dialogue of Christian ethics with philosophy, as well as the contemporary context in which we seek to live as God's people. My basic conclusion is that the Christian ethic is the outworking in life of the theological vision disclosed in and through the narrative given to us in Scripture. This narrative speaks about the triune God of love who stands as the transcendent foundation for human living. The Bible calls us to imitate Christ, who is the revelation of the loving God, because in so doing we fulfill our purpose, which is to be the image of God. And the biblical narrative speaks about the Holy Spirit, who as the concretization of the divine love is poured out on the believing community to transform us into Christlikeness, and hence leads us to embody the comprehensive love that characterizes God's own life.

As this book finds its way into print, I realize again the great debt of gratitude I owe to many people: to the folks at InterVarsity Press, who over the last decade have become not only professional associates but also personal friends; to Professor Steve Wilkens for his helpful comments arising out of a careful reading of an earlier draft; to the administration and staff at Carey Theological College, who since 1990 have given me a supportive context for teaching and writing; to my excellent teaching assistant Paul Chapman for his helpful work on the project, especially in checking bibliographic references and completing the index; to students at NABS (where I taught from 1981 to 1990), at Carey/Regent College (my academic home since 1990) and more recently at Northern Baptist Seminary in Lombard, Illinois, for offering a challenging forum for the ideas presented here; and to my family, who are not only spouse and children to me but also sisters and brother in Christ and copilgrims in the quest to live out the Christian ethical life.

Vernon Grounds was president of Denver Conservative Baptist Seminary during my student days in the 1970s. Since my graduation he has been an ongoing supporter of my work. Yet my experience with Dr. Grounds is not unique. A vast number of people—students, colleagues and friends—bear witness to his keen interest in their lives. But most of all, Dr. Grounds has stood as an example to us all of the deeply felt piety and uncompromising integrity that lie at the apex of the Christian moral quest. Therefore, out of a deep sense of personal gratitude but also on behalf of the many others who have been touched by this modern-day saint, I joyously dedicate this book to Dr. Vernon Grounds.

Soon after joining the NABS faculty, I was privileged to meet Professor James Gustafson at the midwest regional meeting of the American Academy of Religion. Feeling that I lacked the educational credentials to teach ethics alongside of systematic theology, I approached Professor Gustafson with the idea of doing a second doctorate with him. In response, he matter-of-factly stated that I should write a book instead. At long last, I have been able to act on his advice.

Soli Deo Gloria

Introduction

CHRISTIAN ETHICS IN A TRANSITIONAL AGE

As obedient children, do not conform to the evil desires you had when you lived in ignorance. But just as he who called you is holy, so be holy in all you do; for it is written: "Be holy, because I am holy."
(1 PETER 1:14-16)

We are all ethicists. Each day of our lives we face decisions about how we should live. As we do so, we realize that many of the choices we make are not devoid of significance. Rather, we know that somehow and in some way what we do matters. In short, we are continually making decisions that are ethical in nature.

Not only do we sense that we are ethicists, we often feel as if we are being swamped with ethical questions coming at us from every direction. We can't look at the "news" without being bombarded with stories of situations that are ultimately ethical. A recent front page of the local newspaper in a large North American city featured stories about elected officials receiving two pensions, a former evangelical pastor who was dying of AIDS, a political party that had to decide whether to nominate a self-proclaimed witch to run for public office and a scandal involving a well-known sports figure.

Often more excruciating than the "big" issues of the day, however, are the multitudes of ethical questions we must personally process. We are inundated with situations that raise questions about our own lives and our own selves. We continually ask, What should I do in this situation? How should I act? How will this affect who I am? Am I pleased with who I am becoming?

Indeed, to live is to face ethical challenges. So widespread today is the sense that ethical orientations matter that how we respond to moral questions has become the concern of the pollsters. For example, the November 1994 Maclean's/CTV poll of Canadians, published in the January 2, 1995, issue of the magazine, included a section on ethics. Readers were quizzed about a gamut of issues, ranging from cheating on exams to cheating on taxes and cheating on one's spouse. The findings appeared to bring out the moralist sentiments of even the reporter. In the overline to his article he cited one expert who bemoaned that "Canada . . . is becoming 'a nation of greedy, amoral self-promoters.'"[1]

The ethical questions we raise are not always easy to answer. Recently an Anglican priest quipped, "We are bombarded with a host of problems. Every problem that comes our way has an answer which is simple, easy to understand, and *wrong.*"

Knowing this, we can sympathize with Charlie Brown. The baseball game was nearly over. The comic-strip character was getting ready to pitch the final "out." Then Lucy sauntered to the mound. "If you strike out this last guy, Charlie Brown," she said, "you're going to make him very, very unhappy."

By this time, Linus had joined the party. "That's right," he agreed. "Are you sure you want to bring unexpected grief into that poor kid's life?"

Faced with the burden posed by these questions, the hapless pitcher sighed, "Just what I need—ninth inning ethics."

So often we sense that it is the ninth inning. We find ourselves tossed to and fro, pulled here and there by the barrage of questions coming our way. We are burdened by the quandaries life poses. We grow weary from the situations we face. All we want to do is strike out the last player and go home. But once again we are confronted by "ninth inning ethics."

The Ethical Challenge and the Contemporary World

In some respects, the challenge we face is not new. Throughout history people have struggled with ethical questions. In fact, certain ethical issues are perennial. Some of these arise out of social life itself. Humans have always asked, How can we get along with each other? How should we conduct ourselves as we live together? What constitutes proper behavior in social groupings or societies? Other issues are connected with the purpose of life. Since ancient times humans have wondered, What is the "good life"? And how do we best pursue it?

In this sense, then, we are no different from people in other times and other places. To be human means to be confronted by the ethical challenge. Yet, in another sense, we do face a unique challenge. We live at a time in which the ethical life is especially difficult to determine, let alone follow. There is something urgent about our situation.

Our difficulty arises in part from the nature of our contemporary situation. Under the banner of the Enlightenment project, modern science has placed in our hands capabilities that have aggravated long-standing ethical problems as well as introduced new quandaries. Take abortion, for example. Rather than being invented in the late twentieth century, as some people assume, abortion was practiced in the ancient Roman Empire. But modern medical advances have added new moral spins to this practice. Our ability to alert a pregnant woman to the presence of certain fetal disorders prior to birth has augmented the contexts in which would-be parents might consider the "abortion option."

A few years ago, a friend of mine learned through amniocentesis that the child his wife was expecting would be born with spinal bifida. Several members of the medical team immediately advised them to abort the fetus. These people could not understand the couple's decision to give birth to and then raise the child.

Euthanasia provides another example. The idea of "death with dignity" was not coined in our day. But this ancient discussion carries weighty implications when the majority of deaths occur in health-care institutions, when the population is aging rapidly and when politicians are confronted with the limits of funding for health care. We can only wonder if the day is quickly coming when the specter of scarce medical resources will preclude both the choice of giving birth to a child with major medical problems and the possibility of electing to stay alive after being diagnosed with a terminal illness.

Genetic engineering, which forms a third example, was catapulted into the public limelight several years ago by the box-office hit "Jurassic Park." Of course, selective breeding is as old as Jacob's experimentation with Laban's flocks. Yet the mapping of the genetic structures of plants, animals and even humans places a new complexity on old ethical questions. Hailed as a solution for childless couples and promising to eradicate genetic diseases, mastery over the human genetic structure has also introduced new dilemmas—fetal experimentation, to name only one. And imminent discoveries in the field now raise the specter of a super race, for they offer the potential to accomplish what Hitler could only dream about.

The ethical challenge is acute today for a second reason. We are being confronted with a host of questions that our forebears simply did not face. The list is endless. They range from "Who legally owns genetic material once it has been donated for scientific research?"[2] to "Should postmenopausal women be allowed to give birth?"

The nuclear age provides a perhaps even more obvious example. When it was developed in the 1940s, nuclear weaponry was hailed as a way of cutting short a lengthy and costly war. But after the "war to make the world safe for democracy" was won, an entire generation endured the threat of a nuclear Armageddon. In the postwar era, nuclear energy was marketed to a consumer-driven society as the answer to dwindling energy supplies. Since then, however, we have been alerted to the disconcerting truth that nuclear technology produces waste products which will pose health and environmental threats for generations to come.

These situations suggest that the uniqueness of our situation is largely linked to technology. We live in a technological world. Technology has been hailed as a new god, as the key that will unlock human happiness and usher in the utopian society. But while technological advances have given us an unparalleled standard of living, we are also discovering that technology also has a downside—to the extent that its misuse carries the potential of jeopardizing life itself on this planet.

One additional factor contributes to the uniqueness of our situation. We are living in the midst of a crisis in morality. These grave ethical questions challenge us at a time when our society seems to have lost its ethical moorings. Since the Enlightenment, Western society has never been able to boast ethical unanimity. Nevertheless, in the past—until a generation or so ago—some semblance of agreement over certain guiding principles reigned, at least within the wider population. And this "agreement" was based, however loosely, on the ethical traditions of the Bible. That moral consensus, however, has been thoroughly eroded.

The erosion of the older consensus roughly parallels another phenomenon that Christians must take seriously: the declining influence of the church in Western society. So widespread is this decline that many people speak of a "post-Christian" world, perhaps better called a "post-Christendom" world.[3] No longer does Christianity—whether in its doctrinal content or its ethical principles—exercise an all-pervasive influence on society's self-understanding or sense of purpose.[4]

In addition, we appear to be in the throes of a broader cultural transition. We are forsaking the modern era, embedded as it was in the quest for the one, overarching, supracultural truth, including the search for the one, universal ethic. We are embarking on the uncharted waters of postmodernism. In this changing sea, the modern goal no longer provides a fixed point of reference—even if only theoretically—from which to track our course.

In short, we are confronted by the greatest issues humankind has ever faced at a time when the moral fiber of our society appears to be at its weakest. Ethical questions are assaulting us at breakneck speed at a time when people have lost their sense of mooring, their sense of stability and their sense of possessing some platform on which to stand as they make moral decisions.

Yet even when the sky is the darkest a ray of light emerges. Although clouds threaten the moral stability of our society, there are signs that people are beginning to yearn for an ethical foundation for life. For many the quest for an ethic amidst the moral morass has gained a new sense of urgency.

The Ethical Challenge and the Christian

We are all ethicists. We all face ethical questions, and these questions are of grave importance. As Christians, we know why this is so: We live out our days in the presence of God. And this God has preferences. God desires that we live a certain way, while disapproving of other ways in which we might choose to live.

Although everyone lives "before God," many people are either ignorant of or chose to ignore this situation. As Christians, in contrast, we readily acknowledge our standing before God. We know that we are responsible to a God who is holy. Not only can God have no part in sin, the God of the Bible must banish sinful creatures from his presence. Knowing this, we approach life as the serious matter that it is. How we live *is* important. Our choices and actions make a difference; they count for eternity! Therefore, we realize that seeking to live as ethical Christians is no small task.

Nor can we treat the ethical life merely as an individual project. As Christians, we know that we cannot live in isolation from each other. On the contrary, the New Testament clearly teaches that each of us is part of the other. We are a community. More specifically, we are a community under God. This means that together we are responsible to be "holy unto the Lord." We know that our life together ought to reflect the divine character. We are to show what it means to be a fellowship of people whose relationships have been transformed by God's own power. For this reason, not only the decisions we make but the very people we are becoming and the way we live as Christ's disciples is crucial.

We are also a community in the world. Of course, we are responsible before God to be a distinctive community—the people of God. But in our quest to be "separate from the world" we dare not hide in a little Christian enclave. Instead, God calls us to live out our community life in the midst of the world around us. Our mission includes reaching out to and in the name of Christ ministering to people outside our fellowship.

This, then, is our ethical challenge: to be Christians individually and corporately in the specific context in which God has placed us. Our task is to declare the word of God by what we say and how we live. We are to announce and to embody God's will and purposes in the various situations that come our way. This means responding to the crucial issues we face by drawing upon the resources of the Christian faith, so that God might be glorified in our world.

To live as Christians in the contemporary situation requires that we engage with that situation. Such engagement involves a threefold activity that we might summarize with the words *attuning, analyzing* and *applying*.

Engagement with our contemporary situation begins with *attuning*. To speak and embody the word of God in our world, we must become aware of the ethical dimensions of the context in which we live. To this end, we must be a people who listen. We cannot stick our heads ostrich-style into some "holy sand," thinking the world will go away. Instead, we must put our ear to the ground. We must become aware of the depth of the ethical challenges we—and people in our world—face. This listening, however, must engage minds and hearts that are not merely attuned to the world. They must also be attuned to Christ. We must listen to our world through the ears of our Master.

Attuning naturally leads to *analyzing*. To analyze means to seek out the central issue. It involves burrowing beneath the periphery of each situation so as to pierce to its core. When we analyze, we raise the question, What moral principle is at stake here? This requires that we differentiate between the genuine ethical problem that demands our attention and what may merely be our own negative emotional reaction to certain aspects of the situation, a reaction that may be culturally determined.

I remember the day when our thirteen-year-old son declared, "I want to get my ear pierced." When *I* was a teenager, a pierced ear carried a certain message involving ethical overtones. But because this is not the case in my son's world, to respond to his request I needed to set aside my initial emotional reaction. The crucial question was: Is there an actual *ethical* issue at stake here?

To engage in genuine analysis, we need the wisdom and discernment that God provides in response to our prayers.

The process of attuning and analyzing ought to inaugurate the dynamic of *applying*. Our goal is to apply the resources of the faith to the situation at hand. To this end, we must constantly ask, How do the insights we glean from the heritage of our Christian community, as well as the various aspects of our commitment as Christians, assist us in living in this specific context? How do these resources provide direction to us today?

This focus on applying leads to a foundational thesis: *Ethics is theology in action*. Or to turn the statement around, theology is the foundational resource for ethics. Ultimately, ethical living means ordering our steps in every situation of life according to the fundamental faith commitments we share as Christians. It involves putting into practice—living out in the day-to-day realities of our lives—our foundational Christian commitments. And in the end, these commitments are theological.

Ethical living, therefore, entails being conscious of what we have come to believe about God, ourselves and our world, and then acting on the basis of these convictions. It means living conscious of who the triune God is, who I am, who we are as God's people, and what God's program for creation is. Therefore, as we are challenged by ethical questions—what should I (or we) be or do? how should I (or we) live?—we must return to the foundational question—what does it mean to live according to our Christian faith commitments in this situation? what response in this context would be most in keeping with who God is, who we are, and what God's purposes are? To show why this is the case and what this means is the goal of the following chapters.

The first chapter places our search for the Christian ethic in the context of the broader human ethical quest. Our goal here is to summarize the discussion of ethics found within the broader Western philosophical tradition and to show that inaugurating the human ethical quest with reason leads us inevitably back to our starting point. While foundational to all that follows, chapter one is perhaps the most difficult to comprehend. If you find this to be the case, take heart, knowing that many of the difficulties will be illuminated and clarified as you move through subsequent chapters. You may even want to breeze through chapter one quickly at first and then return to it after you have completed reading the book.

The second chapter outlines five major Greek ethical systems that have been influential not only on the Western philosophical tradition in general but also on Christian ethics. In chapter three we turn our attention to the central themes of the biblical vision of the ethical life before perusing three paradigmatic ethical proposals found within the Christian tradition (chapter four) and seven trajectories of contemporary Christian ethical thought (chapter five).

This historical groundwork provides the foundation for setting forth a proposal for a Christian theological ethic. Chapter six moves us more explicitly into the postmodern context, calling for an ethic of integrity while raising the question as to how the revealed ethic of the Christian faith intersects with the moral quest of people around us. With chapter seven we come, as it were, to the heart of the book. Here we lay out the theological foundations upon which the Christian vision of the moral quest is built. This leads us finally to chapter eight, which presents the actual content of the Christian vision—comprehensive love. In the end, therefore, the moral quest leads to the task of reflecting in our relationships the love that lies at the heart of the biblical God. To show why this is the case is the task of the following chapters.

Chapter 1

Christian Ethics & the Ethical Task

So do not worry, saying "What shall we eat?" or "What shall we drink?" or "What shall we wear?" For the pagans run after all these things, and your heavenly Father knows that you need them. But seek first his kingdom and his righteousness, and all these things will be given to you as well.
(MATTHEW 6:31-33)

A man sits in the holding cell on death row. Once a revered teacher, he has fallen into official public disgrace, for he has been convicted of corrupting the minds of the youth of the city and of not believing in the gods the city acknowledges.[1] While waiting for the day when he will be required to carry out the sentence of the court—suicide by drinking poison—the convicted felon receives a visit from a dear friend. The visitor reveals a bold rescue plan several of his supporters have hatched. The conspirators will bribe the guards, free their beloved teacher from the prison cell and whisk him off to a foreign city where he can continue his career. The visitor pleads with the condemned man to cooperate with their scheme. But the teacher remains adamant: He will not support the plan.

The deliberations of this man mark the beginning of the intellectual discipline we now call "moral philosophy" or simply "ethics."[2] And through his illustrious student, Plato, this teacher, Socrates, became perhaps the single greatest influence on the tradition of philosophical ethics that radiated out of ancient Greece.

The Ethical Task

What is ethics? Viewed from the Christian perspective, we could answer, "Ethics is the study of how humans ought to live as informed by the Bible and Christian convictions." Yet *ethics* itself is a broader concept. The English word is the anglicized form of the Greek *ethica,* which comes from *etheos,* meaning "what relates to character."[3] The ancient Greek ethicist, Aristotle, suggested that *ethica* is derived directly from *ethos,* which means "custom" or "habit."[4]

In its more general sense, ethics is often viewed as one major branch of the broader discipline of philosophy.[5] So understood, *ethics* is regularly defined as "moral philosophy." The origin of the term *moral* is the Latin *mos* (adjective *moralis*), which like its Greek counterpart means "custom" or "usage."[6]

Some people differentiate between ethics and morality (or morals). They see the former as more theoretical or general—hence the study of the right and the good—and the latter as more specific and practical, that is, the practice or living out of what one believes to be right and good.[7] Hence *morality* involves the actual living out of one's beliefs that such things as lying and murder are wrong, whereas *ethics* entails the study of why it is that these practices are immoral. In keeping with this distinction, Wayne Meeks describes ethics as a reflective, second-order activity, as "morality rendered self-conscious."[8]

Although *ethics* and *morality* may not be completely synonymous, to set up too strict a distinction between the two is probably arbitrary.[9] As we noted above, the presence of two terms in our language reflects our dual Greek and Latin heritage. Most people tend to use the words somewhat interchangeably.

The tradition of *philosophical* ethics as we know it arose through the deliberations of Greek thinkers in the fifth century B.C., the age of Socrates, who pursued the question of the "good."[10] Specifically, they sought to determine what constitutes a good person. And in this connection they explored what ought to be considered "right." Since Socrates' day generations of philosophers have reflected on morality, moral problems and moral judgments.

The standard textbook definitions of ethics tend to combine these features. Jack Glickman, for example, describes "moral philosophy" as "a consideration of the various kinds of questions that arise in thinking about how one ought to live one's life." Glickman then explains: "We want to know, for example, which actions are right and which are wrong, which activities and goals are worthwhile and which are not, and which actions and institutions are just and which are unjust. At the same time, we especially want to find out how one can *justify* judgments about what is right, good, worthwhile, or just, and precisely what such judgments mean. We also want to know how all these various questions are interrelated. These are some of the main issues of moral philosophy."[11] In addition, moral philosophers throughout history have struggled with the issue of whether or not there is a universal morality that is binding on everyone. And they have sought to discover some wider principle on the basis of which we can justify the correctness of our moral judgments, especially in the face of differing opinions.

Viewed as "moral philosophy"—as the pursuit of questions such as these—ethics is not an exclusively Christian endeavor. One does not need to be a Christian to engage in philosophical reflection on morality. Nor does this endeavor necessarily draw primarily from Scripture or the Christian tradition. Rather, human reason stands at the center of the philosophical ethical enterprise. Ethics as moral philosophy seeks to develop a conception of the ethical life in which all humans (or humans in general) could participate and to which all humans could have access through the use of human reason. And it is especially concerned to provide a rational justification for morality,[12] perhaps in a somewhat scientific manner.[13] We call this broader project "general ethics."

In this chapter we look more closely at general ethics. Our goal is to discover whether the philosophical approach can lead us to a satisfying ethic. Can human reason provide us with a valid conception of the ethical life? And is there a universal ethic to which all people have access through reason?

Aspects of General Ethics

Many ethicists divide general ethics into three major dimensions—

empirical, normative and analytical.[14] The first aspect, empirical ethics or "descriptive morals," as the enterprise is sometimes called,[15] involves the observation of the moral decision-making process with a goal of description or explanation of the phenomena. The empirical ethicist studies how people actually make ethical decisions. This program is not of great interest to us here. We must, however, take a closer look at the other two.

Normative ethics. When we hear or use the word *ethics* we more likely have the second dimension of the ethical enterprise—normative ethics—in view. *Normative,* of course, comes from the word *norm,* which in this context means "standard" or "principle." So normative ethics is connected with the formulation of standards or principles for living. It involves assertions as to what is or is not worth pursuing and what is or is not to be done. We engage in normative ethics whenever we form opinions or judgments about what is right, good or obligatory, and whenever we offer reasons for such judgments. Such discussions lead us to what ethicists label theories of obligation. We also enter the realm of normative ethics when we describe persons, things or acts as "good" or "evil," "admirable" or "despicable." In the language of ethicists, such discussions are about theories of value.[16]

Each day we make judgments of various types. Many of these fall under the concern of normative ethics, for they reflect what we consider to be the norms or standards for human conduct.[17]

Judgments of *moral obligation,* for example, state what someone is morally obliged to do or be. These may be quite particular, referring to a specific person in a specific situation. Thus a counselor might say, "Because your duties repeatedly require you to violate your personal standards, as difficult as it may be, you really ought to resign your employment." Or such judgments may be more general, encompassing a broad range of people or situations. Hence when we say, "Honesty is the best policy," what we are likely asserting is, "People are morally obligated to tell the truth."

Unlike judgments of moral obligation, judgments of *moral value* do not declare what someone ought to do or be; rather they express what we value. If in the context of ethics I say, "My father was a good man," I am stating my conviction that he was morally upright. My declaration is an example of a particular statement of moral value. The old adage,

"Cleanliness is next to godliness," in contrast, forms a general statement of moral value. The speaker thinks that people ought to be concerned with personal hygiene and that they are morally culpable if they do not.

In addition to moral judgments like these, we all make a host of nonmoral judgments each day. They are normative; they set forth what we see as the standard. But they don't express specifically *moral* sensitivities.

Some of these statements are judgments of *nonmoral obligation.* Repeatedly we articulate particular admonitions of this type. We tell others what movies they should view ("You just have to see *Shine!*"), what clothes they should buy ("Don't wear that style; it doesn't look good on you") and so on. Or we offer judgments of a more general type. In teaching the game of football to a group of children, for example, the coach may announce, "When it's fourth down and thirty-five yards to go, you ought to punt!" In each of these cases violating the norm does not entail a *moral* failure. Nor does slavish obedience to it merit a medal for outstanding *moral* conduct. Their nonmoral nature means that such statements, while perhaps interesting, are generally not germane to ethics.

Finally we also make judgments of *nonmoral value.* I happen to own a vintage 1966 Mustang. Were I to say, "My Mustang is a good car!" this would be particular judgment of nonmoral value. Regardless of the opinions of others, *I* value this car. But in contrast to the worthiness of my father, who was an example of moral uprightness, the car's value is of a nonmoral type.

I also own a 1966 Oldsmobile convertible. Without being especially concerned about the year and make of the automobile, I might declare, "Real living is a convertible on a warm summer afternoon." This statement is a general judgment of nonmoral value, in contrast to our earlier declaration, "Cleanliness is next to godliness."

At first glance it appears that such statements, like judgments of nonmoral obligation, have nothing to do with ethics. However judgments of nonmoral value *are* of interest to us in ethics. They are connected to what people consider to be "the good life." And as we will see, the concept of the good life is crucial in ethical decision-making.

Analytical ethics. The third aspect of the ethical discipline is analytical ethics. *Analytical* derives from *analyze,* which means "to take things apart," "to look at the constituent pieces of something." Analytical ethics, therefore, "takes *ethics* apart," as it were. It explores the nature of morality itself. It attempts to develop a theory as to what value judgments mean and how they can be justified.[18]

To this end analytical ethicists pursue questions of definition: What is the distinction between *moral* and *nonmoral?* What do words such as *right, good* and *ought* mean?[19] What are we asserting when we say a person is "free" or "responsible"? Hence analytical ethicists explore questions such as: What does it mean to say something is good? On what basis can I say that the judgment "X is good" is true? But they also seek to determine how such ethical judgements can be established or justified. They raise the question, What forms the foundation for making value judgments? That is, to cite one example, on what basis can we say that the Holocaust was morally reprehensible?

Constructing a Normative Ethic of Doing

With these three aspects of the ethical discipline in view, let us now return to the second, that of normative ethics. Many ethicists see the primary focus of their work as lying here. Some are even more specific. They understand ethics primarily as the attempt to develop standards of conduct. Ethics, they argue, is concerned above all with determining what we should *do.* Consequently they propose what we might call an "ethic of doing."

Proponents of an ethic of doing often sharpen the tools of their trade by seeking the resolution of ethical quandaries. They look for "boundary situations" that seem to present the decision-maker with no ethically justifiable course of action. These situations provide the crucible in the midst of which ethicists can hone their skills.[20] This approach to ethics is sometimes called "casuistry."[21]

* * *

In Europe a woman was near death from a rare kind of cancer. The doctors knew of one drug that might save her. It had recently been discovered by a pharmacist in the same town, who was charging ten times what the drug cost him to manufacture. Although the sick woman's husband, Heinz, borrowed money from everyone he knew, he was able to bring together only half of the purchase price. He even went to the pharmacist and requested that he sell him the drug at half price or let him pay the difference later. But the pharmacist was adamant. "I discovered the drug, and I'm going to make all I can from it," he said. In his desperation, Heinz is considering breaking into the drugstore and stealing the drug.

What should Heinz do?[22]

* * *

One person who did not merely talk about boundary situations but actually faced an ethical quandary was Socrates. In his dialogue *Crito,* Socrates' pupil Plato portrayed the incident we cited at the beginning of the chapter in which the condemned philosopher converses with his friend, Crito. Socrates' response to Crito's overture set the stage for centuries of ethical reflection.

Socrates made three points. First, in response to Crito's largely emotional entreaty, he declared that ethical questions must be settled by reason alone. Second, he countered Crito's appeal to popular support for the conspiracy by asserting that ethical questions are to be answered according to the standards of the person involved, not by consideration for what others think. Third, he rejected Crito's enumeration of the good that would ensue from the conspiracy and the evils that would follow from Socrates' death, declaring that the outcome of an act is irrelevant. The only consideration is whether it is *intrinsically* right or wrong.

In this declaration Socrates delineated what has become a fundamental watershed in ethics, the differentiation between the deontological and teleological (or consequentialist) approaches to ethical decision-making. He set forth the divide between those who declare that the "right" should be done for its own sake and those who base moral duty on some "good" to be thereby attained.[23]

We may use the contemporary question of abortion to highlight the difference between deontological and teleological types of moral reasoning. A couple is in the throes of decision because amniocentesis has determined that the developing fetus has spina bifida. A first person counsels them to go to term and raise the child. "Abortion constitutes murder, and murder is wrong," she argues. A second counselor, in contrast, advises the couple to abort the fetus. "Think about what your baby can anticipate," his argument asserts. "The child will face a series of operations for the first two years of her life. She will always be confined to a wheelchair and will require constant attention. And after all this, she may only live to age six. Consider as well the amount of medical attention that will be expended on this special-needs child, medical resources that could better be spent on someone who could live a normal life."

The first counselor, following Socrates' example, has argued on the basis of a deontological understanding of ethical decision-making. The deontological approach, whose name is derived from the Greek *deon,* meaning "what is due," asks only about the intrinsic rightness or wrongness of an act. Our duty is to do that act which is intrinsically right. The second adviser followed a teleological approach (*telos* means "purpose," "goal"). Teleological reasoning focuses on the consequences of the act. Our duty is to do that act which will bring about the greatest amount of good and the least amount of evil—that act which will result in the greatest balance of good over evil.

Whenever we engage in ethical reflection ourselves or in discussions with others, we should pinpoint whether we (and those with whom we are speaking) are citing deontological or teleological arguments. Although following one approach or the other does not guarantee the outcome of one's deliberations,[24] people on opposing sides of ethical questions often talk past each other because they do not realize they are using different foundational ways of reasoning. Voices on each side of the debate find their opponents' arguments so outlandish that they wonder how any reasonable person could be persuaded by them, while their own arguments, in contrast, are almost self-evidently true. No wonder ethical issues carry the potential to polarize!

The deontological approach. Some people argue that in seeking to make judgments about the moral propriety of acts we need look no farther than the acts themselves. Morality is objective. The morality of any act resides entirely in the act; it is intrinsic and essential to the act. In this view, then, the morality of an act is in no way dependent on the intention or motive of the doer.[25] Instead, the intrinsic nature of each act determines its moral rightness or wrongness. Theories that point to something intrinsic to human actions follow what ethicists call the deontological approach to moral decision-making.

The deontological approach raises a foundational question: How can we know what aspect of the intrinsic nature of an act determines whether it is right or wrong? Although some philosophers have advocated what is often called "act-deontologism,"[26] "rule deontologism" is far more popular. This theory declares that certain rules or principles determine the rightness and wrongness of moral acts. Consequently the ethical life consists in obedience to these rules, whereas unethical conduct is whatever violates them.

Defined in this manner, many Christians embrace rule deontologism. Indeed, they find the rule(s) in the pages of the Bible, the "rule book of life." Yet a person need not appeal to an external authority like the Bible to follow rule deontologism. Instead, philosophical ethicists invoke human reason as the foundation for determining the rules that ought to govern conduct.

Rule deontologism immediately confronts us with a crucial question: How many rules ought to govern ethical actions? How many foundational, ultimate, absolute and universal principles of conduct are either revealed in Scripture or discovered through human reason?

One obvious answer is "one rule." Ethicists sometimes label this position *principle monism*.[27] The principle monist asserts that the whole of morality can be founded on one supreme principle. But what is this one, absolute, foundational principle?

A prominent philosopher who struggled with this question was Immanuel Kant. In fact, so forthright was he in this enterprise that one later commentator asserted that Kant was "the first philosopher to make deontological concepts central in ethics in a clear and uncompromising way."[28] This great German thinker's reflections led him to an ethical proposal at the heart of which was one guiding consideration governing all actions without exception. He called this principle "the categorical imperative." His descriptions of the concept leave no doubt that Kant was proposing a strictly deontological approach to ethics: "A categorical imperative would be one which represented an action as objectively necessary in itself apart from its relation to a further end."[29]

In one of several formulations of the categorical imperative, Kant described it in this way: "Act as if the maxim of thy action were to become by thy will a Universal Law of Nature."[30] Lying behind Kant's statement is his assumption that all our actions arise out of general principles of conduct (maxims) that we accept and that commit us to acting in the described way in every similar situation. For Kant, then, the moral rightness of an act is dependent on our willingness to universalize the rule of action which generates it.[31] Universalizing a maxim entails suggesting that this principle of conduct ought to motivate the action of anyone confronted with a similar choice. Consequently in Kant's view we ought to do only those acts that arise out of maxims that we would be willing to set forth as universal principles of conduct.

In several other contexts Kant reformulated the categorical imperative in a manner that focused more on our treatment of other persons than on maxims or principles of conduct. "Act in such a way that you always treat humanity, whether in your own person or in the person of any other, never simply as a means, but always at the same time as an end."[32] Kant's point, of course, is quite straightforward. Other people are not merely the steppingstones for our own personal fulfillment. Instead they are ends in themselves, that is, they are valuable for their own sakes. Therefore we must always treat others as such and never merely as means toward advancing our own personal ends.

Kant offered yet a third version of the categorical imperative, cast in terms of what he called the principle of the autonomy of the will: "Act always on the maxim of such a will in us as can at the same time look upon itself as making universal law."[33] Through this principle Kant was rejecting as morally worthless every act done out of "inclination," that is, every act motivated by the desire for such benefits as pleasure, power and respect, or out of fear of such perceived evils as injury or death. Of moral value is the act that springs from a firm conviction that it is simply the right thing to do. In short, ethical acts are those that arise solely from our sense of duty.[34]

Perhaps this statement provides the umbrella under which we can subsume Kant's entire ethic. He developed a thoroughgoing deontological ethical theory that focused on one imperative: Always do the act that is motivated by the sincere belief that what you are doing is the right thing to do, right not merely for you but for anybody seeking to act properly in any similar situation.

Although monistic deontologism appears to be an easy ethical system to follow, many people wonder how helpful it actually is in practice. Is the ethical life so simple that we can reduce it to obedience to one rule? In the end Kant proposed an ethic of duty. Ultimately, the categorical imperative states: "Do your duty." Hence in each situation we merely determine what our duty is and do it. But critics reply, Isn't this precisely our difficulty? We cannot always be sure what constitutes our duty.[35] Kant believed that the categorical imperative provides the means to discover what our duty is in each situation. But his critics are not persuaded that he has provided the key to the ethical life.

As Christians we might attempt to improve on Kant's monistic deontologism by introducing what to us seems to be a more serviceable foundational rule: the biblical command to love.[36] We might respond with Joseph Fletcher, "Do the loving thing."[37] But this does not necessarily solve the problem. Just as we cannot always be sure what our duty is, we are not always certain what the "loving" act is. We need instruction—sometimes even boundaries—to help us determine what it means to love.

Perhaps rather than a single principle of conduct there are several rules that determine the ethical life. We might label this alternative *pluralistic deontologism.*[38] Christians who follow pluralistic deontologism generally invoke the Ten Commandments or Jesus' teaching in the Sermon on the Mount as comprising the variety of absolute laws which we are bound to obey.[39]

This approach, whether it be the philosophical or the religious variety, raises a perplexing question: How should we act when two or more of our foundational moral principles seem to be at odds with each other? Ideally, of course, these rules never actually conflict. And some ethicists argue that in fact our fundamental moral obligations never collide *(nonconflicting absolutism).*[40] Yet most of us would admit from personal experience that in actual situations of life we sometimes find ourselves unable to obey all the rules simultaneously. Or we find situations in which exceptions to one or another rule seem to emerge.[41] What do we do when the rules conflict in this manner? What happens when obedience to one rule requires us to violate or claim exception to another rule?

* * *

Suppose you were a member of the resistance movement in Holland during the Second World War. Your role was to provide sanctuary for Jews (and possibly others) by harboring them in the "hiding place" in your house. But you have aroused the suspicion of the secret police. So one day the Gestapo arrives at your door. "We are looking for 'enemies of the Third Reich.' Are you harboring anyone?" they demand.

What principle do you follow in this conflict situation? Do you tell the truth and endanger the lives of all concerned? Or do you lie on the basis of your commitment to protect the innocent, perhaps invoking the precedence of Rahab (see Josh 2:1-7)?[42]

* * *

Conflict situations have led some ethicists to suggest that the rules may not all be equal. They attempt to arrange ethical principles according to a scale of priority. With such an arrangement in place, making ethical decisions becomes easier: when a "lower" rule comes into conflict with a "higher" rule, simply suspend the lower and obey the higher. We may call this suggestion *hierarchicalism*[43] or perhaps "graded absolutism."[44]

At first glance hierarchicalism appears to offer the way out of our problem. It allows us to gather a set of rules that can then govern all aspects of our behavior. And it provides a means of coping with whatever conflict situations may arise. Upon further reflection, however, a crucial question surfaces. Is not this talk about "suspending" a lower rule merely a less onerous way of saying "disobeying" or "violating" that rule? And if under certain circumstances a rule can be "suspended" (read "disobeyed"), in what sense can we speak of it as an ethical *norm?* Aren't norms just that: standards which are to govern all human behavior?[45]

The teleological approach. The perceived difficulties of the deontological approach lead some ethicists to pursue an alternative route. Rather than being bound up with something intrinsic to the act, they propose that the rightness or wrongness of an act is determined by its outcome. In each situation, they advise, determine which course of action will result in the greatest balance of good over evil. These theorists are advocating the teleological (from the Greek *telos,* meaning goal or end) or consequentialist approach to moral reasoning. Teleological theories are built on the assumption that the only ground of moral obligation is the good produced or the evil prevented.[46] The goal of conduct, therefore, is to produce the greatest balance of good over evil.

But, we ask, the greatest balance of good over evil for whom? Whose good should I seek to advance?

One possible answer is: "For you, of course. Seek to advance your own good."[47] We may call this response "ethical egoism." Ethical egoism declares that each person's sole moral obligation is to advance the agent's own welfare. Hence the dictum of ethical egoism is quite simple: Always act in such a manner so as to bring about the greatest amount of good over evil for yourself.

Philosophers often draw a distinction between ethical egoism and what many call "psychological egoism." The latter label refers to the assertion that people are in fact always motivated to act in what they perceive to be their best interest.[48] Defined in this manner, psychological egoism is not an *ethical* theory—a declaration that people *ought* to act in their perceived best interest—but a statement of purported empirical fact.[49] We will look at the move from "is" to "ought" later in this chapter.

Our initial reaction might be to dismiss ethical egoism as sub-Christian and unworthy of further consideration. We anticipate that this theory would lead to a society in which each individual is out to get all he or she can. Contrary to what may be our preconceived stereotype, however, ethical egoists may actually live what by all outward appearances are respectable moral lives. They do not necessarily turn out to be the "let's-live-for-the-pleasure-of-the-moment" types. They may not display the "you-only-go-around-once-so-grab-all-the-gusto-you-can" mentality of the old beer commercial.

On the contrary, ethical egoists could quite possibly think first of their own *long-term* rather than short-term interests. For example, they may slavishly adhere to all the principles of sound capitalist economics, hoping thereby to enjoy a financially secure retirement. They may turn out to be upright citizens who always obey the laws of the land, because they are convinced that this is the way to bring about the greatest balance of good over evil in the long term for themselves.

Ethical egoists may even respond to the gospel invitation and carefully seek to live by the Bible, because they believe that doing so will insure for them the greatest balance of good over evil in the longest term imaginable—eternity. Indeed, ethical egoism might turn out to be quite compatible with Christian teaching. Knowing that a judgment day is coming and knowing that Christ promises rewards to his faithful followers, should we not give our lives to Christ and seek to live as obedient disciples? In so doing, we can make sure that we participate in the best eternal destiny, as we thereby avoid the fires of hell and lay up rewards for ourselves in heaven (e.g., Mt 6:19-20).

Despite these caveats, at one important point ethical egoism does offend Christian sympathies.[50] Our chief consideration in life cannot be to make sure that our actions bring about the greatest balance of good over evil in the long term for ourselves. So doing too easily leads us to use people as means to our own ends. And it eventually lets even altruism degenerate into self-promotion: "I'll help you because in some way doing so will help me."[51]

Perhaps we can avoid this problem by reorienting the focus. Maybe our ethical duty is to act in such a way so as to seek to bring about the greatest balance of good over evil in the world as a whole. This theory is often called "utilitarianism."[52] Its classic statement was penned by John Stuart Mill in his book *Utilitarianism:* "Actions are right in proportion as they tend to promote happiness, wrong as they tend to produce the reverse of happiness."[53]

Strictly speaking, "utilitarianism" is the position that looks to the principle of utility to determine the rightness and wrongness of an act. An act is right or wrong depending on the degree to which it is useful or harmful.[54] In this sense ethical egoism is also utilitarian. Yet proponents of what ethicists call "utilitarianism," such as Mill and Jeremy Bentham, declare that the utility of everyone, and not merely of the agent, forms the criterion for judging whether an act is right or wrong. Hence utilitarians exhort us to do that act which produces the most good or the least evil possible in the given situation.

Since the Enlightenment, utilitarianism has enjoyed wide (albeit not universal) acknowledgment among ethicists. Rightly so, we might think, for the idea that each person ought to seek the good of others rather than focusing on oneself sounds very "Christian." Yet the view is not without problems.[55] Perhaps no difficulty is more debilitating than the potential loss of justice for the individual this theory entails. Acting on behalf of the interests of the greatest number of people seems to provide moral sanction for overriding the concern for justice for each.

A. C. Ewing illustrated the philosophical problem by posing a series of rhetorical questions: "Suppose we could slightly increase the collective happiness of ten men by taking away all happiness from one of them, would it be right to do so? . . . ought an innocent man to be punished, if it would on the balance cause less pain with an equal deterrent effect to punish him than it would to punish the guilty?"[56] This latter question suggests another: Taken by itself, would not the theory of utility justify the conclusion of the high priest Caiaphas, when he advocated that Jesus be crucified in order to forestall the Romans massacring the nation (Jn 11:49-50)?

The potential problems surrounding the focus on acts implicit in utilitarianism has led some ethicists to reintroduce the deontological interest in rules into this basically teleological theory.[57] The resultant hybrid view, *rule utilitarianism,* does not ask which *act* but which *rule* has the greatest utility.[58] Hence proponents of this position seek to set forth that body of rules which if followed would maximize utility. Thus the rules are not to be obeyed because they denote which acts are *intrinsically* right (rule deontologism), but because they indicate which acts have the greater utility.[59]

Regardless of the relative merit of each of these theories in comparison with the others, all teleological theories evoke one telling criticism. They are dependent on our ability to anticipate the results of our actions. Of course we can generally predict with a fair amount of accuracy much of the good and evil that would result from our proposed actions. But, critics reply, can we anticipate all that will result from every act? How well can we accurately forecast the future? Do we really know what balance of good over evil will ensue from our moral choices?[60]

Ethics and Theories of Value

Teleological theories of obligation (and to some extent deontological theories as well) introduce an additional sticky question. If we are to do those acts which result in good (and avoid evil), then we must determine what "good" means. The quest to discover the good leads us to the second dimension of normative ethics, which we introduced briefly earlier, namely, theories of value. Ethicists tell us that to say something is "good" is to acknowledge that we value it. Or stated in other words, we call "good" whatever we have come to value. In this context, the ethical question becomes, What ought we to value and hence call "good"?

Extrinsic and intrinsic value. Before we can speak to this question, we must note a distinction between two types of value[61] that dates at least to Aristotle in the fourth century B.C.

We value certain things and disvalue others not for themselves but because of their relationship to some value external to them. They may assist in bringing that external value into existence for us. I value my 1966 Mustang, for example, because it continues to provide dependable, economic transportation. Ethicists refer to this as *extrinsic value.* Something has extrinsic value when the ground of its value lies in its relationship to another value, that is, when it is valued for its effects.

We value other things, in contrast, because of something intrinsic to them. For example, some people value pleasurable experiences simply because they are pleasurable experiences. Ethicists refer to these things as having *intrinsic value.* Hence, something has intrinsic value when the ground of its value lies within its own nature, that is, when it is valued for itself rather than for its effects.

Obviously judgments about *extrinsic* value are based on other judgments about *intrinsic* value. And discussions about value eventually must arrive at the question of what has intrinsic value. For this reason, philosophers have been chiefly concerned about this topic.

The question of the foundational intrinsic value. In the history of Western ethics, coming to a consensus on exactly what has intrinsic value has not been an easy task. Yet the candidates for this lofty honor have been surprisingly few.

Perhaps the most controversial answer to the question, What has intrinsic value? is "pleasure."[62] Philosophers have repeatedly shied away from this proposal, which is generally called *hedonism,* but often with limited success. Hedonism entails two essential assertions: First, pleasure is always good for its own sake, and pain is always bad. And second, pleasure is the only thing good for its own sake, and pain is the only thing intrinsically bad.[63]

Although our stereotypical image is that of a despicable, rowdy, carousing, sexually indulgent "party animal," a hedonist need not necessarily be sold out to debauchery. Hedonists may in fact be law-abiding citizens. Indeed, Christians may even be hedonists.[64] They may eschew the pleasures of the "worldly" life, but this does not mean that they eschew pleasure itself. Perhaps the life of devotion to God brings them pleasure. Or perhaps they are "eternal hedonists" who eagerly await the unsurpassable pleasure of eternity. En route to the celestial city, they purposefully do what is necessary to insure a pleasurable eternity for themselves. And this goal motivates all their acts, or it determines their moral quest. Like "worldly" hedonists, their ultimate goal is pleasure. They merely have a quite different understanding of what constitutes it.

While thinkers have offered several other theories of value,[65] none has gained the perennial following hedonism enjoys. A second proposal is the so-called *interest theory of value.* This theory asserts that something is good when it is an object of positive interest, that is, when we have a mental disposition of being "for" it. Something is bad, in contrast, when our disposition is to be "against" it. One variety of this theory suggests that the good is what we perceive as satisfying our desires and aims.[66]

A third theory of value asserts that the only intrinsic good is self-actualization or *self-realization.* To be human, this theory suggests, is to have some goal or purpose (a *telos*) for existence. The good life, in turn, occurs as we realize this goal.

Many of the ancient Greek philosophers and the medieval scholastics traveled this route. They viewed the human *telos* from what we might call an "essentialist" perspective: the purpose of our existence determines our nature. Just as the *telos* of an acorn is the oak tree, and therefore the good of the acorn is the mature oak which is its true essence, so also our human *telos* is our good. One classical proposal invokes happiness as the goal of human existence and hence the sole intrinsic value. This understanding of happiness ought to be distinguished sharply from the hedonist view of the good. Rather than the enjoyment of pleasure, in this context, happiness is more akin to the peaceful satisfaction connected with the attainment of harmony in life. J. H. Muirhead succinctly stated the point: "Pleasure is the feeling which accompanies the satisfaction of particular desires; happiness is the feeling which accompanies the sense that, apart from the satisfaction of momentary desires, and even in spite of the pain of refusal or failure to satisfy them, the self as a whole is being realised."[67]

An intriguing alternative essentialist understanding takes on a modern evolutionary tone and places the individual person in a wider social and even cosmic context. Hence Henry W. Wright declared that self-realization involves "the attainment of a progression of ends, each of which includes and supersedes the one before, until the supreme and all-comprehensive ideal is reached."[68] The ends Wright enumerates include (in ascending order): pleasure, culture, altruism, humanitarianism and finally universal progress. And according to Wright the supreme ideal arrives as the person "subordinates his interest to the Universal or Divine Purpose, adopting the latter, so far as it can be known, as his own good."[69]

In contrast to this "essentialist" understanding, certain modern philosophers have given the "self-actualization" theory a decidedly existentialist twist. We have no innate nature, given us at conception. Rather we must decide what we wish to become, and as we integrate our variegated desires we become a self. This, and this alone, is good for its own sake.[70]

A variation of this existentialist approach views the human person as characterized by freedom and hence speaks of the fundamental human purpose as self-determination. "Full personhood" emerges—in the words of Germain Grisez—as we create ourselves "by giving reality to aspects of the self which were previously only possibilities."[71] Yet this is no mere self-centered egotism. Instead, "persons committed to the fullest realization of their personhood," he adds, "will choose in a way that leaves open the possibility of still further self-realization for themselves and others."[72] Similarly, John Wild eschewed shear existentialist relativism and called instead for an "authentic" existence which seeks a "global meaning" which can guide "meaningful action in the concrete world."[73]

Some philosophers offer a third candidate for the highest value. They assert that virtue is the only intrinsic good. As we will see in the next chapter, many of the ancient Greeks offered this proposal in conjunction with their emphasis on the excellence of human reason. The virtuous life, they declared, involves living according to reason. Virtue occurs as reason acts as master over our passions.

The quest for virtue as the highest good very quickly moves us beyond the realm of obligation. It suggests that the goal of the ethicist is not so much that of determining the rightness and wrongness of acts, but more importantly that of discovering the ingredients in the life of virtue.

Constructing a Normative Ethic of Being

Our discussion to this point, climaxing with the question of value, leaves us with the gnawing sense that the quest for a normative ethic of doing may in fact not get us to our goal. The focus on actions leaves us wondering if there is yet another, perhaps even more crucial aspect of ethics. What about the attitudes and motivations from which our actions spring?[74]

Perhaps our uneasiness at this point indicates that our quest initially moved in the wrong direction. So far we have attempted to construct a theory of moral obligation by focusing on human action. This has led us to look at attempts to develop a normative ethic of doing. But supposing the focus of ethics lies elsewhere—in who we *are* (or ought to be)—rather than what we *do?* Perhaps the ethical life is not primarily a function of the actions that people engage in but a function of the kind of people that engage in the actions. Maybe we should turn our focus away from action and become concerned about character and virtue, and only then speak about the actions that emerge from the virtuous person.[75] In short, maybe we should abandon the search for an ethic of *doing* and seek instead to devise an ethic of *being* (or of virtue).[76]

Doing versus being. To see whether or not you resonate with this proposal, let us take a little test, drawing out and updating a situation Aristotle envisioned in the fourth century before Christ.[77]

A man lived in fidelity to his marriage vow throughout their thirty years of marriage. In complete fidelity, that is, except for one night. He was away from home on an extended business trip. In the midst of his loneliness, he met a woman in the bar at the hotel where he was staying. One thing led to another, and the night resulted in a sexual encounter in his hotel suite. Is this man an adulterer?

Your initial response might be to interpret the query as calling for an ethical judgment about the man's *action.* If you reason according to rule-deontologism, you might then rephrase the question: Did the man through this act violate some ethical norm, such as the seventh commandment (Ex 20:14)? That is, is the man guilty of adultery? Or, if you prefer the teleological method, you might ask, Did his act produce a greater amount of evil than of good? Either question could lead to a similar conclusion: the businessman's act was unethical, and consequently he is an adulterer.

But supposing we interpret the question in a different manner. Let us try to understand "Is the man an adulterer?" as inquiring about the *character* of the man: "Is the man a faithful or unfaithful husband?" Posing the question in this manner may lead to a quite different answer. We might reply, "No one act determines a person's character. Indeed, one act of adultery does not mark an otherwise faithful spouse as an adulterer. On the contrary, through thirty years of marriage the man had carefully developed the virtue of fidelity. He is a faithful husband who on one occasion acted against his character and against the virtue of faithfulness he had cultivated."

The first response reflects a commitment to an ethic of doing. The second, in contrast, illustrates a focus on being.

An ethic of being is concerned with what we should be or what we should prefer. Of course it doesn't ignore conduct. But it places conduct secondary to character. Conduct is important both as an expression of character and as a means in its development. For example, suppose that you conclude that courage is a virtue. You want to be a person of courage. Then in each situation of life you will seek to act in a courageous manner and to do whatever contributes to becoming a courageous person.

As this example indicates, an ethic of being gives primacy to value judgments. Whatever place there may be for judgments of moral obligation, they are secondary and are to be derived from judgments about the motives, traits or virtues of moral agents. David Hume may have been expressing sympathy for the quest for an ethic of being when he asserted, "When we praise any actions, we regard only the motives that produced them. . . . The external performance has no merit. . . . all virtuous actions derive their merit only from virtuous motives."[78]

Deontological versus teleological approaches. Just as theorists who advocate an ethic of doing cannot agree as to how to judge acts, so also proponents of the ethic of being differ as to how we are to judge traits. They too disagree as to whether deontological or teleological reasoning is more appropriate.

Some ethicists propose what we may call *trait deontologism.* They argue that certain character traits are intrinsically good. These traits are the virtues that we are all duty bound to develop. Other ethicists are *trait teleologists.* Rather than being intrinsically virtuous, traits are to be measured by their results. The ethical imperative, therefore, lies in developing those traits that produce good rather than evil effects. Here again we must ask, "Whose good?" Some respond: "Your own." Hence *trait egoism* declares that the basic moral virtue is careful concern for your own good. And the attendant virtues include those traits that are the most conducive to your own welfare. Others respond: "The good of all, or at least of the greatest number." Thus *trait utilitarianism* suggests that the basic virtue is the desire to promote the general good.

Recent years have witnessed a marked shift toward concern for an ethic of being among philosophical ethicists. With this shift have arisen reformulations as to the nature and role of virtue in the ethical life. For example, increased awareness of the specifically feminine approach to the moral life led Nel Noddings to advance an ethic of caring. In her proposal, "caring" functions as the wellspring of all attendant virtues and the foundation for actions in specific circumstances. Caring, she argues, is both the expression of our ideal selves and intrinsically good.[79] In a sense Noddings offers an updated trait-deontologism.[80] And in a way that is reminiscent of Kant, she concludes that ethical living ultimately depends on the "will to be good," which she interprets as the will "to remain in caring relation to the other."[81]

Alasdair MacIntyre, in contrast, provides an updated trait-teleological approach. For him the virtues are instrumental to a higher goal, namely, bringing unity to our lives. This unity, in turn, is related to the *telos* of our existence. Consequently, the virtues are "those dispositions which will sustain us in the . . . quest for the good . . . and which will furnish us with increasing self-knowledge and increasing knowledge of the good."[82]

Normative ethics and the pursuit of the good. At each bend in the road, our journey through normative ethics—whether we prefer an ethic of doing or seek to construct an ethic of being—has raised the same haunting question: What is the ultimate foundation for morality?

If we turn to deontological theories, we discover our ethic is dependent on some authority that can declare what is intrinsically right. We require some source for the rule(s) that govern actions or for traits that we should deem virtuous. If our journey leads to teleological theories, we discover that our ethic is dependent on a prior determination of nonmoral value. It raises the question of what we value or what we consider to be the good we want to promote. Ultimately, the quest to determine what we value confronts us with the question of the "good life." For in the end all our values are connected to what we value the most. They contribute to or are aspects of what we ultimately desire. And what we value or desire most defines our conception of the good life.

At first glance it appears that the deontological approach, with its focus on the "right" (whether it be "the right act" or "the right traits"), and the teleological approach, with its focus on the "good" (especially, the final "good" we ought to pursue), are hopelessly divergent.[83] Each seems to subordinate the concern of the other under its own pursuit. If we begin with the right as the key ethical concept, the good becomes descriptive either of the "will" from which duty springs or the reward that follows the performance of duty. If instead we begin with the good, the right in turn becomes the means to maximize the good. Consequently, many philosophical ethicists suggest that the final quest of normative ethics is the search for a convergence between these seemingly opposing directions of ethical reflection.[84]

Often the quest for the good life becomes the point where the approaches converge. Hence, Friedrich Schleiermacher declared that the true order is: the good, duty and virtue. The good, the German theologian asserted, has value in itself. From our perception of the good springs the duty or obligation to strive for it. And when we recognize and perform this duty, habitually virtuous character emerges.[85]

This focus on the good life as the foundational principle is understandable. It is difficult to avoid the conclusion that no matter what it may be, our conception of ethical living is connected to our perspective on the good life. This is obviously true of teleological ethicists, who tell us to do those acts or cultivate those traits that promote the good as we understand it. But this is also true of deontological ethicists. Ultimately they desire to engage in those actions or cultivate those traits that are intrinsically good simply because doing so is the proper way to live as they understand it. Doing what is intrinsically right or being characterized by the right is not only the "right" way of living, it fulfills their vision of the good life: The good life is the life of obedience to one's duty.

In this manner, normative ethics unavoidably leads to the question of the good life: What is the ultimate good toward which we are striving? What is our understanding of the good life? Consequently normative ethics cannot stand alone. It confronts us with the question, How we can justify our ethical judgments? What is the ultimate criterion for normative statements? And finally, what is the "good"? In short, normative ethics leads us to analytical ethics.

Constructing a Justification for Ethics

We have viewed the two major approaches to normative ethics: the ethic of doing and the ethic of being. And we have looked at the two major ways of pursuing questions of normative ethics: the deontological and the teleological patterns of moral reasoning. Our discussion of normative ethics points to a deeper question, the question of analytical ethics: What is the basis for ethical judgments? What is the final court of appeal for making ethical assertions? And what is the "good"? In this manner, normative ethics brings us face to face with analytical ethics.

To the first question, What is the foundation for ethical judgments? ethicists have proposed three major responses. We may call these "naturalism," "intuitionism" and "noncognitivism."

Naturalism. A first possible path to follow in the quest to discover a final court of appeal in ethics is to assume a connection between ethical judgments and what actually "is." Perhaps we can justify normative ethical statements by an appeal to "what is." Perhaps our ethical judgements are somehow rooted in "fact," in the nature of reality or in "the way things are."

The appeal to "the way things are" suggests that ethical concepts can be defined by replacing them with nonethical terms. Ethical judgments, in turn, can be translated into nonethical statements, that is, into assertions of a factual kind.[86] And as pronouncements of fact, these propositions can in some way be empirically verified. In this manner, "goodness" and "the right" come to be viewed as natural properties, which are connected to observable reality. Ethicists refer to this approach as *ethical naturalism.*

For example, when we say "good" we may really mean "what most people desire, favor, like, approve of, or admire." Or when we say "right" we may actually be referring to "what is conducive to harmonious happiness."[87] At least in theory, such statements can be empirically verified. We can take a poll to find out if people truly desire what the ethicist has declared to be good. And we can survey human social interactions to determine if what the ethicist declared to be right actually does contribute to harmonious happiness.

As a philosophical theory, ethical naturalism as we defined it here is a relatively recent contender. However, a less philosophically reflective variety of naturalism enjoys wide use in society. How often do people say, "Honesty is the best policy," meaning, "Truth-telling promotes harmony"—that is, "The world is built in such a way that when people are honest and truthful with one another everybody is better off."

The architects of capitalism, such as Adam Smith, appealed to a wider, cosmic naturalism when they spoke of an overarching harmony built into the fabric of the world. If all members of society seek their own best economic interests, the early capitalists optimistically asserted, the best interests of everyone will be served. Smith believed that in seeking their own economic advantage, people will be led by "an invisible hand" to contribute to the general welfare, even though this goal was not part of their original intentions.[88]

Other popular expressions of naturalism focus the appeal on human nature, rather than the world as a whole. "Humans are just made that way," they declare. Or, "Humans naturally seek their own personal benefit." In all such expressions, the basic idea is the same: We can justify ethical judgments on the basis of "the way things are," and the way things are is in some sense open to empirical observation.

Understood in this sense, naturalism may refer to any approach that couples judgments about the right or the good to what is purported to be "natural." Its proponents assume that we can discover universal principles of obligation, for these are lodged in the very nature of the human psyche and the universe.[89] Or advocates might speak about a fundamental ethical way of being in the world or in relation with others on the basis of what they believe to be a part of our own true nature or what is innate to us (or at least to our ideal self).[90]

One form of this wider naturalism, which is sometimes called *teleological naturalism,*[91] can boast a long pedigree in the history of Western ethics, dating to Aristotle[92] and enjoying prominence in the Middle Ages. Teleological naturalism builds from the assumption that everything is endowed with an innate tendency to grow toward its own ideal, which it therefore possesses in "embryonic" form. "Good" then signifies whatever enables it to fulfill this inborn ideal.

Classical naturalism often comes to expression in what is generally called "natural law."[93] Consider this statement from the pen of a twentieth-century Thomist: "The actions of plants and animals are determined by . . . the law of their nature, or the original determination given to them by the fact of the Creator having endowed them with their specific natures. They must follow their natural tendencies or appetites. This fact leads us to suspect that in man also there must be a law of nature necessitating his actions in a manner consonant with his nature. If so, we shall have found a basis for moral obligation."[94] The author asserts that the foundation for ethical judgments lies in a distinctive feature of human nature and this distinctive feature acts as a type of law that is meant to govern human conduct.

For proponents of this view, natural law is both a scientifically based description of how things normally do behave and a set of precepts as to how they ought to behave.[95] This connection has made natural law theory a perennial favorite among conservative Christian ethicists.[96]

Despite its prominence in the Western tradition, naturalism in its various forms has not enjoyed universal acceptance. Critics maintain that it is beset with one seemingly fatal flaw, the so-called naturalistic fallacy.[97] Ethical naturalism is erroneous, they argue, because it entails moving from natural qualities that things possess to ethical statements about right and goodness. Stated pointedly, ethical naturalism moves from what is to what is good, and hence what ought to be. But, its critics demur, how can we derive "good," and thus an "ought," from an "is"?[98] This question may be read as a problem of logic. The rules of logical discourse will not allow us to deduce an "ought" statement from any number of "is" statements. For example, the observation "Snow is white" does not logically lead to the conclusion that it is good that snow is white or to the judgment "Snow ought to be white."

Lurking within the critique of ethical naturalism is a philosophical or theological problem as well. Can we indeed argue from the "is-ness" to the goodness of this world? Can we move directly from the world as it is (or the world as it potentially is within itself) to the world as it should be? Likewise, can we rightly appeal to human nature as a basis for speaking about human goodness and how humans ought to live? It would seem that we can only do so if we assume that ours is "the best of all possible worlds"[99] or that human nature—or at least the human potential—is untainted by the Fall.

Christians, however, believe that the world is not what it ought to be; rather, humans are fallen creatures living in a fallen world. Indeed, our hope is that neither humankind nor the world is now what will one day be. (We will develop these themes in chapters six and seven.) Consequently, what may appear to be quite natural may also be quite wrong.

Despite what at least on the surface appears to be a debilitating flaw, many Christians do find the appeal to natural law helpful. Ethical naturalism pops up in a variety of discussions. Take, for example, the debate over homosexuality. Some people welcome any scientific evidence which suggests that the homosexual "orientation" may be genetically determined, for they claim that such evidence justifies homosexual activity. Their argument appeals to naturalism: because the homosexual person was born that way—that is, because in this case homosexuality is "natural"—homosexual activity is right.

An interesting variant of naturalism, *metaphysical moralism,* appeals not to the natural but to the supernatural world.[100] According to this view, ethical statements can be translated into assertions of metaphysical or theological fact. Thus *right* does not primarily mean "what is conducive to harmonious happiness" but "what is commanded by God." And "Honesty is the best policy" ought to be translated "God commands that we tell the truth." In other words, the reality to which these ethicists appeal includes more than the natural world. These thinkers look as well to the metaphysical realm of God's preferences.

Metaphysical moralism raises an intriguing theological-ethical question: Is something right because God commands it? Or does God command something because it is right?[101] If we opt for the first alternative, we risk making God a capricious despot. Even if his commands violate *our* sense of right, the sovereign God is still right. In the end this sounds similar to the old dictum "might makes right," and we risk transforming God into a cosmic bully.[102]

* * *

The neighborhood bully has taken a truck belonging to Calvin (of *Calvin and Hobbes* fame). Calvin, looking wistfully on in the distance, remarks to himself, "That no good rotten Mo! He won't give my truck back to me. The oaf will probably break it, too." He then contemplates his course of action: "Should I steal it back? I know stealing is wrong, but *he* stole it from *me.* And if I *don't* steal it back, Mo will just keep it, and that's not fair."

At this point the boy begins to pontificate on ethics. "They say two wrongs don't make a right. But what are you supposed to *do* then? Just let the biggest guy make his own rules all the time? Let might make right?" Finally, a dejected Calvin announces his answer. "That sounds reasonable," he says as he sits on the ground, reconciling himself to the loss of his truck.

* * *

Many philosophers find the other alternative, that God commands something because it is right, equally unacceptable. We then risk introducing a standard to which God must conform. And to do so is to deny God's sovereign deity.[103] This dilemma has led certain ethicists to reject metaphysical moralism out of hand.[104]

Some Christian ethicists offer a "softer" type of metaphysical moralism. Rather than appealing to God's commands, they draw from God's own example. Hence, we might argue, "Because God is love we ought to love as well." We will return to this possibility in chapters six through eight.

Intuitionism. A second alternative, "intuitionism" (or "nonnaturalism"), can be introduced in a few sentences.[105] The simplest definition declares that ethical terms such as *good* are names of objects or qualities observable by intuition, rather than by sense perception or scientific observation.[106]

In other words, an intuitionist claims that we know ethical truth by direct intuition[107] rather than by deductive reasoning. Ethical truth, therefore, is self-evident.

Intuitionists generally point to our reason as the locus of the power of intuition. Hence, they speak of "intuitive reason" or "rational intuition." Obviously the process of intuitive reasoning differs significantly from what we usually mean by "reason." In this latter use of the word, what we have in view is discursive reasoning, that is, the process of moving step by step from premises to conclusions. Intuitive reasoning, in contrast, involves recognizing a particular truth immediately, that is, without observing how it arises from some other truth. Rather than logically deducing it from any other assertions, a self-evident proposition "is evident or true, *by itself* alone . . . it is not an inference from some proposition other than *itself*."[108] Putting the matter simply: with ethics as with many other dimensions of life, "either you see it or you don't."

Perhaps we can better grasp the point when we consider a parallel discussion about the best method for propagating the gospel. Some Christians maintain that the good news is self-evident. The Christian faith, they argue, requires no elaborate rationale or apologetic. We do not convince others to accept our message by bolstering it with "proofs" showing that Christian teaching is compatible with, or can even be confirmed by, what we know about God, the world and ourselves by empirical observation and the scientific method. We simply announce the good news. And the hearer either grasps its truth intuitively or rejects it as nonsense. So also in the realm of ethics. We simply "see" certain things.

But what exactly ought we to "see"? While agreeing on the importance of the power of rational intuition, intuitionists differ as to what exactly we can know through intuitive reason.[109]

G. E. Moore, who is often hailed as the most important twentieth-century proponent of intuitionism, offers a first answer. Above all, what we see is "goodness." Moore is interested in asserting that goodness is self-evident and known through direct apprehension. In a sense Moore's position is reminiscent of Plato's ethical idealism. The ancient Greek philosopher held that the foundational ethical concepts—virtue, justice, beauty and, above all, goodness—are eternal forms that we apprehend ultimately in abstract philosophical contemplation.[110] Despite this similarity, Moore's approach is decidedly different from Plato's. According to Moore goodness resides in human experience, not in an eternal metaphysical realm.[111]

In Moore's opinion goodness, understood as a quality that we assert belongs to something, is a "simple," as opposed to a complex, notion, similar to "simple" notions in other spheres, such as "yellow."[112] As a simple concept, goodness is an undefinable quality, that is, it cannot be defined by describing the parts that compose it. Instead, we apprehend goodness directly. And we know simply by "seeing" whether or not an assertion "x is good" is true. Indeed, if someone were to disagree with us at this point, we could only admonish him or her to "look again."[113]

Obviously for Moore the point of ethics is not to seek to define goodness. What, then, is ethics? According to Moore, ethics (or more specifically, practical ethics) is concerned with questions such as: What is right? What is my duty? What ought I to do? Statements about what is right—that is, ethical judgments—are derived from this direct perception of goodness. Consequently, they can be rephrased in connection with goodness. *Right,* therefore, means "cause of a good result," or more simply "useful." And statements of moral obligation are in the end declarations that "certain kinds of action will have good effects."[114]

Moore represents those intuitionists who propose that through intuition we grasp the foundational moral principles from which we infer ethical judgments about particular acts. These theorists claim that the fundamental principles of ethics are self-evident. Rather than arising as the conclusions drawn from other principles, they are known by intuition. When we understand their meaning, we come to see their truth as well, for we then need no other evidence to know that these principles are true.

Other intuitionists declare that not only goodness but also rightness is an indefinable quality known only through direct apprehension. Thus, we can apprehend directly that doing certain kinds of acts is right without considering the good they bring about.[115] Intuition, therefore, allows us to see the rightness or wrongness of specific acts. Through intuition we know whether or not a proposed act "fits" in a specific situation. Although a decision-maker may need to know certain facts about the situation and the act, ultimately the mind simply "sees" what moral judgment is proper.

Noncognitivism. Perhaps both the naturalists and the intuitionists are mistaken. Perhaps there is no court of appeal for ethical statements. Maybe our judgments are incapable of any rational or objectively valid justification whatsoever, because such statements are not objective assertions at all. Despite their appearances, ethical judgments may not be objective declarations about acts, persons or things at all. And for this reason they may say nothing either true or false. This proposal carries the designation "noncognitivism."

Simply stated, noncognitivists claim that ethical judgments do not carry cognitive meaning. Foundational to their position is the assumption that a statement is meaningful only if it asserts or denies something that is objectively true or false about an object in the universe, so that its truth or falsity can be determined by comparing it with reality. Hence if I say, "There is a fourteen-pound turkey in the freezer downstairs," we can readily discover whether the statement is true or false. According to the noncognitivist view, ethical judgments are *not* of this type. They neither assert nor deny objective fact.

To grasp the noncognitivist position, consider the following examples. Suppose I say, "Rescuing the drowning child was a noble act," or "Mother Teresa is a good person." Or to cite the negative side, suppose I declare, "The killing of innocent babies is wrong," or "Hitler was immoral." According to the noncognitivist theory, I have not said something objective (and hence "true") about the acts of rescuing or killing in themselves. Nor have I really attributed anything objective to Mother Teresa or Hitler. I haven't been making cognitive statements about specific acts or specific persons at all!

If assertions such as these do not ascribe moral properties to acts or persons, what do they describe? Whom or what do they speak about? While denying that normative ethical assertions have cognitive meaning, noncognitivists readily admit that such statements carry great *emotive* meaning. That is, they express emotions, feelings and attitudes. Ethical judgments, therefore, are of the order of outbursts like "Hurray!" or "Bah!" For this reason, many ethicists label the noncognitivist position "emotivism."

Emotivists are quick to point out that we ought to avoid mistaking this view for ethical subjectivism. Although both tie ethical judgments to personal, subjective feelings and attitudes, they are separated by an important difference.[116] This difference lies in the distinction between *expressions* of feeling (e.g., "Yes!") and *assertions* of feeling (e.g., "I am pleased"). Emotivists declare that ethical statements are expressions of feelings, emotions or sentiments, rather than merely being statements revealing the presence in the speaker of such psychological experiences or states. To the emotivist the latter are purely descriptive statements rather than also being value judgments. Because they are purely descriptive, they belong to the realm of psychology and not ethics.

Taken to the extreme, noncognitivism would hold that ethical judgments are nothing more than forceful expressions of the speaker's own emotions. Such statements express the speaker's emotional reaction to something or someone. Hence rather than asserting something that can be verified or falsified, we use ethical statements as a means to express or give vent to our emotions.[117] To say "Hitler was morally culpable" is on the order of an emotional outburst like "Boo Hitler!" We might call this position *radical emotivism.*

In uttering ethical statements, however, we generally intend more than merely expressing our own emotion. We have an additional purpose in view. We hope that the hearer will somehow gain a similar emotional feeling. Thus when we make statements like "Abortion is murder," our intention is not limited to the expression of our emotional revulsion for the practice. We also want the hearer to share the same revulsion. Consequently few philosophical ethicists have gone on record as favoring the radical emotivism described above; emotivists generally prefer some "milder" type.

Some emotivists focus on the implicit command present within every ethical statement. They agree with the radical emotivists that an ethical statement has no descriptive meaning whatsoever. Indeed, its goal is not even to assert the presence of a certain attitude in the speaker. But, they add, every such statement nonetheless harbors an implicit command, calling on the hearer to adopt the same positive or negative attitude present in the speaker. Ethical assertions, therefore, are calculated to arouse feeling and thereby perhaps even to stimulate action.[118]

Other noncognitivists take an additional step. They suggest that ethical statements do carry some descriptive meaning, namely, to indicate the presence of the attitude in the speaker.[119] The purpose of such a disclosure is not merely to command, however, but to evoke approval or disapproval in the hearer.[120] Ethical judgments, therefore, intend to be both expressive and persuasive.[121] We use specifically ethical judgments to evoke the desired response because such statements involve words, like *good,* which carry strong emotive meaning.[122] The persuasive intent of ethical discourse means that ethical disputes need not end in a stalemate, as would be the case if moral judgments were merely expressions of personal feelings. Such discussions can come to a resolution if one participant is able to convince the others to change their moral attitude.

An alternative to these proposals, sometimes termed *prescriptivism,*[123] draws from a slightly different understanding of the function of ethical language. The goal of such language is to guide the choices of others. Hence, according to prescriptivists, ethical judgments are personal evaluations, recommendations or prescriptions that embody an implicit evaluation and an imperative. Such statements remain subjective, of course, for they are the *speaker's* evaluations or recommendations. But they are more than merely subjective, more than simply the expression of personal emotion. Such statements also carry a certain descriptive force. Whenever we appeal to a well-established moral principle, we are invoking something that is already "there," to which we are now—at least implicitly—subscribing and that provides the rationale for acting in a certain manner.

In the words of one prominent proponent, R. M. Hare, "To become morally adult is . . . to learn to use 'ought'-sentences in the realization that they can only be verified by reference to a standard or set of principles which we have by our own decision accepted and made our own." In this manner, "moral judgements provide reasons for acting in one way rather than another."[124]

The contemporary pluralist context takes the prescriptivist approach one step farther. The ethos of the day says that when I offer an ethical judgment, I must realize that my viewpoint is influenced by my own point of reference. It is dependent on where and how I was raised, on my life experiences and on the communities in which I participate. I must realize that because my hearers do not share this standpoint with me, they will likely offer a somewhat different evaluation. We all have a right to our own judgment. But as we talk about the matter with each other, we can at least gain an appreciation for the other person's perspective and perhaps even gain new insights into the life situation under discussion.

Justifying Ethics Itself

Analytical ethics explores the crucial question, How can we justify our ethical assertions? But a deeper query remains: How can we justify morality itself? That is, why be moral? Why be concerned with the ethical life? We might even take this a step further. Perhaps the moral quest is even harmful to ourselves and society, as the nineteenth-century German philosopher Friedrich Nietzsche suggested when he mused, "What if . . . morality itself was the danger of dangers?"[125]

The philosophical justification. Philosophical ethicists often launch their response by invoking some general definition of ethics as the pursuit or determination of "what is conducive to human living" or "what enriches life." The challenge of ethical reflection, therefore, is to present the moral quest as focusing on life as a unified whole, which in turn is seen as the *summum bonum* (highest good) of human existence. Clifford Barrett articulated this viewpoint well: "Nothing can be morally prohibited on any other grounds than that it would detract from this total worth of living, and nothing can be morally insignificant which would make life as a whole more worth living for human beings."[126]

This link between ethics and the "life worth living" suggests that one answer to the question "Why be moral?" lies in our corporate existence. As a result, philosophical ethicists regularly point to the importance of ethics to harmonious social interaction.[127] Ethical living is necessary to produce and sustain the conditions that make corporate human life possible. Ethics promotes social cohesion. Without certain agreed-upon ethical mores, society would disintegrate. Hence preservation of society forms the foundational apologetic for a secular social ethic. Ultimately a society should be concerned that its citizens live ethical lives because its own survival is at stake. The alternative to the promotion of ethics is chaos.[128]

This approach leads us to construct personal morality on the foundation of social ethics. Proponents of this proposal begin by reminding us that we participate in something larger than ourselves, namely, society.

And as members of this corporate whole, we have certain obligations and responsibilities. Therefore we must live the ethical life, because we share social obligations. The discipline of ethics, in turn, seeks to clarify what these obligations are.

But why should *I* be concerned about the well-being of society so as to adopt the moral way of living?[129] Here ethicists in the modern era routinely cite the importance of social cohesion for personal well-being. A well-functioning society provides the necessary context for its citizens to pursue the good life. Only in the context of a stable society can individuals seek their personal well-being. Consequently I should be concerned about the ethical life, because contributing to the well-being of society also fosters my own participation in the good life. Kai Nielsen stated this point crassly: "When we ask: why should we have a morality—any morality, even a completely conventional morality—we answer that if everyone acts morally, or generally acts morally, people will be able to attain more of what they want."[130]

Following this line of reasoning leads inevitably to a teleological ethic.[131] The ethical life contributes to our well-being or to the good life. We ought to be ethical because of the good that living in this manner produces. This response leads likewise to the self as the ground of ethics. The ethical life contributes to my own personal well-being. I ought to act ethically because doing so is to my benefit. And taking this step leads back to human reason as the foundation for ethics. Because the ethical life contributes to my personal well-being—my personal participation in the good life—being ethical is the most reasonable way to live. It "fits" with who we are as humans.[132]

William Frankena articulated this well. His study of philosophical ethics climaxes with the question "Why be moral?" And the only answer the philosopher can offer is "because it is rational." Speaking about a fictitious human person "A" Frankena wrote, "What kind of a life A would choose if he were fully rational and knew all about himself and the world will, of course, depend on what sort of a person he is (and people are different), but if psychological egoism is not true of any of us, it may always be that A would then choose a way of life that would be moral."[133]

And why be rational? While admitting that no reasons can be given for choosing the rational way of life, Paul W. Taylor boldly declared that no reasons *need* be given. He explained: "For knowing that a certain way of life is rational is knowing that one is wholly justified in committing oneself to it. To know that it is rational is already to have all the reasons one could possibly have for living it. . . . The decision to commit oneself to a way of life which is rationally chosen over other ways of life (each of which must be fully known for the choice to be enlightened and hence rational) is the most reasonable, least arbitrary, and best founded decision of all. It is the decision to live the way of life one is most justified in living, all things considered."[134]

Conclusion: The Ethical Cul-de-Sac and the Value of General Ethics

We began our inquiry with general ethics, launching the moral quest solely on the basis of what we could discover through the use of human reason. In this context we raised the foundational philosophical questions: How can we determine what the good life is? Will reason lead to the right understanding of the good life? Is the good life the same for everyone? That is, is there a universal sense of the good life?

Our survey of possible ways of determining the nature of the ethical life, as well as the various theories that could guide the moral quest, led us finally to the question, Why be ethical? And we concluded, "Because the ethical life promotes the good life." This resulted in a further question, Why should I be concerned about the good life? And whose understanding of the good life should I pursue? In the end, our appeal rested on what we see as universally human: to be human, reason tells us, is to promote our own well-being, our own enjoyment of the good life.

This survey suggests that general ethics eventually takes us back to ourselves. The universal question—What is the good life?—always raises the personal question—What do I consider to be the good life? What is the *telos* that ultimately motivates me and my pursuits? What final goal am I trying to accomplish? What purpose drives me? What vision of the good life lies at the end of my quest?

Many philosophical ethicists have observed this. Nowell-Smith, for example, concluded his lengthy treatise on ethics with a blatant acknowledgment that his ethical reflections in the end bring him back to the individual human person: "What sort of [ethical] principles a man adopts will, in the end, depend on his vision of the Good Life, his conception of the sort of world that he desires, so far as it rests with him, to create. Indeed his moral principles just *are* this conception." And this conception of the good life, the philosopher quickly added, is not readily altered by a sheer act of the will: "The conception can be altered; perhaps he meets someone whose character, conduct, or arguments reveal to him new virtues that he has never even contemplated; or he may do something uncharacteristic and against his principles without choosing to do it and, in doing it, discover how good it is. Moral values, like other values, are sometimes discovered accidentally. But the one thing he cannot do is to *try* to alter his conception of the Good Life; for it is ultimately by reference to this conception that all his choices are made. And the fact that he cannot choose to alter this conception neither shields him from blame nor disqualifies him from admiration."[135] Consequently, "The questions 'What shall I do?' and 'What moral principles should I adopt?' must be answered by each man for himself; that at least is part of the connotation of the word 'moral.'"[136]

At first glance, our survey appears to yield a solid foundation for the moral quest. The ethical life means living in accordance with universal human reason. Upon closer inspection, however, we discover that the path we have been pursuing is actually a dead end. We have been walking around in a cul-de-sac. Universal human reason can only lead back to our starting point—the reasonable self.

Perhaps the inevitable circularity of philosophical ethics is redemptive, however. Precisely by leaving us within the human realm through its appeal either to society or to the self, and hence to reason itself, general ethics can point us beyond itself and beyond the merely human. Casting about in this dead-end pursuit raises the question as to whether there might be a transcendent vantage point that can speak to the human ethical quest. Perhaps we must look for a religious or theological foundation for the ethical life.[137] Indeed, a religious vision provides us with a sense of the transcendent, a sense of being connected to something "beyond," something greater than the here and now, something bigger than this life. And this sense of connection with the transcendent can give meaning to our world and to ourselves.

Several strands of contemporary thought confirm that this proposal has promise. Philosophers such as Franklin I. Gamwell have concluded that the justification of moral claims requires a foundational principle that in the end is religious.[138] Many sociologists now realize that religion is crucial to an ordered society and to social stability. Religious insight contributes to the construction of the shared fabric of meaning that characterizes a people.[139] Similarly, psychologists have come to see how important religion can be to personal identity formation.

It is this theological vision that we will pursue in subsequent chapters. But before we do so, we must pause to look more closely at the ancient Greek ethicists who bequeathed to the Christian tradition the heritage of general ethics.

Chapter 2

THE GREEK ETHICAL TRADITION

Jews demand miraculous signs and Greeks look for wisdom, but we preach Christ crucified: a stumbling block to Jews and foolishness to Gentiles, but to those whom God has called, both Jews and Greeks, Christ the power of God and the wisdom of God. For the foolishness of God is wiser than [human] wisdom, and the weakness of God is stronger than [human] strength.
(1 CORINTHIANS 1:22-25)

One day a Jewish traveler arrived in Athens, the famous center of Greek philosophical thought. After debating the foreign teacher in the public marketplace, some of Athens's leading philosophers invited him to join them at the Areopagus. At this gathering they would hear more about the strange new teaching he had been presenting (Acts 17:16-34).

With Paul's arrival in the Gentile world, the Christian gospel discovered the Greek philosophical tradition.

Christianity and the Greek Ethical Tradition

In its general sense, ethics may be defined as "moral philosophy." It involves reflecting on morality, moral problems and moral judgments. Viewed in this broad sense, ethics is not an exclusively Christian endeavor. Philosophical reflection on morality is not limited to Christians. In fact, for the genesis of the dominant approach to the ethical task in our society, we must look to ancient Greece. The Greek philosophers provided the mold that gave shape to the Western ethical tradition.

The early followers of Jesus saw themselves primarily as a continuation of what God had begun with the Hebrew people. Therefore, the foundation for Christian ethics lay in the Old Testament. But as the gospel expanded into the Gentile world, Christians encountered the Greek philosophical tradition. Paul, for example, conversed with Epicureans, Stoics and other Greek thinkers on his missionary forays (e.g., Acts 17:16-21). And as Christianity gained a firm foothold in the Roman Empire, Christians sought to understand the implications of the gospel of Jesus Christ for a context shaped by the philosophical ethics of ancient Greece. In this sense, Greece has formed an intellectual cradle not only for Western philosophical ethics, but for Christian ethics as well.

In general, the ancient Greek thinkers focused their attention on the question, How can we attain well-being? Many of them assumed that as humans we are by nature teleological creatures, ordered toward the attainment of one ultimate end. The ethical quest, therefore, was the attempt to determine how we should best live and act so as to reach our *telos*. This teleological orientation greatly influenced Christian ethics, at least until the dawn of the modern era, when the focus shifted to the question of practical judgment, namely, How can we explain the experience of "oughtness"?[1]

In this chapter we listen to the five major voices in the ancient tradition of philosophical ethics: Plato, Aristotle, Epicurus, the Stoics and Plotinus. Plato offered an ethic of ordered integration. Aristotle devised an ethic of well-being. Epicurus focused on peace of mind. The Stoics were chiefly interested in self-control. And Plotinus explored the ethical life in its connection with divinization or becoming one with the divine. Individually and collectively these five voices formed the context in which the Christian ethical alternative developed.

Plato and Ordered Integration

Many historians date the beginning of the Greek philosophical tradition to the sixth century before Christ and the work of Thales of Miletus (640-546 B.C.).[2] It seems that prior to this time the Greeks did not concern themselves with questions out of which science and philosophy would develop—such as whether permanent substances lie behind the appearances of change—and which would likewise lead to ethical inquiry. Two centuries later, Aristotle credited Thales with originating the search for principles of explanation.[3]

Plato, therefore, was not the first Greek philosopher. Yet this famous student of Socrates was the first to write extensively on the various problems of philosophy.[4] The abiding importance of this fifth-century Greek thinker to the history of ideas is undeniable. One commentator wrote: "Plato in philosophy was a genuine innovator on a scale to which succeeding centuries offer no parallel."[5]

The life of an aristocrat. Plato (428-348 B.C.) was born into one of the most illustrious families of Athens. In fact, his paternal ancestry traced back to the last king of the city.[6] Inevitably, therefore, his own early ambitions would have led him to a career in politics. But he gradually became disenchanted with public service due to the corruption he saw in the Athenian government, climaxing in the sentencing of his beloved teacher, Socrates, in 399. Concerning his rejection of the political vocation, Plato later wrote, "Whereas at first I had been full of enthusiasm for public work, now I could only look on and watch everything whirling round me this way and that. . . . In the end I came to the conclusion that all the cities of the present age are badly governed."[7]

The career of Socrates, both his questioning of the unquestioned presuppositions of the age and his morally upright life, attracted Plato to philosophy. He hoped that "true philosophy" would provide a foundation for eliminating the confusion and error he saw around him.

After the death of his mentor, Plato left Athens to travel, follow the philosophical vocation and vindicate Socrates' life by composing a series of dialogues. He spent the next twelve years in Egypt, Italy and Sicily, as well as Greece. Eventually Plato traced his steps back to his home city. Upon his return he founded his famous Academy, where he taught, with a few brief interruptions, until his death.

Ordered integration and the soul. There are several ways of characterizing Plato's ethical teaching. In a sense it would be proper to say that he set forth an ethic of self-realization.[8] According to Plato the goal of life is to actualize our true nature, together with our many innate potentialities. This suggests that Plato proposed a teleological ethic. Yet it would perhaps be more appropriate to call his proposal an ethic of "ordered integration" or "harmony." For Plato the highest good, whether within the individual or the corporate life, is a well-ordered whole to which each part contributes according to its own capacity.

The quest for ordered integration in the individual human life led to Plato's understanding of virtue. In a typically Greek philosophical manner, Plato distributed the virtues among the constituent "parts" of the human soul (i.e., the human mental life).[9] The rational aspect includes the power of reason—the ability to think clearly as well as to know truth and goodness. Consequently the corresponding virtue is *wisdom,* the ability to exercise the power of reason.

Plato divided the nonrational or passionate aspect of the human soul into the spirited part and the sensuous or appetitive part. The former consists in the power of the will, which includes anger in the face of vice. Hence the corresponding virtue is *courage,* which for Plato is knowing what to do and what not to fear. The sensuous part suggests a third virtue, *temperance,* or the ability to control one's desires.

These three demand a fourth, integrating virtue, *justice.* For Plato, when the appetitive part is subordinated to the spirited, and both are subordinated to the rational part, harmony emerges. The philosopher called this harmonizing virtue "justice." Justice involves the correct balance between authority and submission. And it entails the harmonious functioning of wisdom, courage and temperance as ordered and ruled by reason. Plato's system is summarized in table 1.

Part	Power	Corresponding Virtue
rational	reason	wisdom
passionate		
spirited	will	courage
sensuous	appetite	temperance
		justice (integrative link)

Table 1. Plato's Delineation of the Virtues of the Human Soul

While Plato extolled four distinctive, central virtues, to him these were not four separable traits. Instead they are interrelated and inseparable. Together they comprise one integrated virtuous life.[10] Wisdom and justice are mutually related, in Plato's thinking, for a wise person is one in whom all elements act together in harmony; yet this harmonious activity requires that the person display true wisdom in directing the various elements. Courage and temperance, in turn, are aspects of the wisely regulated actions of the soul, which arise as reason trains the will and as they together control the appetites.

Plato's understanding of the virtuous life led to his conclusion about the source of evil actions: disorder within the soul. Indeed, if the virtuous life arises as reason controls the passions and thereby brings about harmonious action, then evil emerges when nonrational impulses prevail over reason.

More significant, however, is another thesis that arises out of Plato's emphasis on wisdom as the virtue connected with reason, namely, that ignorance is the chief cause of evil actions. According to this understanding, which may actually date to Socrates,[11] we always do what we believe is good. Or to state this in a negative manner, we never set out to do evil. We never do evil voluntarily. If we do an act that is evil and not good, the problem lies with our judgment. Evil, therefore, is simply an error of judgment. In short, then, virtue is the exercise of wisdom, whereas vice is the product of folly.[12]

The ordered society. Plato's concept of justice as the virtue of harmonious action forges a link between the individual and the social dimensions of life. Justice is not merely a personal virtue but is preeminently a social one. More specifically, it is that condition of social harmony that emerges as all participants in society offer their individual contributions to the whole.

In his understanding of how these contributions are to be determined, Plato was no modern-day radical individualist but an aristocratic collectivist. Nor was he a democrat. Having seen first hand the potential deficiency of democracy, Plato regarded this form of government as placing in positions of authority and power those who happen to gain the ear of the ignorant *populus* rather than those who are truly wise.[13]

In place of an egalitarian democracy, Plato envisioned a stratified society. Corresponding to the parts of the human soul, he pictured a division of people within the ideal state into three classes according to their central function in society. Corresponding to the rational part of the soul are the legislators (who manage the public matters), corresponding to the spirited are the soldiers and educators (who protect the society against external and internal enemies), and corresponding to the appetitive are the workers (the merchants, traders and business people whose function is economic and who provide the material needs of the society). On the basis of natural abilities and interests, each citizen is to be a member of a certain class and to contribute to society according to the purposes of that class. Plato even advocated that certain people—especially the rulers—be bred for their future roles in society.[14]

In Plato's ideal society, each class is to exemplify one of the three cardinal virtues introduced earlier—wisdom (the legislators), courage (the soldiers) and temperance (the workers). As its citizens acknowledge their respective stations and live accordingly, the resultant harmony allows society to realize its own integrative virtue, namely, justice. It would be a mistake to localize too rigidly the virtues in their respective social classes, however. Just as all the virtues reside in the virtuous person as an interrelated whole, so also the virtues are present in the well-ordered society as a whole.

While our democratic sympathies lead us to differ vehemently with the ancient thinker, we ought not lose sight of the important point he makes. As Alasdair MacIntyre pointed out, "Plato accepts the fact that moral concepts are only intelligible against the background of a certain sort of social order."[15] The philosopher's drawing together of the individual and the social dimensions of the virtuous life provides a needed corrective to the one-sided individualism of much modern ethical theory. Yet whether the social order is a sufficient background for moral concepts is a question we will need to raise later.

The nature of the good. Plato's description of the ethical life was constructed upon the quest for the good, which like many Greek thinkers he understood as "well-being." The good life is the life of ordered integration. Yet Plato sought to delve deeper into the nature of the good. The philosopher's attempt to determine what exactly is this highest human good eventually led him to another dimension of the philosophical enterprise, metaphysics, and to his famous theory of the forms.

His sustained philosophical pursuit of the good provides historians with a convenient way of dividing Plato's writing career into three stages.[16] Like so many other philosophers, Plato initially asserted that pleasure is the ultimate good (e.g., in the dialogue *Protagoras*). In the second stage of his career *(Gorgias, Phaedo),* however, he radically reversed the hedonism of the first. Because it is transient, pleasure cannot be the essential good the philosopher seeks. In fact, he denied that pleasure is a good at all. Instead of the pursuit of pleasure, Plato advocated a strenuous morality of strict virtue.

In the third stage Plato came to a more balanced position. He realized that although pleasure may not be the absolute good, some pleasures are nevertheless legitimate elements in the good life *(Philebus),* although in the end the philosopher alone enjoys real pleasure. Yet beyond pleasure is a higher standard, Plato added. This higher good is immortality, with regard to which the activities of this life are to be judged.

The good and the forms. The move beyond hedonism points to a specific metaphysical proposal that emerged as the underpinning of Plato's ethic of ordered integration. His understanding of the good arose from his famous theory of the forms (or ideas).

In contrast to the viewpoint of most people today, Plato conceived of reality as made up of two aspects. On the surface, as it were, is the realm of perception or sense experience. This is the realm of the many, which includes individual things or objects. This is also the realm of change or "becoming." For Plato, however, this is less real than the second sphere, the realm of the forms or the ideas. The forms are the eternal, unchangeable essences exemplified by the many individual objects we encounter through our senses. The realm of the forms is the realm of "being." This realm logically precedes that of particular objects.

To cite one example,[17] Plato argued that the concept of circularity antedates our ability to identify circular objects. Our idea of circularity does not correspond to anything in the physical world, because all such objects are subject to change over time. Instead, our concept must be of an unchanging—that is, nontemporal—object. Such eternal objects are what Plato meant by the forms.

Plato theorized that the eternal forms are more real than the changeable objects we encounter, for we must presuppose them in all our explanations of the world. Ultimately, therefore, knowledge is concerned solely with the forms; what we seek to know are these unchangeable realities. Such knowledge is absolute, universal and objective. And the philosopher is the one who has developed the intellectual skills necessary to know them.

As we noted earlier, in good Greek fashion Plato suggested that the goal of anything is to actualize its own nature. To him, this meant that each individual thing is to exemplify the corresponding form. This provided the foundation for his understanding of the good. "Good," according to the Greek thinker, simply means "exemplifying the corresponding form." Hence, a specific tree is "good" if it exemplifies treeness. A good chair is one that exemplifies chairness. However, all objects always remain only imperfect representations of their corresponding form. For example, no perfect circle exists in the material realm. Such a deficiency in exemplifying the corresponding form is "evil." For Plato, to the extent that something is unable to show forth its corresponding form because of some deficiency, it is plagued by evil.

Just as anything is good to the extent that it reflects its form, so also the good for humans consists of exemplifying our form, which is humanness. Ultimately, humanness involves attaining knowledge of the eternal forms. Plato derived this conclusion from his earlier assumption that we are inherently intellectual beings. What sets us apart from the animals is our reason. By means of this power we can attain true knowledge, knowledge of the eternal realm beyond the changeable, physical objects present to our senses and hence beyond the realm of becoming. By using the power of reason we can contemplate the forms and hence gain access to the eternal realm of being.

Plato's metaphysic and his ethic come together in his conception of the Form of the Good. According to Plato the forms comprise a hierarchy. At the apex of this ontological hierarchy lies the Form of the Good or goodness itself. This highest form makes all the others intelligible. The ultimate goal of the knowing process, therefore, is the attainment of knowledge of the Form of the Good. Consequently, the Form of the Good also stands as the goal of our quest for the virtuous life. As Plato declared, "But in my opinion, for what it is worth, the final thing to be perceived in the intelligible region, and perceived only with difficulty, is the form of the good; once seen, it is inferred to be responsible for whatever is right and valuable in anything, producing in the visible region light and the source of light, and being in the intelligible region itself the controlling source of truth and intelligence. And anyone who is going to act rationally either in public or private life must have sight of it."[18]

Yet we must interject one caveat: Attaining knowledge of the Form of the Good is not necessarily within the grasp of everyone. In the end it is the prerogative of the philosophers, who alone are capable of such lofty knowledge.[19]

We may now summarize Plato's advice for the ethical life: Beware of pleasure, especially the pleasures of the body. Seek instead to observe balance and harmony in life, so that you may follow intellectual pursuits, at the apex of which is contemplation of the Form of the Good.

The quest for the good. As we have seen, Plato's ethic is dependent on his metaphysic with its focus on the Form of the Good. In this manner he pinpointed a crucial problem in philosophical ethics, namely, that of the ultimate criterion for ethical judgments. His ethic was motivated by a concern to understand the meaning of the terms we use in making ethical judgments (such as the "good") apart from the particular judgments themselves ("x is good"). As a result his approach was deductive rather than inductive. MacIntyre captured this crucial distinction: "When we inquire about what it is for something to be just or red or equal, the rational first move is to offer examples, to try and find a list of just actions or red objects or cases of equality. But such a list misses the point of the inquiry. What we want to know is not which actions are just, but what it is in virtue of which actions are just."[20]

The only final criterion Plato could offer appealed to the philosopher's apprehension of the Form of the Good. Subsequent thinkers have not always found this answer satisfying.[21] At the heart of the difficulty is Plato's inability to grasp an essential feature of goodness: Our term *good* does not in fact characterize what is. Instead, through it we grope after what ought to be.[22] That is, we seek what is not yet.

Aristotle and Well-Being

Plato may have been the first great ethical thinker. But the honor of being the first thinker in Western civilization to offer a systematic treatise on ethics goes to Aristotle (384-323 B.C.), Plato's greatest pupil.[23] Centuries after his death, he was hailed by Dante as "the master of those who know."[24]

The universal scholar. Unlike Socrates and Plato, Aristotle was not a native Athenian. Instead he was born in the little town of Stagira in northern Greece (or Thrace) and thus on the frontier between the advancing "barbarian" Macedonian empire and the declining "civilized" Greek city-states. The son of Nicomachus,[25] a physician in the court of Macedonia, Aristotle was also trained in medicine. After the death of his father, the eager eighteen-year-old made his way to Athens to enter Plato's Academy for philosophical schooling (368 B.C.).

Aristotle remained at the Academy nearly twenty years, studying, writing and eventually also teaching. But when Plato's death (348) resulted in another person being appointed head of the school, he left Athens. After several years of teaching, travel and biological research, the philosopher was invited to the Macedonian court (343). Philip, the king of Macedonia, wanted a tutor for his son, the young Alexander, who would later conquer the known world.

Although his role at the court probably lasted only three years, Aristotle did not return to Athens until the year after Philip's death (335). Perhaps because Plato's academy was headed by a man with whose point of view Aristotle was not in sympathy,[26] he founded his own school, the Lyceum.[27] The teacher's lecture style—speaking while walking back and forth—earned the school a nickname, the Peripatos (the "covered walk" or "to walk about").[28] The ensuing twelve years were a fruitful time for Aristotle. He engaged in investigation, teaching and writing in almost every branch of knowledge.

Alexander's untimely death interrupted the philosopher's idyllic existence. Now the Athenians' smoldering resentment against their Macedonian overlords burst into flame. Aristotle's association with the Macedonian court made him suspect in the eyes of the city leaders. They charged him with various acts of impiety.[29] But before the case could be tried, Aristotle, refusing to follow the path trod by Socrates nearly eighty years earlier, left the city again. Lest the Athenians sin twice against philosophy, as Aristotle supposedly remarked, he exiled himself to the town of Chalcis in Euboea. The following year he died at the age of sixty-three.

The world of form plus matter. Aristotle's ethical thought was deeply embedded in his conclusions in another branch of reflection, metaphysics, which he spoke of as "first philosophy." In his opinion, metaphysics is foundational to the scientific enterprise, for it supplies the first principles of the sciences.

Aristotle proposed a seemingly slight, yet far-reaching alteration of Plato's understanding of reality. He agreed with his mentor that the unchangeable, eternal forms are more perfect than changeable objects. He also believed that the goal of every natural thing is to exemplify perfectly its own corresponding form. And like Plato, he declared that contemplation of unchangeable essences is the highest human activity. But Aristotle rejected his mentor's suggestion that the forms exist outside of specific objects. According to the younger philosopher, individual objects are a unity of form and matter.

Aristotle's rejection of Plato arose in part from his understanding of causation and, in turn, of substances. Causation was crucial, because the discovery of causes provides the first principles that the philosopher is seeking. The conclusions Aristotle drew at this point played a significant role in philosophical reflection from the Middle Ages until the dawning of the modern era.

Everything that is, Aristotle said, exists because of four causes,[30] not merely one or two, as some of his predecessors had erroneously thought. He labeled these four the material, the formal, the efficient and the final. By *material* cause he meant simply the elements of which the object is compounded. But rather than focusing attention here—as the atomists, for example, had done—Aristotle determined that a more important cause was the *formal,* that is, the form or pattern that shapes the material into the object. The formal cause is what makes a ceramic bowl, for example, a bowl rather than merely a lump of clay. In addition, there is the *efficient* cause, the actual agent—such as the potter—whose activity produced the object. But above all, Aristotle pointed out, every object exists because of a *final* cause, which determines its purpose or *telos*—its *raison d'etre.*

Like other philosophers, Aristotle sought to account for the changeableness of objects in the world of senses while noticing that objects have a certain durableness to them as well. As a result, he differentiated between the *substance* of an object and its *accidents.* A substance is the permanent substratum underlying the changeable qualities—color, texture, size and so on—that we can perceive with our senses. We must not equate the concept of substance with physical matter, however. Rather than being merely matter, an object exists because of the presence of what Aristotle called its *form.* A form is the purposive element that shapes an object and brings it into actual existence. Every object, therefore, consists of form plus matter.

Another way of understanding matter and form is through the distinction between potentiality and actuality. According to Aristotle, all objects are potentially whatever they have the capacity to become, even before they attain their potential. Hence, an acorn is a potential oak tree even before it takes root and grows. "Matter" is the potentiality that can become an actuality when it takes on its appropriate form. Contrary to what we might anticipate, the philosopher declared that the actual (the form) logically precedes the potential (the matter). That is, the chicken precedes the egg—not temporally, but logically—because the chicken is the goal latent in the egg, the actuality of which the egg is a potentiality.

Here Aristotle differed sharply with Plato. The forms do not inhabit an eternal realm of their own separate from the present, visible world, he concluded. Instead they inhere in the specific objects of sense experience.

The human telos. Aristotle's metaphysic carried important implications for ethics. He rejected Plato's assertion that moral reflection presupposes an independently existing "good." Instead, "good" inheres in the activities of daily living. Therefore, it can be discovered only through diligent study of human life.[31]

The philosopher developed what we have already characterized as a teleological, that is, a goal-oriented ethic. In fact, as we noted above, the philosopher believed that everything in existence—and not just humans—is made with a purpose, for each exists due to a final cause.

His ethical proposal began with the question about the purpose or function of the human person (our final cause). And to discover the answer, Aristotle raised the question, What is desirable as an end in itself rather than the means to some further end? What is the self-sufficient goal of our desires, that which if attained we would desire nothing else? The philosopher's answer came as the result of an empirical investigation of what humans do in fact desire. In contrast to several of his predecessors, his conclusion was not simply "pleasure"—Aristotle was no pure hedonist—but "happiness" *(eudaimonia):* "Happiness then is the best, noblest, and most pleasant thing in the world."[32]

We ought not to mistake Aristotle's concept for what people today so often mean by the word "happiness," namely, the inner feeling or somewhat transitory mood of "being happy." Rather, as we might expect from a Greek thinker, the philosopher understood happiness as "well-being." Happiness involves both living (or behaving) well and faring well.[33] And in keeping with the Greek tradition, he described this well-being in conjunction with the intellect. Happiness is not a static state of being but an activity. Perfect activity produces perfect happiness. Therefore, the highest happiness arises through the activity that is connected with our highest good.

But what is the human good? Aristotle's answer built from his analysis of our use of the term *good* itself. *Good* refers primarily to excellence in the performance of whatever activity is essential to the nature of the performer of the activity. Hence, the activity that is essential to the nature of a teacher is teaching. And consequently a good teacher is one who teaches excellently.

Like most Greek thinkers of his day, Aristotle argued that the activity that is characteristically human—the activity that separates us from other living things—is reflection or contemplation. The human is the rational animal, to cite his famous definition, and as a result our purpose lies in the exercise of rationality or reason. While not ignoring the "inferior" aspects of human existence that are connected to our biological nature and the satisfaction of which are necessary preconditions of contemplation, Aristotle asserted that our supreme happiness emerges through the blossoming of our rational nature. Happiness, therefore, must be explained in terms of reason: it involves the full realization of our human rationality. The happiness all humans seek, therefore, lies in excellence in performing the activity of thinking. It involves fulfilling well our proper human function[34] as rational beings.

The virtue of excellence. Aristotle's purpose-centered ethic leads us directly to his concept of virtue and the virtuous life. He declared that human happiness or the human good is the "activity of soul exhibiting excellence [virtue],"[35] which means, as we have just noted, that happiness is the effective exercise of reason.[36] Because the good life entails excellence, "excellence" informs Aristotle's concept of virtue, which plays a central role in his ethic.

The philosopher's understanding of virtue was informed by his teleological ethic. For him a virtue is a quality that allows whoever possesses it to function well—to perform its proper function effectively—and hence to gain well-being and happiness. Thus virtues do not carry a strict moral sense. Rather, they include all the various good qualities of character, including such traits as wittiness and cordiality (or friendliness), as well as the more traditional virtues such as courage, temperance and truthfulness.[37]

Following Plato's lead, Aristotle connected the central virtues to the human soul, which in typically Greek fashion he also divided into rational and nonrational parts. The rational aspect is the sphere of the intellectual virtues, whereas the nonrational is connected to the moral virtues.

The rational aspect of the soul includes the "scientific" or "knowing" dimension (i.e., contemplation). Consequently, the virtuous life involves *theoretical wisdom* or the knowledge of eternal realities. Within the rational soul is also the calculative dimension (deliberation). Here the corresponding virtue is *practical wisdom* or prudence, which Aristotle defined as the ability to choose proper means to attain right goals. The nonrational aspect of the human person, in turn, consists of the appetitive or emotional dimension, in which the virtuous dispositions of character are to be operative, and the vegative dimension (i.e., physical growth), for which there are no corresponding virtues. See table 2.

Part	**Function**	**Corresponding Virtue**
Rational		Intellectual virtues
scientific	calculation	theoretical wisdom
calculative	deliberation	practical wisdom
Nonrational		Moral virtues
appetitive	emotion	character dispositions
vegative	physical growth	(none)

Table 2. Aristotle's Delineation of the Virtues of the Soul

Aristotle's manner of dividing the soul suggests how it is that virtue is central to our attainment of the goal of our existence and hence to our well-being. Virtue facilitates us in the task of actualizing our form as human beings. In fact we attain our purpose through the development of virtue. The ideal life includes above all exercising theoretical wisdom as we contemplate eternal realities by gaining intuitive knowledge of first principles and scientific knowledge of the theorems that arise from that knowledge. The ideal life involves as well the exercise of practical wisdom as we make right decisions in accordance with reason. Equally necessary in this enterprise is the development of the moral virtues as we keep our desires and emotions in tune with reason. This last enterprise is the specific topic of ethics.

While reason—that is, the contemplative life—provides our final purpose, Aristotle emphasized the importance of developing dispositions of character (the moral virtues), which belong to the nonrational aspect of the soul. The philosopher agreed with Socrates and Plato that bad behavior is the result of ignorance[38]—at least sometimes. Yet by distinguishing moral virtue from intellectual virtue, Aristotle indicated that the ethical life requires more than knowledge.[39] Not only must we *know* what is right, we must also *choose* to do the right. This requires the presence of proper dispositions of character, and these do not belong directly to the rational part of the soul. In the end, the virtuous life arises through the cooperation of reason and will. The moral virtues are the specific domain of the will. But they are to be governed by reason or the intellect.[40] In this manner, the good life requires both intellectual and moral excellence.

Aristotle is convinced that we can develop into virtuous persons. This is possible in part because of the power of will. As humans we are able to act voluntarily. (Something is voluntary when it is not done under compulsion nor through ignorance.)[41] Because we voluntarily choose between good and evil, moral states are likewise voluntary: "Therefore virtue also is in our own power, and so too vice. For where it is in our power to act it is also in our power not to act, and *vice versa*."[42]

In addition to the will, we possess a natural capacity toward virtue, which according to Aristotle makes it possible for us to develop into virtuous persons. Yet this capacity is only a potentiality. To actualize our potential requires that we exercise our will properly, that is, that the will be directed to a right end by rational moral principles. In this manner, the will can lead us to engage in a right act, which Aristotle saw as involving the performance of the right thing to the right person in the right way to the right extent and for the right purpose.[43]

Yet one right act does not produce a virtuous life. Nor do our wills remain forever free. Instead, the habits we develop over time dispose the will in one direction or another. For this reason the life of happiness requires the cultivation of virtuous dispositions of character. This occurs through training and the building of good habits as we repeatedly do right acts. Moral virtues are simply the positive habits we have formed.

In short, virtue is a habit that arises from the natural capacities of our soul and that is formed as we voluntarily act under the guidance of rational moral principles.[44] And our innate potential to develop moral virtue, in turn, makes moral instruction possible.

As we have noted, Aristotle acknowledged the connection between right acts and the development of virtues. Yet his chief concern was virtue rather than merely right acts. As a result he elevated disposition as the crucial factor in making ethical judgments about a person. A right act can occasionally be performed by a nonvirtuous person, he argued, but that act alone does not make the person virtuous. Similarly, a virtuous person may occasionally commit an act of vice, but such an act does not brand the person unvirtuous. For this reason, Aristotle would have considered the faithful husband who committed an isolated act of adultery (whom we mentioned in the previous chapter) fundamentally virtuous, despite the one instance of vice.

Aristotle agreed with Plato that virtue involves excellence. Yet he did not stop with this idea. For Aristotle the excellence of the moral virtues consists in habitual moderation,[45] that is, in the "golden mean." Virtue, then, to cite his words, "is a state of character concerned with choice, lying in a mean, i.e., the mean relative to us, this being determined by a rational principle, and by that principle by which the man of practical wisdom would determine it."[46] Virtue is always a mean between two extremes—a vice of deficiency and a vice of excess—both of which lead us to do wrong and eventually contribute to unhappiness. To cite one example, courage is the mean between cowardice (which is a vice of deficiency) and foolhardiness (the corresponding vice of excess).

One trait, justice, is not the mean between two extremes but is the sum of all virtue, and its absence is the sum of all vice.[47] While Plato defined justice as the harmonious ordering of the individual soul, in Aristotle's thinking justice is a social virtue. At its heart, this virtue consists in voluntarily doing what is good for, and avoiding what is harmful to others.[48] Justice likewise involves fairness and lawfulness. Table 3 sorts virtues and vices according to Aristotle's concept of the golden mean.

Vice of Deficiency	Virtue (Moderation)	Vice of Excess
cowardice	courage	foolhardiness
insensibility	temperance	licentiousness
stinginess	generosity	prodigality
meanness	magnificence	vulgarity (the ostentatious display of wealth)
humility	highmindedness	vanity
lack of ambition	wholesome ambition	overambitiousness
impassivity	gentleness	irascibility
self-deprecation	truthfulness	boastfulness
boorishness	wittiness	buffoonery
contentiousness	friendliness	flattery
shamelessness	modesty	bashfulness
maliciousness	righteous indignation	enviousness
injustice	justice	injustice

Table 3. Aristotle's Golden Mean[49]

Like Plato, Aristotle conceived of the individual life of virtue as embedded in the social dimension of human existence. In fact, in his ordering of the branches of knowledge, the philosopher placed ethics as a subdivision of a comprehensive science he labeled "politics," which likewise contained the studies of economics and politics proper. At the same time Aristotle acknowledged that human communities are composed of individuals. And he knew that unless the parts are good the whole cannot be perfect. Consequently in his ordering of academic studies, ethics, as the science of individual good, provides the foundation for the investigation of the principles of human society.[50]

The philosopher's understanding of the proper society built from his assertion that humans are naturally gregarious. We form communities with other humans—first families, then villages and finally the state—for ends that seem good to us. Because we are naturally gregarious, we can properly fulfill our human potential only as we live within communities. In this sense, the ethical life must be social, and the virtues involve good conduct directed toward others.[51]

The highest expression of the social process is the state. According to Aristotle, the state is not merely "an association of people dwelling in the same place, established to prevent its members from committing injustice against each other, and to promote transactions." Instead, in typically Aristotelian language, he added that it should be "an association intended to enable its members, in their households and the kinships, to live *well;* its purpose is a perfect and self-sufficient life . . . and that, we hold, means living happily and nobly."[52]

Aristotle and the fallacy of naturalism. Aristotle's ethic of the actualization of well-being may rank as the greatest expression of ancient Greek thought, and its longevity as an influential statement of philosophical ethics is unsurpassed. Although overshadowed by the influence of Plato during the patristic era of Christian history, Aristotelian ideas reemerged in the Middle Ages, largely due to the work of the Christian thinker Thomas Aquinas. Aristotle's ongoing importance to Western thought has been evidenced more recently in the work of the twentieth-century philosopher Alasdair MacIntyre.

Yet in the opinion of many critics, the ethic proposed by the great Greek thinker suffers from several problems.[53] Two of these are the most debilitating. The first is connected to the foundation from which it draws. As we have seen, Aristotle's proposal is teleological. The ethical life is connected to our human telos, to the goal of our existence. While fundamentally oriented to a goal, Aristotle's ethic is nevertheless naturalistic. Our human telos is in its entirety already present within us, being the latent potentiality that is ours from the beginning. Like all naturalistic philosophical ethical proposals, his is hard pressed to avoid being dashed on the rocks of the naturalistic fallacy. In the end, Aristotle would have us do the impossible, namely, to move from an "is" which is totally immanent in our being to the "ought" that we are ethically required to actualize.

The second problem builds from the first. Critics rightly point out that Aristotle's teleological ethic is also eudaemonian. The philosopher's view of the ultimate goal of human existence is happiness. By elevating happiness as the ethical ideal, critics charge, Aristotle's proposal runs aground on the shoals of the "hedonistic paradox." In the final analysis, like pleasure, happiness—even understood as "well-being"—cannot be pursued directly. There is no road that we can take which will lead to happiness. Instead it is a byproduct. It arrives, sometimes even unexpectedly, as we engage in other activities that may only remotely be connected to what we might assume to be the pursuit of happiness.

Despite its plausibility, this criticism may be a bit wide of the mark. Aristotle did not in fact extol happiness as the object of our human quest. He too saw true happiness as a byproduct, and therefore he sought to determine what led to the well-being we all desire. Aristotle found the answer in our human function, that is, in the goal of our existence. He concluded that this involved excellence in the active exercise of the faculties of the soul, so that as reason leads to habitual moderation, we might enjoy the contemplative life.[54] This, he concluded, is the life of happiness.

But this conclusion leads us back to the problem we outlined above. It is precisely here that Aristotle is thrown back to the naturalism with which he began. Contrary to what he proposed, the goal of our existence is not latent in our nature waiting to be actualized. Nor does habitual moderation offer us the way to finding our highest good. And the contemplative life as Aristotle conceived it does not necessarily mark the actualization of some innate human nature we all possess as a potentiality. Viewed from the perspective of Jesus, only the pursuit of God's reign and God's righteousness carries the promise that "all these things will be given you as well" (Mt 6:33).

Epicurus and Peace of Mind

According to the book of Acts, upon his arrival in Athens, Paul discovered two flourishing philosophical traditions, the Epicureans and the Stoics. The first of these owes its name to an apparently withdrawn and frugal philosopher who avoided the public spotlight and chose to live much of his life teaching in the serenity of his own garden. Lauded by his students, Epicurus has even been hailed as the "apostle of common sense"[55] because of his unwavering commitment to the assumption that all knowledge arises from our senses, rather than from any innate ideas that philosophers like Socrates and Plato claimed we possess. The world, we might say, is simply what it appears to be. Further, Epicurus elevated the study of ethics to the exalted status of being our most important human occupation.[56] That "Epicurean" would later be equated with excess and even debauchery ranks among the greatest ironies of the history of ancient philosophical ethics.

The life of a serene sage. Concerning Epicurus (341-270 B.C.), scant information is available.[57] His father, Neocles, was one of the colonists sent from Athens to the island of Samos in the middle of the fourth century. Hence Epicurus was an Athenian by birth, although he may have been born on Samos. In either case, he spent perhaps the first twenty years of his life on the island. After the death of Alexander (323), the Athenians—in all likelihood including Epicurus—were driven out of Samos. Consequently the troubled years that followed saw the budding thinker in Athens and in the coastal towns of Asia Minor (now Turkey) pursuing philosophical study. In 311 Epicurus gathered a few disciples and eventually returned to Athens (306), where he resided until his death.

Following in the footsteps of Plato and Aristotle, Epicurus founded a school in Athens. Unlike theirs, however, his school was located in a secluded garden, which for the philosopher and his students—both men and women[58]—served as a serene refuge from the turmoil of the outside world in the era after the decline of the Greek city-states. It is a tribute to the far-reaching influence of Epicurus that the school remained true to the principles he taught for over five hundred years.[59]

Epicurus drew his foundational viewpoints from two important Greek thinkers of the age of Socrates, Democritus (c. 460-370) and Aristippus (c. 435-356). From their ideas he developed an ethic that espoused serenity or peace of mind, in contrast to the focus on contemplation of eternal knowledge that characterized Plato and Aristotle.

An austere hedonism. The beginning point for Epicurus's ethic lay in Aristippus's hedonism. Against Socrates, Aristippus observed that human nature is such that all people quite naturally seek what they believe will give them pleasure and avoid what will result in pain. Rather than bemoaning this situation, he declared that pleasure, understood as the feeling that results when the appetites are satisfied, is the highest good. His advice was to maximize the bodily pleasures of the moment, for these, and not the memory of past pleasures or the anticipation of future experiences, are the only ones that are real.[60] Virtue, in turn, is servant to the pleasure principle. For virtue is simply the capacity to choose the right pleasures.

Like his predecessor, Epicurus was a thoroughgoing hedonist. He agreed that pleasure is the sole ultimate good and pain the sole evil. He likewise agreed that virtue is simply "the art of pleasure," to borrow MacIntyre's description.[61] All virtuous conduct is empty and useless, except as it contributes to the pleasantness of one's own life.[62]

But here the agreement ends. Epicurus's advice about choosing the right pleasures differed radically from Aristippus's. In a sense the wise sage turned his predecessor's hedonism on its head. Rather than elevating the state of happiness resulting from satisfaction of the appetites, Epicurus focused on the mental life. Hence pleasure does not entail "continual drinking and dancing, nor sexual love, nor the enjoyment of fish and whatever else the luxurious table offers . . . rather, it is produced by the reason which is sober, which examines the motive for every choice and rejection, and which drives away all those opinions through which the greatest tumult lays hold of the mind."[63]

Several sobering considerations led Epicurus to this startling conclusion and resulted in the development of his austere hedonism. The philosopher asserted that more important than the *intensity* of pleasure is its *duration.* This realization led to a new appraisal of bodily experiences. Although not discounting physical pleasures, experience led him to see that the pursuit of such pleasure leads eventually to frustration. What is worse, physical pleasures are often accompanied by an even greater amount of pain. Consequently, Epicurus rejected Aristippus's appeal to what is the most intense sensual pleasure of the moment as the criterion for judging what is good.

Further, while agreeing that the body is the source or root of all pleasure, Epicurus concluded that the pleasures and pains of the mind are more significant than those of the body. The foundation for this lay likewise in Epicurus's preference for duration instead of intensity. Whereas bodily experiences are only momentary and fleeting, the powers of memory and anticipation elongate mental experiences. Hence, physical pleasure may provide momentary enjoyment. But when the sensation ends, the mental pain that arises from the withdrawal of the pleasurable experience often surpasses the pleasure itself.

As a result, Epicurus advocated passive or negative over active or positive pleasure,[64] the removal of pain rather than the stimulation of sense pleasure. In his estimation, our ultimate goal cannot be the attempt to create a constant succession of intense physical pleasures, for this is simply unachievable. Instead, our quest ought to be for serenity or peace of mind, which he described as freedom from trouble in the mind and pain in the body.

Epicurus taught that future considerations are of great assistance in the development of serenity in the present. When bodily experiences produce more pain than pleasure, the true sage should be able to compensate by means of mental pleasures that outweigh the pain. This is only possible, however, if the mind is not disturbed by fears for the future.[65] But how can we achieve such freedom from fear?

Radical materialism. Epicurus observed that the most disturbing anticipations of the future arise from our terror of death and our fear of the displeasure of the gods. Combating these superstitions requires a true understanding of the universe. For this Epicurus turned to the fifth-century philosopher Democritus, who taught what we might call "materialistic atomism."[66] Democritus stood in a long line of ancient thinkers who sought to give a rational explanation of the world in purely material terms,[67] that is, without appeal to the gods or to supersensible concepts (i.e., to supposed realities that lie beyond our senses). He theorized that the universe consisted of uncreated, indestructible bits of matter ("atoms") which combined and recombined to build all that is.[68]

On the basis of the theory of atomism,[69] Epicurus, like his predecessor, denied that some divine providence governs the world.[70] Even the gods are made of atoms. As a result, they neither reward nor punish humans. The gods do not control or even interest themselves in human life, and therefore events have purely physical rather than theological explanations.[71] If anything, the gods are models of the serene life that characterizes the goal of the sage's quest. Consequently Epicurus thought it possible to speak about good and evil without appeal to such metaphysical concepts as the will of the gods, supernatural laws or divinely imposed ideals of human duty.[72] Indeed his ethic was not one of duty at all but of concern for what we must do to live the good life.[73]

In Epicurus's opinion, true knowledge of the world—that is, radical materialism—can dispel our human fears. Above all we do not need to fear death. Because there is no divine retribution, we ought not to be terrorized by what supposedly comes after death. In fact his strict materialism led Epicurus to reject any idea of personal survival after death, for even the soul is made up of atoms, which dissipate when we die.[74] Nor do we need to live in terror of the anticipation of death. Epicurus came to this conclusion in a somewhat convoluted manner: "Death, the most dreaded of evils, is therefore of no concern to us; for while we exist death is not present, and when death is present we no longer exist. It is therefore nothing either to the living or to the dead since it is not present to the living, and the dead no longer are."[75]

Epicurus's unflinching attack on the religious superstition pervasive in his day and his adamant attempt to free humans from the fear of death won this eulogy from Lucretius, who was perhaps his most devoted later follower: "When human life lay foul before men's eyes, crushed to the dust beneath religion's weight . . . a man of Greece first dared to raise the eye of mortal against her, first stood ground against her. Not all god's glory, his lightning, heaven's rumble and rage, could stop him; rather they rasped his heart to keener courage, and made him a pioneer eager to burst the bolts on nature's door."[76]

Prudence and the value of friendship. Rather than the exploitation of pleasurable sense experience, Epicurus's "hedonism" consisted of the quest for a peaceful, pain-free existence. To this basically negative ethic he could only add that through study and personal effort a person could acquire the requisite virtues of the serene life. Most important on his list was prudence, the root of all other virtues.[77] Prudence is merely the application of a true understanding of the world to the personal life. The prudent person knows that we, and neither blind destiny nor the gods, control our own personal happiness. Prudence leads the sage to avoid besetting pain and choose the right pleasures, namely, whatever facilitates serenity and peace of mind.

Epicurus also advocated the cultivation of friendship, which he saw as the crown of the perfected life.[78] Yet the friendship the philosopher championed appears quite shallow and inconsistent.[79] It is largely based on self-interest or mutual utility, rather than mutual trust. Nor is it to be equated with the fuller communitarianism of Plato and Aristotle. Epicurus's model sage does not fall in love, beget a family or enter into political life. Rather, Epicurean friendship consists largely in the fellowship of the small philosophical fraternity that by withdrawing into simple living can pursue serene leisure and peace of mind.

In short, Epicurus's ethical advice was: Seek the life of serenity and peace of mind, and enjoy the company of a few good friends. In the end, then, although like Aristippus before him Epicurus advocated the pleasure principle, his ethic was quite different from the antinomianism and wild debauchery that has come to be associated with his name. Epicurus was not an "Epicurean." Yet, the fact that his teachings could come to be connected with a less austere hedonism indicates how difficult it is to set out on a road to pleasure that does not eventually lead to Vanity Fair.

The Stoics and Resigned Self-Control

Perhaps no philosophical tradition was more widely espoused in the first-century world than Stoicism. Commenting on the era after Aristotle, one historian even asserted, "The philosophy of the Hellenistic world was the Stoa; all else was secondary."[80] As this quotation suggests, "Stoic" derives from the "stoa poikile," the designation for the painted porch on the north side of the market place in Athens where the philosophers gathered. It was here that Zeno of Citium disseminated the ideas that came to bear the name "Stoic." The great nineteenth-century ethicist Henry Sidgwick suggested that the popularity of Stoicism was in part because the theory "bound the common notions of duty into an apparently complete and coherent system, by a formula that comprehended the whole of human life, and exhibited its relation to the ordered process of the universe."[81]

Living according to nature/living according to reason. For the genesis of the Stoic tradition many historians look to Zeno of Citium (c. 335-264 B.C.).[82] Rather than being a Greek, Zeno was a Semite, the son of a Phoenician merchant. He was forced by a shipwreck to land in Athens.[83] There he studied with the leading teachers of the day before launching out on his own.

Like many thinkers of his day, Zeno taught that the ultimate goal in life is wisdom. But unlike his contemporaries, he defined wisdom as living according to nature, rather than contemplating the eternal forms. He believed that reality is rational, for nature is governed by the laws of reason. Our lives, in turn, are guided by providence. Rather than futilely attempting to resist providence, the wise person willingly submits to it.

Where did this seminal idea lying at the heart of Stoicism come from? Foundational to Stoicism was a deterministic understanding of reality. Like Democrites, the early Stoics were materialists. They believed that everything in existence was made of material substances *(physis).* Although they may have accepted the standard theory of four basic elements (earth, air, fire and water), they were most interested in the third of these, which they regarded as the ultimate substance. In this sense, therefore, the Stoics were actually materialistic monists.[84]

The basic substance at the foundation of everything was not Democritus's shower of atoms but "fire." Yet we ought to avoid understanding this too literally. The world the Stoics envisioned was completely rational; everything that occurs is directed by a rational purpose, and all things are ordered according to an underlying, determining rationality. *Fire,* therefore, was their designation for the rational, molding principle (the *logos*) penetrating everything.[85] Hence, the word also carried the idea of "fate" or "providence," and was even linked to the divine.

The metaphorical use of the word *fire* allowed some Stoics to tie the physical universe to the Greek high god Zeus in a somewhat pantheistic manner. In their view the universe was fashioned by the permeating force of the divine spirit and ordered by divine law.[86] It was, therefore, both material and divine.[87] Regardless of the fine points of their metaphysical outlook, the Stoics were rational determinists.

This fundamental determinism led to the Stoic understanding of the human ideal. Some historians interpret the Stoics within the broader Greek tradition that exposed a basically eudaimonian outlook, differing only in that their vision of well-being involved a condition of undisturbed happiness.[88] Others offer the more likely suggestion that the Stoic concept of the good life draws from another Greek emphasis, namely, the concern for virtue for its own sake, especially virtue connected to practical wisdom or the wise application of knowledge to life.[89]

In any case the Stoics taught that the key to the good life lies in conformity to universal reason. Thus the good life consists of living "according to nature," that is, according to the principle of the universe bound up with fire or fate. The Stoics assumed that we have access to this rational principle of the universe through our own reason. Consequently, living "according to nature" means allowing our human reason—as the connecting point with the divine reason that permeates the universe—to govern our lives.

The resignation of the true Stoic. In typical Greek fashion, the Stoics pitted reason against the nonrational or irrational aspect of the human soul, which they saw as focused on the desires and the emotions. Human nature, like everything in the universe, is fundamentally rational. The affective dimensions of the human soul—especially pleasure, sorrow, desire and fear—are irrational and hence incompatible with human nature. Therefore the rule of reason involves the strict control of our desires so as to free us from and even eliminate these irrational aspects. The rejection of the irrational dimensions of the human soul led the Stoics to disdain the pursuit of pleasure and with it any ethical system, such as Epicureanism, that elevated pleasure to the status of being our human good.

Reason controlling the desires and emotions, in turn, determined the Stoic understanding of virtue. Because human assent or "will" is the one thing in the universe that escapes determinism, virtue involves conscious assent to the inevitable order of things.[90] This virtue is to be sought for its own sake, for it alone constitutes the good life. A virtue is a "perfect good," that is, a good which is perfectly harmonious, for it harmonizes with the universal will. The quest for this kind of harmonious living led the Stoics to deny that such goals as health, wealth and pleasure could be classified as virtues, because these are inherently neither beneficial nor injurious. Instead, they cited the traditional virtues such as justice, courage, temperance and knowledge. More practically, virtue consists of controlling our reactions or practicing self-control. Above all, the virtuous person keeps the emotions in check. The Stoic expresses neither joy nor sorrow regardless of the outward circumstances.

But why this disdain for emotion and desire? The answer lies in the goal of life. There are only two major roads to contentment: we must either "get what we want" or "want what we get."[91] In contrast to their hedonist rivals (including the Epicureans), the Stoics opted for a softer variety of the second alternative: We must accept without any stirring of our emotions or desires whatever comes our way. Hence living according to reason in a deterministic world means seeking to be content within oneself. The virtuous person finds happiness in himself or herself, rather than in the external world, which brings both joy and sorrow, success and failure, fulfillment and want. The way to overcome this seemingly capricious world is by mastering oneself, that is, by becoming master of one's passions, desires and emotions. And the way to master the desires is through resignation.

When we achieve sublime unity with cosmic reason through the contemplative life, we become truly free. Nothing can harm our true self. Therefore, neither the forces of nature nor the fall of empires need disturb us. In the midst of it all, we remain steadfast, noble, invincible, fearless and serene.

The duty of world citizenship. The Stoic outlook made possible the development of a sense of universal citizenship, together with the concept of natural law. At the heart of Stoicism was the idea of a universal reason, a fundamental rationality behind everything. This opened the door to seeing humans as people of the one cosmos (a *cosmopolis*) rather than merely citizens of various specific nations. Operative within this universal cosmos is the universal law of reason. In fact, the Stoics may have been the first Greek ethical teachers to introduce the idea of an all-pervading law governing the universe, as well as human action.[92]

This idea led the Stoics to the ethical concept of duty: humans are morally obliged to conform to universal reason. Yet this duty was more than merely personal. Because all humans form one community with a common law, as "citizens of the universe" we ought to fulfill the duties to each other that this common citizenship requires.[93] Such responsibilities of citizenship include discharging the obligations of one's station in life and society.

Above all, therefore, the Stoics elevated duty. In fact, "Stoic" came to be equated with the person who does his or her duty at all cost. Although present in the teaching of the Greek Stoics, this was more specifically the concern of Stoicism in the Roman world.

Self-control and natural law: the Roman Stoics. Perhaps no Greek philosophical-ethical tradition resonated so well with the Roman soul, with its emphasis on jurisprudence, as Stoicism. A long line of Roman thinkers from Cicero (106-143 B.C.) to Seneca (c. 4 B.C.-A.D. 65) and Marcus Aurelius (A.D. 121-180), emperor of Rome from 161 until his death, came to be numbered with the Stoics. Consequently, Stoicism in a sense marked the transition from the ancient Greek focus on good and virtue to the more modern conception of ethics as concerned with duty and adherence to law.[94] In addition, philosophy came to be seen as the healer to which people turn out of a sense of their own moral weakness.[95]

Perhaps the greatest ethical teacher among the later Stoics was

Epictetus (A.D. 50-138).[96] The scanty known details of his life[97] depict a person who reflected well the Stoic outlook of coming to terms with one's fate. Epictetus was probably born in the Greek city of Hierapolis in Phrygia (Asia Minor or what is now Turkey). When he was a child, his parents apparently sold him as a slave to a Roman soldier who served in the court of the emperor Nero. While a slave, Epictetus was allowed to attend the lectures of a Stoic philosopher. After the death of his master, he gained his freedom. Having already achieved some fame as a philosopher, he remained in Rome as a teacher. Upon Domitian's eviction of the philosophers from Rome, Epictetus moved to Nicopolis and founded a school, where he taught until his death.

Foundational to Epictetus's ethic was his distinction between what does and what does not lie within our control. Specifically, we can control our attitudes toward events but not the events themselves.[98] Only what is in our control is relevant to ethics. The opening lines of his *Enchiridion* announce the fundamental inner freedom we possess, in contrast to the outer situation over which we have no control: "There are things which are within our power, and there are things which are beyond our power. Within our power are opinion, aim, desire, aversion, and, in one word, whatever affairs are our own. Beyond our power are body, property, reputation, office, and, in one word, whatever are not properly our own affairs. Now, the things within our power are by nature free, unrestricted, unhindered; but those beyond our power are weak, dependent, restricted, alien."[99]

Epictetus was convinced that personal contentment is not contingent on external circumstances. Instead it arises from an inner aspect of the human soul, namely, the unconquerable or invincible will. Hence, like other Stoics of his day Epictetus spoke about a governing faculty within the soul (the will), which is to rule according to right reason.

The Stoic philosopher asserted that for the will to govern rightly, we need to gain a proper perspective on the universe. This proper perspective involves the acknowledgment of divine providence directing the world.[100] This trust allowed Epictetus to view life as a spiritual exercise ordained by God. Such knowledge also leads us to face life without anger, envy or pity. Instead of succumbing to these emotions, the virtuous person lives in "resignation to life," knowing that in the end the worst that life affords is death. Epictetus likewise emphasized self-sufficiency. We ought to muster our own resources to face the challenge that life entails.

Like other Stoics, Epictetus believed that the key to the life of resignation lies in detachment from material goods and physical pleasures, for these lie beyond our control. Hence he offered this appraisal of our angry reaction to people who we think have wronged us: "Why, then, are we angry? Because we admire the goods of which these men rob us. For, mark you, stop admiring your clothes, and you are not angry at the man who steals them; stop admiring your wife's beauty, and you are not angry at her adulterer. Know that a thief or an adulterer has no place among the things that are your own, but only among the things that are another's and that are not under your control. If you give these things up and count them as nothing, at whom have you still ground to feel angry?"[101]

Equally important in the process of eradicating the irrational aspects of our soul is the practice of self-control. Epictetus's advice is as follows: "If, therefore, you wish not to be hot-tempered, do not feed your habit, set before it nothing on which it can grow. As the first step, keep quiet and count the days on which you have not been angry. 'I used to be angry every day, after that every other day, then every third day, and then every fourth day.' If you go as much as thirty days without a fit of anger, sacrifice to God. For the habit is first weakened and then utterly destroyed."[102]

Resignation to a "perfect" world. In the end, then, the Stoics were determined to accept the world as it now is with resolute detachment. This ethos lives on. It is evident whenever we are advised to "keep a stiff upper lip" in the face of life's tragedies.

Why is this the best way to live? According to the Stoics, the world as we know it is the product of divine reason, and therefore it is in a certain sense perfect.[103] Consequently, the wise philosopher does not hope or anticipate a better world in the future—whether in this life or beyond death. Nor does the sage strive to create a better world in which the inequities of the present are overcome. These inequities are neither good nor evil; they simply *are.*

The goal of the Stoic outlook was to live within the world as it is, not to change it. Hence, Stoicism could not form the cradle for a truly transformationist ethic. For such an ethic to arise would require the invasion of the Christian gospel and its vision of a future kingdom of God.

Plotinus and Unity with the Divine

When Jesus walked the pathways of Palestine and later when his disciples were gathering in small house churches throughout the cities of the Roman Empire, Greek philosophy was at its zenith. Two hundred years later, the Greek philosophical tradition was beginning to run out of steam. The last great effort of the Greek genius found its articulation in the work of Plotinus.[104] As a philosophical system of thought, this last proposal stands as the antithesis of the materialism lying at the foundation of the Epicurean and Stoic alternatives. But in so doing, it marks a return to and a deepening of the Platonism with which our discussion began.

The life of a mystic. What we know about the life of Plotinus (205-270) comes exclusively from the short biography Porphyry placed at the beginning of his collection of his master's writings, the *Enneads*. The opening line of this biography sets the stage for the philosophical teachings that follow in the volume: "Plotinus seemed ashamed of having a body."[105]

Plotinus lived during one of the most confused and difficult periods of the Roman Empire.[106] He was probably born in Lycopolis, Egypt. After a lengthy study in Alexandria, which had become the philosophical center of the Greek world, the young philosopher set his sights on investigating the intellectual traditions of the East. He hoped to accompany the emperor Gordian on an expedition to Persia, but his plans were interrupted by the assassination of the ruler in 244.

With some difficulty Plotinus then made his way to Rome, where he taught and served as a spiritual counselor until his death. He was partially blind and perhaps in part as a consequence spent much of his time in solitary meditation.[107] During his teaching career he enjoyed some notability, even gaining the favor of the emperor Gallienus. Porphyry, his most famous student, later became an important antagonist of several church fathers, including Jerome.

The Neoplatonic alteration of Plato. Neoplatonic ideas appear in the teachings of many thinkers from the death of Plato to Proclus Diadochus (A.D. 410-485).[108] Prominent among them were Philo Judaeus (c. 25 B.C.-A.D. 40), who sought to harmonize Scripture and Greek philosophy, and Plutarch of Chaeronea (c. A.D. 46-120) who proposed a similar congruence of philosophical reflection with the popular Greek religions. But it is with Plotinus that we find the flowering of Neoplatonism.

Plotinus's philosophy exemplifies the slight yet far-reaching alteration of Plato indicative of Neoplatonism as a whole. The philosophers who taught in Plato's Academy after his death inaugurated a tendency to go beyond the ancient teacher by linking the divine with his Form of the Good. The final result was a philosophical understanding of reality that carried theological and even mystical overtones.

This innovation at the heart of Plato's philosophy carried significant ethical implications.[109] It obviously altered the conception of the human good. According to the Neoplatonists, the good life entails a flight from the material world and sense experience to an increasingly closer relationship to this ultimate principle.

In a sense this was not new. The ancient master himself taught that the good life consists in turning away from the realm of the senses to contemplate the eternal forms. Yet his principle of harmonious integration left open a place for the sensible world. For Plato sensible objects belong to the realm of becoming and hence they simply cannot perfectly reflect the forms. They are only evil in a negative way, namely, in that they lack goodness. Consequently, the task of the true philosopher, while focusing on contemplation of eternal truth, involves ordering life in all its various dimensions, including bringing a degree of goodness and beauty to the sensible realm. In addition, because the life of ordered integration encompasses both individual and social existence, the philosopher is also to fulfill this ordering, integrative, harmonizing role in human society.

In Neoplatonism, however, this changes. Plato's followers came to view matter not merely as lacking in goodness. It is itself evil. Plotinus spoke of formless matter as the "first evil," from which arises the "second evil," the body. And the influence of the body is the cause of all the evil in the soul's existence.

The revision of Plato moved to his epistemology as well.[110] According to Plato anything is knowable to the extent that it is real. Consequently, as the mind advances from particular things in our senses to abstract essences, thought becomes more definite and clear. For example, understood from a Platonic perspective the various individual trees we see are less real than their abstract form—treeness. When we look at a particular tree, our conception of "treeness" is not fully crystallized, because that tree is not a perfect representation of treeness. But as our mind moves from particular trees to treeness itself, our conception becomes clearer because we are now contemplating treeness in its pure form apart from the deficiencies that characterize every particular tree. And Plato believed that in this way the human mind could even come to know the highest form, the Form of the Good, which is the highest mode of human existence.

Plotinus disagreed. All thought, he observed, involves duality—the duality of thinker and object thought. Therefore the unity lying behind all reality cannot be apprehended through the power of thought, but only as we transcend thought, only as we lose all consciousness of the self in a mystical or ecstatic union with that unifying principle.

The human predicament. To understand Plotinus's mysticism, we must view the metaphysical perspective that provided its basis. The foundation of the thinker's philosophical vision is the concept of the One. In a way reminiscent of the similar proposal of Philo,[111] Plotinus spoke of the One as the orientation point. It is completely ineffable and beyond description, for it transcends all predicates, even the predicate "is." The One is not an essence *(ousia)* but is beyond essences and being.[112] At the same time it is in some sense divine. And it is the eternal source of all being, as well as the measure of all things.

All reality, in turn, is the result of a series of logical (rather than temporal) emanations from the One. The first of these emanations is Intelligence *(nous),* which is roughly comparable to the realm of Plato's forms. The second emanation is Soul *(psychē),* which we might view on one level as the life principle animating the entire physical universe and in which we participate through our personal soul. At the end of the chain of emanations is Matter, which because it is devoid of form lies closest to nonbeing.

In this hierarchy of being, humans are in a sense stuck in the middle.[113] As composite beings consisting of soul and matter, we belong partially to the realm of spirit and partially to the realm of matter. Our true being does not lie in the material dimension, however, but in the intellectual, or perhaps better stated, in the spiritual. While acknowledging that we are intellectual creatures, Plotinus declared that our true fulfillment does not come as we satisfy our intellectual curiosity. More than seekers of knowledge, we are essentially "desire."[114] And the true object of our soul's desire is the One.

Our soul desires the One as the perfection we lack. In this way, we might say that the One is the "source" of the soul. Nevertheless, because we are caught within material bodies, the soul does not necessarily look upward to the higher realm. Instead we orient ourselves by looking downward to the evil regions of matter.

The return to the One. According to Plotinus, all creation is a cyclic movement *from* the One and *to* the One. More important, because the soul is a microcosm of the universe, the cyclic rhythm perceivable throughout the universe is imbedded in our own ontological structure. The soul is designed to return to the One.

The return involves a turning inward. It is an "introspection," a journey into the "center of the soul," to cite Plotinus's words.[115] This journey involves three stages. The first is a negative movement, a separating of the self from the realm of multiplicity—that is, of sense experience—into the intelligible realm.[116] Here we leave behind the world of matter for the interior world of thought. But this step is insufficient. The soul does not return to the One through the pursuit of knowledge alone. To the first, therefore, must be added a second stage. This involves a separation from an even loftier multiplicity, namely, from reasoning itself. Thereby the soul moves deeper within to a realm in which even thought disappears.

These two steps do not yet bring us to our goal, however. Both are merely the preparation for the third. They lead to an interiority in which the soul has attained the point of utmost simplicity within itself. This, in turn, opens the way for union with the One, which Plotinus likened to inebriation. Or, to use another analogy, it is similar to being so absorbed in one's reading that one is no longer aware of reading.[117] Such a union involves the intellect going beyond itself into the nonintelligible. But the most appropriate word to describe the experience is *ecstasy,* understood in the original sense of standing outside oneself.[118]

In the return to the One, the last veil of multiplicity is lifted. The soul takes flight to its true home, the One, from which it came. Because it involves the overcoming of the subject-object dualism, for Plotinus the experience is closer to sensing a presence[119] than engaging in an act of knowledge. When this occurs, Plotinus declared, "the contemplative is suddenly swept by the wave of The Intelligence beneath and carried on high and sees, never knowing how; vision floods the eyes with light but it is not light that shows some other thing; the light is itself the vision."[120] In this experience the soul becomes divine.[121]

Plotinus reported having experienced the ecstatic union he advocated: "Often I awaken to myself by escaping from my body: thus cut off from other things, in the intimacy of my self, I see a beauty that is as marvelous as can be. Above all, then, I am convinced that I have a higher destiny; my activity is the highest degree of life; I am in union with the divine and, once I have reached this peak of activity, I fasten to It above the other intelligible beings."[122]

The virtues of the mystic. True to the Greek philosophical tradition, Plotinus advocated the cultivation of the virtuous life. Not surprisingly, however, he saw the purpose of this enterprise as related to the soul's ascent to the One. In its desire to flee evil, that is, to "flee from here," the soul seeks to become "like the divinity," which means becoming just, holy, prudent—in a word, "virtuous."[123] In this manner, Plotinus made the moral quest subservient to the intellectual, and external conduct became the servant of interiority.

Plotinus acknowledged the importance of cultivating the "civil" virtues. Traits such as practical wisdom (prudence), courage, temperance and rectitude (justice)[124] are necessary for us to live well in society. By limiting and moderating our desires and passions, and by delivering us from erroneous opinion, these virtues "order our lives for the better." He was even willing to concede that in a sense, the possession of civil virtue makes a person "godlike."[125]

But because the civil virtues facilitate living in the world of multiplicity, they form only the substratum of the ethical life. The chief concern of the soul is not to live well in society but to move beyond its evil "mingling" with the body. Plotinus, therefore, was more interested in the virtues as far as they are connected to the "purification" of the soul[126] so that it might become truly like the divine. With this goal in view, the mystic seeks to cultivate these virtues from the perspective of their role in facilitating union with the One.

Viewed from this vantage point, wisdom (or prudence) is no longer merely the ability to judge well in the practical matters of life. This aspect of the virtue does not lead to divinization. More important, wisdom involves the contemplation of the eternal forms.[127] Similarly, temperance is no longer limited to the control of pleasure, which focuses merely on bodily existence. The virtuous person develops the kind of temperance that leads to the isolation of the soul from the body and its desires.

For Plotinus only this higher understanding of the virtues can facilitate the soul becoming truly divine, whereas the civic virtues merely lead us to become good humans. Hence he wrote concerning the true mystic, "In a word he does not live the life of one who, according to civic virtue, is a good man. He forsakes that life and chooses another in its place, the life of the gods, for his wish is to become like to the gods and not to good men. Likeness to good men is likeness of one image to another image that comes from the same model. But likeness to God is likeness to the model itself."[128]

Although Plotinus stood at the end of the Greek philosophical tradition, his ideas did not die with the triumph of Christianity over pagan Rome. Through its influence on Augustine and others, a metamorphosed Neoplatonism seeped into the Christianized Western intellectual tradition. It provided a philosophical foundation for the new Christian mysticism, which often involved a strict asceticism that deprecated the material realm, including the body. And even where mysticism has not taken root, Christians have been affected by a concentration on personal interiority or the cultivation of the interior life similar to what Plotinus advocated. Table 4 offers a summary of the Greek ethical-philosophical tradition.

The Greeks and the Christian Tradition

Nearly nine hundred years mark the span of time from the birth of Thales to the death of Plotinus. During this era, intellectual artisans laid the foundations of Western civilization. The concrete these builders so carefully troweled into place consisted of the conviction that the exercise of human reason, which focuses on clarity of thought and rigor of argument, is the best means at our disposal for answering questions, solving

Name	Metaphysical Background	Nature of the Human Person	Type of Ethic	Conception of Virtue
Plato	hierarchy of forms	rational vs. passionate	ordered integration	4 virtues, justice
Aristotle	form + matter	rational animal	well-being	golden mean/ well-function
Epicurus	atomism/ hedonism	purely material	peace of mind	pleasure/pain/ friendship
Stoicism	determinism	will	live according to nature	self-control
Plotinus	return to the One	soul as a microcosm	becoming divine	civic + higher

Table 4. The Greek Tradition of Philosophical Ethics

problems and progressing toward a higher level of human existence.[129]

By Plotinus's death, the vibrancy of the Greek intellectual tradition had begun to dissipate. In the meantime a new spiritual force had been loosed, the gospel of Jesus Christ. This transformative message was birthed by a quite different but equally potent progenitor, the historical trajectory of the relationship the Hebrew people enjoyed with the God who had entered into covenant with them.

The Greek tradition would live on. But it would no longer be the single most determinative influence in society. At times it would struggle against the Christian alternative and either gain a partial victory or suffer a temporary defeat. More often, however, it would simply find itself co-opted by Christian thinkers, who put the Greek ethos to their own use—or, dare we say, whom it put to its own use.

Chapter 3

ETHICS IN THE BIBLE

My command is this: Love each other as I have loved you. Greater love has no one than this, that he lay down his life for his friends. You are my friends if you do what I command. . . . You did not choose me, but I chose you and appointed you to go and bear fruit—fruit that will last.
(JOHN 15:12-13, 16)

Charlie Brown was sitting comfortably in a chair in the living room when he heard a noise in the kitchen. Checking it out, he caught Snoopy in the act of raiding the refrigerator. "Hey what are you doing?" he asked. "You can't just take things out of the refrigerator." Pulling out his Bible, the boy added, "Look, it says here in Exodus 'Thou shalt not steal.'"

Snoopy, being knowledgeable in the Bible as well, took the book out of the boy's hand, flipped forward a few pages and pointed Charlie Brown to Deuteronomy 25:4. While his master read, "Thou shalt not muzzle the ox while he treads out the grain," Snoopy slipped away and resumed a comfortable position atop his dog house.

Having finished reading the verse, Charlie Brown realized what had happened. "I don't see you treading out any grain," he hollered.

Snoopy interrupted his meal long enough to reply, "It got me out the back door."

* * *

As we said in chapter one, ethics is not an exclusively Christian enterprise. Many people have sought to determine and then to follow the ethical life. We have viewed this wider interest through the lenses of the tradition of philosophical ethics that finds its genesis in ancient Greece. Our concern, however, is to move beyond general ethics to set forth a Christian ethic. Although the Christian ethical tradition developed in a culture that was indebted to the Greek philosophers, Christians have always looked primarily to the Bible as the foundation for living. Therefore, if we would develop a Christian ethic for today, we must engage with Scripture.

Like Snoopy, each of us has probably been guilty from time to time of misusing the Bible. We have all probably used Scripture simply to get ourselves "out the back door" in the situations of life. But sensitive Christians want the Bible to be the instrument through which the Holy Spirit guides them into godly living. Indeed, a central goal of the Bible is to instruct the believing community about ethical living. Scripture, consequently, is foundational to Christian ethics.

Most Christians would agree that the Christian ethical tradition rests upon the Bible. But what does this statement mean? What is the biblical ethic? And how do we move from the Bible to contemporary living?

Our first impulse might be to propose that biblical ethics consist in the precepts, principles and laws for human conduct contained in the Scriptures. We will take up this suggestion more explicitly in chapter seven. Suffice it to say here that many Christian ethicists find this approach to be an oversimplification of how the Bible interfaces with life. In recent years scholars across the theological spectrum have observed that whatever else it may be, the Bible is a narrative. It recounts a story that includes a beginning, a middle and an end.[1] Instead of abstracting the laws found in Scripture from this story so as to assign a universal status to them, these thinkers conclude that the Bible's ethical teachings are embedded within that narrative and are understandable only in the context of the biblical story.[2]

These Christian ethicists take the idea a step farther. They are convinced that the central focus of the biblical narrative is Jesus Christ. Consequently, for them ethics viewed from a biblical perspective is concerned with the manner of life that is incumbent on the community of faith as it is revealed in the story of Jesus. As R. E. O. White declares, "The essence of biblical morality is not a legal system, a written code, an abstract moral philosophy, but a spirit and a loyalty, a vision and faith, incarnate in the inexhaustibly rich and varied personality of Jesus."[3] Or, in the words of the Roman Catholic scholar Robert J. Daly, Christian ethics is "the science and the art of reflecting on and living out the practical aspects of existence in Christ."[4]

Our main task in this chapter is to indicate how the lines of the Bible's ethical teachings converge in Christ. We do so by exploring the central ethical themes present in the biblical narrative.

The Moral Life and the Hebrew Scriptures

The church owes its existence to ancient Israel, for, following Jesus' lead, the early believers saw themselves as the continuation of what God had begun in the Old Testament era. They were convinced that in Jesus the story of God at work in human history had reached a new level. Motivated by this belief, the early Christian community explored the implications of the gospel and of Jesus' teachings for life in their historical context. But in this task they looked to ancient Israel, claiming that the Hebrew Scriptures cradled an understanding of what it meant to live as the people of God in the world.

For this reason our survey of the biblical foundation of Christian ethics must start with the Hebrew Scriptures. Yet we do not begin with Old Testament ethics per se. In a sense, any reference to "Old Testament ethics" is a misnomer. As Walter Kaiser notes, "There is no abstract, comprehensive concept in the Old Testament that parallels our modern term 'ethics.'"[5] Instead we must look to the Old Testament story line. Bruce Birch speaks for many scholars when he notes, "We do not have in the Old Testament abstract, philosophical discourses on morality or codified, theoretical systems of ethics. We have materials that tell the story of Israel or witness from within that story."[6] Rather than searching for whatever timeless principles of conduct may be sprinkled throughout the Hebrew Scriptures, therefore, our goal is to summarize the central themes within the Old Testament narrative that shaped the ancient Hebrew understanding of what it meant to be the people of God in the world. This understanding, in turn, provided the cradle for the ethical teachings of Jesus and the subsequent reflections of the early Christian community.

The basic theme: God in covenant. Foundational to all that the writers of the Hebrew Scriptures say about what we might call the ethical life is the theme of covenant.[7] Indeed, we could suggest that the entire biblical narrative recounts the story of the covenant. The curtain rises with a covenantal relationship between God and humankind (Gen 1:27-30), set in the context of God's act in creating the heavens and the earth "in the beginning" (Gen 1:1). Through Noah, God later renewed the universal covenant (Gen 9:9-11). But of special significance is God's covenant with Israel, who as the offspring of Abraham was to be the nation through whom God would bless all peoples (Gen 12:1-3). The German Old Testament scholar Walther Eichrodt declares that the concept of the covenant "enshrines Israel's most fundamental conviction, namely, its sense of a unique relationship with God."[8] It is no surprise, therefore, that the understanding that they were a people in covenant with God provided the foundation for ethical reflections among the ancient Hebrews.

At the heart of the covenant idea was the realization that Israel's relationship to God was due entirely to divine grace.[9] The most powerful covenant-creating event in Israel's narrative was clearly the exodus. God rescued the people from bondage in Egypt, and, above all other experiences, this event constituted them as God's covenant people. From this point on, the covenant found its basis in God's gracious initiative in salvation. The declaration "I am the LORD your God, who brought you out of Egypt, out of the land of slavery," repeatedly served to introduce the divine injunctions about life in the covenant community (e.g., Ex 20:2). But Israel knew that the Exodus, and hence the covenant itself, was the outworking of God's own lovingkindness and mercy.[10] Beginning at Sinai, the Old Testament story became the narrative of the fidelity of God to the covenant, even in the face of the failure of Israel.

The covenant was no one-way street, of course. Being God's covenant-partner—being the recipients of divine grace—placed obligations on Israel. This realization led to the "teaching" about the "way."[11] Kaiser is surely correct in noting, "Old Testament ethics is concerned with the manner of life that the older covenant prescribes and approves."[12]

Above all, the covenant meant that Israel was to be a "holy assembly" (Ex 12:16).[13] Indeed, the people in covenant with a holy God must likewise be holy.[14] Holiness involved obedience to the covenanting God as motivated by love and gratitude (Deut 6:5, 20). Covenant obedience was expressed through careful attention to the divine will revealed at Sinai and in the Torah.

In contrast to the Greek philosophers, therefore, the Hebrews did not set out to search for the good life, viewed as the final goal of human existence. Nor did they focus on the cultivation of a set of virtues as the best means to the good. Instead the Old Testament people were concerned with righteousness. And this righteousness involved the obedience of holiness.[15]

Obedience included separating themselves from all that is profane or defiled, including the worship of other gods. It also meant being consecrated for God's own use.[16] Being God's holy people did not end with the God-ward direction of life, however. Being in covenant with God demanded that Israel be a holy community, a people who knew that covenant status must translate into proper conduct toward others. Holy living extended to all dimensions of human interaction, including aspects as diverse as family life and commerce. And holiness demanded concern for the less fortunate; it placed limits on vengeance (Deut 25:3); it even required proper care for animals (Deut 22:1-4).

In short, being God's holy covenant partner allowed no bifurcation between temple worship and daily life. Being Yahweh's "guest" on the sabbath required both a right attitude toward God and proper conduct during the week. It involved not only a pure heart but also clean hands, not only the avoidance of idolatry but also truthful dealings with others: "Who may ascend the hill of the LORD? Who may stand in his holy place? He who has clean hands and a pure heart, who does not lift up his soul to an idol or swear by what is false" (Ps 24:3-4).

The "blameless walk," therefore, was highly social: "LORD, who may dwell in your sanctuary? Who may live on your holy hill? He whose walk is blameless and who does what is righteous, who speaks the truth from his heart and has no slander on his tongue, who does his neighbor no wrong and casts no slur on his fellowman . . . who keeps his oath even when it hurts, who lends his money without usury and does not accept a bribe against the innocent" (Ps 15; cf. Ps 51:6; 66:18; 118:20; 141:2-4).

As these considerations suggest, holiness did not focus primarily on blind obedience to an externally imposed set of laws as ends in themselves. Instead it involved taking seriously the responsibility implicated in receiving the gift of divine grace. Hence the covenant law served a higher purpose. It was a signpost indicating what it meant for Israel to be holy—that is, distinctive from the nations. Keeping the law, therefore, was not a means to *becoming* God's covenant people. Rather, Israel was constituted as a people by their relationship to Yahweh. The laws provided guidance and instruction so that the community might apprehend and live out the implications of being in this covenant relationship.[17] By living out the implications of the covenant, Israel could fulfill its God-given mission to serve as teacher, model and even mediator for the nations.[18]

Living as God's covenant people meant living in relationship with God as God's covenant partner. Indeed, this formed the goal of the covenant. As Kaiser notes, "The covenant aims to establish a personal relationship, not a code of conduct in the abstract."[19] And more important than any ideal norm as a measurement of conduct was God's relationship with Israel in which God had shown himself faithful over time.[20] Above all, therefore, being God's covenant partner meant modeling life after the divine pattern embodied in the narrative of God's dealings with Israel. It involved patterning human life according to the ways of the covenanting God. Even the law itself was embedded in the flow of the narrative of the covenant.[21] Consequently, not merely the divine will, but the character and activity of God lay at the foundation of the Old Testament perception of proper living.[22] God's covenant people were to be holy because the covenant-making God had shown himself to be holy (Lev 18:5-6; 19:2-4).[23] Life in covenant, in short, was to be the imitation of God.[24]

Throughout the history of the covenant with Israel as depicted in the biblical narrative, God had revealed the divine character. Thereby, in the history of the covenant, God had shown Israel what is good (e.g., Mic 6:1-8).[25] The Hebrew prophets saw this clearly. The Covenant-maker whom they had come to know was faithful (Jeremiah), just (Amos), loving (Hosea), holy (Isaiah) and merciful (Micah).[26]

Drawing these characteristics together, the Old Testament writers presented this God as above all compassionate. In fact, compassion arising out of the divine love depicted the foundational relationship of God to the covenant people. The theme of the compassionate God is evident in a formulation that stood at the center of the faith of the Hebrew community, which according to the book of Exodus had its source in God's own self-affirmation. After revealing the divine name to Moses on Mount Sinai, Yahweh described himself as "the compassionate and gracious God, slow to anger, abounding in love and faithfulness" (Ex 34:6). The declaration that God abounds in love and is filled with compassion is found repeatedly throughout the Old Testament, constituting as it were its central theological affirmation (e.g., Neh 9:17; Ps 86:15; 103:8; 111:4; 116:5; 145:8; Joel 2:13; Jon 4:2; Is 54:10). Concerning this, Williston Walker concluded, "Nothing therefore is more prominent in the Old Testament than the ascription of compassion, pity, mercy, etc. to God. The people may be said to have gloried in it."[27]

As these observations suggest, the focus on God-in-covenant led to a distinctively historical perspective among the ancient Hebrew people.[28] If God had entered into covenant with Israel, then the story of this people is the history of the covenant. More specifically, it is the history of the Covenant-maker's resolute faithfulness to the covenant. Because God is faithful, the Old Testament people concluded, the righteous will eventually triumph over their enemies.

We cannot overestimate the importance of the covenantal theme for Old Testament ethics. By providing a theological foundation for holy living, the conviction that God had entered into covenant with Israel forged an indissoluble link between inward belief and outward conduct. As the book of Proverbs emphasizes, wisdom (understood in the practical sense of knowing the proper way to live and as a result living properly)[29] begins with reverence for God.[30] The story of God's dealings with Israel likewise provided the Old Testament writers with a transcendent theological reference point—embedded as it was in a specific history—for concepts such as justice and impartiality.

Above all, the conviction that God had entered into covenant with Israel led to a theological understanding of the "good." As we noted in the preceding chapter, the Greek philosophers linked the good with such human-oriented ideals as personal well-being and peace of mind. Unlike the Greek philosophers, the Hebrews carefully avoided resting their delineation of the moral life on an assumption of our human moral capabilities. They drew instead from the revealed character of God.[31] Whatever conception of the "good life" the Hebrews may have had, it was always connected with life in covenant with the God of Israel's history.

The Hebrew approach came to clear expression in Jesus' statement "Seek first [God's] kingdom and his righteousness, and all these things will be given to you as well" (Mt 6:33). In this short statement our Lord summarized the Hebrew outlook and relegated the Greek pursuit of the good to the status of being a by-product of something even more fundamental, namely, the quest for righteousness in relationship with the Fountain of all righteousness, the covenant-making God. By making this connection, the Old Testament provided a theological grounding for the lively discussion with the Greek philosophical tradition that would occupy Christian thinkers.

The supporting themes: personal sin and social solidarity. Paralleling the acknowledgment of the covenant-making God was a profound perception of human failure. For the ancient Hebrews sin was fundamentally Israel's waywardness or refusal to live up to their covenant responsibilities. The people of Israel had shown themselves to be faithless in the face of God's faithfulness. Rather than consecrating themselves as a holy people, they served other gods. And instead of imitating their righteous God in the various relationships within the community, they did not act justly.

As we noted earlier, Israel's covenant responsibilities were codified in the law. This suggests that the biblical authors did not look to obedience to the law itself as the goal of human existence. Rather this goal lay in being faithful covenant partners of the covenanting God. The purpose of the law was to indicate that the covenant brought responsibilities toward God (e.g., the first four of the Ten Commandments) and toward others (hence the last six commandments). Nor did the laws *constitute* Israel as the covenant people. Rather, as the biblical narrative itself indicates, Israel's covenantal relationship to God preceded the codification of law. This relationship provided the context in which the law became important. The law offered guidance in living out Israel's identity as God's covenant partner.[32] For this reason violation of any one individual law, while it damaged the relationship between Israel and God, did not in itself necessarily invalidate the covenant, which was primarily dependent on the faithfulness of the covenanting God.

This understanding of the role of the law led to a deeper awareness of the nature of sin, an understanding that would later permeate Jesus' teaching as well as the ethic of the New Testament. Sin is not merely the outward transgression of a law; it is primarily inward defilement.[33] Sin consists of a misdirected heart. For this reason, after his terrible acts of adultery, deceit and murder, David confessed to the God who had chosen him as king over Israel, "Against you, and you only, have I sinned" (Ps 51:4). Aware from the downfall of his predecessor, Saul, that God required more than mere outward obedience, he acknowledged that his heart was defiled and was sorely in need of renewal: "Create in me a pure heart, O God, and renew a steadfast spirit within me" (v. 10).

David's example suggests that the Old Testament understanding of proper human existence brought together the individual and the corporate dimensions of life. In contrast to many modern Christians, the ancient Hebrews had a keen sense of the interplay between the individual and the group. Life as the covenant people meant that each member of Israel participated in a corporate people, a community. The ancient people of God were characterized by what Walter Kaiser terms "corporate solidarity."[34] Simply stated, they knew that they were interconnected. Because of this fundamental solidarity, the whole group comprised a unit (e.g., 1 Sam 5:10-11), which could function as a whole through a single representative figure. At the same time, what one person did affected the group, whether in implicating all in sin or effecting a blessing upon all.

This corporate solidarity is evident in Isaiah's response to his vision of the holy God. Not only did he declare, "I am a man of unclean lips," he also confessed, "I live among a people of unclean lips" (Is 6:5). Similarly, when pleading with God to honor the promise to restore Jerusalem, Daniel not only acknowledged his own sins but offered a lengthy recitation of the sins of his people Israel: "O LORD, the great and awesome God, who keeps his covenant of love with all who love him and obey his commands, we have sinned and done wrong. We have been wicked and have rebelled; we have turned away from your commands and laws. We have not listened to your servants the prophets" (Dan 9:4-6).

The social solidarity of the Old Testament has an ethical dimension beyond the fundamental unity of the people in culpability for their failure to live out their covenant obligations. Such solidarity means that God's covenant people do not realize their true being as individuals but as members of the community. This understanding added a new level of reciprocal responsibility between the individual and the group. Thomas

Ogletree draws out the implication: "our wholeness as moral beings cannot be abstracted from the moral soundness of the community to which we belong."[35] Hence, members of the ancient covenant community were not only united in failure; they were also united in the promotion of the well-being of the group.

Yet the individual was not lost within this profound sense of corporate solidarity. The emphasis on the corporate people was balanced by an equally important focus on the individual member of the community. According to the Old Testament, not only are all participants in the group, each stands before God, and this responsibility before God constitutes each one as an individual person.[36] With Jeremiah and Ezekiel,[37] this perspective, which pervades the entire biblical narrative,[38] came to succinct expression. Hence, through the prophet God voiced the individual person's responsibility for one's own sin: "The soul who sins is the one who will die" (Ezek 18:4).

This sense of individual responsibility opened the way for the concept of the righteous remnant within the rebellious nation. Even though the nation turns away from God, the faithful Covenant-maker will preserve an obedient remnant of the people (Ezra 9:8; Is 11:11; Jer 23:3; Zech 8:12). Early in Israelite history God had given to Solomon a promise that the action of the faithful few—the remnant—would benefit the wayward many: "if my people, who are called by my name, will humble themselves and pray and seek my face and turn from their wicked ways, then I will hear from heaven and will forgive their sin and will heal their land" (2 Chron 7:14).

The concept of the remnant, in turn, gave rise to what R. E. O. White sees as the "pinnacle of Old Testament ethics,"[39] the voluntary suffering of the guiltless as the means toward the regeneration of the nation. The idea of the suffering of the innocent on behalf of the people found its most forceful expression in Isaiah's Suffering Servant poems: "But he was pierced for our transgressions, he was crushed for our iniquities; the punishment that brought us peace was upon him, and by his wounds we are healed. We all, like sheep, have gone astray, each of us has turned to his own way; and the LORD has laid on him the iniquity of us all" (Is 53:5-6).

Isaiah may not have known the identity of this righteous sufferer.[40] But according to the New Testament, the sinless one who voluntarily suffers for the people and thereby brings regeneration is Jesus, "the Lamb of God who takes away the sins of the world." And the early Christians believed that the risen Christ had called his followers to participate in his sufferings.

The climactic theme: the eschatological perspective. The foundation of the Old Testament ethic lay in God's past action of constituting Israel as the covenant people. However, the story did not end in the distant past. The ancient people of God developed a keen orientation toward the future. They anticipated that God would again act in a glorious manner for their salvation. One day, the prophets declared, God would bring renewal to the covenant people who have failed their Covenant-partner. The future renewal would not be merely a retrieval of some golden age in the past, however. Instead, the prophets directed their hope toward the dawning of the complete reign of the sovereign God over all the earth and toward the role of Israel in that reign.[41] This anticipation, which focused on the coming of the Messiah, provided an eschatological perspective to ethics.[42]

The eschatological perspective is evident in the repeated prophetic call to right living in the present on the basis of the promise of God's future activity. In fact we might suggest that the essence of the prophetic vision was to announce God's intentions for the future so as to call Israel (and the surrounding nations) to an ethical response in the present. The hope of a future participation in God's kingdom entailed grave ethical implications. It meant that moral decisions carried consequences for the future. Only the righteous could anticipate participating in the messianic era (e.g., Dan 12:2). Consequently the prophets summoned the community to the kind of living that was appropriate to their expectation of the coming of God's reign. Such living might even contribute to its realization.[43]

The growing eschatological anticipation led finally to the realization that God's vindication of the righteous and judgment upon the wicked may not come in this life. The righteous one may go to the grave crying out for God's intervention. Nevertheless, the prophets held out the hope that even if the divine response does not come now, God will surely act on behalf of the covenant people at the end of the age.

Jesus and the Moral Life

With its eschatological focus the Old Testament ethic ended on a hopeful note. The Hebrew people anticipated a day when God would act decisively on their behalf. The remnant in Israel kept the hope alive, even as they sought to prepare themselves for that great day. In faithfulness to the covenant, God responded to this expectation, the New Testament evangelists declared, by sending Jesus.

The report of the life, death, resurrection and exaltation of Jesus lies at the center of the Bible. In the same way this report forms the heart of biblical ethics. With this in view we turn our attention to the ethic of Jesus. My concern in these paragraphs is not to provide an exhaustive survey of Jesus' ethical teaching. Instead it is to discover what themes lay at the foundation of that teaching so as to indicate how Jesus stands at the fulcrum of the flow of biblical ethics. Wolfgang Schrage notes that the criterion and basis of New Testament ethics is God's saving act in Jesus Christ.[44] In keeping with this observation, we want to discover the christological foundation for an understanding of what it means to live as God's covenant people. Indeed, when the prophet of Nazareth came into the world, he not only articulated the way of life for the new people of God, he also embodied it.

The context: Jesus and the Jewish religious leaders. We can understand the significance of the ethical teaching of Jesus only when we place it in the context of his sustained disagreement with the religious teachers of his day, especially the scribes and Pharisees, as to what it meant to live in covenant with God. Ernst Käsemann summarized the situation in a poignant manner: "Jesus . . . broke through the piety and theology of his contemporaries, and brought God's promise and love in place of the Mosaic law, his own endowment with the Spirit in place of casuistry, and grace in place of good works."[45] This disagreement quickly led the Jewish religious leaders to oppose Jesus' ministry and eventually resulted in their decision to instigate his death.

Despite what Käsemann inferred, Jesus and his enemies did not disagree about the fundamental importance of the law as set forth in the Hebrew Scriptures for life within the covenant community. Instead they differed about the implications of the Hebrew Scriptures for living as God's people and about the nature of the divine will.[46] As Eduard Lohse pointed out, "Jesus did not think of calling the validity of the law into question. But he attacked the hypocrisy of those who supposed they had done enough when they had responded to the law's demand by casuistic interpretation and application."[47] Consequently Jesus sought to correct his hearers as to the nature of righteousness, God's purpose in giving the law and the proper interpretation of the law itself.[48] In short, Jesus intended to rectify his opponent's mistaken teaching about what marks the appropriate ethical response to the covenant-making God.[49]

Our Lord disagreed with the Jewish leaders he encountered about who actually are the people of God. The Pharisees and scribes viewed themselves as the truly righteous ones with whom God was pleased. They were righteous because only they obeyed the strictures of Jewish piety and followed the law to the letter. Jesus, in contrast, proclaimed that God's people are not those who appear to be righteous, but the ones who are penitent. God accepts those who humble themselves and cry for mercy; God rejects the proud who claim they have no need of forgiveness.

In a poignant parable Jesus put this disagreement in sharp relief. In contrast to the Pharisee who exalted himself through his supposedly pious prayer, the tax collector could not even look toward heaven but humbly entreated, "God, have mercy on me, a sinner." Jesus then drew a pointed conclusion: "I tell you that this man, rather than the other, went home justified before God. For everyone who exalts himself will be humbled, and he who humbles himself will be exalted" (Lk 18:14).

In keeping with this, Jesus' concern consistently went beyond any simple discussion of the rightness and wrongness of isolated acts. Instead he desired to speak about the doer, for the first consideration was not *what* should be done but *who* is doing it.[50]

A helpful example is Jesus' response to the lawyer who inquired of Jesus, "Who is my neighbor?" (Lk 10:29). The questioner's goal was to determine the limits of the circle of those whom he was to love. Jesus, however, refused to become involved in such casuistry. Through the ensuing parable, he reversed the direction of the question. Of central interest is not "Who is my neighbor?" but "To whom can I be a neighbor?"[51]

Jesus likewise disagreed with his contemporaries about human merit and divine rewards.[52] Many of the Jews of his day believed that God would reward those who strictly obeyed the regulations set forth in the Jewish religious tradition. Consequently they meticulously determined what the law of God required and forbade, and they slavishly fulfilled the strictures they devised. They assumed that in this manner they were gaining divine favor.[53]

Jesus denied that humans can make any claim on God whatsoever. We can never put God in our debt, he declared. Nor can we hope to merit God's favor by what we do. Strive as we might, we will never make ourselves righteous in God's sight: "Unless your righteousness surpasses that of the Pharisees and the teachers of the law you will certainly not enter the kingdom of heaven" (Mt 5:20). Yet Jesus' message remained hopeful. We can be righteous, for God freely bestows divine favor on us by sheer, unconditional grace. Righteousness is God's gracious gift.

At the heart of Jesus' interaction with his opponents was a foundational disagreement over the intent of the law. The Jewish religious leaders were quite happy to content themselves with outward acts. They believed that God requires meticulous conformity to the standards of conduct set forth in the law. Jesus, however, was unwilling to stop with outward conduct. Instead his teaching pierced to the core, to the inward dimension of human existence. Not public performance but the person behind the public façade is ultimately important. Not mere outward conformity to the law but inward piety marks true obedience to God. Jesus was primarily concerned about character, motivation and the heart.

Jesus' concern for the heart was born from his insightful perception that the source of wickedness lay within the human person. Unless this "interior" problem is remedied, "exterior" obedience will not endure long: "Make a tree good and its fruit will be good, or make a tree bad and its fruit will be bad, for a tree is recognized by its fruit" (Mt 12:33). Jesus also was aware of the uncanny human propensity for self-deception. Humans can sincerely believe they are obeying the law but in fact have missed its intention. Or, worse yet, they can willingly disobey the law even though they appear outwardly to be living according to it. He accused the Pharisees, for example, of such disobedience to the spirit of the Fifth Commandment ("Honor your father and your mother"). They were willing to abrogate their responsibility to provide for parents by declaring the financial resources earmarked for them *Corban,* that is, "a gift devoted to God" (Mk 7:11).

No wonder Jesus repeatedly bemoaned that the seemingly impeccable actions of the Pharisees and scribes hid hearts that were cold, callous and deceitfully wicked. He applied Isaiah's words to his contemporaries: "These people honor me with their lips, but their hearts are far from me" (Mk 7:6).

Above all, however, Jesus knew that inward piety and not outward conformity to the law marks true obedience to God, because God's intent focused on establishing right relationships. The Covenant-maker desires to enter into a person-to-person relationship with the people of the covenant. Mere obedience to laws cannot mediate this kind of relationship. Perhaps this lay near the heart of what Jesus was trying to say to the Pharisees and scribes of his day. The Master pointed out that fidelity to the intricacies of the law as the religious leaders perceived them was not what interested God.

God was not looking for their strict refusal to travel beyond a certain distance on the sabbath, for example. Honoring the sabbath may be a means through which to offer the heartfelt response God desires. But what the Covenant-maker desired was covenant partners who had a heart for God and therefore who reflected the divine heart in all their relationships.

Finally, Jesus disagreed with his contemporaries over the theological foundation for the ethical life. The Jewish religious leaders he encountered honored God as the divine lawgiver. God was the originator of the law. God had entrusted to Moses the tablets on Mount Sinai. In their understanding, the ethical life, in turn, was the attempt to please this Lawgiver through strict obedience to the divinely given law.

Jesus went beyond this understanding. He proclaimed that God is a heavenly Father whom to know is to trust, love and obey with gladness from the heart. In so doing, Jesus reoriented the direction of the ethical life. Because the Father is the God of all goodness and truth, the ethical life emerges from an intimate relationship with this God and not through slavish obedience to rules forming an intermediary between God and humans. Jesus invited others to share his confidence in the divine favor toward humankind that God had already freely shown. We might say that for Jesus the ethical life arises as our response to God's demonstration of love, grace and favor toward us, rather than as our attempt to win God's favor through acts of obedience. And this response consists above all in seeking God's reign and God's righteousness. As people do this, they discover that God has already freely given them all they truly need.

In his discussions with his opponents Jesus did not seek to demonstrate the truth of his position by logical analysis. Instead he focused on the appeal that moral truth makes to the heart. He proceeded on the assumption that truth will make its way into the hearts of those who are willing to believe. To this end he repeatedly used stories and parables, rather than logical syllogisms and elaborate intellectual proofs.

An ethic of the kingdom. Jesus weighed the teachings of the religious leaders of his day and found them wanting. But what did he offer in their place? What kind of ethic did he propose?

Most scholars today acknowledge that at the center of Jesus' ministry lay his announcement of God's reign, which marked the inauguration of an eschatological epoch (e.g., Mk 1:14).[54] This suggests that whatever else it may have been, the ethic our Lord set forth was an ethic of the kingdom.[55] According to L. H. Marshall, "All the ethical teaching of Jesus is simply an exposition of the ethics of the Kingdom of God." His teaching spoke about the way in which people "inevitably behave when they actually come under the rule of God."[56] And R. E. O. White intimates that Jesus' articulation of a kingdom ethic was his unique contribution to ethical thought.[57]

The Synoptic Gospels present Jesus' mission as primarily directed toward the kingdom of God. At the foundation for all that Jesus said and did, therefore, lay his belief that God was acting on behalf of the covenant people. God's reign was near at hand. In its fullness this reign remained future, for it would be universally present when the Son of Man arrives. Yet Jesus taught that God's reign was nevertheless present: People could already enter the kingdom (Mt 11:12). Therefore the message of the kingdom—of God's action in human history—entailed a call for response. Jesus declared that entrance into the kingdom comes through repentance and faith (Mk 1:15), which results in a changed heart and life. This change entailed total devotion to God, rather than mere legalistic penitential zeal.[58]

This focus carried ethical implications.[59] For Jesus the good life is not the quest for happiness but the pursuit of God's kingdom (Mt 6:33). The good life is life under God's reign or life in accordance with the will of the

King. Even our Lord's injunction "believe the gospel" carried with it an ethical aspect: Those who would respond rightly must be governed by the gospel.[60] Goodness, then, begins with the heart, which is the wellspring of action (Mk 7:21; Lk 6:45). With this in view Rudolf Schnackenburg concluded, "The real ground of moral obligation is the perceptible saving action of God in Jesus' coming and activity, his revelation of redemption, which is both historical and eschatological, and which guarantees the accomplishment which is to come."[61]

According to Jesus, being his disciple meant participating in the reign of the heavenly King. And life under his lordship entailed not merely a new way of thinking but a radical conversion that led to willing obedience to his Father's will (which was in part expressed in Jesus' commandments).[62] Hence the Master taught his disciples to pray, "Your kingdom come, your will be done on earth as it is in heaven" (Mt 6:10).

Jesus summarized the King's will in the double command to love,[63] which Rudolf Schnackenburg claimed is "the core and climax of the whole of moral doctrine."[64] Summarizing the entire Old Testament law in the command to love God and one's neighbor may have been unique to Jesus' message.[65] In any case, for him the central ethical principle of the ethic of the kingdom is heartfelt love for God and others. The citizens of the kingdom are those who love God from their heart and who love others as themselves. Such love, however, is no mere inward affection. Instead it involves humble service to God and the neighbor.

Jesus prescribed an ethic for a community who lived in expectation of the eschatological future and who had come to experience the inbreaking or initiation of that future in the present.[66] Life in the kingdom impinges on all aspects of human relationships. Hence Jesus spoke about such social institutions as marriage and divorce.[67] Kingdom citizens also ought to find true security in God rather than possessions.[68] Those who seek God's kingdom will also experience the care of the divine Sovereign (Mt 6:33). Riches, in turn, are not the key to the good life; on the contrary, they bring perils. Hence Jesus taught that rather than being an asset, affluence can actually become a hindrance to kingdom participation. Nowhere is this more evident than in the case of the rich young man who left Jesus' presence because he valued his possessions more than kingdom citizenship (Mt 19:16-22). Concerning this, Jesus remarked, "It is easier for a camel to go through the eye of a needle than for a rich man to enter the kingdom of God" (v. 24).

Jesus' interaction with the young man reminds us of a further dimension of the kingdom ethic. "If you want to be perfect," our Lord said, "go, sell your possessions and give to the poor, and you will have treasure in heaven. Then come, follow me" (Mt 19:21). The ethic of the kingdom requires assisting the needy. The King wills that those whom he has blessed with material possessions use these gifts for the sake of others.

An ethic for the family of God. Jesus clearly declared that the King of whose kingdom his followers are citizens is not some distant tyrant. Instead this King is none other than Jesus' own heavenly Father, and consequently he is their loving Father as well. Further, Jesus' message of the kingdom demanded repentance and faith on the part of its hearers (Mk 1:15). But this response entailed forsaking self-righteousness and humbly accepting God's gracious provision—like little children receiving the kingdom as an undeserved gift (Mt 18:1-5; Mk 10:15; Lk 18:17). Thus the kingdom message with its call to repentance and faith readily flowed into the idea that the inauguration of discipleship involved entering a new family by being "born again" (Jn 3:1-8). Through the new birth—being "born of God"—Christ's disciples had become God's children (Jn 1:12-13).

In keeping with these considerations, we may view Jesus' ethical teaching from the perspective of participation in God's family. This perspective suggests that Jesus, proclaimed an ethic for the family of God. According to Jesus the foundation for true living lies in participation in a family as children of the One he called "Abba" (Father).

According to Jesus, presence in God's family brings certain privileges. Above all, God's children can place their trust in the Father's goodness. Childlike faith in a loving heavenly Father formed the context for Jesus' teaching about earthly wealth and material possessions. Only foolish people boast in the accumulation of material things as the source of their security, he asserted (Lk 12:13-21). Instead, taking their cue from the birds of the air and the flowers of the field, God's children look to their heavenly Father, who cares for them and graciously provides for their needs (Mt 6:24-34).

Trust in the Father should likewise lead Jesus's disciples to pray in a new way. The Pharisees offered elaborate prayers as an act of piety or a sign of righteousness (e.g., Mt 6:5). God's children, in contrast, pray so as to tap into the unlimited resource of their loving heavenly Father (Mt 7:9-11).

Jesus taught that presence in God's family carried ethical implications. At the basis of the family ethic was the principle that family membership naturally involves family resemblance. Similar to the Old Testament focus on the imitation of God, Jesus exhorted his disciples to resemble their heavenly Father as children naturally resemble their earthly fathers. For example, he appealed to God's love for the unjust to challenge his hearers to an ethic of unbounded love: "Love your enemies and pray for those who persecute you, that you may be sons of your Father in heaven. He causes his sun to rise on the evil and the good, and sends rain on the righteous and the unrighteous" (Mt 5:44-45; cf. Lk 6:32-36). In fact family members are to be like their Father in everything: "Be perfect, therefore, as your heavenly Father is perfect" (Mt 5:48).[69] Birger Gerhardsson has pointed out the radical nature of this injunction. Our Lord demanded that the disciple be "complete, undamaged, undivided, and unimpeachable in the attitude of one's heart and, as a result, in all one's doings . . . 'perfect.'"[70]

The family resemblance extends to siblings as well. As children of a common Father, Jesus' disciples are to realize that they belong together. Because they are one family, his followers are to treat each other as brother and sister. The principle of family solidarity goes deeper than merely being kind to each other. Ultimately a family ethic requires participation in the family itself. Hence Jesus' moral ideal can only be corporately fulfilled.[71] Jesus' disciples can truly live as his followers only in relationship to others. They live out the Christian ethic together.

Participation in God's family, therefore, ought to lead to a special family solidarity among Jesus' disciples. Jesus commanded his followers to love each other. Indeed, drawing from the Old Testament itself, our Lord placed love for others second only to love for God (e.g., Mt 22:37-40). Familial love is not merely an emotion, however, but a strong mutual loyalty or a pledge to stand with one another as those who belong together. Family solidarity also brings the duty to forgive.[72] Here again disciples merely follow the example of their heavenly Father. Just as God has forgiven their great debt, so also they must forgive each other the debts which in comparison are minuscule (Mt 18:21-35).

Family solidarity carries a far-reaching implication for other human relationships. Jesus' ethic demanded that his followers view participation in the divine family with utmost seriousness. No longer ought his disciples to follow the Old Testament pattern of viewing the physical family as the closest human bond. Jesus taught that more important than physical ancestry and who one's parents are is spiritual ancestry—who one's heavenly Father is (e.g. Lk 3:7-8; Jn 8:31-59). As a result, the disciples' primary family is no longer based on earthly kinship ties, for no other relationship ought to rival membership in God's family. The disciples' fundamental relationship as participants in God's heavenly family must be to him and by extension to each other.

Jesus therefore admonished his hearers, "Anyone who loves his father or mother more than me is not worthy of me; anyone who loves his son or daughter more than me is not worthy of me" (Mt 10:37). Yet he promised to his loyal disciples a larger, spiritual family to compensate for the loss entailed in leaving their natural family for the sake of discipleship: "I tell you the truth, no one who has left home or mother or father or children or fields for me and the gospel will fail to receive a hundred times as much in this present age . . . and in the age to come eternal life" (Mk 10:29-30). What the Master demanded of his followers, he fulfilled himself. He too forsook family for the sake of obedience to the Father's will. Rather than attaching himself to his physical mother and siblings, he counted as his true family "whoever does the will of my Father in heaven" (Mt 12:50).

While focused on the family of God, Jesus' ethic does not end with God's family. Instead it leads to a widened concern. Disciples are committed to God's task of reconciliation. Just as they have experienced peace through receiving God's unmerited favor, so also they should desire to become peacemakers. Thus Jesus declared, "Blessed are the peacemakers, for they will be called sons of God" (Mt 5:9).

An ethic of imitation. Viewing Jesus' teaching as setting forth an ethic for the family of God leads to an additional perspective. Jesus' ethical teaching gives birth to an ethic of imitation: Disciples are to imitate their Master. In so doing, they are actually imitating God.[73] R. E. O. White claims this perspective is "the nearest principle in Christianity to a moral absolute," for it "remains the heart of the Christian ethic."[74] But determining exactly what the *imitatio Christi* entails requires further reflection.

Throughout his ministry Jesus pointed to his own example as the pattern for ethical living. In addition to offering them his teaching, Jesus directed his disciples to his own conduct. Thus he challenged his disciples to love each other according to the pattern of his love for them (Jn 13:34; 15:12). He likewise admonished them to obey their heavenly Father after his example of submission to the Father's will, which would even take him to the cross.[75]

Our Lord dramatized or exemplified the life he desired for his disciples through certain symbolic acts.[76] Perhaps none of these is more poignant than the occasion when he washed the disciples' feet (Jn 13:1-11). In first-century Palestine it was customary for the host to place a servant at the door to wash the feet of the guests as they arrived from their journey over the dusty streets of the city. In the upper room that night no servant met Jesus and his friends at the door. For their part the disciples were too caught up in disputing with each other as to which one was the greatest to perform this menial task (Lk 22:24). So Jesus rose from the table, wrapped a towel around his waist and one by one washed the feet of these cantankerous men. When he had finished, he announced the symbolic nature of his act: "Now that I, your Lord and Teacher, have washed your feet, you also should wash one another's feet. I have set you an example that you should do as I have done for you" (Jn 13:14-15).

The ethic of imitation is not completed as the disciple follows Jesus' example, however.[77] The ultimate motivation for ethical living lies beyond mere patterning one's conduct after the example of a great leader. It arises from the kind of devotion that connects disciples to the Lord at the deepest level of their person: disciples are devoted to Christ. And this leads to increasing conformity to their Lord.

Jesus himself pointed in this direction.[78] After washing their feet in the upper room, he did not admonish his disciples simply to love as they had *seen* him love. Instead his words were, "As I have loved you, so also you must love one another" (Jn 13:34). They were to love as he had loved them, that is, as each of them had personally experienced his love directly. The moral ideal Jesus embodied was not merely an example that his followers had observed. More importantly, it was a quality they had experienced. They knew firsthand the love of their Master. Such experiential knowledge could elicit heartfelt love and devotion in return.

The goal of devotion supplied the ultimate rationale for Jesus' emphasis on inwardness. Conduct flows from character, he taught, but true character arises from devotion. Indeed, devotion to the Master became the wellspring for the development of Christlike character in his disciples. In short, Jesus' followers were not motivated to follow their Lord by admiration for a historical person who had done some great deeds. Instead their discipleship was the outflow of personal gratitude and love to the one whose love they had experienced. Such discipleship opened the way for the New Testament focus on incorporation into Christ and conformity to Christ.

The ethic of devotion provides the link between Jesus and his disciples in every era. The dynamic of devotion means that we no longer stand outside the biblical story. Unlike the manner in which we may observe the plot of a good novel or even follow the biography of a great hero, we are not mere uninvolved observers of the gospel narrative. Instead, we are participants in the gospel drama as those who, like the early disciples, are the recipients of Christ's love. We have been touched firsthand not only by the moral ideal Jesus embodied but by the Risen Lord himself.

Consequently we do not merely admire Jesus as we might admire other historical figures such as Gandhi, Albert Schweitzer or Mother Teresa. We do not simply draw inspiration or a pattern for living from his life as we might do from theirs. The Christian ethic does not look to Jesus solely as a historical example whom we seek to emulate. We do not look to him only as the main character in a story from a bygone era on whose life we can reflect and thereby draw instruction. Rather he has loved *us* and has sacrificed his life for *us*. To this personal experience of Jesus' great love, we find ourselves compelled to respond with gratitude and love. Hence, rather than merely patterning our lives after his, we enter into relationship with him. In this relationship we desire to live as Christ would have us live, that is, to have Christ formed in us.

This ethic of devotion has characterized Christians throughout the ages. Christ's followers have consistently differentiated between other model persons (such as the patriarchs, the apostles and the martyrs), whose memory they bore in their hearts, and Jesus Christ, who through his Spirit had made his abode in their hearts.[79] Thereby the Christian ethos has intensified and personalized the biblical concept of the presence of God among God's people. The divine presence is none other than the indwelling reality of the living Lord Jesus Christ mediated through his Holy Spirit.

The ethic of devotion to Jesus likewise forms the most direct bridge to the Old Testament ethic of the imitation of God. The foundation of this connection lies in Jesus' mission as the beloved Son in whom the Father is well pleased (Mk 1:11).[80] Endowed with the divine Spirit, Jesus revealed the character of the holy God, who is loving, merciful and compassionate. Thereby he incarnated the divine life. As a consequence Christ serves as the model for all human living. And by pouring out the Spirit on his followers, the Risen Lord mediated to them the divine dynamic that made possible the imitation of the God revealed in Jesus of Nazareth.

The Ethic of the Early Church: The Example of Paul

"If the ethical teaching of Jesus is a newly-opened spring of moral inspiration fresh and inexhaustible, fed from the deep reservoirs of Israel's long experience," commented R. E. O. White, "then apostolic ethics represents the channelling of that renewing stream out into farther lands."[81] Indeed, just as Jesus' ethic drew from the storehouse of Israel and the Old Testament, so also the Master's teaching formed the foundation upon which the New Testament writers built. As the gospel moved beyond the confines of Palestine, the early believers came face to face with the question, What does it mean to be a disciple of Jesus of Nazareth and thereby to acknowledge the God of Israel in the context of a pagan world? In response, they channeled the stream that flowed from the Master's own life into the discipleship task within that environment.

The apostle Paul was, of course, not the only early Christian leader to reflect on the significance of Jesus' life, death and resurrection for living as the people of the new covenant. Yet he stands as perhaps the most striking and influential example of those who took up this challenge. For this reason I will focus my attention on the basic orientation toward the Christian life that emerges from his writings in order to see the christological focus of Paul's understanding of how Christians should live—that is, of what we might call ethics or the moral life.[82]

Salvation: the basis of the moral life. The ethic of the early church arose out of the steadfast belief that in Christ the covenant-making God of Israel had acted on behalf of humankind. God's glorious plan for the ages was now unfolding, and this cosmic plan centered on Jesus Christ. Its intent was to call a people from among all nations, a people who would belong to God. The New Testament ethic grew out of the concern of the early disciples to live in the light of God's glorious act as God's eschatological covenant-partners.

According to Paul, God's mighty act was fundamentally soteriological. God had acted for human salvation. This glorious act emerged in the context of human moral failure and sin. Humans had become captives of sin. Like an alien power sin holds them in its evil grasp, instills in them hostility toward God and leaves them helpless to remedy their situation (Rom 7:14-24). In the midst of human moral failure and depravity, however, God had acted definitively. This divine action disclosed God's own righteousness: "For in the gospel a righteousness from God is revealed" (Rom 1:17; cf. 3:21). God has confirmed his righteousness, Paul declared, by demonstrating definitive faithfulness to the covenant (e.g., Rom 9—11).[83] Hence the Pauline ethic was radically theological; it arose out of the awareness that a person's entire life and being are dependent upon God's sovereign redemptive power.

Although God's display of divine righteousness involves judging human sin (Rom 1:18), for Paul its focus is Christ, and through Christ it centers on the Holy Spirit. This focus begins in the past—with the narrative of Jesus, who shared the human situation. Central to this past narrative were the cross and resurrection. In his crucifixion Christ took human sin upon himself, so that sinful humans might be reconciled to God. And in his resurrection Christ made it possible for his followers to enjoy a new life. J. Paul Sampley indicated the significance of the cross for the apostle: "The death and resurrection of Jesus Christ is the primary reference point in Paul's thought world. Paul sees past, present, and future in the light of that pivotal event. For the Apostle, believers relate to the death and resurrection of Christ as the formative event in their past."[84]

For Paul salvation extends from the past into the present. As a result of the cross and resurrection, Christ's followers enjoy a new moral dynamic within themselves—the Holy Spirit, who is the Spirit of Christ.

Through his Spirit, therefore, Christ is present with his followers. And because of the indwelling Spirit of Christ, they are united with Christ in his death and resurrection (Rom 6:1-14).

According to Paul the horizon of salvation moves beyond even the present. In fact the present gains its significance as the time between the past and future. In Christ's death and resurrection the new aeon has dawned. But the old aeon remains operative until Christ's future *parousia,* his return in glory. In the meantime the present form of the world is passing away and the new creation has begun.

Salvation forms the great "indicative" in Paul's thought: The God who is faithful to the divine purposes has acted in Christ on the behalf of sinful humankind and through Christ has poured out the Holy Spirit in the hearts of those who are "in Christ." Believers have died with Christ, and they will one day be raised with him.

This great indicative provided the basis for the "imperative" indissolubly linked to it:[85] Believers are now to live in a manner in keeping with the eschatological salvation they have received. Their behavior is to reveal the new life that God has graciously given them and which one day will be theirs in its fullness. As those who will be raised with Christ, they already can "live a new life" (Rom 6:4). Therefore Paul enjoined his readers to live in the light of the coming day (e.g., Rom 13:11-14; 1 Cor 7:29-31). In this manner the eschaton casts its beams of light into the present and is made evident in the "already" of the moral life of the believing community.[86]

Christlikeness: the goal of the moral life. In a sense the Pauline imperative is simply the admonition to those who are "in Christ" that they live accordingly—as those who *are* "in Christ." The moral imperative of living "in Christ" suggests that for Paul the Christian life is a dynamic. It involves, to borrow his words to the Colossian believers, "Christ in you the hope of glory" (Col 1:27). The Pauline moral imperative focuses on a radically new reality. Far beyond merely a rearrangement of features of one's former life, being "in Christ" involves a "new creation" (2 Cor 5:17), which God himself brings into existence.[87] Paul likened this divine act to God bringing life out of death (Rom 4:17; Eph 2:1-10). The goal of this dynamic is nothing less than perfect conformity to Christ, becoming like Christ in one's entire being.

For Paul, therefore, at the heart of the moral life is the imitation of

Christ (e.g., Rom 15:7; 2 Cor 10:1; Eph 5:25), or the imitation of God after the pattern of Christ (Eph 4:32-5:2). In keeping with this focus, the moral life is served as believers pattern their lives after those who are following Christ and become patterns for each other to follow. Thus he could admonish the Corinthians, "Follow my example, as I follow the example of Christ" (1 Cor 11:1; cf. 1 Cor 4:16-17; Phil 3:17; 1 Thess 1:6-7; 2:14).[88]

Christlikeness includes possessing the "mind" of Christ: "Let this mind be in you which was also in Christ Jesus" (Phil 2:5 NKJV). Having the mind of Christ has to do with the believer's attitude. Paul admonished his readers to pattern themselves after the one who "did not consider equality with God something to be grasped, but made himself nothing" (Phil 2:6-7). But for Paul the Christlike mind also has a more intellectual side: "We demolish arguments and every pretension that sets itself up against the knowledge of God, and we take captive every thought to make it obedient to Christ" (2 Cor 10:5).

Christlikeness also entails exhibiting the character of Christ. More specifically, Christ must be formed in his disciples by the Holy Spirit. Hence when Paul lists the fruit of the Spirit—"love, joy, peace, patience, kindness, goodness, faithfulness, gentleness and self-control" (Gal 5:22-23)—Christians rightly find in these traits a description of Christ, for many of these words are elsewhere used to speak about Christ.[89]

Being made like Christ, however, does not occur in some private sphere of the quiet life. For Paul, Christ's mind and character are formed in disciples as they are involved in the believing community, as well as in the ministry their Master has entrusted to them. In fact, the apostle anticipates that believers will engage in the work of Christ even to the point of suffering persecution for their Lord (2 Tim 3:12). In so doing, however, they are merely sharing in the fellowship of Christ's sufferings (Phil 3:10; cf. 1 Pet 4:13).

Spiritual conflict: the context of the moral life. As the suffering motif suggests, being made like Christ does not occur without a struggle. Indeed, according to Paul the Christian life entails spiritual conflict. This conflict pitches the "Spirit" against the "flesh": "For the sinful nature desires what is contrary to the Spirit, and the Spirit what is contrary to the sinful nature. They are in conflict with each other, so that you do not do what you want" (Gal 5:17).

Paul's word *flesh (sarx)* carries a variety of meanings depending on the context in which it occurs. Sometimes it refers simply to the material that makes up physical bodies or to the human body itself.[90] More important, it can also stand for the whole human person in the purely physical aspect of existence. Hence *flesh* can also refer to this-worldly, earthly existence, especially its frailty, limitations and mortality.[91]

When the word appears in the context of moral conflict, however, we must be careful to avoid reading into it purely physical connotations and thereby localizing the source of evil in the physical dimension of human existence, in contrast to a supposedly "spiritual," immaterial aspect.[92] Paul did not intend to set up a strong dichotomy between the material and the immaterial. Nor did he assume an ethical dualism that locates the evil impulse in the physical dimension of human existence. Instead Paul's teaching arose out of the Hebrew and Semitic anthropology that could view the one human reality from various standpoints.[93] Rather than referring to the physical as such, the use of "flesh" as an ethical principle, arising out of the idea of human weakness and mortality, refers to human moral weakness and vulnerability to sin.[94] "The flesh" signifies the human person as frail and hence as susceptible to temptation and readily coming under the captivity of sin. Thus it refers to the human person in our propensity to give evil opportunity and hence to fall away from God.

From this understanding it is only a short step to the eschatological meaning that lay at the heart of Paul's dichotomy between flesh and Spirit. These terms describe two kinds of existence. The first is conditioned by the present age, which is already passing away. The second, in contrast, describes the believers' new existence that is ours through union with Christ by the indwelling Spirit.[95] No wonder in this in-between era the "flesh" is in mortal combat with the "Spirit."

For Paul the flesh becomes the enemy of the Spirit in two interconnected ways. As the source of insatiable desires (Rom 13:14; Gal 5:16-17, 24), it is the means through which sin gains mastery over the human person (e.g., Rom 7:25). As the source of self-sufficiency—hence, of confidence in one's ability to attain righteousness through obedience to the law—it provides the foundation for prideful independence from God (Phil 3:3-4) and from God's gracious saving act in Christ.[96] For this reason Paul not only warned his readers against living to gratify the desires of the "flesh," he also admonished them to avoid self-commendation (2 Cor 10:18) and boasting in anything (Rom 3:27; 1 Cor 1:29) except the cross of Christ (Gal 6:14; cf. 1 Cor 1:31; 2 Cor 10:17).[97]

The spiritual conflict that characterizes the Christian life is not solely an individual matter. It is not merely a conflict within the heart of the individual believer. On the contrary, Paul's main concern in his discussions of flesh and Spirit was with life within the believing community. Therefore Paul's admonition to "walk" in the Spirit—which is his most common way of describing or urging ethical behavior[98]—called on believers to act in love toward each other. And the resultant "fruit of the Spirit" includes love, joy and peace being acted out within the people of God.[99]

There is another dimension to spiritual conflict. Lying behind the struggle believers sense within and among themselves is an external conflict—a cosmic battle—in which they are often unwitting participants. Paul spoke about this conflict as "spiritual warfare." Believers have enlisted on the side of God and therefore are enemies of the spiritual hosts arrayed in opposition to God:[100] "For our struggle is not against flesh and blood, but against the rulers, against the authorities, against the powers of this dark world and against the spiritual forces of evil in the heavenly realms" (Eph 6:12).

The presence of the conflict in which believers are engaging leads to one of the apostle's central ethical directives, the repeated admonition to "put off/put on" (e.g., Rom 13:11-14; Eph 4:22-24; Col 3:9-10). Believers must "put off" one reality and "put on" another: Put off the flesh, and put on the spirit. Put off the old life, and put on the new. Put off the works of the flesh, and put on the Lord Jesus Christ. Put off the deeds of darkness, and put on the deeds of light. In this vivid manner Paul characterized the Christian ethic as forsaking the old life so as to live in a new manner. Here again we are confronted with an eschatological ethic.

Love: the manner of the moral life. But what is this new manner of living? Here Paul returned to the central description that Jesus received from the Old Testament and passed on to his disciples. The fundamental moral principle is love.

In a sense in announcing an ethic of love Paul built on Jesus' conflict with his opponents. Like Jesus, Paul affirmed the law; the law had in no way been abrogated (Rom 3:31). The law represents the norm for living. Hence the apostle could say, "The commandment is holy, righteous and good" (Rom 7:12). And in admonishing believers Paul readily drew from the Hebrew Scriptures as authoritative writings (e.g., 2 Cor 8:15; 9:9).[101]

Like his Lord, however, Paul espoused a christological understanding of the law. The positive role of the law in salvation emerges only when it is viewed in the light of Christ and his coming (cf. Gal 3:19-25).[102] Thus the law must be seen through the lenses of the gospel, that is, through the role of Christ as the fulfillment of the law (Rom 10:4)[103] and above all through the cross and resurrection of Jesus Christ.[104] Viewing the law in this manner allows one to realize that the law was never meant to be the agent of human salvation. Righteousness could never be attained by human efforts to obey the law; instead, it is God's gracious gift for all who are "in Christ."

The apostle declared that the law fulfills only a circumscribed ethical role, namely, that of marking the boundaries. Thereby the law points out—even stimulates—human failure, inability and sin. The sole result is condemnation (Rom 7:5-14). The law can inform as to what the boundaries are, but it is unable to prevent the transgression of these boundaries. In this context Paul recited his own experience of knowing what is right but doing what is wrong (Rom 7:14-23). This experience could only lead him to cry out, "What a wretched man I am! Who will rescue me from this body of death?" (Rom 7:25).

For Paul, then, the law is severely limited. The apostle, following Jesus' own teaching, was indicating that because they are by nature external to the human person, laws can never create the kind of relationships that God desires for humans. Laws can only point out the boundaries in the midst of which truly godly relationships can arise.

Paul adamantly declared that only the Spirit—and not the law—can give life (Rom 8:1-4). And the life that the Spirit gives is characterized by love. Indeed the Spirit sets us free to love.[105] According to Paul love is the "most excellent way" of living (1 Cor 12:31), greater than even faith and hope (1 Cor 13:13).

Consequently, the apostle reiterated Jesus' teaching about the centrality of love for others. In so doing he drew his Master's teaching to its logical conclusion, namely that love is the fulfillment of the law: "Let no debt remain outstanding, except the continuing debt to love one another, for he who loves his fellow man has fulfilled the law. The commandments . . . are summed up in this one rule: 'Love your neighbor as yourself'" (Rom 13:8-9; cf. Gal 5:13-14). This does not mean that the multiple laws of the Hebrew Scriptures are reduced to one new law. Nor does this suggest that the individual commandments are absorbed into such an overarching law. Instead Paul indicates that love recapitulates the Old Testament law. And by being the bond that unites the individual commandments into a unified whole, love provides the perspective from which believers understand the law.[106]

Why love? Paul seems to offer a threefold answer. In keeping with the ethical teaching of the Old Testament and of Jesus, Paul agreed that love is crucial because it characterizes God. The narrative of God's great action on behalf of sinful humankind reveals the greatness of the divine love. As we love, we imitate God. This confirms that as the eschatological Spirit creates a people who reflect the very character of God—which is love—the intent of the law comes to fulfillment.[107]

Further, love lies at the heart of the Pauline ethic because of his assumption that the community of faith is the primary context for living as believers.[108] Despite his repeated focus on the individual, the apostle did not conceive of Christ's followers living an isolated, solitary existence. On the contrary, believers are called *together* in Christ, called to be the *ekklēsia* (assembly or church). Realizing that they form the one body of Christ (e.g., 1 Cor 12:12), believers are naturally to contribute their gifts to the common good (1 Cor 12:5), practice mutuality (Eph 5:21) and evidence such Christlike traits as self-sacrificial concern for each other (Gal 2:2; Phil 2:1-11), even to the point of giving up their personal rights for the sake of others (1 Cor 10:23-33).

In a word, such community life is the life of love. And love is merely life in community.[109] Victor Paul Furnish captured this crucial dimension of the Pauline ethic: "The believer's life and action are always in, with, and for 'the brethren' in Christ. For him, moral action is never a matter of an isolated actor choosing from among a variety of abstract ideals on the basis of how inherently 'good' or 'evil' each may be. Instead, it is always a matter of choosing and doing what is good for the brother and what will upbuild the whole community of brethren."[110] Paul's ethic has rightly been termed "the ethics of life in the community."[111]

The third reason for the focus on love is apparent in the climax of Paul's hymn to love.[112] Whereas all other aspects of Christian existence will one day cease, love will carry over into the new aeon. This indicates that of the various dimensions of the moral life, love alone provides insight into the coming age. Indeed, love is the actual quality of the age to come.[113] Hence for Paul where love exists the new aeon is present. And the moral life is eschatological living: It involves living now as those who belong to the age to come.

Self-discipline: the means to the moral life. While the apostle denied that the law can produce the ethical life, Paul did not advocate a life devoid of "law." Paul was no antinomian.[114] In the words of Gordon Fee, "To be 'Law-less' does not mean to be lawless."[115] On the contrary, for the apostle the ethical life also includes diligence and self-discipline.

Repeatedly Paul enjoined his readers to be diligent (1 Tim 4:15), to work hard at their salvation (Phil 2:12) or to make every effort (2 Tim 2:15). Above all he spoke about self-discipline. He compared the Christian life to an athlete who disciplines himself in preparation for the competition (1 Cor 9:27). In this context Paul indicated by personal testimony that he controlled himself—even beat his body and made it his slave (v. 29). R. E. O. White described Paul's perspective on the matter: "Plainly, the Christian has exchanged the outward compulsion of imposed regulations for the inward constraints of a very high ideal. Yet this *is* a liberation, since the compulsions are now from within the self, and exercised by an ideal freely accepted."[116]

According to Paul, then, the Christian has replaced external law with an even greater form of diligence: self-discipline. But why follow the disciplined life? The apostle's response invokes the goals believers ought to have in view. The intermediate goal of self-discipline is ministry, being able to be faithful servants of Christ who are busily engaged in the work their Master has entrusted to them. Faithful servants know that certain activities, while not necessarily evil, do not contribute to ministry: "'Everything is permissible'—but not everything is beneficial. 'Everything is permissible'—but not everything is constructive" (1 Cor 10:23).

* * *

I was raised in the parsonage. When I was a teenager my parents occasionally requested that I refrain from certain activities that they did not necessarily consider evil but that they knew would injure my father's ministry. This appeal shed a new light on the matter. My parents could have set down a legalistic framework and simply forbade me to do these things. But they did not. They appealed to my respect for my father and for the ministry which we as a family shared. Thereby they challenged me to exercise internal discipline, a challenge that has remained a guiding factor for me. Repeatedly I return to the question of expediency: Will this activity promote the ministry or hinder it?

* * *

Regardless of our chosen occupation, the vocation of all believers is the ministry. For Paul this shared goal of desiring to minister as Christ's servants requires that we live diligently and practice self-discipline.

Paul's horizon, however, linked the intermediate to the eschatological. The final goal of the Christian life is participation in the glorious future salvation. His desire to gain an eternal dwelling in God's new community motivated the apostle to exercise self-discipline and diligence. Hence he reported that the reason he makes his body his slave—extending the metaphor from the Olympic runner—is "so that after I have preached the gospel to others, I myself will not be disqualified for the prize" (1 Cor 10:27).

Yet for Paul the bottom line lay beyond any reward he might receive. Above all, he suggested, believers practice self-discipline because they desire to please Christ. The reward Paul wanted to gain was the praise of his Lord.

This leads us back to the ethic of imitation we found in Jesus' teaching. For Paul the ethical life entails diligence and self-discipline motivated by love for Christ. For this reason it is characterized by consecration. Christians live as they do because they have dedicated themselves to the person of Christ and to the God who has reconciled them in Christ. Consequently, believers are to live "worthy" lives—worthy of their calling (Eph 4:1), worthy of the God who has called them (1 Thess 2:12), worthy of the Lord (Col 1:10) and worthy of the gospel of Christ (Phil 1:27).

The Holy Spirit: agent of the moral life. As we noted earlier, Paul built on Jesus' disagreement with the Pharisees about the efficacy of the law.

Human attempts to obey the law and thereby gain righteousness—which was the way of the Pharisees—are doomed to failure.[117] For Paul the law's inability to produce life arose in part out of the radicality of human sin. The law is powerless to produce righteousness because it is "weakened by the sinful nature [flesh]" (Rom 8:3). Humans are "dead" in transgressions and sins" (Eph 2:1). The ethical implication is grave: No human can conceivably fulfill the Christian ethic.

What is the solution? Paul himself raised this question: "Who will rescue me from this body of death?" (Rom 7:24). According to the apostle the answer rests with the Holy Spirit, who is poured out in the lives of those who through faith have been united with Christ. The Spirit is the agent of righteous living. Paul knew this from personal experience. He testified, "The law of the Spirit of life set me free from the law of sin and death" (Rom 8:2). The Christian ethic, then, entails life in the Spirit. Christ came, Paul declared, "in order that the righteous requirements of the law might be fulfilled in us, who do not live according to the sinful nature but according to the Spirit" (Rom 8:4).

According to Paul the Spirit is the link between the indicative and the imperative.[118] The same indwelling Spirit who mediates salvation through the believers' union with Christ also provides the divine power necessary for Christian living. The indwelling Spirit enables us to live on a new plane of existence (Rom 8:2-4; Gal 4:6). As a result Paul's ethical imperatives boil down to our appropriation of the Holy Spirit. Rather than being drunk with wine, we are to be "filled with the Spirit" (Eph 5:18). If we "live by the Spirit" we will not gratify the "desires of the sinful nature" (Gal 5:16).

Appropriating the indwelling Spirit is the way to Christ-mindedness, for "those who live in accordance with the Spirit have their minds set on what the Spirit desires" (Rom 8:5). In this manner Paul's focus on the Spirit leads back to the ethic of Jesus, for living by the Spirit—that is, being led by the Spirit—confirms that believers are God's children (v. 14); we are members of God's family. Those who are united with Christ through the Spirit are experiencing moral transformation, for they are being changed into the image of Christ (2 Cor 3:18).

For Paul the Spirit's role extends to the specific situations of life. The Spirit is the believers' guide into the very "how" of right conduct.

Through the Spirit believers are able to discern God's will and perceive what constitutes proper behavior. In this way those in whom the Spirit dwells can live out God's claims in everyday life (hence Rom 8:4-9, 13-14; Gal 5:16; Col 1:10).[119]

The Spirit is also the prime link between the past, the present and the eschatological future. The same indwelling Spirit who facilitates the union of believers with Christ in his death is also the "down payment" guaranteeing their eschatological participation in Christ's resurrection (Rom 8:11; 2 Cor 1:22; 5:5). This link indicates the profound connection Paul drew between Christ and the Spirit (e.g., 2 Cor 3:17). In fact we might say that Paul's pneumatology was a radical extension of his Christology. H. Wheeler Robinson rightly concluded, "Paul's doctrine of the Spirit as active in the regeneration and sanctification of the believer united with Christ through faith and baptism, is his most important and characteristic contribution to Christian anthropology."[120]

Consequently Paul's ethic is not only radically theological, it is also radically soteriological. As a result it is not only radically christological but also radically pneumatological. Hence we might capsulize the ethic of Paul—as well as of the New Testament as a whole—in the phrase "By the power of the indwelling Spirit, be (that is, become) who you are."[121] Because the Holy Spirit is "the absolutely essential constituent of the whole of Christian life," to cite Gordon Fee again,[122] the Christian ethical life is the life of holiness—the life of the people who are holy unto the Lord—in fulfillment of the Old Testament quest.

Chapter 4

MODEL CHRISTIAN PROPOSALS

"Love the Lord your God with all your heart and with all your soul and with all your mind." This is the first and greatest commandment. And the second is like it: "Love your neighbor as yourself." All the Law and the Prophets hang on these two commandments.
(MATTHEW 22:37-40)

"Take and read," chanted the child's voice from a neighboring house beyond the garden of the Villa Cassiciacum in which a man was weeping in despair. His pursuit of wisdom and his quest for truth had led him steadily toward the Christian faith. But his unwillingness to let go of the licentious lifestyle he had enjoyed since his youth held him back. "Take and read," came the admonition again.

"This cannot be merely the words of a child's game," the man concluded, "but must be God's own voice." He hurried back to the place where he had left a copy of Scripture. The book fell open, and he read the familiar words of Paul: "Let us behave decently, as in the daytime, not in orgies and drunkenness, not in sexual immorality and debauchery, not in dissension and jealousy. Rather, clothe yourselves with the Lord Jesus Christ, and do not think about how to gratify the desires of the sinful nature" (Rom 13:13-14). As he read the text, light infused the man's heart, and all the gloom and doubt that had lodged in him vanished.[1]

In this way the person destined to become the most influential Christian thinker since the apostles—Augustine—was converted to Christ. Augustine's writings would shape all subsequent theology, and the intellectual cast he would set for the faith would provide the context for one of the most significant articulations of the Christian ethic.

* * *

Christians have always looked primarily to the Bible as the foundation for their ethic. Yet throughout most of church history Christian ethicists have articulated their conclusions concerning the nature of the life of discipleship cognizant that they lived in a context shaped by and indebted to the philosophical tradition that dates to ancient Greece. As a result many thinkers have grappled with the question as to what connection—if any—ties biblical revelation to the quest for a philosophical ethic. Their reflections have yielded a wide variety of proposals.

A survey of the entire Christian ethical tradition lies beyond the scope of this chapter. Instead we will concentrate our gaze on three such offerings. These three proposals represent the central ways classical Christian thinkers have sought to construct a theological ethic within the context of the world around them.[2]

Augustine: Ethics as the Love of God

Alasdair MacIntyre claims that "the paradox of Christian ethics is precisely that it has always tried to devise a code for society as a whole from pronouncements which were addressed to individuals or small communities to separate themselves off from the rest of society."[3] If MacIntyre's appraisal is correct, much of the credit for transforming the Christian ethic into a system of morality upon which an entire civilization could be built must go to Augustine (A.D. 354-430). In the words of Henry Sidgwick, "an important part of Augustine's work as a moralist lies in the reconciliation which he laboured to effect between the anti-worldly spirit of Christianity and the necessities of secular civilisation."[4] Augustine was perhaps the first Christian to engage wholeheartedly in this endeavor. For his attempt he has been hailed as the first Christian philosopher to formulate the faith into a comprehensive framework.[5]

Like the apostle Paul, whose life his own paralleled in several significant ways, Augustine was not raised a Christian but came to faith through a dramatic religious experience. After conversion both Paul and Augustine became powerful articulators of Christianity whose influence extends into the present. Indeed, if Paul is the most significant apostle of the church, Augustine is the most important theologian the church has produced.

Seeking truth.[6] Aurelius Augustine was born on November 13, 354, in the small agricultural town of Tagaste near Carthage in northern Africa. Although his father, Patricius, was not a believer, Augustine's mother, Monica, was a devout Christian who faithfully prayed for her son. But his wayward early life gave little indication that Augustine would eventually play such a formative role in the shaping of Christian ethics.

After studying the classical poets and orators at the school in Madaura some twenty miles south of his home, the seventeen-year-old Augustine moved to the more metropolitan context of Carthage to continue his education in rhetoric. While reading one of the works of the great orator Cicero, Augustine discovered the philosophical quest that Cicero's rhetorical style was designed to convey. The ancient orator's conclusion that happiness is not only the possession of truth but questing after it launched Augustine's own pilgrimage.[7]

The young thinker's search for wisdom, as well as his concern for the problem of evil, which he would take with him his entire life, led him to embrace Manichaeism, a system of religious and philosophical thought that originated in Babylonia.[8] The Manichaeans propagated a radically dualistic outlook. They described the cosmos as engulfed in a conflict between two equally eternal primal principles: light and darkness, good and evil, truth and error, or, to use the biblical language, God and Satan.[9] Because it was rational (as opposed to being dependent on faith in divine revelation),[10] this dualistic understanding was initially attractive to the philosophically minded Augustine. It likewise held out promise, because it appeared to free the individual from personal responsibility for evil.[11]

Eventually Augustine became disillusioned with the conditions he experienced in Carthage.[12] So in 383, aged twenty-seven, he set out for Rome in order to open a school of rhetoric and to continue his own studies. In the meantime he grew increasingly dissatisfied with Manichaeism. The final parting of ways came after an interview in which the Manichaean leader Faustus could offer only evasive answers to the questions that troubled the young thinker.[13]

Although Augustine put Manichaeism behind him, its ghost continued to haunt his philosophical reflections. His fears of lapsing back into what he saw as the Manichaean heresy continually led him to shy away from any suggestion that evil had actual existence.

In Rome Augustine turned to Greek philosophy.[14] At first he flirted with the skepticism propagated by Plato's successors at his famed Academy. However, he could find no solace in a view that denied the possibility of knowledge.[15]

At the conclusion of his Roman educational experience, Augustine received an appointment as professor of rhetoric at Milan in northern Italy (384). There he was introduced to the writings of the Greek Neoplatonists—probably Latin translations of Plotinus and Porphyry. This Greek philosophical system held greater promise than skepticism and served to remove his last lingering Manichaean sympathies.[16] Although he could not accept such aspects of its teaching as the idea that the human person is part of the World-Soul,[17] Neoplatonism offered an understanding of evil that provided Augustine with a way of escape from Manichaeism. Consequently Neoplatonism remained the single most significant philosophical influence on Augustine's thinking.

More important than his encounter with the Neoplatonists, however, was Augustine's contact with Ambrose, the bishop of the city. Ambrose was instrumental in Augustine's dramatic conversion (September 386), and on Easter Sunday 387 Ambrose had the privilege of baptizing the future theologian.

Shortly after embracing Christianity, the new convert left Milan to return to his former home country. His plans were temporarily interrupted by the untimely deaths of his mother and later his son. He did return home, however, and soon thereafter he entered the priesthood, being ordained a presbyter in the community of Hippo Regius, where he founded what may have been the first monastery in Africa.[18] In 391 he yielded to popular pressure and became the assistant to Valerius, bishop of Hippo. When Valerius died, Augustine was named his successor (395). He served in this post until his own death on August 28, 430, which occurred as the invading Vandals were laying siege to the city.

Defending the faith. Augustine lived during an era of great tensions. The church found itself caught in successive waves of theological strife, and Augustine's ordination plunged him into the thick of the conflicts that were threatening its peace, if not its very existence.

One theological quarrel, the Donatist controversy,[19] actually predated Augustine by half a century; yet it demanded his attention for some two decades (393-412).[20] The genesis of the controversy lay in the Diocletian persecution (303-305). During this short-lived attempt to suppress Christianity, church leaders often escaped martyrdom by handing over copies of the Bible to their Roman oppressors or pouring a libation to the emperor.[21] A group within the church considered such acts to be sheer apostasy. They were willing to welcome any such *traditor* back into the fold only through rebaptism, in contrast to the more lenient Catholic practice of simply prescribing some appropriate penance.

The dispute was especially acute in North Africa, where the installation of a suspected *traditor* as bishop of Carthage eventually led to the consecration of Donatus as rival bishop (313). This situation revealed an important difference over ecclesiology that separated the two groups. The Donatists viewed the church as a visible community of the elect who were to be separate from the world. They also argued that the validity of a sacrament was dependent on the spiritual condition of the officiating priest, specifically, that he be holy and in good standing with the church.[22]

The smoldering dispute broke into flames as Donatists became involved in uprisings in 371 and again in 388. In the context of the latter revolt, Augustine spoke out against what he considered to be the false teaching of the Donatists. Augustine countered the "pure church" ecclesiology of his opponents by claiming that the true church is an invisible number within the mixed company of the visible church. As for the efficacy of the sacraments, he countered that the priest's part was merely instrumental. So long as the sacraments were administered within the church, their purity was guaranteed by Christ himself, even if they were dispensed by a schismatic or heretic.[23]

While the church was seeking to recover from internal theological strife, the empire faced a more tangible, external threat. Invading hordes of barbarians were shaking the foundations of its very existence. Eventually Rome itself was affected, for on August 24, 410, Alaric and the Visigoths sacked "the eternal city." The threat of political and social collapse provided the defenders of the older religions of the empire the occasion to launch a vigorous attack against the Christian faith. The calamities that had overtaken Rome following the triumph of Christianity, these critics asserted, were signs that the older gods of the empire were angered over the success of the new religion.

Augustine responded by composing his magnum opus, *The City of God,* which took fifteen years to complete (411-426).[24] In arguing that the Christian faith was not the culprit, he drew from the biblical analogy of the two cities, Babylon and Jerusalem, to set forth a distinction between the human city—represented now by the Roman Empire—and the true City of God, which alone is eternal. Augustine invited his readers to divest themselves of the great myth of the founding of Rome and to view the fall of the city from the perspective of God's hidden intentions.

The threats to the city of Rome brought Augustine face to face with a second theological conflict, the Pelagian controversy,[25] which would consume his energies until his death. The theological altercation began after the arrival in Rome in 384 of an effective and popular teacher from Britain named Pelagius. In the wake of the barbarian invasions Pelagius and his disciple Celestius were among the crowds of refugees seeking shelter in North Africa. Celestius's attempt to propagate his master's teachings drew Augustine's fire and eventually led to a twelve-year debate with one of his former pupils, Julian of Eclanum.[26]

At the heart of the quarrel was the understanding of sin. Rather than a "substance" that could be passed on from generation to generation or could influence human nature, Pelagius described sin as a quality of individual human actions. Adam's sin, he argued, did not alter human nature but is spread simply through imitation.[27]

Augustine saw in his opponent's view an overly optimistic anthropology that was dangerous because it suggested that humans are capable of being justified without God's grace.[28] To combat this grave error, Augustine declared in no uncertain terms that although we were created sinless and without imperfections, because of Adam's sin we are unable to live as we ought, for our will is bent away from God. We therefore stand in need of divine grace—of God's merciful work on our behalf.

Augustine's struggle against heresy and his apologetic for the faith provided the context for and the major themes of his ingenious way of carving out a coherent statement of Christian ethics. To this end he sought to bring together the biblical faith and the Greek philosophical tradition. To see how he accomplished this feat, we must look to his appropriation of the Neoplatonism of his day.

The Christian Neoplatonist. Augustine has repeatedly been called a Christian Neoplatonist.[29] His ethical understanding, while thoroughly Christian, reveals a deep indebtedness to this philosophical system. In fact Thomas Bigham and Albert Mollegen go so far as to assert, "The Augustinian theological ethic is a deep and real synthesis of Neoplatonism and the New Testament."[30] As a Christian thinker Augustine sought to press philosophy into the service of faith.[31] In the process the Neoplatonic outlook influenced his understanding of Christianity.[32]

At the heart of Augustine's thought was his appropriation of the Neoplatonic focus on ultimate knowledge as a mystical intuition of the divine.[33] This was tied to a basically Neoplatonic ontology, which viewed reality as a hierarchy of being resembling a pyramid. The higher objects on the pyramid participate more completely in being. Beneath the pyramid lies only nonbeing, which is "nothing" or pure "nothingness." At the apex of the hierarchy is pure being or what Plotinus called "The One."

Further, the Neoplatonic view of reality equated being with the good and nonbeing with evil. Hence, The One, which is the fullness of being, is also the perfect good. In so far as everything that is participates in being, every existing thing is good—good, that is, to the extent that it participates in existence.

According to Augustine, The One standing at the apex of Plotinus's hierarchy of reality is none other than the Christian God. This God is also the highest good.[34] As a result Augustine asserted that the human *summum bonum* is God or, perhaps better stated, the enjoyment of God.

His concern for the supreme good reveals the basically eudaemonian orientation of Augustine's ethic,[35] as well as his indebtedness to the Greek philosophical tradition. Indeed the church father defined the object of the quest of moral philosophy as "the supreme good, by reference to which all our actions are directed. It is the good we seek for itself and not because of something else, and once it is attained, we seek nothing further to make us happy. This, in fact, is why we call it our end, because other things are desired on account of this *summum bonum,* while it is desired purely for itself."[36]

Augustine postulated that humans seek after God by nature. And we find blessedness only when we come to behold God, that is, as we are "inwardly illuminated and occupied by his truth and holiness."[37] Only then do our strivings cease, for in the contemplation of God we find the goal of our existence. At the beginning of his *Confessions,* Augustine stated this sublime idea in an eloquent prayer, "Thou hast formed us for Thyself, and our hearts are restless till they find rest in Thee."[38]

Augustine's Christian Neoplatonism also provided the foundation for his response to the problem of evil, which question drew his attention from the beginning to the end of his intellectual quest.[39] Insofar as God—who is good—created everything that is, all beings (including the devil, the church father would add) are good.[40] Evil, therefore, is not something that actually exists; it is not an objective reality. Instead, evil is purely negative; it "exists" only in beings that are themselves good. The negativity that is evil can take the form of the disruption of order in nature or the disordering of nature. Hence, evil occurs when any being is deprived of its order or when its original nature as God created it becomes corrupted.

Likewise, the negativity we call "evil" is the privation or absence of good. It is a defect in something that is good or the lack of what something ought to possess. Augustine offered this example: "In the bodies of animals, disease and wounds mean nothing but the absence of health; for when a cure is effected, that does not mean that the evils which were present—namely, the diseases and wounds—go away from the body and dwell elsewhere: they altogether cease to exist; for the wound or disease is not a substance, but a defect in the fleshly substance—the flesh itself being a substance, and therefore something good, of which those evils—that is, privations of the good which we call health—are accidents."[41]

Moral evil, in turn, emerges as good creatures fall away from their true moral nature and therefore lack the moral goodness that ought to characterize them. Hence, vice is the corruption of our good nature.[42] Like evil in general, vice has no objective existence but is a privation of good in the human will. Augustine drew from his earlier example of a purely physical evil to illumine this point: "Just in the same way, what are called vices in the soul are nothing but privations of natural good. And when they are cured, they are not transferred elsewhere: when they cease to exist in the healthy soul, they cannot exist anywhere else."[43]

The love of God and the ethical life. On this basically Neoplatonic foundation Augustine built his understanding of the Christian ethic. In a word this ethic is *love,* more specifically, *the love of God.*

The phrase "the love of God" is grammatically ambiguous. Does it mean "God's love for us" or "our love for God"? For Augustine it involves both. God's love for us and our love for God are integrally connected. They form two sides of a seamless ethical garment.

To see why this is the case, we must realize that at one fundamental point Augustine's view forms a stark contrast to the older Greek ethical tradition. From Socrates onward the Greek outlook elevated knowledge as the pathway to wisdom and hence to the ethical life.[44] The great philosophers believed that at least to some extent the human moral problem was due to ignorance; evil is an error in judgment. Consequently the antidote to evil is knowledge, for correct knowledge leads to correct action or virtuous conduct. As a result the Greek thinkers viewed ethics as the study of whatever fosters virtuous living. Beneath the surface of this understanding of the ethical task is a presupposition that forms the guiding dictum of enlightened humanism in every age, namely, that if people obtain knowledge of the right they can and will do the right.

Augustine was too heavily influenced by the Bible to adhere slavishly to this principle. He came to see that the human moral problem is not merely ignorance.[45] We do not only lack knowledge of what is right, we also lack the ability to do what the law commands. And as a result, we cannot do what we know we ought to do. In fact, humans can knowingly and freely choose what is evil. We have the uncanny knack of knowing what we ought to do, even anticipating the unwholesome consequences of an evil act, and yet choosing to engage in conduct we clearly perceive will be to our own detriment and to the detriment of others.

Why is this? Being a good biblical thinker, Augustine countered the ethical optimism of the Greek tradition by appeal to the pessimistic anthropology he derived from Paul's critique of the law. But he articulated the biblical doctrine of depravity in Neoplatonic terms. Augustine located the source of evil deeds in human passion[46] and ultimately in the misdirected will. Hence the human moral problem lies in a privation within the human will. The will is not what it ought to be; it is bent in the wrong direction.

To grasp what Augustine meant, we must return again to his Neoplatonic ontology. As we noted earlier, Augustine argued that because God is absolute being—that is, the One who possesses "supreme and original existence"—God is also the highest good.[47] For Augustine this meant that the ethical life consists in the will directed toward God. This is our *summum bonum.* The sad fact is, however, that our human will is directed toward lesser objects. Whether these be the lusts[48] of the flesh or the lusts of the mind, the result is the same. Instead of desiring God with our whole heart, our will is directed toward something that is not God. In this sense, the will is evil. This situation is what Augustine called "concupiscence" or sin.

Augustine's concept of sin places the problem of evil squarely within the human will. The will, and not the things the will desires, is evil. Augustine provided this helpful explanation: The will's "defections are not to evil things, but are themselves evil; that is to say, are not towards things that are naturally and in themselves evil, but the defection of the will is evil, because it is contrary to the order of nature, and an abandonment of that which has supreme being for that which has less. For avarice is not a fault inherent in gold, but in the man who inordinately loves gold. . . . Consequently he who inordinately loves the good which any nature possesses, even though he obtain it, himself becomes evil in the good, and wretched because deprived of a greater good."[49]

Augustine located even the cause of the turning of the will from the Creator to the creature within the will itself. This turning is a defect of the will, simply because it is not natural, that is, it moves against what the will ought in fact to be. Being unnatural, it marks a privation of the good will, and hence, it is voluntary.[50]

According to Augustine, any solution for concupiscence requires a redirection of the will and a reorientation of our affections. To desire God above all means that we must set our affections on God alone. Hence the ethical life arises out of love for God. Consequently Augustinians of every age can sing heartily, "More love to thee, O Christ." Through love for God the affections are drawn upward toward God and the will is set on God.

Loving God results in the will always conforming to God's will. Augustine capsulized his point in the well-known dictum "Love, and do what you will" *(dilige, et quod vis fac).*[51] By this Augustine meant that when we truly love God we desire to act in a manner that pleases God. When our will is set on God alone, what we want to do—what pleases us—is nothing else than what God views as right. When we love God, we can indeed do as we please.

For Augustine, therefore, love is central to ethics. Love is both the chief virtue and the fountain of all other virtues, for virtue is "nothing else than perfect love of God."[52]

To explain how this is the case, Augustine simply reinterpreted the four virtues of the Platonic tradition,[53] viewing them as restatements of the great Christian virtue of love for God:[54] "Temperance is love giving itself entirely to God; fortitude is love bearing everything readily for the sake of God; justice is love serving God only, and therefore ruling well all else, as subject to man; prudence is love making a distinction between what helps it towards God and what might hinder it."[55] Yet by redefining the cardinal virtues in this manner, Augustine was also declaring that they are first clearly understood in the light of the gospel.[56]

Related to love for God, of course, is love for neighbor. Here again the church father drew from scriptural teaching. Yet Augustine did not view love for others as an independent movement of the will but as "a sort of cradle of our love to God."[57] Although love for God is foundational, he noted that the love of others may actually reach maturity or perfection first.[58]

And what is the source of such love for God? Here Augustine turned to the other side of the ambiguous declaration "The Christian ethic consists in the love of God." The love for God which issues forth in the ethical life is a supernatural gift God bestows. Only God can redirect our affections and draw the human will. We can live ethically, then, only as we become the recipients of God's grace. In short, ethics is God's love for us; the ethical life comes as the gift of divine grace.

The true philosophy. We have already suggested that the Augustinian proposal marks an attempt to Christianize the Neoplatonism the church father found at the apex of the Greek philosophical tradition. Just as Augustine's metaphysic was a "Pauline" or Christianized form of the Neoplatonic hierarchy of being, so also his view of the ethical life was a Christian version of the Neoplatonic myth of the eternal return. The ecstatic union with The One occurs as God draws our will to love goodness itself, the pure being who is the only fountain of pure goodness. Coming home to The One is nothing else but God's refocusing of our will on himself as the Source of our being.

According to Augustine, the glorious reality toward whom our quest is ultimately directed is none other than the God of the Bible. Consequently what the pagan philosopher Plotinus desired, we know as the Christian ethical life, the return of the will to the highest good—the Christian God. And what the pagan philosophers sought as the virtues of the human soul are ultimately found only in the Christian ethical life, which is the life of love.

Our sketch leads to a crucial question: To what extent was the church father able to bring together what he saw as the best of the reigning Neoplatonic philosophy of his day with what he found in Scripture? Some historians conclude that Augustine's answer to the great ethical quest of antiquity turns out to be more Neoplatonic than biblical. Thomas Bigham and Albert Mollegen, for example, suggest that in the end he seems to define virtue as "rewarded self-fulfillment" and thereby squeezes the biblical ethic of love into the mold of the Platonic idea of *eros*.[59]

Although he was undeniably influenced by Neoplatonism, in one crucial respect Augustine remained to the end a *Christian* thinker. He knew that the Christian ethic was more than merely a restatement of conclusions to which the Greek philosophers had gained access through reason. Instead the gospel of Jesus Christ had taken the church father beyond what the philosophers offered. They may have correctly pointed to the *summum bonum*, the object of the heart's quest, but they failed to disclose the power necessary to attain it. Augustine knew that the restless human heart can reach its repose only as it comes to be touched by divine grace.

Francis Palmer Clarke's appraisal, therefore, is clearly on target: "True philosophy not only shows man what is his true end, but provides him also with the means for attaining it. It is mainly in this that the superiority of Christianity to Platonism is to be found. Thus the ethics of Augustine is not a mere intellectual analysis of the good or of the principles of morality; it is an exposition of the Christian revelation, the means for attaining the end. For Christian philosophy considers revelation as an enlightenment of the reason . . . and equally in the moral sphere, as a source of strength for the will to enable it to attain what else it must fail of."[60]

Thomas Aquinas: Ethics as the Fulfillment of Our Purpose

If Augustine is the greatest theologian the church has ever produced, Thomas Aquinas (1225-1274) is the most influential Roman Catholic thinker who has ever lived. Augustine set the agenda for the theological and ethical discussion of the entire Western tradition. Aquinas developed the system of thought that would evoke the most crucial debate within that tradition.

A controversial scholar.[61] The thinker whom Vernon J. Bourke terms "the outstanding ethician of the thirteenth century and perhaps of the whole Middle Ages"[62] was born in the castle of Roccasecca near Aquino, Italy. Hence, although his given name was Thomas, the location of his birth has provided an equally common way of designating him—Aquinas.[63]

In 1231 Thomas's parents enrolled him as an oblate in the Benedictine monastery of Monte Cassino, where he supposedly was to remain the rest of his life and perhaps eventually become abbot.[64] But eight years later war between the pope and the Holy Roman Emperor temporarily closed the abbey. Young Aquinas left the monastery to complete his study of the liberal arts at the newly established secular university in Naples, which was the first center of learning to propagate the entire philosophical work of Aristotle. In Naples Aquinas encountered the reform-minded Dominicans, whose efforts focused on the intellectual life and the universities rather than monasteries, as was the practice of many of the traditional orders.[65]

After a year-long struggle with his family,[66] Aquinas turned his back on monastic life and in 1244 became a Dominican. Accordingly, he set out for Paris, arriving in the summer of 1245. Whether he remained in the French city for a time[67] or went on to study in Cologne, Germany, is unclear.[68] In any case, when the famous philosopher Albert the Great was sent to Cologne in 1248 to found a house of philosophical studies, Aquinas became his pupil.

The gifted student remained with Albert the Great until 1252, at which time, upon Albert's recommendation, he returned to the Dominican convent of St. James in Paris to complete his academic preparation. This probably involved writing a commentary on the Gospels (1252-1254) and then commenting on the standard theological treatise of the day, the famous *Sentences* of Peter Lombard (1254-1256). This work completed, the promising young scholar received his license to teach from the University of Paris (1256) and inaugurated his career as a professor of theology in Paris, thereby fulfilling his lifelong desire to be a teacher of divine wisdom.[69] What followed was what Timothy McDermott calls "one of the most packed and prolific philosophical and theological careers in history."[70]

Three years later Aquinas returned to Italy, perhaps to teach at the Papal Curia or in the Dominican houses.[71] In any case, between 1259 and 1268 he served at four different locations and visited several others. During this time, he met William of Moerbeck, a fellow Dominican and the translator[72] of the works of the Greek philosopher Aristotle, who at this point was generally viewed as an enemy of Christianity. Aquinas, in turn, began a series of commentaries on these translations.

In an era when Aristotle's ideas were suspect, especially in Paris, the Dominican scholar proved to be a controversial thinker. Aquinas's work evoked the opposition of the Augustinians, who were the reigning theological and philosophical teachers of the day. In the heat of the intellectual battle Aquinas returned to Paris in 1268. But in 1272 the attacks of the Augustinians and other pressures led to his dismissal from teaching duties in the French city.

The Dominican Order commissioned their gifted teacher to establish a new house of studies in Naples. Late in 1273, however, Aquinas suddenly suspended his writing and teaching career.[73] A few months later (March 7, 1274), while en route to the Council of Lyons to which he had been summoned by Pope Gregory X, he died at the Cistercian monastery of Fossanova, not far from the place of his birth. Meanwhile Aristotle's philosophy had fallen into disfavor. As a result, Aquinas's teachings were condemned three years after his death, first by the bishop of Paris and then by the archbishop of Canterbury.[74]

Although fiercely attacked during his lifetime, Aquinas's views eventually received broad acknowledgment. Fifty years after his life came to a premature end, he was canonized by Pope John XXII (July 18, 1323). In 1567 Pope Pius V pronounced him the Angelic Doctor of the church, and in 1880 Pope Leo XIII named him Patron of Catholic Schools. In this manner, the theologian who during his life had been drummed out of his teaching position emerged as patron saint of the Roman Catholic Church's educational institutions.

The turn to existence. As we noted above, the intellectual mood of Aquinas's day was dominated by the legacy of Augustine and, by extension, the philosophical method that originated with Plato. Although indebted to it at several points, Aquinas was highly critical of this tradition. He rejected what he saw as "Platonic errors," which, he was convinced, were responsible for most of the philosophical aberrations of his day. These errors centered on one fundamental misstep, the "flight from existence."[75] In Aquinas's estimation, Plato erroneously separated "being" from "becoming."

As we noted in chapter two, the Platonists divided reality into two realms: the world of sense experience, change, material objects—hence the realm of becoming—and the world of essences, the unchanging, the ideas—that is, the realm of being. By elevating the latter over the former, the Platonists were in effect declaring that reality is fundamentally essence rather than existence.

Building on this foundation, the Platonists elevated intellectual knowledge above knowledge derived from or concerning sensible objects (objects in the senses). Because their understanding of what is truly real was structured according to thought—according to the abstractions of the human intellect—they sought to move beyond the world of sense experience so as to contemplate the eternal forms and ultimately the form of the good (God). According to Plato the specific objects we contact through our senses cannot lead us to such knowledge. The senses only yield knowledge of changeable particular objects, rather than knowledge of the changeless eternal essences (i.e., the forms). Aquinas found this problematic because the use of reason or thought alone cannot bring us to know existence.

The Platonic tradition also separated the soul from the body. According to the Platonists the real person is the immortal, immaterial soul. This soul simply uses the body[76] that houses it for a time, while longing for the great day when it casts the body aside. Then the soul, enabled to contemplate the eternal, immaterial forms unencumbered by the body, will enjoy true knowledge.

For an alternative to the Platonism of his colleagues, Aquinas turned to Aristotle. He drew from the great philosopher's claim that reality consists of "form" plus "matter," or "essence" plus "existence." The forms or eternal essences do not populate some special realm beyond the world of sense experience, Aristotle argued. Instead, they inhere in objects. And every object consists of its essential form plus material "stuff."

Aquinas's basic Aristotelianism led to his this-worldly epistemology (theory of how we come to know): "Now it is natural to man to attain to intellectual truths through sensible objects, because all our knowledge originates from sense."[77] Or to put this comment into the form of a philosophical dictum, we have no knowledge of essences except through the gate of sense experience.

The metaphysical assumption that all things are a composite of form and matter occasioned Aquinas's understanding of the nature of the human person. In contrast to the Platonic anthropology with its focus on the soul apart from the body, Aquinas declared that the human person is soul plus body.[78] This does not mean that the person is two beings, however, but one entity, a composite, for the soul is the form of the body.[79] The soul is the spiritual substance through which the composite human individual exists; the presence of the soul animates the body, whereas the body, in turn, exists in and through the soul. Viewed from the perspective of existence, therefore, we might say that the body is in the soul, rather than the soul in the body.[80]

Aquinas's epistemology, coupled with his understanding of the human person, had far-reaching implications for his view of the human ethical task. He agreed with Plato that the soul is an intellectual substance whose purpose is knowing. But against the entire Platonist philosophical tradition, he then asserted that the soul is unequal to its task apart from the body. Because the soul knows truth only as it comes to know sensible objects (objects in our senses), knowing is mediated through the world of sense experience. The Thomistic knower, therefore, is neither a pure thinker nor a pure mind, but a composite of soul and body. As Anton Pegis notes, for Aquinas the activity of the human person consists in "knowing the world of sensible things," rather than "thinking abstract thoughts in separation from existence."[81]

A Christian Aristotelian ethic. Henry Sidgwick characterizes the ethic of

Thomas Aquinas as "Aristotelianism with a Neo-Platonic tinge, interpreted and supplemented by a view of Christian doctrine derived chiefly from Augustine."[82] Whatever truth there may be in this appraisal, Aquinas's chief mentor was the Greek thinker he often spoke of as "the Philosopher." Following Aristotle, Aquinas placed ethics within the context of the *telos* or goal of existence. For this reason, some historians classify his as an ethic of self-realization[83] or a teleological ethic.

The Thomistic ethic begins with the foundational Aristotelian insight that agents always act with a specific end in view: "Every agent, by its action, intends an end. For in those things which clearly act for an end, we declare the end to be that towards which the movement of the agent tends."[84] Further, each existing thing has a purpose. Each is designed to act for some specific goal. And each naturally "tends" toward this purpose; that is, it strives to fulfill its *telos* or to actualize its potential. To cite a mundane example, the *telos* of an acorn is "oak tree," for each acorn is a potential tree and "strives" to become a tree.

From here the medieval Aristotelian made the jump to ethics. The *telos* of any existing thing is its "good." In this manner Aquinas bridged the gap between "is" and "ought." Knowing what something is also entails knowing what it ought to be. In fact, knowing what it ought to be—that is, knowing what the ideal of its species is and hence that toward which it is directed—is the only way of determining what something is.[85] Like his mentor, Aquinas then added that the highest good and the fountain of all goodness is God. Consequently, as things tend toward their natural end they are actually tending toward God. For this reason Aquinas could conclude that "all things are directed to the highest good, namely, God, as their end."[86]

Aquinas walked with Aristotle yet another step, namely, in the application of this basic teleology to the specifically human good. Aristotle had argued that the human person is form plus matter, that is, soul plus body. Although the medieval thinker developed a strong sense that humans are composite beings, as we have seen, he nevertheless maintained the basic Greek focus on the soul as constitutive of human existence. Because this soul is an intellectual substance, the goal of existence is not merely physical maturity but intellectual knowledge. Or perhaps more appropriately stated, the activity that most actualizes the human purpose is knowing.

According to Aquinas, the highest "object" we can know—and thus the goal or object of our quest—is God.[87] Consequently, he concluded, "the end of the intellectual creature" is "to understand God."[88] While primarily an intellectual activity, this "possession of God" also involves the satisfaction of the will, which in the process is moved by reason toward the only true good. This situation, Aquinas concluded, constitutes true happiness.[89] The attainment of such blessedness, however, is not possible in this life,[90] because in the here and now we simply cannot see God face to face.[91] Nor does the beatific vision which comes with the reception of eternal life arise apart from divine grace.[92]

Already here we begin to see the Christian use to which Aquinas was putting the system of his Greek philosophical mentor. Aristotle declared that the goal of human existence is happiness, which he understood largely as living and faring well. Aquinas was in basic agreement with this assessment. Yet a major difference separated the Christian theologian from the pagan philosopher. In a sense, the Aristotelian human *telos* was largely internal: Happiness involves actualizing an internal potential. And God—that is, the Unmoved Mover—merely serves as the uninvolved object of the agent's desires. Aristotle's Christian disciple, however, asserted that human happiness derives ultimately from God and through the active working of God.[93] As the contemplation of the God who is absolute truth, the chief end of the human person is directed toward an external reality who is our highest end and therefore our "good." Hence, for Aquinas our ultimate goal—the good life—is not merely the internal well-being that results from the rule of reason in the soul. Instead it leads us beyond ourselves (including our innate potentiality) to an external Good[94] whose grace is operative in our lives.

Not only did Aquinas more closely connect the highest good with God, he also identified this God. In contrast to the pagan philosopher, the Christian thinker declared that the ultimate good toward which all things—including humans—are directed is no one else but the God of the Bible.

Ethics and the human telos. The Bible likewise provided Aquinas with the tools by which to appraise the actual situation of the human person.[95] In so doing he followed the typical medieval differentiation between the image and the likeness of God, which drew from Irenaeus's exegesis of Genesis 1:26.[96] In keeping with this view, Aquinas declared that God's original design endowed humans with not only the natural powers (especially, reason and will), which form the divine image. Humans also enjoyed God's supernatural gift of righteousness, which marked the divine likeness.[97]

As a Christian, Aquinas also knew that something went wrong in God's design: Adam fell. According to the Christian teacher, the Fall means that humans have lost the likeness of God. We no longer enjoy the supernatural gift of righteousness. Nor can we now love God as we should.[98] However, the image of God remains intact. Therefore, the natural powers—especially our intellectual capabilities—were not destroyed by the Fall.

Humankind in the original state:	supernatural gift (righteousness)
	natural powers (reason and will)
Humankind in the Fall:	\\\\\\\\\\\\\
	natural powers (reason and will)

Table 5. The Thomist Anthropology

A "right reason" ethic.[99] This understanding of the human person and the Fall has far-reaching philosophical implications. According to Aquinas, even in the fallen situation human reason remains operative. By using reason fallen humans have access to a certain, albeit limited, truth of God. Hence Aquinas believed that human reason could move from sense experience of the world to a demonstration of God's existence, as well as to whatever must be true about God as the First Cause of the world.[100] We must quickly add, however, that Aquinas knew that reason can only take us so far. For complete theological knowledge—and hence the restoration of the supernatural gift as well as attainment to the vision of God—we are dependent on divine revelation.[101]

Building from this same anthropology, Aquinas suggested that human reason likewise provides access to certain levels of ethical truth. Fallen humans retain some capacity for virtue, as well as at least a certain aptitude for loving God.[102] As a result, even without the infusion of special divine grace, humans can expect to attain a degree of ethical living, specifically, whatever is in accord with reason.

This formed the foundation for the Christian thinker's appropriation of the Aristotelian tradition of virtue language. It also provided a way of blending the Greek cardinal virtues with the medieval focus on the Christian virtues of faith, hope and love. By synthesizing Greece and Jerusalem in this manner, Aquinas combined what had previously been two disparate frameworks into one unified whole reflecting his own overall ethical theory.[103]

Following Aristotle, the medieval thinker spoke of a virtue as a habit[104] or disposition that facilitates the achievement of the goal of existence.[105] This understanding arose from an important Thomistic contention concerning human freedom: "But the rational powers, which are proper to man, are not determinate to one particular action, but are inclined indifferently to many."[106] What then moves the powers to their particular ends? "Habits"—which according to Aquinas are the enduring traits of character inclining the agent to act in one characteristic manner rather than another.[107] Habits that direct the agent toward good ends or assist us in actualizing our human goal are termed "virtues."

Aquinas drew a close relation between the virtues and reason. Proper living involves pursuing the human good by employing our rational powers. Living in accordance with reason entails comprehending and consequently desiring our only perfectly fulfilling and satisfying good. Like the Greek philosophical tradition before him, Aquinas's broad understanding of the good life led to a similarly broad understanding of the virtues. These included the intellectual virtues, the abilities related to the power of reason, including understanding (i.e., the ability to discern principles), science (or the ability to deduce conclusions) and wisdom (the facility of judging and ordering truth).[108]

Of greater direct interest to the discipline of ethics, however, are the moral virtues, the habits related to the "appetitive" part of the human soul. According to Aquinas this dimension is equally important, for good deeds require not only that one's reason be well disposed through the exercise of intellectual virtue but also that the appetite be well disposed by means of moral virtue.[109] In the category of "moral virtue" the Christian ethicist placed the great cardinal virtues of the Greek ethical tradition: prudence (reason controlling itself so as to reason well about and command good moral actions), justice (reason controlling the will so that it habitually wills what is good for others), and temperance and fortitude (reason controlling the passions).[110]

Aquinas's description of sin follows. Simply stated, sin is acting contrary to reason. A vice, in turn, is a habitual sin. It involves being disposed in a manner not befitting our nature as beings with a telos. Or we might say that sin is acting contrary to law, realizing that for Aquinas law is an expression of reason. This connection surfaces in his basic definition of law: "Law is nothing else than an ordinance of reason for the common good, made by him who has care of the community, and promulgated."[111]

According to Aquinas the one "who has care of the community," of course, is God, for God governs the whole community of the universe. This Christian perspective leads to Aquinas's focus on law. At the foundation of all law[112] is the "eternal law," the divine plan by means of which God governs all creation.[113] The eternal law is not merely external to God, however. Rather Aquinas seems to be suggesting that God's own "mind" is in a sense reasonable. God acts in a rational manner—in accordance with a certain logic. In this sense we might say that God's will is reason itself.[114]

In so far as God wisely orders all creation, we speak of events of nature as "rational." However, Aquinas is more concerned with creatures, such as humans, who rationally direct themselves to an end. He uses the term "natural law" to refer to the participation in divine law that properly belongs to rational creatures.[115] Natural law entails both the laws which emanate from our human, rational nature, as well as the judgments that people quite naturally make. As examples we could cite "the law of self-preservation" and even the yearning to know God.[116] But above all, natural law includes the human tendency to order life through the regulative function of reason and thereby participate in God's regulatory law.

Two other terms round out Aquinas's discussion of the law.[117] "Human law" consists of the various laws human reason devises from the natural law to achieve certain ends. Aquinas argued that personal happiness and human society require a humanly formulated code of conduct. Finally, the "divine law" involves those precepts, such as the Ten Commandments, that God gives to us for our betterment through revelation.

Aquinas believed that to a limited though real extent the natural human can be a person of virtue. By using our innate human powers, we can develop the intellectual virtues and the cardinal moral virtues (prudence, justice, temperance and fortitude). Although the cardinal virtues are necessary for proper living, they come up short. Through cultivating these virtues alone, we cannot attain our natural human good.[118] Instead prudence, justice, temperance and fortitude only lay the foundation for a truly virtuous character.

The fullness of ethical living requires three additional, surpassing virtues: faith, hope and love. The medieval tradition referred to these as the "theological virtues." Whereas the cardinal virtues foster the development of our intellect and appetite according to the dictates of reason and human nature, the theological virtues direct us toward our supernatural end, namely, toward God himself and our spiritual union with God.[119] The two categories differ in one additional, crucial respect, namely, in their accessibility. Through the innate power of reason, everyone has access to the natural virtues. The theological virtues, however, lie completely beyond our attainment. For their presence in us, we are dependent on the infusion of divine grace.[120]

Christian ethics and the philosophical tradition. By developing what Sidgwick calls an "Aristotelianised Christianity,"[121] Aquinas modeled a second paradigm, a second Christian response to philosophical ethics. He attempted to build a composite ethic by a process of addition, attempting to combine the best of the Aristotelian tradition with what the church taught on the basis of biblical revelation.

Above all Aquinas declared that the natural virtues require the addition of the theological virtues, which come solely as God's gift. This marked a crucial departure from Augustine, who under the rubric of *love* reinterpreted the four cardinal virtues of the Greek ethical tradition. Aquinas, in contrast, treated the theological virtues (faith, hope and love) separate from and in addition to the natural virtues.[122] The implications of this innovation are far-reaching. According to the Thomistic view the truly ethical life God intends requires more than the best that reason has to offer. We need the truth available only through revelation and the additional ethical dynamic available only to the Christian by God's grace.

The affirmation of the universal human quest for the ethical life remains foundational to the Thomistic approach. Convinced of the value of human reason, Thomists readily admonish people to employ reason in seeking the ethical life. They believe that our innate human powers have a role to play in the quest for truth and virtuous living. But Thomists quickly point out that every natural ethic, every conception of the good life we construct on the basis of reason or by drawing from insights into our human nature, is insufficient. Just as a theological *summa* requires that we add to the insights of natural theology the further truth about God known only by revelation, so also we must augment the ethic of reason with a dimension that is distinctively Christian.

* * *

The Thomist Case Against Abortion

Aquinas's approach to ethics carries far-reaching implications for how Christians should take a stand on moral issues in a secular world. The question of abortion, which has proved to be such an important issue for Roman Catholics, offers a helpful example. Does involvement in this debate violate the principle of church-state separation? Does it entail a religious group's seeking to impose their specific theological viewpoint on the wider society? From a Thomistic perspective the answer is clearly no.

In keeping with Aquinas's anthropology the Thomist argues against abortion on the basis of reason, not revelation. Reason—that is, the best scientific findings available—leads to the conclusion that the fetus is human life. Because it is human, the fetus has certain rights, not the least of which is the right to life. The role of government is to defend the right of the fetus and to demand through legislation that citizens of the land act justly toward the fetus. Prolife legislation, therefore, is required by reason, not revelation.

Of course Christians would also appeal to people to act with love. Hence a Thomist might admonish a woman who is contemplating an abortion to do the loving thing, namely, out of love for her child to carry the fetus to term so that the human being developing in the womb might live. But because love is a theological virtue that no government can legislate, this appeal moves beyond the realm of civil authority. There can be no legislating of the biblical injunction "Love your neighbor as yourself."

* * *

Luther and the Reformers: Ethics as Believing Obedience

If Augustine is the most significant theologian of the postapostolic era and Thomas Aquinas is the most important thinker the Middle Ages produced, then Martin Luther must rank as the most noteworthy churchman of postmedieval Western Christendom. The pious monk's search for a gracious God and his subsequent stand against pope and empire unleashed a potent force in Europe that marked a watershed in Western history.

The focus of the Protestant Reformation was primarily theology, not ethics. Perhaps for this reason classical historians of ethics often overlook luminaries such as Luther and Calvin,[123] leaving the task of assessing their contributions to surveys of Christian ethics.[124] Nevertheless, the Reformers' claim to having recovered sound biblical teaching in areas such as soteriology (our understanding of salvation) carried implications for their view of the Christian life as well. In fact, their rethinking of the nature of Christianity was so radical that we may speak of the Reformation ethic—especially that carved out by Martin Luther (1483-1546)—as a third proposal alongside of those set forth by Augustine and Aquinas.

The making of a Reformer.[125] The man whom Roland Bainton speaks of as the medieval figure who ushered in the modern age[126] was born in 1483 in Eisleben, Saxony, the mining district of Germany. The event which was to shape Luther's future occurred twenty-two years later. While returning to Erfurt, where he was preparing for the legal career his father had charted out for him, Luther was nearly killed by a lightning bolt. Instinctively the young student cried out to the patron saint of miners: "St. Anne, help me! I will become a monk." Two weeks later he entered the Augustinian monastery.[127]

Life in the monastery did not quell the wrestling in Luther's heart. Instead he continued to be tormented with the question as to how a person could stand in holiness before a righteous, demanding God.[128] Sometime during the years 1513 and 1519, Luther's lectures on the Bible led him to the answer to his quest: The biblical phrase "the righteousness of God" does not refer to God's demanding justice but to his mercy and grace. This grace—and this grace alone—enables us to stand before the righteous God, for God ascribes righteousness to us apart from our strivings. This insight proved fatal to the reigning theology of the church and sparked the Reformation.

Luther's actual struggle with the Roman Church began in 1517, when he posted the Ninety-five Theses on the door of the castle church in Wittenberg. Thereby he publicly questioned the church practice of granting indulgences and, by extension, even the power of the papacy. Four years of conflict climaxed in his appearance before the Imperial Diet at Worms. In response to the demand that he repudiate his writings, Luther uttered the words that have been memorialized in the title of Roland Bainton's classic biography: "Unless I am convinced by Scripture and plain reason—I do not accept the authority of popes and councils, for they have contradicted each other—my conscience is captive to the Word of God. . . . Here I stand. I cannot do otherwise."[129]

Branded as a heretic, Luther found refuge in the Wartburg castle, where he began translating the Bible into German. Meanwhile in Wittenberg the Reformation proceeded in earnest, led at first by Luther's colleagues Philipp Melanchthon and Gabriel Zwilling, and later by the great Reformer himself. The "seamless robe of Christ" (Western Christendom under the direction of the pope) was rent.

Luther spent the remainder of his years consolidating the gains of the Reformation, as well as combating the errors of both the papists and the "enthusiasts," the radicals who desired to take the reforms to greater lengths than he. On February 18, 1546, the Protestant hero died, bequeathing the task of reform to a new generation of leaders—such as the great Reformer in Geneva, John Calvin (1509-1564)—who continued along the trail Luther had blazed. Through it all, the German leader never lost sight of his great discovery of God's justification of sinful humans by grace alone through faith. This theological doctrine formed the foundational principle for the entire Reformation ethic.

The protest against autonomous reason. As the term *Protestant* indicates, the Reformation was born out of protest. The Reformers weighed the reigning theology of the medieval church and found it wanting. In a sense the movement constituted a thoroughgoing protest against the elevation of autonomous reason that had characterized the grand synthesis between Jerusalem and Athens—between biblical faith and the philosophical tradition—accomplished by the thinkers of the Middle Ages, especially Thomas Aquinas. While not originating in questions about proper conduct and the good life, this protest spilled over into ethics as well and eventually led to a radical rethinking of the Christian understanding of the ethical life.

The Reformers were not the first to voice doubts about the Thomistic synthesis. On the contrary, they were heirs to a debate that predated their fight by two centuries.

Aquinas's writings were hardly dry when Duns Scotus (1266-1308) inaugurated what would become a long line of thinkers who modified the great medieval thinker's vision of the reasonableness of the universe and of the God who had created it.[130] Duns Scotus focused on God's will, rather than reason, as providing the foundation for morality. Ethicists often term this position "voluntarism."

More significant was the critique of William of Ockham (c. 1280-1349). Ockham rejected the claim implicit in Thomism that so close is the connection between divine and human reason that were we able to gain access to God's mind we could understand its operative logic. This assumption made the living God of the Bible into something of a "civilized Aristotelian." Rather than being the epitome of rationality and logic, Ockham claimed, God is inscrutable will.

Ockham's proposal carried important implications for ethics. The moral law is simply what is commanded or prohibited by God's will. And what is right can ultimately be known only through knowledge of God's decrees.[131] In the end, therefore, no valid ethic can be constructed apart from theology. In this manner, Ockham advocated an ethic of divine authoritarianism, which Bourke characterizes as: "God is the boss and whatever he wills to be right is what is morally good."[132]

Ockham's voluntarism found echo in the Lutheran Reformation. Luther, who himself had been educated in the Nominalist tradition of Scotus and Ockham, refused to acknowledge reason as the arbiter of morality,[133] for the ethical life does not consist in obeying prescriptive norms devised through philosophical reflection.[134] Consequently, for Luther and his colleagues if Christian ethics was to become truly Christian, it had to be freed from philosophical ethics—from the misguided eudaemonistic attempt to construct ethics upon the human quest for happiness.[135]

The foundation for this thoroughgoing critique of reason lay in certain central theological convictions. In somewhat different ways both Luther and Calvin spoke about a hidden, unknowable God whose decrees are fixed in the shrouded mystery of eternity and whose ways are higher than human reason can fathom. The sovereign God commands according to God's own good pleasure and will. This God does not need to justify the divine commands at the bar of human reason. In fact, sometimes God refuses to supply any rationale whatsoever for the directives that come our way. Indeed such commands require no rationale or justification beyond the fact that they are God's own injunctions.[136]

A penetrating application of the Reformation ethic came three hundred years later in a little book, *Fear and Trembling,* written by the Danish Lutheran thinker Søren Kierkegaard.[137] Kierkegaard illustrates the priority of obedient faith over reason through the narrative of Abraham and Isaac. In the familiar Bible story God commanded the patriarch to offer his son as a sacrifice. In response to the divine directive Abraham set out with Isaac to the appointed place. At each step of the way to Mount Moriah, Abraham could only trust and obey the God whose command seemed so unreasonable. Kierkegaard points out that when judged by the categories of traditional ethics Abraham was a sinner—a murderer. Yet the Bible extols the Old Testament patriarch as the paradigm of faith. Consequently Kierkegaard concludes that the Christian life cannot consist in reasoned philosophical reflection on morality. Instead it involves complete abandonment to God and trusting obedience to God's directives.

Following in the footsteps of Abraham, Reformation Christians passionately sing "Trust and Obey." The ethical life involves faith—trusting that God knows what is best—and obedience—doing what God says simply because God's way is best.

Luther's voluntarist ethic draws from another theological foundation as well—anthropology. Earlier we noted that differentiating between the image and the likeness of God allowed Aquinas to salvage our natural human powers (reason and will) from the Fall. Their exegesis of the Hebrew text, however, prohibited the Reformers from perpetrating this distinction. Their reading of Scripture led them to the conclusion that the Fall has affected us in our entirety (which is the meaning of the

Reformation doctrine of total depravity).[138] Sin's power extends to every dimension of human existence, so that no aspect of the human person—not even reason—remains untainted, as Paul indicated when he declared that "their foolish hearts were darkened" (Rom 1:21).

Consequently the Reformers taught that no humanly devised path leads directly to the ethical life. Not even reason can offer a trustworthy guide for living. On the contrary, living in a manner that pleases God may at times entail acting against reason or against our natural inclinations. Nor do we obey the divine law so as to satisfy our desires, as Aquinas suggested. On the contrary, because our desires are corrupted by the Fall, our quest for happiness may be antagonistic to what God commands.[139]

The Thomistic view	The Reformation view
\\\\\\\\\\\\\\\	\\\\\\\\\\\\\\\
natural powers (reason)	\\\\\\\\\\\\\\\

Table 6. The Fall: Thomism vs. the Reformation

An ethic of grace. The question of merit formed a crucial focus of Luther's disagreement with the Roman Church. From his reading of Scripture the Reformer concluded that none of our works are meritorious, for all that we do is the product of a fallen, depraved human nature. Even the best of what we can attain through the employment of our natural powers always falls short of God's glory. All of our righteousness—every attempt to please God and live up to God's standards—is like filthy rags.

Nor can we look to obedience to the law to win moral uprightness, Luther added. Because of human depravity the divine law is incapable of fostering in us obedience to God. Although it can command us to do right, the law cannot insure our conformity to God's standard. As a result Luther pointed out that all human activity must be done in faith, and no one dare presume that he or she is pleasing to God on the basis of such activities.[140] In short, against the optimistic anthropology of the medieval thinkers, the Reformer declared that we are destitute of the resources necessary to live ethically.

This did not mean that Luther and the Reformers were antinomian or had no place for the law. On the contrary, the law plays a foundational role in Reformation ethics. Luther spoke about two specific "uses" of the law—the general and the theological.[141] The law fulfills a general use, in that it acts as God's gracious restraint on sin. Hence Luther taught that human government "bears the sword" so that through the rule of law humans might not become as sinful as they otherwise would be.[142] More significant, however, is the theological or salvific use. The law serves as the prelude to the gospel; it acts as a schoolmaster bringing us to Christ. According to Luther, God's law shows us how we ought to be disposed or how we ought to live. But in so doing, it indicates how woefully short of God's glory we fall.

At this crucial point Luther extolled divine grace, upon which we are dependent even in living the Christian life. By showing us our sinfulness, the law leads us to see our desperate need for God's gracious justification. It points out how our motives and actions are always tainted by sin, so that we can never justify ourselves by claiming that we acted purely or rightly. Instead we can only cry out for the divine grace freely available in Christ and cast ourselves on the justifying God. For this reason believers know they are *simul iustus et peccator,* "always sinner" yet "always justified" by God's grace.[143] For Luther, being justified does not mean that we are in fact good but that God accounts us as good; rather than holding our sins against us, in Christ God freely forgives us.[144]

The theme of justification provides the theological foundation of Luther's ethic. For the great Reformer all ethics is based on God's forgiveness of sin, that is, on the relationship God establishes with us through the forgiveness God has made available to us in Christ.[145] Paul Althaus began his monumental study by summarizing the importance of this principle: "Luther's ethics is determined in its entirety, in its starting point and all its main features, by the heart and center of his theology, namely, by the justification of the sinner through the grace that is shown in Jesus Christ and received through faith alone. Justification by faith determines Christian ethics because, for the Christian, justification is both the presupposition and the source of the ethical life."[146]

For Luther we cannot do God's will by striving to keep the law (or by making pilgrimages to holy places or purchasing indulgences). Instead God's will is that we humbly acknowledge our sinfulness and in faith accept God's gracious provision. Only when we have laid hold of Christ in faith do we love God and do good works.[147] Indeed, in faith we receive God's love so that we might pass it on to our neighbor.[148] Hence in contrast to Aquinas, for Luther virtuous character is not a habit acquired through the performance of right deeds but a new nature given by God through faith.[149]

Luther's dictum that the Christian is always simultaneously sinner and justified by divine grace had far-reaching consequences for his view of the Christian life. Knowing that our actions are always tainted by sin, we can never hope for perfection in this life, not even in the individual moments of life. For this reason we never "progress" beyond the need for repentance. Instead the Christian pilgrimage consists in the life of continual repentance as well as the experience of God's justifying grace.

His focus on the reception of grace in each moment of life meant that Luther eschewed the idea of living according to prescriptive norms determined through rational reflection and applied in advance to life situations. Instead Luther advised that at every step of our journey we seek to listen carefully so as to discern the voice of God instructing us concerning what is right and then diligently attempt to act accordingly. When we intently seek to do God's will as those who know that even our best efforts are tainted with sin, we can "be a sinner and sin boldly, but believe and rejoice in Christ even more boldly, for he is victorious over sin, death, and the world."[150] And it is this trust which is pleasing to God and makes our actions good in God's sight.[151]

An ethic of the individual. The Reformation ethic elevated the individual to center stage. Until the modern era life was defined largely in accordance with the network of social relationships that bound people together in a variety of ways and mediated to each person well-defined status within society. As a result, to the ancient and medieval thinkers the ethical ideal consisted in each person functioning in, contributing to and deriving personal identity from the group. The importance of the individual lay largely in that person's role as a microcosm of the whole and as a functioning element within the whole.

Beginning with the Reformation a new interest in the individual as such emerged in the Western philosophical tradition. Each person came to be viewed as an autonomous, "freestanding" individual who possessed myriad rights, including the legal power to enter into social, political and economic contracts. Consequently, modern people derive their personal identity from the choices they make as individuals—that is, the contracts into which they freely enter. And these contractual relationships, which occur in the context of competing possibilities, mark our personal pilgrimages and constitute our individual life narratives.

* * *

The year is A.D. 800. A traveler arrives in a village some distance from his home. The village leaders desire to know who he is and why he has come to their town. He produces a letter from the leaders of his own village and explains its contents. "I am Stan, son of Richard of Alpena, pastor of the Alpena parish," he declares. "I too have been schooled for pastoral service, and have been sent by my superiors to seek answers to certain perplexing questions about the Scriptures from the monks at Lansing. I hope to arrive at the monastery tomorrow, Lord willing. Should the abbot request that I stay in Lansing, my superiors will be pleased that I do so. Otherwise, I am expected to resume my duties in Alpena upon my return in a month or two."

The year is 1997. A group of students at the theological college are going around the circle introducing themselves before they commence the ethics class. The professor begins: "Hi! As you know, I'm Stan. I was born January 7, 1950, in Alpena, Michigan. Because my father was a pastor, we moved several times when I was growing up. Upon completion of high school in Greeley, Colorado, I decided to attend the University of Colorado at Boulder, for I was planning to become a nuclear physicist. But after a year's break from my studies, during which I traveled with a youth evangelism group (1971-1972), I sensed God's call to ministry. To prepare for ministry, I changed my major to philosophy. After graduating in 1973, I attended seminary in Denver. During my seminary studies I became increasingly interested in academic pursuits. In 1975 I met Professor Wolfhart Pannenberg, who invited me to come to Munich for doctoral work, which I began in 1976. From Munich the Lord took me to the pastorate in Winnipeg (1979) and two years later to a teaching position in Sioux Falls, South Dakota. After nine years (1990) I accepted appointment to the faculty of Carey/Regent College in Vancouver. In 1972 I married one of the women on the evangelism team. We have two children."

* * *

Luther introduced a radically new conception of human life and thereby opened the way for the modern focus on the autonomous individual. He highlighted the experience of the individual stripped of all social relations, standing continually and immediately before God[152] and being the recipient of God's salvation. Consequently the individual became the central subject of ethics. The Reformation model is based on the assumption that we live each moment in the very presence of a God who calls each human to make responsible choices in the situations of life.

Luther himself formed the exemplar of this life-before-God. In the crucible of decision at the council at Worms, with his status in the church and perhaps even his life hanging in the balance, Luther remained resolute. From that day on the hero of the Reformation faith became the individual saint with Bible in hand facing the crucible of decision, conscious of standing solely before the God who alone—rather than pope, council, emperor, society or even the entire world—is able to judge.

Three centuries later Kierkegaard raised anew the Lutheran banner in extolling the Knight of Faith who realizes that he or she stands alone before God. In the decision to obey God, Kierkegaard boldly declared, the Knight of Faith refuses to hide behind the furtive attempt to live the ethical life as codified in the great philosophical ethical systems (which, ironically, in Kierkegaard's time were devised by the Lutheran philosophers Kant and Hegel).

According to Luther, the individual upon whom the ethical burden rests inhabits two realms simultaneously. The Reformer spoke of these as the sphere of law in which sin is to be restrained and the sphere of grace where we can experience forgiveness. Although we ought not simply to equate these two with the civil and the ecclesiastical spheres—indeed, the former includes the various dimensions of human existence in the "world"—they loosely parallel the governing authority of state and church.[153]

Appealing to Romans 13:1-5, Luther offered this description of the two: "For God has established two kinds of government among men. The one is spiritual; it has no sword, but it has the word, by means of which men are to become good and righteous, so that with this righteousness they may attain eternal life. He administers this righteousness through the word, which he has committed to the preachers. The other kind is worldly government, which works through the sword so that those who do not want to be good and righteous to eternal life may be forced to become good and righteous in the eyes of the world. He administers this righteousness through the sword. And although God will not reward this kind of righteousness with eternal life, nonetheless, he still wishes peace to be maintained among men and rewards them with temporal blessings."[154]

Proper service within the two kingdoms requires an understanding of the goal of each. The duty of the Christian while acting as magistrate in the "secular" realm is to uphold the law and mete out due punishment for offenders, for in this manner sin is restrained. But the duty of the Christian who is ministering the gospel is to declare God's gracious forgiveness in Jesus Christ. Confusing these two kingdoms, Luther added, risks creating great confusion, for persons who do so "would put wrath into God's kingdom and mercy into the world's kingdom."[155]

Despite his teaching about the two kingdoms, Luther did not develop a thoroughgoing Christian social ethic. He did acknowledge that because God wills that we live in an orderly manner rather than in chaos, the Creator instituted "orders of creation" (e.g., marriage, family and community). Yet, while he elevated these as integral to God's will for the world, for Luther the natural orders are important chiefly because they provide the contexts in which individuals are to respond to the gospel message and the gift of faith, and in so doing help others. Luther's chief concern, therefore, was to admonish Christians to obey God in the situations of life within the structure of their own particular calling.

This focus on personal conduct as the concern of ethics left little place for talk about a specifically Christian ethic for human social orders, such as government or economics.[156] Nor was Luther willing to identify the gospel with any specific program of social organization.[157] Rather, he seemed to assume that the social orders operated according to a "secular" law that God had placed within them. Thereby he treated the political, economic and social dimensions of life as if they operated according to their own self-justifying rules.[158] Hence Luther declared that the gospel preacher ought not to call politicians to obey a specifically Christian law but rather ought to summon them to follow the more general law God had established for human government, which could be known through the application of reason.[159]

In this manner the Reformation concentration on the individual set the stage for a bifurcated morality built on a distinction between the realm of individual ethical decision and a seemingly autonomous, "secular" social realm. Like Abraham whom God commanded to sacrifice Isaac, the individual believer is the recipient of God's absolute and sometimes suprarational commands within the concrete situations of life. This experience, and not the "Christianization" of the social orders, was Luther's goal. This is evident even in Luther's theory of the two kingdoms, for the sole inhabitant of and thus the point of contact between the "secular" and the "spiritual" kingdoms is the individual Christian.[160]

The Calvinist alteration. The task of integrating the broader outline of Luther's proposal into a more elaborate, multidimensional ethic fell to the great Genevan theologian John Calvin. The foundation for Calvin's development of the Lutheran ethic lay in two related extensions he drew out of the deposit he had accepted from other leaders of the Protestant cause.

The first ethical extension had to do with the understanding of the law. In addition to acknowledging the general and theological uses so central in Luther's thought, Calvin, following Melanchthon and Martin Bucer,[161] saw yet an additional purpose: The law instructs believers about God's will for holy living.[162] As a result, Calvin declared that Christians express their gratitude for God's gracious mercy through voluntary—albeit imperfect—obedience to the law.[163] The addition of the "third use" of the law provided the foundation for the Reformed understanding of sanctification as growth in obedience to divine precepts, especially as codified in the Ten Commandments.[164]

The second extension marked a further development of Luther's understanding of the presence of divine law in the secular orders (natural law). Calvin agreed with Luther that God had placed within creation and the human heart laws which facilitate a properly ordered existence. In keeping with the doctrine of depravity, he then added that fallen humans can only discern the various aspects of the natural law with differing, yet always partial, degrees of clarity.[165] Christians, however, know the divine will more clearly, because they find it announced in Scripture. In this matter Calvin linked the natural law (or the law within) to biblical revelation, declaring that ultimately the content of the two is identical.[166]

The connection between natural law and biblical precept fostered a stronger social ethic among Calvinists than Lutherans developed. The convergence of the natural and the revealed law suggests that society ought to be ordered in accordance with Christian ethical guidelines, for such an ordering is in line with the nature of society as created by God.

It is no accident, therefore, that Reformed Christians, more so than their Lutheran counterparts, have been transformationists. Calvinists have sought to mold human society in accordance with what they saw as Christian principles of human social interaction. As R. H. Tawney notes in his monumental work, *Religion and the Rise of Capitalism,* Calvin believed that the task of the Christian is simultaneously that of disciplining one's personal life and creating a sanctified society.[167]

A third Christian proposal. I have indicated that the ethical proposals of Augustine and Aquinas represent two paradigmatic ways in which Christian thinkers have responded to philosophical ethics. The Augustinian ethic represents the attempt to "Christianize" the philosophical tradition. The Thomistic ethic appeals to revelation to augment what God has made available to all humankind through the light of reason.

But what if human reason has no direct access to God and truth? Indeed, what if the wisdom of the world is opposed to the wisdom of God? In a sense the Reformation ethic built from this assumption. The Reformers believed that the Fall extends to every dimension of human life, including human reason. As a result, we dare not always trust human ethical reflection. What we need is divine revelation to guide us, for humans were created to obey God—to follow God's precepts, which are most clearly known only through revelation—and to do so from hearts that know the gracious forgiveness and justifying mercy of God. Viewed from this perspective, our pursuit of the true ethic requires that we reject the wisdom of the world—including the philosophical tradition—casting ourselves on God's gracious provision in Christ and listening to the voice of God coming to us through divine revelation.[168]

The Classical Thinkers and Us

Seen as representing three typical Christian responses to the moral aspirations of people around us, Augustine, Aquinas and Luther become more than mere historical relics. They are not simply curious examples of how thinkers in the past sought to engage in Christian ethics. Instead these church leaders serve as paradigms of the options set before us as well, as we attempt to engage critically with the ethical traditions prevalent in our culture.

Thus whenever Christians seek to draw from and reformulate in Christian terms the moral quest they see evidenced in the "best" philosophical thought of the day, they are following a course similar to that charted by Augustine in the early 400s. If Christian ethicists are convinced that all humans can attain a certain level of morality, even though the fullness of the moral quest requires the application of the gospel, they are falling in line with an approach pioneered by Thomas Aquinas in the late Middle Ages. But Christians who conclude that the divine revelation disclosed in the gospel—and this revelation alone—provides the foundation for a life that honors God are more in tune with Luther in his dismissal of all human striving for goodness in favor of casting oneself solely on God's mercy and grace.

Chapter 5

CONTEMPORARY CHRISTIAN PROPOSALS

Therefore, since we are surrounded by such a great cloud of witnesses, let us throw off everything that hinders and the sin that so easily entangles, and let us run with perseverance the race marked out for us. Let us fix our eyes on Jesus, the author and perfecter of our faith.
(HEBREWS 12:1-2)

During the fourth decade of the twentieth century, a thinker who has been described as "a theologian's theologian"[1] voiced a biting complaint about the reigning theological ethic of the day. In what has since become a classic—if not somewhat overstated—characterization of the Social Gospel, H. Richard Niebuhr declared, "A God without wrath brought men without sin into a kingdom without judgment through the ministrations of a Christ without a cross."[2]

While intending to focus on the theological foundation for the movement, Niebuhr's indictment pierced to the heart of the ethical agenda of the Social Gospel, namely, its attempt to bring about a "Christianization" of the social order in the United States. But in so doing, his comment uncovered the deeper issue at stake. Niebuhr and the Social Gospelers differed at a foundational level, that of the nature of the Christian ethical task itself.

The critique Niebuhr articulated in 1937 is endemic of a deep chasm that has separated architects of theological ethics since the advent of the twentieth century. Christian thinkers have differed in their understanding of exactly what ought to be the focus of the ethical life mandated to them by their Lord. In this chapter we peruse the ethical landscape of the century by taking a cursory look at the writings of several thinkers whose work is representative of certain of the main motifs that have dominated ethical reflection. Specifically, we will trace seven major trajectories that emerged and continued in one form or another as the ethical discussions of the century unfolded.

An Ethic for the Christianization of the Social Order

The advent of the twentieth century witnessed the ascendancy of the ethical orientation that viewed the Christian ethical life as primarily directed "outward." Concerned Christians sought to take seriously the biblical teaching that love for neighbor is the measure of one's love for God. And love for neighbor does not stop with doing good deeds for individuals in need but involves seeking to eradicate the social ills plaguing one's neighbors.

Consequently, the turn of the century was an "activistic" age. Awakened by the great evangelical revivals of the 1900s, Christians stood at the forefront of a host of social causes. They saw themselves leading the charge against the powers of darkness that were attempting to subvert God's intentions for human social well-being.

Walter Rauschenbusch and the Social Gospel. As the title of the book containing H. R. Niebuhr's allegation indicates—*The Kingdom of God in America*—the turn to social activism rested on a specific theological concept, God's reign. Advocates of the Social Gospel were hopeful that human cooperation with the divine Spirit would advance the work of God and spread the divine rule. This motif, the progress of the kingdom of God on earth, had already provided a powerful theological motivation for Christian social activism through much of the nineteenth century. No wonder the idea emerged as a driving force in the fledgling Social Gospel movement. Perhaps no one came to epitomize the growing evangelical fervor for social reform more than Walter Rauschenbusch.

The son of a German Lutheran minister who had become a Baptist shortly after emigrating to the United States, young Rauschenbusch quite naturally set out to become a minister himself. His first pastoral call brought him to Hell's Kitchen, a particularly impoverished section on the west side of New York City. His firsthand exposure to the underside of

American laissez-faire capitalism worked in him a deep social concern: "When I saw how men, hard, toiled all their life long toilsome lives, and at the end had almost nothing to show for it; how strong men begged for work and could not get it in the hard times; how little children died—oh the children's funerals! they gripped my heart . . . why did the children have to die? . . . And in that way, gradually, social information and social passion came to me."[3]

In 1891 Rauschenbusch spent several months in Germany where he came under the influence of Albrecht Ritschl, especially the German liberal theologian's emphasis on the ethical kingdom of God. Upon his return to the United States, Rauschenbusch threw himself into the budding "Social Gospel" movement, becoming its most theologically able exponent.[4] Through his writings he sought to apply the ethical aims and ideals of the kingdom of God to concrete social life in industrial America.

Rauschenbusch's most influential work was *Christianity and the Social Crisis* (1907). After alerting the reader to the extreme gap between wealth and poverty in America, the author made the bold assertion that the Christian task is "to transform human society into the Kingdom of God by regenerating all human relations and reconciling them in accordance with the will of God."[5] Hence he called on Christians to work for the salvation of economic structures that perpetuated poverty. In so doing they could foster a revival in which not only individual souls but entire corporate entities and social structures would repent and be saved.

In his second major book, *Christianizing the Social Order* (1912), Rauschenbusch offered specific suggestions for the revival he envisioned. He called for the socialization of major industries, support for labor unions and the abolition of an economy centered around greed, competition and the profit motive. Such changes would mark the gradual Christianization of the social order, leading American society to ever closer approximation to the kingdom of God, which in *A Theology for the Social Gospel* (1917) he equated with "humankind organized according to the will of God."[6]

The Christianization of society. As a coherent phenomenon the Social Gospel movement did not outlive its most famous proponents. Its legacy has lived on nevertheless, especially in the ecumenical social ethic to which it gave birth. The most prominent bearer of this social ethic has been the World Council of Churches (WCC).

The connection between the Social Gospel and the WCC is actually indirect, coming via the Life and Work movement. Several prominent Social Gospelers were in attendance at a gathering known as the Edinburgh Conference (1910), which created the Life and Work movement for the purpose of encouraging greater unity among Christians involved in social witness and action. The statements from the movement's Stockholm Conference (1925) incorporated central Social Gospel themes. Later as Life and Work became a part of the fledgling WCC, it brought with it the legacy of concern for the Christianization of the social order. Consequently, social ethics has remained prominent in ecumenical circles, as is evidenced by the consistently high place social issues have enjoyed on the WCC agenda.[7]

Although the concern for the Christianization of the social order lived on, the theological orientation of the Social Gospel movement toward the kingdom of God as the foundation for this understanding of the Christian ethical mandate waned. In fact, neo-orthodox impulses led the participants in the Oxford Conference of the Life and Work movement (1937) to warn against identifying the kingdom of God with human institutions.

As a result in WCC documents other motifs have replaced the focus on the kingdom of God so characteristic of the Social Gospel movement. Some of the most significant of these have been drawn from Christian theological anthropology. Hence the Amsterdam Assembly (1948) appealed to our creation as free beings responsible to God to issue a call for a "responsible society" in which freedom and justice prevail. In so doing the assembly elevated this ideal as the criterion for judging all existing societies.

More recently WCC social ethicists have viewed human society in the context of a sustainable natural environment. To this end thinkers have looked to trinitarian theology as providing the theological grounding for the instrumental value of creation.[8]

Despite the insertion of other foundational theological concepts, with the discrediting of the Social Gospel theme of the earthly kingdom of God, the older ethical vision of a Christianization of society has lost much of its punch. In fact, ecumenical statements often leave the impression that theirs is a social ethic in search of a theological foundation, rather than being the thoroughgoing theological ethic for which the older Social Gospel held out promise.

The Ethic of Transcendence

The guns of August 1914 sounded the death knell of the progressivist optimism that pervaded the Social Gospel movement. The kingdom of God would not come through the conversion of social structures. In the ensuing decades a loosely knit coalition of thinkers formed, drawn together by their rejection of what they saw as the culture Christianity of liberalism. Although they charted their own individual courses, these theologians were united in the conviction that the price of the attempt to Christianize the social order had been the loss of the Word of God—the voice of the Transcendent One—thundering the good news of reconciliation to humankind hopelessly lost in sin. Because they sought to recapture certain doctrines that had been central to the older Christian orthodoxy, the movement is now generally known as neo-orthodoxy.

Nowhere was the necessity of hearing anew the transcendent voice of God more crucial than in the area of the Christian life. Hence neo-orthodox theologians have called for a break with the ethical approach of liberalism. In keeping with their rediscovery of the foundational theological themes of the Protestant Reformation, they proposed nothing short of a radical Reformation ethic that centers on obedient listening to the divine command. In the words of historian Edward LeRoy Long Jr., "They all posit the importance of revelation and vehemently reject the validity of autonomous moral deliberation; they all derive the content of the moral norm from the will of God and somewhere in their discussion use the idea of command in connection with that will; they all stand in the Reformation heritage in which justification by faith is a central concept."[9]

Karl Barth: ethics as the command of God. The thinker who launched the attack on theological liberalism and with it on the ethic of the Social Gospel was the Swiss pastor-turned-theologian Karl Barth (1886-1968). Barth's goal was to call the church to listen anew to the Word of God, to the message that breaks into our world from the God who is utterly distinct from us.[10] Consequently his theology focused on the transcendence of God, the lordship of Christ and the givenness of revelation. This theological agenda carried far-reaching implications for Barth's ethic as well. According to Barth, theological ethics (which encompasses Christian ethics) has as its task "to understand the Word of God as the command of God."[11]

Barth did not view ethics as a separate discipline in addition to but as the flip side of theology. In his *Ethics* he boldly stated, "Theological ethics is itself dogmatics, not an independent discipline alongside it."[12] In the sections in his *Church Dogmatics* devoted to ethics,[13] he indicated that he is merely setting forth the ethical implications of the particular doctrinal matters under consideration, specifically, the doctrines of God and creation.

Like his theology, Barth's theological ethic has a radical christological center. Christian ethics, he insisted, cannot be relegated to the status of being a subdivision under the broader rubric of general ethics,[14] which brings to light the universality of the ethical impulse. Christian ethics cannot be vindicated by appeal to some general ethical criterion. Nor is the ability to distinguish good from evil the glorious mark of human superiority to the animals, as many philosophical ethicists have maintained. According to Barth all human strivings for the good are merely the vain attempts of a fallen and depraved humankind to attain self-justification. Humans are simply not able to give the answer to the ethical question, for this answer is God's electing and sanctifying grace alone.[15]

In his early lectures on ethics Barth declared—against the tradition of philosophical ethics—that the good is nothing other than obedience to the divine command.[16] But he had a specific understanding in view. He was not referring to the biblical commands as universal imperatives. In Barth's estimation, to treat the scriptural injunctions in this manner or to engage in casuistry is to exchange the divine will for a fixed and unbending set of prescriptions, that is, to fall into legalism and even idolatry.[17] Instead these commands are witnesses to the fundamental command that comes to us in each moment of our lives.[18] As the "absolute, personal, and living will of God" confronts us, we are faced with a decision, "a decision for or against *God*."[19] The good news, Barth added, is that in confronting us with the divine command, God accepts us—justifies us. Indeed God's love is revealed to us in the command.[20]

Lying behind this intriguing approach was Barth's profound theology of grace. At the foundation of his understanding of ethics lay our status as those who have been elected in Christ and in Christ are in covenant with God.[21] Indeed, for him ethics is a counterpart to the doctrine of election.[22] The divine act of election, Barth asserted, carries with it the divine command. God commands us to be what he himself in his grace has chosen us to be. Consequently, the basis for morality does not lie in our ability, Barth argued, but in our response of faith to the Word of grace which God speaks in Jesus Christ.[23] Hence the Christian ethic consists of living in grace and through that grace being free to be what by God's grace we actually are.

Christian living always occurs in the concrete situations of life. According to Barth, "The good is a question which is directed to us and which we must answer with our *act,* with an act which for its part is always concrete and *individual.*"[24] In this manner, Barth sought to reconnect being and doing, acting and existing, for in his estimation humans exist as they act.[25]

While Christ is the center of Barth's ethic, creation provided its context. Barth drew a connection between creation and the covenant, which in turn led to his alternative to natural law ethics. The covenant, he wrote, "is the goal of creation," whereas creation is "the way to the covenant." Barth then explained that while the free love of God is the inner basis of the covenant, creation is its *external* basis. By this he meant that creation makes the covenant "technically possible; that it prepares and establishes the sphere in which the institution and history of the covenant take place; that it makes possible the subject which is to be God's partner in this history, in short the nature which the grace of God is to adopt and to which it is to turn in this history."[26]

On this basis Barth offered a two-sided appraisal of the moral significance of the natural world and human institutions. These are not the covenant itself, and hence they do not possess meaning and good in themselves. Nevertheless God's covenant of grace depends on them, and as a result they contain morally significant patterns. Consequently Barth rejected any attempt to build a Christian ethic on natural law; yet he was able to draw important ethical inferences from the structure present in the natural world.[27]

James Gustafson: ethics in service to God. Perhaps no other twentieth-century thinker has cast as long a shadow as Karl Barth, not only in theology but in theological ethics as well. To the name of Barth we could add other significant thinkers whose theological ethic advanced an agenda similar to his. Several of these persons—such as Emil Brunner[28] and Reinhold Niebuhr—were contemporaries of the great Swiss theologian. One person whose major work appeared later and who therefore took up the basic neo-orthodox mantle in a new context is James M. Gustafson.

Like Barth before him (and explicitly conscious of this connection), Gustafson criticized those traditions in ethics—whether they be philosophical or theological—that operate from the presupposition that the human person is the "measure of all things."[29] Traditionally ethicists have understood this dictum as implying that God's chief concern is human well-being and that the rest of creation exists for our sake. To Gustafson this "anthropocentricism" involves "a denial of God as God." It denies the God who is "the power and ordering of life in nature and history which sustains and limits human activity, which 'demands' recognition of principles and boundaries of activities for the sake of man and of the whole of life."[30]

Like Barth, Gustafson sought to draw from the Reformation heritage, especially that of John Calvin, to restore ethics to a consistently theocentric perspective. Why the Reformed tradition? Gustafson found in it three laudable emphases: a sense of a powerful Other, the centrality in the religious and moral life of piety or the religious affections (i.e., an attitude of reverence that implies a sense both of devotion and of responsibility), and an understanding of human life in relation to God which requires that all human activity be ordered in relation to the divine purposes.[31] In addition Gustafson followed his neo-orthodox forebears in mining from the Reformed tradition an awareness of the depth of the "human fault."[32]

On this basis Gustafson offered a radical alternative to the anthropocentricism he discovered not only in Catholic natural law theories and the Social Gospel but also in Calvinist appeals to special providence and even the older neo-orthodoxy.[33] In contrast to these, Gustafson wanted to articulate a position that "does not see the purposes of the ultimate power to coincide perfectly with our interpretations of what constitutes human well-being."[34] Rather than God and the universe existing for our sake or for the sake of our salvation, Gustafson asserted the opposite: we exist for the sake of God. Our chief end, he declared, reminiscent of the Westminster

Catechism, is "to honor, to serve, and to glorify (celebrate) God."[35]

Consequently, following his theological mentor Julian N. Hartt, Gustafson asserted that the primary task of religious morality is "to relate to all things in a manner appropriate to their *relations* to God."[36] To this end he set as his program the development of an adequate understanding of God, an adequate interpretation of humankind in relation to God and an appropriate pattern of ethics. Like that of Barth, Gustafson's pattern centers on human consent to divine governance (i.e., obedience to God). He believes that this theocentric focus transforms the human moral question into concern for "what serves the divine purposes." And it determines that ultimately the moral life consists in discerning the purposes of God and then joining in these purposes.[37]

While deeply indebted to Barth, Gustafson refused to follow slavishly the great theologian's lead. For example, Barth's theological ethic contained a strong corporate dimension, for its foundation lay in the principle of corporate election, the election of humankind in Christ. More overtly than Barth, however, Gustafson sought to move beyond the individualism endemic to modern ethics, and on the basis of a keen awareness of the social character of human experience[38] retrieve the social character of the ethical life. As a result he was interested in the role of virtues in the development of the moral life within human community.[39]

Perhaps an even more significant departure from Barth lay in the place Gustafson gave to human experience. Reminiscent of Schleiermacher and drawing directly from Jonathan Edwards, religious experience provided the launching pad for his theological ethic. Specifically, Gustafson appealed to the religious sense of dependence on an ultimate power beyond ourselves, a power that bears down upon us, sustains us, orders our relationships, sets the conditions for human activity and provides a sense of direction.[40] To name this power, Gustafson invoked the traditional Christian "symbols of God"—God as Creator, Sustainer, Governor, Judge and Redeemer.[41]

As Gustafson's use of experience suggests, the American thinker was much less pessimistic than Barth about the value of general ethics. He posited no radical contradiction between nature and grace, but a continuity. Nature, Gustafson argued, is redirected or transformed by grace. Hence the solution he proposed for the "human fault" does not negate the natural. Instead it lies in "a governing and reordering of our natural desires, loves, natural instincts, and aspirations."[42] As a result, although he shared the Reformation concern that Christian ethics not slip into legalism, Gustafson found a positive place for moral principles as general rules that can find application in changing historical conditions.[43] And nature can enjoy a normative significance as a source of moral norms.[44]

Love as the Christian Norm

While some thinkers were exploring theological ethics from the perspective of obedience to the divine command, others were thinking through the content of that command. Certain ethicists concluded that the Christian ethical life could be summed up in the royal law of love. These thinkers elevated to center stage the agapaic ethic that has always played a significant role in Christian thought. For them love constituted the Christian norm. Those who pursued this route form a third trajectory of contemporary ethical thought.

The name most commonly associated with the reappropriation of the Christian concept of love in the early twentieth century and the precursor to others who built on the theme is Anders Nygren (b. 1890). In his widely read work *Agape and Eros,*[45] the Swedish Lutheran thinker drew a sharp contrast between the biblical and the Hellenistic understandings of love and sought to show that the unmotivated—free and gracious—love of God is the fundamental category of Christianity.[46]

Nygren laid down the categories in the context of which the theological discussion of love developed. But he left to other thinkers the task of developing an agapaic theological ethic.

Paul Ramsey: an ethic of in-principled love. At midcentury the paradigmatic statement of an agapaic theological ethic emerged from the pen of Paul Ramsey. This book, *Basic Christian Ethics,*[47] launched the writing career of one of America's most distinguished Christian ethicists.

In his work Ramsey echoed certain fundamental themes of neo-orthodoxy. Like Barth's, his primary concern was to construct a truly biblical ethic—one that is self-consciously rooted in the Scriptures, especially in the biblical concepts of the covenant and the reign of God.[48] Like other midcentury thinkers, Ramsey was cautious about draping any particular proposal or social program with the mantle of being *the* Christian approach.[49] And in a typical neo-orthodox manner he viewed his project as an attempt to rearticulate the christocentric ethic of the Reformation.[50]

His biblical and christological foundation led Ramsey to the theme of "obedient love" as the central concept of Christian ethics.[51] In so doing, he presented what Long termed an ethic of "in-principled love."[52] Ramsey's goal was to set forth an agapaic ethic that does not eliminate all appeal to rules but grounds moral rules, sets of rules ("rules of practice") and even moral institutions in the Christian understanding of love. For this reason his position is sometimes characterized as a "rule agapism."[53]

But what exactly is Christian love? For the answer Ramsey turned to the biblical injunction to love one's neighbor as oneself. Such love, he declared, involves "neighbor-regarding concern for others" or "disinterested regard" for another person.[54] Thus Christians are to aim at their neighbor's good just as unswervingly as they by nature wish their own.[55] They are to abandon the prudent regard for the self and willingly practice an "enlightened unselfishness."[56]

By defining love in this manner, Ramsey self-consciously constructed a deontological ethic, one that is primarily concerned with the "right" rather than the "good." As a result, while upholding the christocentric orientation he derived from Scripture, he declared his openness to making common cause with the philosophical tradition, especially idealism.[57] But Ramsey's program involved a radical transformation of philosophical ethics. For him Christian neighbor-love (and not some philosophical principle such as concern for the self or even the quest for the greatest good for the greatest number) defines what is right or obligatory.[58] Thus according to Ramsey, the Christian ethicist does not seek to dissuade a hedonist, for example, but to turn hedonists from persons who think only of their own pleasure into those who give pleasure (which is the greatest good they know) to their neighbors.[59]

Ramsey's agapaic ethic likewise transforms the concern for moral norms or principles. For Ramsey there is but one fundamental ethical principle, that of neighbor-love. As a consequence, the moral ideal does not arise from rules of conduct but from the self-regulation of persons unconditionally bound to their neighbors.[60] Rules do have their place, Ramsey admitted, insofar as they embody love. Therefore acting in violation of a rule may result in weakening the rule and consequently weakening love itself. Yet the foundation for any moral rule or set of rules governing a sphere of human activity does not lie in an appeal to natural law or in rational reflection on general human moral experience, he averred, but on its relationship to love.[61]

Ramsey, therefore, offered a nuanced stance toward natural law. He admitted that philosophical reflection can lead to insights into such ethical concepts as justice and that the Christian may make use of the ethical insights of natural law theorists. But the agapaic ethicist adamantly asserted that natural law can never occupy the ground floor of Christian ethics—this position must be reserved for love[62]—for no natural law can fully encompass all the demands of Christian love.[63]

This focus on the normative value of love led to a fluidity not found in other, more rigid, rule-oriented ethical proposals. Ramsey wrote, "Christian love whose nature is to allow itself to be guided by the needs of others changes its tactics as easily as it stands fast; it does either only on account of the quite unalterable strategy of accommodating itself to neighbor-needs."[64]

Christian love provided Ramsey with a starting point from which to tackle other modern philosophical questions as well. Foremost among these were personal rights and the quest for virtue. The agapaic ethicist asserted that in Christian ethics rights are "derived backward" from a consideration of neighbor-love. This approach brought about a radical shift from rights to duties, "from claiming to giving one's own."[65] Any claim to possess rights, he declared, is actually a claim "that my neighbor possesses them in me. If my neighbor possesses them in me, these rights are my duties, duties to myself which also, if they are Christian duties, I owe to my neighbor for Christ's sake."[66]

While expressing an interest in virtue theory even to the point of suggesting that virtue flows out of love, Ramsey refused to endorse the equating of the ethical life with the cultivation of personal virtues so prominent among the ancient philosophers. On the contrary, he seemed to dismantle the entire Greek tradition with one sharp blow when he asserted that reason and moral intelligence were not part of our original endowment as humans but came into existence as a consequence of the Fall.[67]

Ramsey's chief concern with virtue ethics, however, lay deeper. Rather than the product of the careful cultivation of character traits or habits, to use the Thomistic language, love of neighbor is always a "present decision."[68] Yet despite this critique, the agapaic ethicist did highlight certain virtues—above all, humility and faith—as contributing to neighbor-love. These, he concluded, have a place within the framework of an agapaic ethic.[69]

Joseph Fletcher and "situation ethics." The first name that in the minds of many people emerges with the mention of an ethic of love is not Paul Ramsey's but that of Joseph Fletcher. In 1966, the onetime dean of Cincinnati's St. Paul's Cathedral and later professor of social ethics at the Episcopal Theology School in Cambridge, Massachusetts, produced what his publisher touted as an "explosive" book that "will offend some, excite many, and challenge all!" *Situation Ethics: The New Morality*[70] lived up to the hype. Upon its appearance, the book created quite a storm—albeit largely beyond the walls of academia.

In an essay published three years before his famous book, Fletcher differentiated his approach from the traditional method in Christian ethics. According to his characterization the older model, which Fletcher labeled "casuistry," begins with the Christian ideal, formulates a set of working principles for conduct and then reflects on how these rules would be applied to specific situations. Fletcher, in contrast, intended to turn that process upside down: "We start with the situation empirically and inductively in all its contextual particularity, then we attempt to hammer out a few tentative working principles 'generally' valid, and only in the end, in an even more open way, do we refer in fear and trembling to the ideal. And of the ideal itself we see but one principle, a monolithic norm or standard against which every other principle has to be checked in the concrete situation. The one judge is 'agapeic' love."[71]

What resulted from Fletcher's inversion of the traditional ethical method was an "act agapism," a radically contextual ethic in which the moral agent determines how best to act "there and then"[72] in the specific situation itself.

On what basis is this determination made? Act agapism offers a simple answer—love. In each situation the moral agent seeks to determine what is the most loving thing to do. Hence the goal of ethical reflection is to determine what Fletcher called "contextual appropriateness," that is, neither the good nor the right, but the "fitting."[73]

Fletcher did not see his ethical theory as especially new or radical.[74] In his view situationism charts a middle course between legalism and unprincipled antinomianism.[75] Yet Fletcher was chiefly interested in undermining the former alternative, for he was convinced that throughout the centuries legalists have dominated Christian ethics.[76] Thus act agapism has no place for absolute moral principles (besides the general norm of love). All such "norms" are mere "rules of thumb,"[77] similar to the know-how of a wise sports player, and hence are to be altered according to the circumstances.[78] Instead of relying on norms, therefore, Fletcher declared that "the indicative plus the imperative equals the normative." He then explained his catchy dictum: "Love, in the imperative mood of neighbor-concern, examining the relative facts of the situation in the indicative mood, discovers what it is obliged to do, what it should do, in the normative mood. What is, in the light of what love demands, shows what ought to be."[79]

The descriptions of love Fletcher offered do not differ greatly from those found elsewhere in the Christian tradition. Basically it consists of benevolence or goodwill. Love may likewise be equated with justice, in that justice is simply love distributed.[80] Such love is disinterested, impartial, inclusive and indiscriminate; it wills the neighbor's good whether or not we like him or her.[81] Ultimately we do not direct this kind of love toward others for our sakes or for theirs, but for God's.[82]

Fletcher's act agapism has been hailed by convinced adherents and railed against by skeptical critics.[83] Some of the protests were based on misunderstandings of his actual position or were triggered by his radical statements on certain issues, especially those related to human sexuality. More germane are criticisms that point out the lack of theological foundation evident in Fletcher's work.[84] Fletcher did make a fleeting attempt to set forth a christological basis for his position. Christian love, he declared, is motivated simply by gratitude for what God has done for us in Christ.[85] But perhaps the book's author himself noted its chief fault, namely, that *Situation Ethics* falls short as a presentation of a specifically *theological* ethic. Indeed, as Fletcher himself admitted, "Situationism is a *method*, not a substantive ethic."[86]

The Ethic of Discipleship

Most Christians would likely agree that the Christian ethic is in some sense an ethic of love. Most would likely also add that the Christian life is somehow connected to discipleship: Christians are to follow after their Lord. For this reason discipleship has been a recurring theme in Christian ethical thought. But how is discipleship to be understood? The growing number of thinkers struggling with this question compose a fourth trajectory within contemporary theological ethics.

Charles Sheldon's novel *In His Steps* embodies what we might see as the classic nineteenth-century answer to the question, What is Christian discipleship? According to Sheldon, discipleship entails confronting social ills after the manner of Jesus, that is, by answering the question "What would Jesus do?" As we have seen, to twentieth-century ethicists chastened by the horrors of destructive wars and the disintegration of society, this simple approach seemed neither credible nor workable. Yet the ethic of discipleship did not disappear from the purview of Christian thinkers.

Dietrich Bonhoeffer: ethics as holy worldliness. His imprisonment in 1943 and subsequent death at the hands of the Gestapo in the waning days of the Nazi regime interrupted the career of one of Germany's most promising young thinkers, Dietrich Bonhoeffer (1906-1945). Despite the fragmentary nature of his writings, Bonhoeffer's ethical reflections live on in such works as *The Cost of Discipleship*,[87] completed while he directed an illegal seminary on behalf of the Confessing Church, and *Ethics*,[88] a reconstruction based on incomplete manuscripts concealed from the Gestapo, as well as his less formal *Letters and Papers from Prison*.[89]

Christology provided the unifying thread for Bonhoeffer's writings, as it did for Barth's.[90] Throughout his life Bonhoeffer wrestled with the question: Who is Jesus Christ?[91] To it he gave an unswerving and basically Lutheran answer: Christ is the One in whom God reconciled the world to himself.

More difficult was the related question: Where is Christ present? His first answer was ecclesiological: Christ is in the believing community.[92] But a second theme—Christ's presence in the world—soon joined the first.[93] These christological postulates provided the foundation for Bonhoeffer's typically Barthian conclusion that the Christian ethic begins with the divine command and obedience to that command.[94] But they led to his un-Barthian insistence that the Christian life entails following

Christ back into the world and thereby participating in his messianic sufferings.

Bonhoeffer set the stage for his ethical position in the vivid contrast between "cheap grace" and "costly grace" he presented in *The Cost of Discipleship.* "Cheap grace" refers to mere "churchianity," for which the German thinker provided this piercing description: "Cheap grace is the preaching of forgiveness without requiring repentance, baptism without Church discipline, Communion without confession, absolution without personal confession."[95] "Costly grace," in contrast, is the message that salvation is costly. It cost God his Son, and it demands from us obedience, that is, a life of discipleship.

With these words the young German took direct aim at the Lutheran church of his day, which in his estimation had elevated grace at the expense of discipleship. Against the perpetrators of this error, he appealed to Luther himself, who, Bonhoeffer claimed, discovered costly grace when he returned from the cloister to the world. At that point the great Reformer learned that "the only way to follow Jesus was by living in the world."[96]

In prison Bonhoeffer reflected further on the meaning of the Christian ethical life. He concluded that the contemporary experience of a world "come of age" demands a radical discipleship characterized by "holy worldliness."

To understand Bonhoeffer's call for a Christian "worldliness," we must see it as the application of his fundamental christological axiom to the life of discipleship. For the German thinker, the chief temptation Christians face is the lure to withdraw from the world into pious enclaves or to view religion as one dimension of existence alongside of others. But Christ is found in the world and not merely in some special, religious sphere. Consequently the gospel is not a call to be "religious." Nor are Christians to strive for a detached, disengaged piety that seeks to elevate them above humankind. Rather than the cultivation of asceticism or the attempt to serve God merely in some sterile religious sanctuary or in an isolated, sheltered Christian enclave, to be a Christian means to participate in the life of the world. The church, Bonhoeffer argued, is "to stand in the center of the village."[97]

In his typically lively style, Bonhoeffer declared that we must "drink the earthly cup to the lees," for only in so doing is the crucified and risen Lord with us.[98] He acknowledged that such participation in life on earth means enjoying the goodness of living.[99] But more important, holy worldliness entails sharing in the sufferings of God in the life of the world.[100] Living as a true disciple means following in the steps of "the man for others" and becoming vulnerable in service to the world, for "the Church is her true self only when she exists for humanity."[101]

For Bonhoeffer true discipleship emerges as we become aware of the close relationship between the "penultimate" and the "ultimate," between the present world and the eternal reality, which gives it meaning. We live as those who belong wholly to this world, while keeping in view a vision of the ultimate reality. This connection means that Christians must avoid both the total rejection of and any complete sanctioning of the penultimate, present world,[102] the realm in which God's goal of justifying the sinner by grace alone is to be experienced and served. As we do so, our lives become a participation in God's encounter with the world.[103]

Bonhoeffer's call for holy worldliness was not a license for immoral or indulgent living. Rather, his focus lay squarely on the path of true Christian faith. Viewed in this light, being a "worldly" Christian involves abandoning "every attempt to make something of oneself, whether it be a saint, a converted sinner, a churchman (the priestly type, so-called!) a righteous man or an unrighteous one, a sick man or a healthy one." Instead, by "taking life in one's stride . . . we throw ourselves utterly into the arms of God and participate in his sufferings in the world."[104] Participating in the suffering of God in the world requires stretching ourselves to the limit, and this necessitates living "close to the presence of God." Only by being "in Christ," Bonhoeffer concluded, can we gain the strength to face the challenges of life.[105]

James McClendon: ethics as disciples in community. All Christians share a desire to live as Christ's followers, even if not to the extent set forth in Bonhoeffer's call for holy worldliness. Yet thinkers standing in the radical Reformation tradition have led the way in elevating discipleship to the very center of the Christian life.[106] However, the understanding of discipleship typically found among the heirs of the radical Reformation is not the individualistic piety often present in more mainline Protestant circles. Instead these thinkers—together with certain voices from other traditions[107]—tend to place on center stage a theme Bonhoeffer discovered through his experiment in illegal theological education, namely, the importance of the believing community to the construction of a discipleship ethic.

The Baptist theologian James William McClendon offered an interesting twist on this ethic of community discipleship. In contrast to both Bonhoeffer and the influential Mennonite thinker John Howard Yoder (to whom he acknowledges his indebtedness), McClendon approached the ethical task through the doorway of narrative theology. In fact, he distinguished himself as a narrative thinker before turning specifically to ethics, as indicated by the title of an early book *Biography as Theology: How Life Stories Can Remake Today's Theology* (1974).

In the 1980s McClendon turned his attention to the formidable task of constructing a narrative ethics. His efforts crystalized in a work bearing the descriptive title *Ethics: Systematic Theology, Volume One* (1986),[108] which formed the foundation, in turn, for a follow-up volume, *Doctrine: Systematic Theology, Volume Two* (1994). This sequence illustrates the important contention McClendon shares with certain other contemporary thinkers that ethics precedes doctrine chronologically (albeit not logically).[109] The Baptist thinker explained the proper order of theological inquiry: "We begin by finding the shape of the common life in the body of Christ. . . . This is ethics. We continue with the investigation of the common and public teaching that sanctions and supports that common life."[110]

This terse definition of ethics indicates the direction in which McClendon's theological ethic moves. The basis from which it arises is McClendon's Baptist heritage. This heritage includes a strong focus both on discipleship "as life transformed into obedience to Jesus' lordship" and on community "as daily sharing in the vision."[111] In keeping with this focus, McClendon displaced the modern emphasis on decision-making in favor of the shared life of the Christian church.[112]

McClendon acknowledged that Christians live in several realms simultaneously—the natural order, the human social world and the eschatological new world God established through Jesus' resurrection.[113] This observation led to a division of Christian ethical reflection into the categories of body, social and resurrection ethics. At the center of Christian morality, however, stands Jesus' resurrection, which provides us with "a new ground, a new outlook, a new dynamism"[114] leading to the transformation of both bodily and social life.

The place where this transformation occurs is in the life of the believing community. For Christians, McClendon asserted, the gathered church is the link connecting body and social ethics—connecting the moral self and social morals.[115] The Christian life emerges "in the self-involving common practices that draw the disciples of Jesus Christ into solidaristic union in their obedient following of him."[116]

Hence, drawing from McClendon's own suggestion, we might characterize his as "an ethic for disciples in community."[117] And this ethic is a narrative ethic, he argued, because through the interaction of its three strands, it displays the marks of a narrative: character (embodied selfhood), social setting (the believing community) and incident or circumstance (God's action upon us in Jesus' cross and resurrection).[118]

The Ethic of Liberation

As a distinct movement the Social Gospel did not survive the onslaught of its neo-orthodox critics. Yet the ethos it embodied did not die. We noted earlier how the movement bequeathed its legacy to the ecumenical social ethics of the World Council of Churches. Its vision of a society in which the marginalized enjoy justice has lived on in another form as well, namely, in the various types of liberation ethics that emerged in the final third of the twentieth century.

Some of the architects of liberation thinking, such as Martin Luther King Jr., were directly influenced by the Social Gospelers, especially Walter Rauschenbusch.[119] Others such as Gustavo Gutiérrez may never have read the writings of this American hero.[120] In any case, the proponents of liberation push the Social Gospel's call for a truly just society in new directions in an attempt to meet what they see as the needs of the situation confronting them. In so doing, they constitute a fifth distinctive trajectory of contemporary ethical reflection.

Martin Luther King Jr.: an ethic of militant nonviolence. In the United States the name that above all others has become associated with the political struggle of marginalized people is that of the Baptist pastor and social activist Martin Luther King Jr. (1929-1968). King was a controversial figure during his lifetime. Yet since his untimely death at the hands of an assassin, the nation has come to acknowledge the great importance of King's leadership in the civil rights movement during the turbulent decade of the 1960s and his commitment to nonviolent resistance in the struggle on behalf of racial equality for African-Americans.

King's untiring work was an outgrowth of Christian theological convictions that provided the foundation for his understanding of ethics. As a practitioner more than a theorist, he was not interested in carving out an elaborate theological ethic. Nor did he focus his energies on formulating elaborate answers to the standard ethical questions about the nature of the good. Instead his concern lay with the more immediate and concrete problem of how to know and do the good in specific situations,[121] especially situations involving social justice. Hence, anticipating the liberation theologians, he sought to engage theology in the practice of social ethics. In fact, for him, all ethical thought is but a method to eliminate social evil, and the ethical life is primarily the implementation of this method.[122]

King's commitment to social ethics was born out of his understanding of the gospel.[123] King believed that one of God's primary purposes is the establishment of a just economic and social order on earth. Such a social order promotes the development of every human person[124] after the model revealed in Jesus, who is our human ideal. This understanding provided King with a criterion by which to appraise the justice of all humanly devised laws: "How does one determine when a law is just or unjust? A just law is a man-made code that squares with the moral law or the law of God. An unjust law is a code that is out of harmony with the moral law. . . . Any law that uplifts human personality is just. Any law that degrades human personality is unjust. All [racial] segregation statutes are unjust because segregation distorts the soul and damages the personality. It gives the segregator a false sense of superiority, and the segregated a false sense of inferiority."[125]

Because the implementation of God's program requires human involvement, social justice became for King the primary ethical task. This goal, he added, is stymied by certain evil structures, including economic individualism, as well as attitudes and habits, such as apathy toward the poor, practical materialism and ignorance of the situation of others. The challenge for ethics in this context, King concluded, is to set forth a moral method to oppose evil structures and attitudes such as these and thereby bring about change.

Motivated by the Christian vision, King's goal was not "black power" but a racially inclusive community—racial integration.[126] He believed that because all persons are created in the image of God, they are inseparably bound together.[127] In his estimation this ideal is not merely the substance of the gospel, however. It encapsulates the purpose of the American nation as well. Hence King's goal was nothing less than "fashioning a truly Christian nation."[128]

The method King advocated for moving from injustice to justice and thereby bringing about the restoration of what he called the whole "beloved community" was nonviolent resistance or militant nonviolence. He was convinced that this tactic provides the best way to combine the moral and the political so as to bring about true justice.[129] But to King nonviolence was more than merely a pragmatic means to the goal of justice.[130] Rather, he elevated what he called "conscientious nonviolence" to a central normative concept.[131]

But why nonviolence? King offered several reasons. One was quite pragmatic. Nonviolence can achieve results in situations where violence would only be futile. In a situation of fear, hatred, violence or irrationality, King argued, only nonviolence can release a respect for the law by bringing people to believe the laws are right: "Here nonviolence comes in as the ultimate form of persuasion. It is the method which seeks to implement the just law by appealing to the conscience of the great decent majority who through blindness, fear, pride, and irrationality have allowed their consciences to sleep."[132]

Further, because the struggle is ultimately against evil powers and not humans, King declared that his goal was not victory over his human opponents but victory over the source of conflict, leading to reconciliation with his opponents.[133] This purpose is best served through nonviolence. Not only does it facilitate morally strong persons in resisting evil, but because it refuses to sow new seeds of bitterness and thereby breaks the chain of hate, it is the best way to bring about reconciliation between victim and perpetrator. Violent methods, in contrast, only heighten the hostility. King explained: "The problem with hatred and violence is that they intensify the fears of the white majority, and leave them less ashamed of their prejudices toward Negroes. In the guilt and confusion confronting our society, violence only adds to the chaos. It deepens the brutality of the oppressor and increases the bitterness of the oppressed. Violence is the antithesis of creativity and wholeness. It destroys community and makes brotherhood impossible."[134]

Above all, however, King advocated nonviolence because it comes closest to embodying the Christian ideal of love *(agapē)*, which includes the possibility of suffering. Indeed, he asserted that nonviolence involves the willingness to accept suffering upon oneself rather than inflict suffering on others.[135] It is ultimately this aspect that transforms nonviolence from merely an alternative means of violence into what for King was a way of life, or, as James Hanigan noted, a "spirituality."[136] But for this transformation to occur, the nonviolent resistor must renounce not only all physical violence but also all violence of spirit,[137] so that love itself can be the motivation for nonviolent resistance.[138]

As in the case of Jesus himself, nonviolence motivated by love can bring about great good. King summed up his entire ethic when he declared, "Suffering becomes a powerful social force when you willingly accept that violence on yourself, so that self-suffering stands at the center of the nonviolent movement and the individuals involved are able to suffer in a creative manner, feeling that unearned suffering is redemptive and that suffering may serve to transform the social situation."[139]

Gustavo Gutiérrez: an ethic of liberation. In 1968 in the city of Medellín, Colombia, the bishops of the Catholic Church in Latin America shocked the world by condemning the church's traditional alliance with the ruling powers of Latin America and by describing the situation in that part of the world as "institutionalized violence" against the people.[140] In many countries the widening gap between the rich and the poor was being met with a "second violence"—revolutionary movements to overthrow oppressive regimes. In an attempt to declare what roles Christians should play in this revolutionary situation, Gustavo Gutiérrez, a Peruvian priest and theology professor, published *A Theology of Liberation.* With it a new theological movement was born. The close link between theology and ethics in liberation theology is evident in one of the guiding dictums of the movement: theology is "a critical reflection on Christian praxis in light of the word of God."[141]

An underlying assumption of liberation theology is that theology must be contextual, that is, it must be intrinsically linked to a specific social and cultural situation. This stance is based in part on a theory called the "sociology of knowledge," which declares that knowledge always tends to reflect the vested interests of the knower.[142] In order to rise above this self-enclosed framework, people must subject their own social-environmental conditioning to scrutiny and criticism, that is, exercise a "critical consciousness."[143]

This process was pioneered in the late 1950s and early 1960s by Paulo Freire, a Catholic educator in northeastern Brazil. Convinced that the poor themselves must take the first steps in dealing with their plight, he engaged in what he termed *conscientization* or "making aware." Because poverty is caused by a few privileged persons defending their status, Freire declared, the poor must liberate themselves from their "dominated-conditioned mentality" and free the rich from their "dominating-conditioned" mindset.

Building on Freire's work, Gutiérrez declared that, because of its particular situation, the task of Latin American theology was to respond to the question of the "nonperson": "the human being who is not considered human by the present social order—the exploited classes, marginalized ethnic groups, and despised cultures."[144] The Peruvian priest explained: "Our question is how to tell the nonperson, the nonhuman, that God is love, and that this love makes us all brothers and sisters."[145]

But has not this always been the task of the Christian church? To understand Gutiérrez's point we must recall that Latin America has historically been predominantly Roman Catholic. In Gutiérrez's estimation, despite its claim to the contrary the Catholic Church is not "neutral" but actually has always taken the side of the status quo, that is, of the oppressors who foist structural poverty and institutionalized violence upon the poor and marginalized.[146] The question, therefore, was not whether the church should "get involved in politics" but whose side it was to take.

Gutiérrez's response to this question is uncompromisingly clear. In the current revolutionary situation characterized by class struggle and conflict, the church must cast its lot with the oppressed. Why? At this point the fundamental theological foundation for Gutiérrez's ethic emerges. God has demonstrated that he is on the side of the poor. To prove his point, the liberation theologian appealed to the biblical story of liberation, thereby linking God closely with history. In the great Old Testament events such as the exodus, Gutiérrez explained, God actually entered into history, liberating his people from bondage and oppression. Above all, God entered history in Jesus Christ.[147] God's historical activity on behalf of the poor did not end in the past, however. According to the liberation theologian, God is active today wherever the poor and marginalized are being liberated.

Consequently, for Gutiérrez "the poor deserve preference not because they are morally or religiously better than others, but because God is God, in whose eyes 'the last are first.'"[148] Although God loves all people, he identifies with the poor, reveals himself to the poor and sides with the poor against every oppressor who would exploit or dehumanize them.

This focus on God as the liberator of the marginalized goes hand in hand with Gutiérrez's reinterpretation of another doctrine foundational to the liberationist ethic, salvation.[149] Actually the Peruvian priest articulated a broad understanding of this theological concept. Salvation is God and humans working together within history to bring about the full humanization of all relationships. In Gutiérrez's estimation, however, the church has generally offered a truncated view of salvation, speaking of it solely in "quantitative" terms in an attempt to "guarantee heaven" for its faithful adherents. The Latin American situation, in contrast, requires that salvation be reinterpreted in qualitative terms—as commitment to the kind of social transformation that fosters "liberation from all that limits or keeps human beings from self-fulfilment."[150] Every action that works toward the goal of abolishing unjust, oppressive, exploitive and alienating social structures is in this sense liberating and hence salvific.[151]

Involvement in social transformation has another purpose as well. According to Gutiérrez, it is "the only way to have a true encounter with God."[152] God, he boldly asserted, can be encountered only in and through "conversion to the neighbor."[153] Therefore by joining with God's cause in the world, we are actually joining with God.

The main tools of Christian mission in the world are the denunciation of oppressive social structures and the annunciation of God's will for total liberation from everything that dehumanizes people. But contrary to the strict nonviolent stance preached by Martin Luther King Jr., Gutiérrez admitted that while violence is never ideal, it is sometimes a necessary last resort in the struggle for justice. Consequently he refused to criticize those who were taking up arms against the violence of the established order. His argument is simple: "We cannot say that violence is all right when the oppressor uses it to maintain or preserve 'order,' but wrong when the oppressed use it to overthrow this same order."[154]

Rosemary Radford Ruether: an ecofeminist ethic. Beginning in the 1970s, certain feminist thinkers used language similar to Gutiérrez's to call for the liberation of another marginalized group—women. But rather than focusing on economic injustice as did their Latin American counterparts, feminists zeroed in on the distinctive oppression prevalent in gender relationships. For this reason, the cutting edge of feminist ethics has tended to be the search for egalitarian and participatory models of social structures that can replace the hierarchical and patriarchal structures they find dominant throughout most of human history.

One leading voice in the feminist cause has been a prolific author and theology professor at Garrett Evangelical Theological Seminary, Rosemary Radford Ruether. In recent years Ruether has imported the feminist approach into the discussion of another grave issue of contemporary ethics—ecology. Of course, Ruether is not the only Christian theologian to enter the realm of ecology.[155] What is important about her work is its blending of feminism and environmentalism into what Ruether and others have termed "ecofeminism."[156] By bringing these two strands together, ecofeminism, in Ruether's words, "explores how male domination of women and domination of nature are interconnected, both in cultural ideology and in social structures."[157] Her task as an ecofeminist, in turn, is to "continue the struggle to reconcile justice in human relations with a sustainable life community on earth."[158]

Contemporary environmental ethicists approach their topic through many avenues, many of which are self-consciously religious or theological. As the title of her book *Gaia and God* indicates, Ruether's ecofeminism is representative of those who hark back to the ancient religious idea of Gaia, the Greek earth goddess.[159] Yet the feminist theologian did not discount totally the Christian tradition. Instead Ruether wanted to separate the legacy of those within classical traditions who struggled with injustice and sin from what she called "the toxic waste of sacralized domination."[160]

Nor is Ruether's vision limited to anticipating a new ecological awareness. Viewing all the patterns of destruction that reign in our world as interconnected, her goal was nothing less than a far-reaching reordering of society in all its dimensions. This social reordering would involve a fundamental restructuring of our social relations so that they are changed from systems of "domination/exploitation" to ones of what she called "biophilic [i.e., earth-friendly] mutuality."[161] Such a transformed society would foster "just and loving interrelationship between men and women, between races and nations, between groups presently stratified into social classes, manifest in great disparities of access to the means of life."[162]

If this is its goal, what provides the foundation for an ecofeminist ethic? Ruether sketched several theological themes that could work together to transform our "culture of competitive alienation and domination" into one of "compassionate solidarity."[163]

Appealing to the ancient philosophical concept of the human person as a microcosm or a fragment of the "cosmic soul,"[164] Ruether built from the idea of the fundamental interrelatedness of all things. Hence like many other theological environmentalists, she spoke about our kinship with the entire universe. Yet rather than focusing on the mystical monism that often arises in environmentalist circles, she looked more to the growing scientific awareness of our natural interdependency with all creation. On this basis she proposed an innovative task for human ethics, namely, that of mandating to humans the role of imagining and feeling the suffering of others, as well as of finding ways to bring about mutually enriching cooperation.[165]

Ruether's ecofeminist ethic draws likewise from a disjoining of sin and death. Death, she argued, is natural. Therefore we must replace the erroneous idea that humanity is culpable for human finitude, as well as understandings of salvation that focus on recapturing a supposedly lost immortality. In their place she elevated what she saw as the ancient Hebrew view "that mortality is our natural condition, which we share with all other earth beings, and that redemption is the fullness of life within these finite limits."[166]

Rather than being lodged in human finitude, Ruether declared, sin is fundamentally the distortion of relationship or even "wrong relationship."[167] In sin we absolutize our own rights to life and power rather than seeing our fundamental interrelatedness with others. We misuse our freedom so as "to exploit other humans and the earth and thus to violate the basic relations that sustain life."[168] This leads to the cycle of violence and the construction of systems of control.[169]

Two traditions within Christianity provided Ruether's basic understanding of the divine. These gave rise to the twin motifs of God and Gaia. God, the masculine, transcendent voice of power and law speaking on behalf of the weak,[170] arises from the biblical theme of covenant. This covenantal vision stipulates the place of humans in the cosmos as that of caretakers who neither create nor own the rest of life but are accountable for its welfare to God, who is the divine source of life.[171] The sacramental tradition yields the Gaia motif, which for Ruether is akin to the immanent voice of the divine—"the personal center of the universal process," "the Great Self" or "the Matrix of life"[172]—beckoning us into communion.

For a truly constructive ecofeminist ethic, Ruether concluded, both of these "holy voices"—God's and Gaia's—must be heard.[173] Yet living as we do at the close of an era in which Gaia has long been silenced by God's voice, and given the urgency of the current crisis, there is no doubt which of the two must speak more loudly. In the end, therefore, Ruether's ecofeminist ethic requires the "patient passion" that only Gaia can teach. And the ecofeminist ethic is motivated by neither optimism nor pessimism about the prospects for the future, but by committed love, love for the communities of life in which we participate and above all love for "our common mother, Gaia."[174]

The Ethic of Character

One of the surprising trends in recent years has been the keen interest in virtue and character formation, that is, the renewed quest to develop an ethic of being. Of course the strong focus on the "theological virtues," especially love, present throughout the Christian tradition kept Christian ethicists from abandoning totally all discussion of the cultivation of Christlike character. Yet their tendency throughout the modern era has been to follow the lead of their counterparts in the philosophical tradition and allow questions of conduct and the morality of actions to dominate their reflections.[175] Since the 1970s, however, an abrupt about-face has transpired, constituting a sixth major trajectory of contemporary theological ethics.

Voices from beyond the church. Character, of course, is not an exclusively Christian concern. Indeed the development of an appropriate ethic of being (or virtue ethic) has always been a part of the tradition of philosophical ethics that owes its genesis to ancient Greece. It is not surprising, therefore, that the contemporary retrieval of this interest would not be limited to theological ethicists. Voices from two quarters beyond the church have been especially articulate in calling attention to virtue and character.

A first voice is that of contemporary feminism. In recent years certain feminist thinkers have questioned what they see as a male bias in our understanding of moral reflection and action. Like feminists in other disciplines who critique the academic tradition for universalizing the male experience,[176] these thinkers are convinced that male dominance in the conceptualization of ethics and the ethical life has led to the erroneous assumption that males and females share a similar approach to morality.

Carol Gilligan has been a leading exponent of this enterprise. In her controversial book *In a Different Voice,* Gilligan took to task the widely acclaimed work of Lawrence Kohlberg as typifying the privileging of the male vantage point in moral development theory.[177] She argued that the male outlook approaches ethical questions from a "justice perspective," leading to an ethic of rights and formal reasoning. The female approach, in contrast, tends to view life primarily from a "care perspective," born from a concern with preventing harm, maintaining relationships and providing care. This leads to an ethic of responsibility, compassion or care. In keeping with this discovery, Gilligan offered an alternative to Kohlberg's typology in the form of a six-stage series with three levels of moral development focusing on "care."

Obviously, the elevation of *care* as a—if not the—central ethical concept marks a definite turning to an ethic of being or virtue. This move is readily evident in a book from the pen of Nel Noddings, *Caring: A Feminine Approach to Ethics and Moral Education.*[178] As the book title suggests, Noddings's goal was to develop a type of virtue ethic[179] that builds from[180] and centers on what she saw as the natural, innately feminine—if not universally human—impulse to care[181] and to live in the context of caring relationships.

In constructing her ethic, Noddings consciously bypassed the traditional attempt among philosophical ethicists to develop a set of universalizable moral judgments: "To care is to act not by fixed rule but by affection and regard."[182] Nor did she discuss the rightness or wrongness of acts. Instead, her "ethic of caring locates morality primarily in the pre-act consciousness of the one caring."[183] And she carefully differentiated her proposal from Christian agapism: "There is no command to love nor, indeed, any God to make the commandment. Further, I shall reject the notion of universal love, finding it unattainable in any but the most abstract sense and thus a source of distraction."[184] Instead she set forth a philosophical ethic of care drawing solely from the human—and especially female—experience of caring, believing that this experience provides a sufficient foundation.[185]

In contrast to the feminist call for a new (feminist) virtue ethic in their critique of the philosophical ethical tradition, the highly respected ethicist Alasdair MacIntyre sought to spark a retrieval of that tradition. In his widely read work *After Virtue*,[186] MacIntyre bemoaned the ascendancy of "emotivism" in contemporary culture. By emotivism MacIntyre was referring to "the doctrine that all evaluative judgments and more specifically all moral judgments are *nothing but* expressions of preference, expressions of attitude or feeling, in so far as they are moral or evaluative in character."[187]

To combat this erroneous understanding of the nature of ethical assertions, MacIntyre reintroduced the "lost morality of the past."[188] For him, this older morality is not embodied in the modern quest to determine what are the rules we ought to follow. Instead it lies in the ancient Aristotelian teleology (recaptured by Aquinas) with its desire to answer the question: What sort of person am I to become?[189] Hence MacIntyre called for a return to virtue ethic. But the ethic he envisioned builds from a communal tradition nurtured in "heroic narrative."[190] By an appeal to a higher cosmic order, heroic narrative is able to embed each of the virtues in a harmonious understanding of human life in its totality[191] and to speak about what constitutes the *telos* or good of a human life in its entirety.

MacIntyre is convinced that this kind of virtue ethic is more in keeping with the contemporary discovery of the centrality of narrative to personal identity formation.[192] Each of us lives out a story that runs from our birth to our death, and each of these stories has its own particular meaning. This means that we are accountable for our actions and experiences, and because our stories are interconnected, we are also accountable to each other. The narrative dimension of human life also means that we are all on a lifelong quest for the good life. The virtues, therefore, are those traits that enable us to learn "what more and what else" the good life is.[193]

Stanley Hauerwas: an ethic for a peaceable people. Alasdair MacIntyre, the *philosophical* ethicist, leaves us without a definitive answer to the central ethical question: What is the good life? Instead he envisioned an open-ended search: "the good life . . . is the life spent in seeking for the good life,"[194] especially as a bearer of the tradition of which we are participants.[195] Stanley Hauerwas, the *Christian* ethicist, likewise drew from narrative and tradition. But he sought to say more. The goal of our quest does not lie in some generic human or natural law ethic,[196] for there is no such thing as universal ethics.[197] Our goal, he boldly asserted, is found in the community of faith, as it bears witness to God's peaceable kingdom[198] and as we find our role in God's story.[199]

Before relocating to the divinity school at Duke University, Hauerwas taught at Notre Dame.[200] In this creative context the Methodist thinker launched into his program of drawing out the insights of the emerging narrative thinking for theological ethics. As a result he became, in the opinion of Paul Nelson, "the most significant and influential exponent of narrative among contemporary Christian ethicists."[201]

Hauerwas's program evidences two important similarities to thinkers we have already mentioned. Somewhat similar to McClendon, Hauerwas claimed that ethics must come at the beginning rather than following after theological reflection.[202] With MacIntyre, in turn, Hauerwas shares a fundamental commitment to virtue ethics. For him the central ethical question is not so much "What constitutes a good action?" as "What constitutes a good person?" And, similar to MacIntyre, for Hauerwas the "good person" is related to a narrative community (and hence a tradition).

The foundation for Hauerwas's theological ethic lies in his acceptance of narrative as a "perennial category" by means of which to understand personal identity formation as well as the role of convictions—especially religious convictions—in this process.[203] Hauerwas found an insightful parallel between stories and human living in the world. In both, a narrative account binds together in an intelligible pattern seemingly contingent events and actors.[204] How this operates in a story is obvious, for a story *is* the narrative it tells. But so also the self. The conflicting roles and loyalties that the self confronts during the course of life require a unifying dynamic. And this is exactly what our personal narrative with its intertwining of subplots and characters provides.[205]

This means that rather than being static or given realities, the self and personal character develop through one's personal history.[206] To describe how this happens and thus link personal identity with ethics, the Duke theologian introduced three interrelated concepts—character (or virtue), vision and, of course, narrative.[207] By "character" he meant the cumulative source of human actions,[208] that is, "our deliberate disposition to use a certain range of reasons for our actions rather than others."[209] But life also entails "vision,"[210] for how we view the world and ourselves influences what we are becoming. According to Hauerwas, however, our vision does not arise *sui generis.* It is formed and given content by "the stories through which we have learned to form the story of our lives."[211] By not only describing the world in the present but also indicating how it ought to be changed,[212] narratives challenge our own self-deceptions as well as encourage us.[213]

But where do we encounter the narratives that ought to form us? Here Hauerwas's specifically Christian orientation surfaced. The Christian community embodies the narrative of God at work in history for the sake of the world. The basic task of Christian ethics, therefore, is to assist the church in being just what it is—the church[214]—the people in whom "the narrative of God is lived in a way that makes the kingdom visible."[215] This task, however, requires that the church be a peaceable people, a people of character. Hence Hauerwas declared that the church must become "a community capable of forming people with virtues sufficient to witness to God's truth in the world."[216] And this leads once again to the concept of narrative.

Crucial to becoming this people are the narratives of the community—

the stories of Israel and especially the story of Jesus "into" which we are to live and which are to live through us[217] so that by learning to imitate Jesus we might learn to imitate God.[218] For this reason the Bible is crucial to the Christian community. In it we find the traditions and narratives which form our lives[219] and which provide continual guidance for our corporate and individual lives.[220]

Again the question emerges, however: Why narrative? For the ultimate answer to this question Hauerwas could only return to God's chosen means of self-disclosure. Narrative is central to Christian character because it is the medium through which God has chosen to reveal himself. Because of the narrative character of God's activity and of our own lives, through these narratives we learn the truth about God and ourselves.[221] And as we do so, we are molded into God's peaceable people.

Evangelicals and the Ethical Task

In a sense there is no specifically evangelical motif in contemporary ethics. That is, evangelical ethicists have not coalesced around a single approach to the ethical task. In fact, we could quickly find evangelical thinkers among the proponents of each of the six motifs we have surveyed in the chapter. At the same time, evangelicals do bring something unique to the discussion. For this reason we may view evangelical ethics as a separate, seventh trajectory of thought in contemporary theological ethics.

Carl F. H. Henry: thankful obedience to biblical precepts. In 1947 a young professor at Northern Baptist Theological Seminary in Chicago published a short treatise that exploded like a bombshell in the beleaguered camp of fundamentalism.[222] In *The Uneasy Conscience of Modern Fundamentalism,* Carl F. H. Henry chastised the movement for its lack of a social program. He claimed that its humanitarianism—its benevolent regard for the interests of humankind—had evaporated.[223] Imbued with the lofty conviction that "the redemptive message has implications for all of life," Henry called his colleagues once again to engage the gospel with the world. He envisioned nothing less than the reemergence of "historic Christianity" as a vital "world ideology."[224] True to his own vision, the evangelical thinker did not confine his interests to a "pure," disengaged theology but devoted equal attention to Christian living in the world—to ethics.[225]

Lying at the foundation of Henry's theological ethic is his understanding of divine revelation. The evangelical theologian is convinced that God has both acted in history and has spoken to humankind. And Henry understands this dynamic in basically rational categories. Revelation is rational communication from a rational, transcendent God to rational human beings, who due to our creation in the divine image can come to understand the divine communication despite sin.[226] According to Henry the rational, living God[227] "shares his mind" with us, giving to us the truth about himself and about us.[228] Because God has spoken, revelation is likewise rational, and hence it is propositional, meaningful,[229] objective,[230] conceptual,[231] intelligible and coherent.[232] The repository of this revelation is Scripture. Because the Bible is God speaking to us, Henry asserted, God is its ultimate author. Consequently it is inerrant or totally trustworthy in all that it teaches.

The evangelical theologian offered a succinct summary of his epistemology: "Divine revelation is the source of all truth, the truth of Christianity included; reason is the instrument for recognizing it; Scripture is its verifying principle; logical consistency is a negative test for truth and coherence a subordinate test. The task of Christian theology is to exhibit the content of biblical revelation as an orderly whole."[233]

The implications for ethics of this theological orientation are patently obvious.[234] Like that of every topic of human knowledge, the basis for ethics lies in the objective character of divine revelation found in the Bible, which defines the content of God's will and our human duty.[235] The objectivity of revelation means that ethical norms are objective and hence not dependent on circumstance.[236] As a result we can obtain rational knowledge of ethical standards and need not flounder in a sea of "secular" relativity: "The ethics of the Hebrew-Christian theistic revelation commends itself to logical thought because its coherence avoids the conflicts which lurk in the speculative accounts of the moral claim. It rises above the interior contradictions of secular ethics and provides a new integration of the legitimate elements of the moral situation."[237]

The objectivity of biblical revelation means that the ethical enterprise focuses on discovering the will of God for human living as God has revealed it in the pages of Scripture. Hence Henry's central goal as a Christian ethicist is nothing less than to bring all of life under the divine will as revealed in Scripture. But how does the Bible reveal the divine will?

Although Henry seemed to offer several answers to this question,[238] at the heart of his response is an appeal to the Old Testament concept of the divine covenant with humankind, which elevates biblical law as the expression of the divine will for us.[239] At the center of the biblical law stand the Ten Commandments, which are universally binding on all humankind.[240] But equally important are the teachings of Jesus, especially the Sermon on the Mount, in which our Lord reiterates the divine law set forth in the Old Testament.[241] According to Henry, "The Sermon expresses . . . the only righteousness acceptable to God in this age or in any. As such, the Sermon condemns the man in sin, is fulfilled by Christ's active and passive obedience, and serves as the believer's rule of Christian gratitude in personal relations."[242] As a result the Sermon provides us with guidance "not only in the disposition it intends, but in its precepts and commandments."[243]

Yet Henry is not a pure legalist; he does not understand the law itself as expressing the fullness of God's will for us. Instead, as Jesus' own life displays,[244] our human duty is to love.[245] The precepts of the Bible merely define love or indicate what love actually entails. Against the agapaic ethicists of his day the evangelical thinker asserted: "Love, as the Bible exposits it, is not something as nebulous as moderns would have us think. . . . No believer is left to work out his moral solutions by the principle of love alone. He has some external guidance from Divine revelation. . . . Love is in accord with the biblical ethic when it devotedly seeks to obey fully the Divine commands." Hence Henry concludes, "The content of love must be defined by Divine revelation. . . . What the Bible teaches gives trustworthy direction to love of self, of neighbor, of God."[246] And this biblical teaching is primarily found in the biblical commands, such as the Sermon on the Mount: "The Sermon is an exposition of the deeper implications of the moral law, and hence a statement of the practical way in which *agape* is to work itself out in daily conduct here and now." In the end then Henry elevated obedience to the law, because for him it is the sign of our love and gratitude to the God who has rescued us from sin.[247]

Although his major treatise on ethics bears the title *Christian Personal*

Ethics, Henry's love ethic ingrained in him a concern with social ethics.[248] He believes that Christianity ought to foster social transformation, touching even politics, business and work. The biblical view, he declared, elevates both individual conversion and social justice,[249] which to Henry entails not only ministry to the victims of injustice but also commitment to the task of remedying and eliminating the causes of that injustice.[250] In Henry's estimation fidelity to the social and political implications of the biblical message demands that Christians voice an "authentic challenge to the status quo."[251]

At one fundamental point, however, Henry's social activism differed from the direction advocated by many voices in mainline Protestant circles. Henry maintained that a Christian social ethic begins with the individual: personal spiritual regeneration forms the foundation for social transformation.[252] Consequently he called on the church to avoid attempting to wield direct pressure on government or public agencies. Instead the church ought to look to its individual members "to fulfill their duties as citizens of two worlds."[253]

Oliver O'Donovan: living in the light of the resurrection. Twenty-nine years after Carl Henry published his *Christian Personal Ethics,* Oliver O'Donovan, Regius Professor of Moral and Pastoral Theology in Oxford, England, produced a volume entitled *Resurrection and Moral Order: An Outline for Evangelical Ethics.*[254] As the book's subtitle indicates, its author took up Henry's concern to develop a thoroughly evangelical ethic. While sharing this basic agenda, O'Donovan's approach differs markedly from that of his American predecessor. According to the British evangelical thinker, Christian ethics is evangelical because it arises from the gospel itself. The gospel, with its focus on Christ's death and resurrection, forms the Christian ethic in that it announces a new, objective situation in creation, creates a new subjective situation in the human heart and sets forth the form of the Christian moral life.[255]

According to O'Donovan, the beginning point for Christian ethics lies in an objective reality proclaimed in the gospel. The salvation God achieved in Christ's death and resurrection presupposes and reaffirms the "order of creation." By this phrase the British thinker meant humankind in our context as the ruler of the ordered creation God has made.

Salvation does not end there, however. It leads as well to our destiny, namely, the eschatological fulfillment of the created world in God's kingdom. As a result Christian ethics looks backward and forward. It respects the natural structures of life in the world, while looking forward to their transformation.[256]

For O'Donovan morality is linked to our participation in the created order[257] as those who are aware that Christ's resurrection has not only ushered in God's kingdom but also restored and fulfilled the order of creation. Our hope, therefore, is not that we might be redeemed *from* creation but that *creation* might be redeemed. For this reason O'Donovan's proposal involves a coalescing of a creation ethic with a kingdom ethic.[258]

"Redeemed creation does not merely confront us moral agents," O'Donovan boldly asserted, "but includes us and enables us to participate in it."[259] Thus the objective foundation of ethics is augmented by a subjective dimension. In addition to the objective redemption of the created order, Christian ethics arises out of a subjective reality also proclaimed in the gospel, namely, the presence of the Holy Spirit in the believer and the church.

In typical evangelical fashion O'Donovan described the Spirit as God at work within us confirming and applying God's act in Christ. The Spirit makes redemption a present reality in our lives.[260] And the Spirit evokes our free response as moral agents to this new reality,[261] for he elicits our obedience to Jesus' moral authority as the bearer of God's own authority.[262]

The gospel proclamation of God's renewal of both the world order and the moral agent indicates as well the "form" of the moral life. O'Donovan wrote: "If the gospel tells of agents rendered free before the reality of a redeemed universe, then the form which their agency assumes will correspond *both* to the intelligible order which they confront *and* to the freedom in which they act. The form of the moral life will be that of an *ordered moral field* of action on the one hand, and of an *ordered moral subject* of action on the other."[263]

Like many Christian ethicists, O'Donovan invoked the biblical concept of love at this point. He saw the ordering principle—that which confers unifying order both upon the plurality of a person's actions and upon the acting person—as the ideal of love as taught in Scripture. Love, he argued, is the fulfillment of the moral law as well as the form of the virtues.[264] And love moves us in the eschatological direction marked out by God's saving work in Christ's death and resurrection. Love, which is the true moral life of the Christian community, ultimately entails our participation in the divine life of love, which is the goal of humankind and of the restored creation.[265]

O'Donovan's quest for an "ordered moral field of action"—a unity to the many specific moral actions in which a person engages—led him to acknowledge a role for the moral law. But this law is more than a collection of rules or a catalogue of moral claims. Any such focus on disconnected rules is not true morality but sheer legalism.[266] Instead, by "moral law" O'Donovan meant a comprehensive moral viewpoint,[267] a unified expression of the order of the created reality in which we act. This moral viewpoint brings order into our field of action by showing the relationship among the situations we face.[268] For the evangelical thinker the Bible guides us toward such a comprehensive moral viewpoint,[269] not by providing a list of commands and prohibitions but by leading us to the supreme principle of order that unifies the obligations of the moral law—the double command to love.[270]

Because the life of love unifies the virtues, love likewise provides the ordering principle for the moral subject.[271] But although in this manner love unites an ethic of doing with an ethic of being, O'Donovan clearly gives priority to doing. In his estimation a person's character is known only through his or her acts.[272] Consequently he concluded that "knowledge of the agent's character . . . cannot contribute to *deliberative* moral thought. It contributes to *evaluative* moral thought only because that kind of moral reflection supposes a closed narrative of actions from which the character has already emerged clearly into view, so that each element in the narrative can be interpreted in the light of the whole."[273] But because prior to death the narrative of one's acts is never complete, we can make only provisional evaluative statements about an agent's character.

What, then, is the function of an ethic of character? O'Donovan offered a unique answer that returned him to his beginning point in the gospel: "Thought about moral character plays a central role in repentance. . . . The observer's distance, which removes us from the deliberative situation, can . . . give us a perspective from which to review our own past lives. We can form judgments . . . on what kind of character our history has disclosed, and these, rather than judgments on particular acts, are what will make us feel most acutely the need of salvation."[274]

Lines of Convergence in Contemporary Theological Ethics

As we noted at the beginning of this chapter, a deep chasm divides contemporary Christian ethicists. Despite a shared legacy that includes luminaries such as Augustine, Aquinas and Luther, Christian thinkers continue to differ with each other about the focus of the moral quest. We cannot simply overlook the foundational divergence separating ethicists like Barth and Henry, for example, from, say, Rauschenbusch and Ruether. At the same time, however, our study also indicates that certain lines of convergence are emerging. And these suggest some of the themes that ought to inform our construction of a Christian ethic for our day. Three interrelated dimensions are especially important in setting the stage for our subsequent discussion.

First, Christian ethics in the last hundred years has shown a marked movement from "doing" to "being." This convergence is manifested, for example, in the growing rejection of the assumption (which provided much of the impulse for the Social Gospel) that social action is the single—or even the central—concern of Christian ethics in favor of a renewed emphasis on the foundational importance of developing the inner life. This shift is paralleled by a corresponding rethinking of Christian discipleship. For many ethicists, more significant than the quest to follow Jesus' own example is the concern to exemplify Christlike character (e.g., McClendon).

Second, in the last hundred years Christian ethics has displayed a marked shift away from the focus on the individual moral actor to a relational ethic. Christian ethicists (including evangelical thinkers such as Henry) are increasingly disinclined to see morality solely as a matter of personal conduct, or the goal of ethical reflection as growth in "personal holiness," understood as increasing conformity in conduct to a set of rules. Instead a growing number view the moral life as entailing right relationships, leading to genuine concern for the well-being of others (e.g., Gutiérrez) and even all creation (e.g., Ruether).

Connected to this development is a corresponding shift away from the emphasis on ethics as the fulfillment of one's duty and toward a rediscovery of the centrality of love to the ethical life (e.g., Ramsey). The convergence on a relational ethic is paralleled by a growing interest in the role of communities in moral development, both as transmitters of ethical traditions as well as the location of the ethical life itself (e.g., Hauerwas).

Finally, and paralleling the other two, the last hundred years have witnessed a shift away from the present as the focus of ethical inquiry toward an orientation that draws from the goal of human existence. A growing number of ethicists no longer see the task of ethical discourse as determining the proper response to ethical quandaries the moral agent faces in the here and now. Instead they see their task as drawing from a vision of who we are to become and thereby setting forth an understanding of the moral quest itself. This shift is evident, for example, in the resurgence of interest in the older Aristotelian concept of ethics as the realization of our human *telos* (e.g., MacIntyre). But it is more forcefully displayed among Christian thinkers who look to the eschaton and view ethics as living in the light of God's glorious future (e.g., O'Donovan).

Insofar as such themes are in keeping with divine revelation in Scripture, they suggest that the Christian ethic is an eschatological ethic of transformation. Hence our moral quest begins with the vision of God's eternal purposes for all creation, and it involves the reordering of ourselves and the world we inhabit in the light of that glorious vision. To the construction of such an ethic we now turn our attention.

Chapter 6

CHRISTIAN ETHICS & THE CONTEMPORARY CONTEXT

Paul then stood up in the meeting of the Areopagus and said: "Men of Athens! I see that in every way you are very religious. For as I walked around and looked carefully at your objects of worship, I even found an altar with this inscription: TO AN UNKNOWN GOD. *Now what you worship as something unknown I am going to proclaim to you."*
(ACTS 17:22-23)

By all outward appearances the chief executive officer of the giant savings and loan association was a model citizen. He made generous gifts to worthwhile causes such as the work of Mother Teresa. He was an ardent crusader in social issues, including the fight against abortion and pornography.

Above all he "cared for" his family, especially their financial needs. So prominent were his relatives on the corporation's payroll that during the 1980s the family took home some $34 million for their services. His oldest son was one such beneficiary of his position. Although a college dropout with little experience, the young man ascended to the helm of the business, enjoying annual reimbursement in the $1 million range.

The CEO's ardent conservative political loyalties did not prevent him from donating to the campaigns of those whose ideology differed from his own. One powerful liberal U.S. senator was the special benefactor of his financial benevolence. When asked whether his generous contributions went to buy influence, he publicly replied, "I want to say in the most forceful way I can: I certainly hope so."[1]

* * *

Our task in this chapter is to launch the process of carving out an understanding of the Christian ethic in the context of the wider ethical discussion that has been the focus of our attention throughout the first five chapters. The goal of our reflections is to discover what a truly biblical vision of the ethical life entails within the contemporary context. En route to this goal we will need to address several crucial issues, some of which have surfaced in our discussion so far.

We begin the constructive process by looking more closely at the situation in which we now seek to live as ethical Christians and to proclaim our Christian ethic. This context is characterized above all by a reemerging public interest in ethics, which in turn is leading to the attempt to develop a community-based ethic of being.

This contemporary concern will provide a jumping-off point for our specifically Christian proposal. But for it to function in this manner we must show in what sense the human moral quest provides a connecting point for the Christian ethical vision. In particular we will indicate that despite the human-centeredness of all general ethics, the human moral quest is essentially the search for the will of God, and therefore the Christian ethic marks the transformation of general ethics. More specifically, naturalism, with its appeal to creation, reemerges at this point as an appropriate bridge to the Christian moral vision, rooted as it is in the new creation.

With this connection in place, we will round out our discussion by showing how the Christian ethic fulfills the contemporary quest for a community-based ethic of being. Doing so, however, leads us beyond the interface between Christian ethics and philosophical ethics. We must consider other communitarian ethical systems, specifically, the religious ethical traditions. Consequently the chapter concludes with an appeal to the

Christian vision of God as triune as the basis for our affirmation of the uniqueness of the Christian ethic.

The Contemporary Context of Christian Ethics

As the trajectories sketched in chapter five suggest, Christians today engage in ethical reflection and discourse in the midst of a changing landscape. Many observers have concluded that we are living in a time of transition, that a new intellectual and cultural ethos is emerging in society. This new social situation commonly bears the label *postmodern.* If this is the case—if we are living in a postmodern world—then our task is to think through the Christian ethic in a manner that takes seriously the challenges the new reality brings our way.

Two aspects of that changing landscape are most significant as shapers of the ethical climate of postmodernism: the reemergence of public interest in ethics, which is leading to a restructuring of the ethical quest.

The reemerging public interest in ethics. We appear to have entered the age of ethics. People throughout our society have grown acutely aware of the ethical dimensions of contemporary life and consequently have become increasingly willing to speak the language of ethics. Hence Christian moralists are not the only ones today who would find questionable the attitudes and actions of the CEO in our opening narrative. Many people who claim no connection to Christianity would likewise label such conduct blatantly unethical.

The emergence of ethics as a concern throughout society is evidenced by front-page news items that repeatedly deal with ethical problems or situations that carry ethical overtones. The concern for ethics has also invaded the political realm. In fact during election campaigns the quest to gain the "ethical high ground" over one's opponents is very noticeable.

The blossoming of ethical concern is likewise evident in the renewed interest in ethics as a field of inquiry. We are witnessing a renaissance of the classical study of ethics. More importantly, ethics has invaded a variety of divisions of the academic curriculum. Entire new specialties have grown up almost overnight. Today medical ethics, business ethics, environmental ethics and legal ethics are not only serious endeavors but required curricular components in respected professional schools across the land. The growing interest in reflecting on the moral issues that surround these professions has produced new areas of specialization and new vocational opportunities. These burgeoning fields have made ethics a "growth industry."

Underlying the mushrooming interest in the academic study of the ethical disciplines is a broadly based realization that ethics has gained a new sense of urgency. Wearing his prognosticator hat for the New Year's weekend edition of *The Vancouver Sun,* columnist Douglas Todd joined many other voices in predicting that in the coming year (1995) the public ethical discussion would "explode." This discussion, he predicted, would be fueled by the belief that our worsening situation requires concerted action: "More than four out of five North Americans believe a decline in morals is the continent's gravest problem and that ethics should be taught in schools."

Why a specifically *public* discussion? According to Todd, the old guardians of morality have lost credibility, a situation that casts us on our own to hammer out a new ethic: "Most people no longer believe a single religious institution can be the final authority on morality. So discussion of ethics will shift more to the wider, public domain." And what shape will this discussion take? Todd answered: "Through thousands of courses, conferences, books, newspaper columns, government hearings and meetings, we'll struggle over values."[2]

The concern for a community-based ethic of being. The recent resurgence of public interest in ethics has been paralleled by a reconsideration of the actual goal of the human ethical quest. In our day both professional and lay ethicists have grown increasingly uncomfortable with the prospect of continuing to engage in the ethical task in the manner their immediate predecessors pursued. Douglas Todd's remark "We'll struggle over values" bears witness to the nature of this transition. The renewed interest in ethical reflection has produced a reconceptualizing of the ethical task, which has come on the heels of the phenomenal upheaval in ethical thinking that occurred throughout the twentieth century.

A crucial dimension of this shift involves the move from the focus on "doing" that dominated Western ethical discourse during the modern era to a concern for "being."[3] As we noted in chapter five, many contemporary ethicists today—as represented by secular voices, including Nel Noddings and Alasdair MacIntyre, and by religious figures such as

Stanley Hauerwas—no longer view the rightness or wrongness of specific actions as the central feature of the ethical task. Instead an increasing number of ethicists are concerned about character ideals (or virtues) such as friendship and cooperation, or they elevate the quest for "values" as the central ethical concern. In keeping with this shift, J. Philip Wogaman recently declared, "The question is, where do we *ultimately* get our values?" He then explained: "We do not have a basis for making ethical judgments until we can ground our conception of the good and of moral obligation on an ultimate framework of valuation."[4]

Paralleling this ethical revisioning is the advent of a new quest for spirituality. In the modern era people expunged the remnants of the supernatural from their worldview and focused attention on the scientific method as the means to unlocking nature's secrets. At the same time they threw themselves into the enjoyment of an ever-rising "standard of living," understood, of course, strictly in economic terms. But in recent years the children of the Enlightenment have launched a search for the key that can unlock the door to *spiritual* vitality and power. People today rush from guru to guru in an attempt to learn how best to develop their own inner person. This search includes the goals of greater fortitude, higher virtue, personal character formation and enhanced relationships with others. Like the new ethical mood, the new moral quest focuses on "being" rather than "doing."

The transition from doing to being has paralleled the philosophical shift away from the Enlightenment focus on knowledge understood as dispassionate, objective certainty. In the eighteenth century Immanuel Kant suggested that humans ask three central questions: What can I know? What should I do? And what can I hope for?[5] Enlightenment ethics sought to answer the second question—the question of the ethical life—on the basis of a prior answer to the first. Thinkers today are no longer sure that this method is feasible. For an alternative many are looking to the third question, seeing in it a possible foundation for searching out the answers to the question of ethics. And contrary to what we might expect, this proposal is not the exclusive domain of religious ethicists but is gaining adherents among secular thinkers as well.

Robert Kane provides a case in point. As a chastened secularist he declared, "We simply do not know enough to ground ethics necessarily in human reason and knowledge alone; and centuries of failure in trying to do so have led many to relativism, skepticism, and nihilism."[6] Rephrasing Kant's third question to read "What should we aspire to?" Kane turned to the realm of human aspiration for the guiding principles of a new, postmodern ethic. For his vision of the ethical life he drew from the Latin root of the term. In that "aspiration" signifies a "going outward of the spirit," Kane proposed the image of "our spirits reaching beyond the finite perspectives we inhabit toward an objective reality and objective worth that are always only partly revealed to us."[7] He explained: "By living in certain ways, by loving and seeking excellences in our various practices and traditions, cultures and ways of life, we may 'embody the truth' in the sense of attaining objective worth, without being sure of having attained it."[8]

With the new interest in spirituality the center of ethics is shifting away from the individual actor and the quest for the one true ethical theory. These are being replaced by a new focus on the community in the midst of which, and according to the ideals of which, personal character finds its reference point. In the end, the newer voices assert, ethical judgments arise from and must be articulated in accordance with the belief structures of the community in which a person lives. As Wayne Meeks remarked poignantly, "Making morals means making community."[9] Why? According to Meeks, "Individuals do not become moral agents except in the relationships, the transactions, the habits and reinforcements, the special uses of language and gesture that together constitute life in community."[10]

In this manner the current restructuring of ethics pierces to the very heart of the modern "decisionist" ethic, with its focus on doing. The ethic of doing, communitarian thinkers argue, presupposes a basically Enlightenment view that understands the human person as a morally empty vessel waiting to be filled through the acts in which he or she chooses to engage. Communitarian ethicists repudiate this anthropology in favor of a community-based understanding of the moral life. They argue that personal identity and character do not first emerge as the product of choices we make as autonomous agents but actually precede our acts. The Mennonite thinker Harry Huebner stated the point sharply: "When we engage in moral activity, we act on the basis of our perceptions and our beliefs. We act on the basis of who we are as social/moral beings and on the basis of the characters into which our communities/families have shaped us."[11]

Communitarians do not deny the importance of the language of obligation. Instead their concern is that such language find its proper ground. In their thinking obligation is not primarily connected to the individual agent nor to the corollary concept of inherent individual rights. Instead obligation flows out of a person's presence in a community and builds from the implications of this presence for being a person of character. Although reflecting a specifically Christian perspective, Huebner's words nevertheless articulate the more general communitarian view: "If obligation is a community matter, that is, if what we ought to do derives from the kind of people we have committed ourselves to be . . . then what we do or do not do is not determined by the rights we and others as individuals have or do not have. Rather, our moral obligation then comes from the character of the community which we have given shaping power over us. Then what we do does not have its origin in what we can legitimately claim, but in what we have been graciously given and in turn are inspired to give."[12]

In a multicultural context the focus on a community-based ethic leads to the new ethical pluralism of the postmodern ethos. In a situation in which multiple communities exist side by side, ethical discourse becomes a discussion of the moral practices of differing communities. The underlying assumption, of course, is that what appears wrong from one vantage point, when viewed from within the community that practices the act, may actually be right.

An episode of *Star Trek: The Next Generation* provides an especially illuminating illustration of this tendency. An accident has robbed Lieutenant Worf of the use of his legs, which in the Klingon culture means he is as good as dead. In keeping with his cultural mores, Worf has decided to end his life. And he has asked the first officer aboard the *Enterprise,* Will Riker—who is also his friend—to assist him in the death ritual. Riker, of course, is loath to do so. According to his moral framework this constitutes a reprehensible act of suicide. Riker goes to his own commanding officer, the ship captain Jean-Luc Picard, for advice. In the conversation that ensues, the good captain seeks to help his second in command view the situation from Worf's perspective within the context of the Klingon community with its particular set of beliefs, mores and rituals. What appears immoral to Riker, given his embeddedness in one particular moral community, is perfectly acceptable to the Klingon Worf.

Do postmodern ethicists offer any way whereby we might move beyond the impasse posed by competing moral communities? Is there anything that transcends the multiplicity of social groups that exist side by side in our global village and thereby can bring humans from differing communities together? The *Star Trek* episode presented one commonly presented postmodern response: "friendship." Picard appeals to Riker to remember that he is Worf's friend and to do whatever act is most in accordance with the ideal of friendship.

Douglas Todd concluded the essay I cited earlier by invoking a similar postmodern solution to the problem of multiculturalism. He wrote, "We'll debate everything from euthanasia to sexuality, poverty to business, in an effort to hammer out shared values that will enhance neighbourliness and, let's hope, the common good." With these words Todd inadvertently appealed to the one goal that all societies share. He used the word *neighbourliness* to characterize that common goal.

We could draw Picard's advice and Todd's prognosis together by invoking the postmodern buzzword *community.* As terms like *neighborliness* and *friendship* suggest, all communities seek to foster a common goal—*community.* They desire that humans live together in a spirit of neighborliness and friendship. This goal is universal even though the specific mores that determine what exactly community, neighborliness and friendship are may be culturally determined.

These two characteristics of the contemporary social ethos—the renewed interest in the ethical quest and the focus on a community-based ethic of being—provide the context in which we must set forth an appropriate understanding of the Christian ethic. En route to our goal we must tackle the foundational questions that these aspects of our situation introduce.

Christian Ethics and the Human Ethical Quest

The resurgence in interest in ethical discourse and the quest for an overarching ethic of community (or neighborliness) raises again a foundational question that has followed us throughout the pages of this book. Viewed from the Christian perspective ethics may be defined as the study of the ethical life as informed by the Bible. But the ethical life is not an exclusively Christian concern. Although the Christian ethic may offer a unique perspective on what it means to live ethically, the search for a truly appropriate human ethic has stood at the center of a long and robust public debate since the days of the ancient Greek philosophers, and it comprises a crucial focus of every major religious tradition. We must ask, therefore, What is the connection—if any—between the Christian ethic, which we claim arises out of God's self-disclosure in Scripture, and the seemingly universal human ethical quest so evident in the broader discussions of our day?[13]

Our sketch of the paradigmatic proposals in the Christian tradition (chapter four), as well as our outline of developments in the twentieth century (chapter five), indicated that this question has been a perennial concern of Christian thinkers. They have repeatedly explored the connection between the specifically Christian approach to ethics and the philosophical tradition that devises a purportedly natural—or general—ethic. Like our forebears, therefore, we must seek to determine what "Athens" indeed does have to do with "Jerusalem."

The ethical quest as a universal phenomenon. The beginning point for our constructive engagement with this question lies in the universal sense of oughtness that seems to characterize human existence. This experience forms a bridge linking the concerns of the philosophical ethicists to the Christian ethic.

Ethicists in the modern era have repeatedly noted the presence in humans of what they describe as a sense of "oughtness."[14] These thinkers theorize that we all are burdened with an inescapable sense that we are called to live "morally." We sense that our actions have ethical importance, that they are either "good" or "bad," "right" or "wrong." Try as we will, we simply cannot avoid this situation. This sense of being conditioned by the category of the moral, this "moral conditionedness," ethicists have postulated, is a universal human phenomenon. In short, to be human means to be a moral creature.[15]

Ethicists often note further that the phenomenon of moral conditionedness is closely connected to the systems of laws, customs and mores humans develop in their social contexts. The specific social sanctions themselves differ from society to society and from culture to culture, of course, for despite certain similarities, there is no single, universal human code of conduct.[16] Nevertheless the phenomenon of morality is universal. Every society seeks to regulate human interaction through the devising of moral strictures, so as to promote a culturally agreed-upon understanding of proper interpersonal relations. These varying moral codes and social mores bear witness to a sense of oughtness that underlies them all. Indeed the differing codes of ethics constitute the variegated human response to the common sense of moral conditionedness.

As the British ethicist N. H. G. Robinson noted, "Behind all the diversity, unless I am mistaken, there is, there must be an objective and original claim which imposes upon man the sense of 'ought' and so some sense of human dignity and social justice. This claim is not itself, however, an explicit system of specific moral laws. Such a system arises at a logically subsequent stage as, in his creative response to this original claim, man seeks to articulate a moral code by which to live."[17]

This observation carries a far-reaching implication. Because a universal sense of moral conditionedness precedes and lies behind the construction of the variety of systems of morality found in human societies, this sense—which drives the human ethical quest—forms the foundation for what we have referred to as a "general" or "natural" ethic. But it is precisely at this point that our foundational question emerges: What is the relationship of this quest to the Christian ethic, which we claim is grounded in divine revelation? Or to formulate the issue more specifically, what is the relationship between the attempt to construct a proper response to our moral conditionedness with the biblical focus on living as a special people in covenant with the God of the salvation narrative?

In chapter four we pinpointed three major answers to this question present in the Christian tradition.[18] One alternative suggests that the ethic disclosed in the biblical revelation reframes what is found in a different form in the great tradition of philosophical ethics. A second possibility is to view the human response to the sense of moral conditionedness as helpful and valid as far as it goes or within its own sphere, while acknowledging it as insufficient and hence in need of the additional truth of Christian revelation. Finally, we might simply reject the human ethical quest as pure idolatry, as a sign of our destitute need for the revealed ethic found exclusively in the Bible.

Which of these alternatives—if any—provides the proper approach to the human ethical quest? To reach an answer, we must look more closely at the phenomenon of general ethics, appraising it from a Christian perspective.

General ethics and the will of God. At first sight it would seem that Christians ought to find much in general ethics to affirm. It is only right that humans be concerned about cultural mores, moral norms, standards of conduct or codes of ethics. These constitute the variegated human response to the sense of moral conditionedness we all share.

Our Christian faith offers a theological foundation for such a positive appraisal in the conception of God as Will. We firmly believe that the ultimate origin of all moral distinctions lies in nothing else than the will of God. Ultimately all human ethical concern arises solely from a theological foundation, specifically, the conception of God as moral, that is, as a God who has "preferences." The God we know and affirm wills certain things and abhors others. This God calls all humans, in turn, to align themselves with the divine will. Our desire ought to be that God's will be done "on earth as it is in heaven," to allude to the words of the Lord's Prayer.

At the heart of the Christian doctrine of creation is the idea that the universe exists by the will of God. The Hebrew Scriptures present the act of creation in a manner similar to a monarch issuing commands. This is evident in the creation account in Genesis 1. At each stage in the creation process, the narrator declares, "And God said . . . and it was so" (Gen 1:3, 6, 9, 14-15, 20, 24). God speaks, and the power of the divine will brings creation into existence.

This suggests that the divine will is not some "extra item" added to the world. God's will does not collide with the world from beyond, as if it were an externally imposed, alien demand having no connection with the created realm. On the contrary the will of God lies at the very foundation of the world, for the world exists solely by the divine will. As the worshipers in the heavenly court in the seer's vision put it, "You are worthy, our Lord and God, to receive glory and honor and power, for you created all things, and by your will they were created and have their being" (Rev 4:11).[19]

Viewed from the biblical perspective, therefore, existence and ethics are not two separate concerns. Instead they are integrally connected. The ethical life involves living according to the divine will that provides the foundation of our very being as God's creatures populating God's universe.

On this basis we can conclude that the sense of moral obligation lying behind all human ethical systems is nothing less than the impact of the divine will upon human life. The sense of moral conditionedness arises because we exist by the will of God. And this divine will—the divine preference—forms the foundation for morality. Our existence as the product of the divine will leads to the sense of moral obligation which drives the seemingly natural human ethical quest. Human moral codes, in turn, stand as valiant attempts to take seriously the seemingly preconscious and often unacknowledged sense of the divine will that both calls all things into existence and calls humans to account as moral creatures.

This connection forges the link between Christian ethics and general ethics. Their common genesis in the divine will means that the revealed ethic of the Christian faith and the general ethic of the philosophers occupy the same ground and traverse the same territory. The Christian ethicist and the philosopher are ultimately concerned about the same thing, namely, the proper human response to God's claim on our lives or the determination of what constitutes living according to the divine will. Whether or not they are consciously aware of it, whenever people engage in ethical reflection they are in fact seeking to determine God's intention for human life and conduct. They are ultimately searching for the answer to the fundamental questions of theological ethics: What does God will that we be and do? And how should we live as those who exist by God's own will?

The "good" and the divine will. At first glance, however, it may appear that we have stretched the connection too far. In chapter one we noted that philosophical ethics is largely interested in the category of the good, for it involves basically the search for goodness. Consequently any positive appraisal of philosophical ethics requires that we be able to provide a link between the philosophical concept of the "good"—together with the attendant quest for the good—and the Christian category of the "will of God." On what basis can we assert that the philosophical discovery of the good is in fact related to the divine will?

The answer to our query draws from a distinction between what is (ontology) and how we come to know what is (epistemology).[20] From the perspective of ontology what Christian ethicists denote as "the will of God" precedes, or is foundational to, what the philosophers speak of as "the good." Goodness is entirely dependent upon and derived from the divine will. Nevertheless the actual way in which a person comes to know the good and the divine will may occur in the opposite order. Knowledge of goodness may in fact come before awareness of God's will. A person may obtain knowledge about what is the good before acknowledging that the good is in fact the content of God's will.

This epistemological reversal does not alter the truth that God's will is the foundation for all goodness and forms the goal of the human quest for the good. Even when a person's first grasp of the divine will comes indirectly—through the quest to determine the true nature of goodness or the good life (i.e., philosophical ethics)—the fact remains that what he or she is actually seeking and even coming to know is nothing else but the will of God (which is the explicit topic of Christian ethics).

Just as Paul drew from the pagan poets of Athens to address the quest for the unknown god, so also Christians can confidently conclude that lying at the foundation of the quest for goodness displayed in philosophical ethics is the will of the God revealed in Jesus of Nazareth. Consequently we can affirm the sincere human search for the good, for we know that the quest for goodness is nothing less than the search for the divine will.

The anthropocentricity of general ethics. Despite this fundamentally positive evaluation of general ethics, we must also express a grave reservation about the philosophical ethical enterprise. General ethics is flawed by an all-pervasive defect, namely, its "anthropocentricity" or fundamental human-centeredness. James Gustafson pinpointed the problem: "The dominant strand of Western ethics . . . argues that the material considerations for morality are to be derived from purely human points of reference. In terms of good or value the question is, usually, What is good for man? or What is of value to human beings?"[21]

This anthropocentric orientation is noticeable in two aspects integral to the philosophical approach. First, general ethics is anthropocentric in that it presupposes a human-centered understanding of the distinguishing characteristic of the human person. Endemic to the philosophical tradition is the tendency to operate from an anthropocentric, rather than a theological, anthropology. Because it seeks to elaborate whatever ethical system can be discovered through the use of human reason, general ethics assumes that the distinguishing characteristic of the human person lies in some dimension of human existence (e.g., the experience of being moral agents) or in some power that humans supposedly possess (such as rationality).

As we noted in chapter two, the elevation of reason as the mark of humanness was especially evident in the Greek philosophical tradition which has been so influential on Western ethics. Plato, for example, elevated the rational when he spoke of the goal of human existence as the contemplation of eternal forms. Aristotle in turn defined the human person as the rational animal. Although the centrality of reason remained, much of the ethical thinking in the Enlightenment—including Kant's philosophical ethic[22]—was generated by the parallel focus on human moral agency.

In contrast to the philosophical approach, Christian ethics does not start from the assumption that the distinguishing characteristic of the human person consists in our rationality. Nor does our essential humanness lie ultimately in our experience of being moral agents. Instead the definitive human characteristic lies in a relationship for which we were created, namely, community or fellowship with God. To use the language of the Hebrew Scriptures, we are to be God's covenant partners (see chapter three). This divine desire to enter into covenant with us even stands at the foundation of our status as morally conditioned beings.

From the Christian perspective, therefore, the ethical life does not arise out of any innate human characteristic or any integral aspect of our existence. Instead its genesis lies in our divinely given purpose as those called to live in the presence of, and responsible to, God. The Christian message is that God created us with a destiny, with a goal for our existence, namely, that we enjoy a special covenantal relationship with the covenanting God, that we live in fellowship with our Maker. Our creation by God with a special destiny is what marks us as ethically responsible.

A second aspect of the anthropocentricity of general ethics is its human-centered understanding of the basis and goal of the ethical enterprise. The philosophical approach begins and ends with the human person, the self. The foundational presupposition of every natural ethic is the reality of the human person. This is the case whether the focus be human nature, the human condition or a specific understanding of some supposedly innate human *telos.* In the same way the objective or goal of every natural ethical system tends to be the attempt to foster the actualization of our essential nature, the working out of our condition or the attainment of a perceived innate *telos.*

Aristotle's eudaemonian ethic of self-realization forms a striking example of the anthropocentricity of philosophical ethics. As we saw in chapter two, at the foundation of the Greek philosopher's ethical reflection was the quest to determine the *telos* of the human person, which Aristotle concluded is "well-being" ("living and faring well"). The ethical life, in turn, is the attempt to achieve this *telos,* that is, to promote personal (and social) well-being.

By beginning and ending with the self, the enterprise of philosophical ethics seeks to assist the self in becoming "better." To this end general ethics explores what it means to be "good," and applied ethics, in turn, seeks to assist us in fulfilling the universal human goal of becoming a good person.

The Christian ethic, however, departs radically from this focus on the self with its attendant agenda of making human beings "good." By its very nature Christian ethics must begin and end with God. It finds both the basis and the goal of ethical living in God. Christian ethical reflection draws from a biblical understanding of what God is like and what God's purposes are. Hence its concern is the discovery of the divine will. The purpose of such deliberation is to advance the ways of God in the world, so that God may thereby be glorified.

In short, whereas general ethics is necessarily anthropocentric, Christian ethics must be thoroughly theocentric.[23] This foundational distinction requires that a movement from philosophical to Christian ethics be accompanied by a corresponding, radical rethinking of the nature of ethics. As James Gustafson declared in his adamant call for a theocentric ethic, "Theocentric ethics could defend the view that the material considerations of moral life are almost totally related to what is good for us, what is right in person-to-person relations. One would be able so to restrict the considerations of ethics if the Deity were for man above all other things. But if the Deity is not bound to our judgments about what is in our interests, then theological ethics is radically altered. It may no longer be ethics at all in the traditional sense of Western culture and Christianity."[24]

The Christian transformation of the ethical quest. Our deliberations to this point have led us to a yes/no response to general ethics. Understood from a Christian perspective, its search for the good is ultimately the quest for the divine will and therefore is laudable. Yet the human moral quest erroneously begins and ends with the human person. Where does this leave us in our pursuit of the relation between the revealed Christian ethic and the philosophical tradition? And how can we articulate the Christian moral vision in the contemporary context? Is there a position in between the wholesale rejection of the ethical search of people around us and the simple embracing of whatever results from that search?

In a word our answer to these questions is "transformation." Christian ethics marks the *redemption of,*[25] or perhaps better stated, the *transformation of,* natural ethics. The Christian ethic is able to affirm, while not becoming captivated by general ethics, because it carries transformational power. The Christian moral vision transforms general ethics in that it refocuses the universal human ethical quest.

To understand the transformational role of the Christian ethic we must state again the biblical vision of God's central goal for human existence. According to the Bible the highest purpose of life is community—fellowship with God through Christ and hence fellowship with others, as well as with all creation. Christian ethics, in turn, is the exploration of the implications of this divine purpose for our understanding of the ethical life. By engaging in such reflection, Christian ethics redirects our eyes away from the self so that we might focus on God. Hence it redirects the human ethical quest, raising it above the anthropocentric preoccupation with the self to the theocentric concern for God and the divine will as revealed in Jesus Christ.

In the transformative process Christian ethics does not depreciate or set aside the moral aspirations of human beings. Instead it reorients the human quest for the good by refocusing our ethical vision. The Christian ethic draws our gaze away from the self (which can only lead us into an ethical cul-de-sac) and points our eyes toward the transcendent foundation of our quest. By placing our "natural" human aspirations on their only sure foundation and directing them toward their only proper goal—the God revealed in Jesus Christ—Christian ethics fulfills these ethical aspirations.

In transforming our human ethical aspirations, the Christian ethic unifies the otherwise disjointed field of philosophical ethics. In chapter one we noted how ethical systems generally divide into two basic types—those with a focus on actions and those that elevate virtues or character. We saw likewise that traditionally the philosophical discussion has led to a division of the ethical life into a quest for the right (or duty) and the pursuit of the good (or virtue).

By redirecting our vision toward the God revealed in Christ, Christian ethics resolves the tension between an ethic of doing and an ethic of being. It overcomes the fragmentation of general ethics into a set of duties and a set of virtues. By pointing to Christ as the foundation of the ethical life, Christian ethics shows that moral obligation and virtuous living are united, fulfilled and completed in the Christian ethic of love, for love encompasses both act and character. Love is both something we do—we act lovingly—and a set disposition or dimension of our character—we love.

The Christian vision, therefore, is neither a life of slavish devotion to duty nor the attempt to cultivate the proper set of virtues. Instead the ethical life emerges as we desire to be transformed according to the image of Christ. For the Christian the Lord Jesus Christ—and neither a list of virtues nor a delineation of duties—is the focus of the ethical life.

Paul seems to have understood this distinction. When offering that great list of Christian virtues—"But the fruit of the Spirit is love, joy, peace, patience, kindness, goodness, faithfulness, gentleness and self-control" (Gal 5:22-23)—the apostle does not split the ideal character into a series of independent traits. He does not present these virtues in the form of a checklist, a series of items that we can tick off one at a time. On the contrary, Paul treats them as a unity, as is evident from his use of the collective singular term *fruit* that focuses on the inner unity of the nine items he lists.[26] Together these traits constitute the *fruit* of the Spirit, "the lifestyle of those who are indwelt and energized by the Spirit," to cite

F. F. Bruce's description.[27] This composite fruit is nothing less than Christ's own character made present in us through the indwelling of his own Spirit.

The Christian transformation of general ethics also entails lifting the standards of morality above the anthropocentric level to their true source—God. Every anthropocentric ethic suffers from the loss of a transcendent reference point from which to derive its conception of the ethical life. Indeed, for its understanding of the good no general ethic can appeal beyond the human realm, whether this be the ideal solitary person or the ideal corporate society. Nor can any such ethic draw from anything higher than the specifically human for the meaning of ethical concepts such as love or justice. Thus if we operate within the confines of general ethics, our court of appeal can rise no higher than the human person or human society for the content of ethical ideals, including what it means to act justly or even to love one's neighbor.

In the Christian ethic, in contrast, the human does not serve as the ideal point of reference. On the contrary the ultimate court of appeal for the ethical life lies beyond the human. It is nothing less than the divine nature as embodied in the narrative of God's actions toward humankind. As a result central ethical concepts such as justice and love find their definition from the biblical story of God acting in human history, which reveals God's own character.

Jesus' words enjoining his disciples to love their enemies as well as their friends offer a clear example of this appeal to the ways of the God of the biblical narrative. In this situation, our Lord based his teaching in the way his heavenly Father acts: "You have heard that it was said, 'Love your neighbor and hate your enemy.' But I tell you: Love your enemies and pray for those who persecute you, that you may be sons of your Father in heaven. He causes his sun to rise on the evil and the good, and sends rain on the righteous and the unrighteous. . . . Be perfect, therefore, as your heavenly Father is perfect" (Mt 5:43-48).

The appeal to God and God's character as the foundation for human morality carries another implication. It undercuts any attempt to ground ethics solely on legalistic strictures. While the Christian ethic does not deny the importance of laws, its focus lies elsewhere. The Christian ethic places the emphasis on the obedience to laws, even human laws, found in many human ethical systems within a higher context. Paul capsulized this radical perspective when he set forth the Christian dictum: "So . . . whatever you do, do it all for the glory of God" (1 Cor 10:31).

From naturalism to a Christian ethic. The discussion in chapter one of ethics as a general human phenomenon netted the conclusion that the philosophical approach invariably leads to a cul-de-sac. Then followed a hint as to what may serve as the pathway out of that dead end, namely, the introduction of a transcendent—that is, religious—vision as the foundation for ethics. We have been implicitly exploring that previously undeveloped theme. But is there no explicit, specific connection between general ethics and the Christian ethic? And if there is, what exactly forms the connection between the universal human ethical quest and the Christian vision?

To discover the path from the general to the revealed, from natural ethics to a specifically Christian ethic, we must return again to the discussion of analytical ethics introduced in chapter one. In that context, we mentioned three basic attempts in the philosophical tradition to determine how ethical assertions can be justified. The first of the three, naturalism, derives every ethical *ought* from an ontological *is*. Hence naturalism suggests that ethics moves from "what is" to what we ought to do or be.

Viewed from a Christian perspective, naturalism has much to commend it. More readily than intuitionism, naturalism makes ethical judgments a topic for discussion and deliberation, thereby opening the door (at least theoretically) to the development of a consensual ethic, an understanding of the ethical life born of the give-and-take of life together. In contrast to its other rival, noncognitivism (or emotivism), naturalism presupposes the fundamental objectivity of ethical assertions. In arguing that moral judgments have as their basis what is built into our humanness or into the nature of the world, naturalism assumes that moral judgments have some link to the world beyond the subjectivity of the speaker.

It is not surprising, therefore, that many Christian thinkers find in naturalism a promising bridge to Christian ethics.[28] Evangelical ethicists, for example, readily laud naturalism for what they perceive to be its close affinity to the biblical suggestion that all humans have access to a creation-based ethic.[29] Many evangelicals agree that by nature humans possess a sense of morality, which arises out of God's universal self-disclosure in creation and the human conscience. Some theologians refer to this aspect of the divine self-disclosure as "general revelation."[30]

Although finding a foundation in several biblical texts (e.g., Mt 19:4-12; Mk 7:18-23; 1 Tim 4:1-5; Jas 3:9), these thinkers look to Paul for the clearest statement of the moral ramifications of general revelation. In his great case against humankind, the apostle declares that humans are "without excuse" before God. Their responsibility to God arises from God's prior act of self-disclosure in creation: "For since the creation of the world God's invisible qualities—his eternal power and divine nature—have been clearly seen, being understood from what has been made" (Rom 1:20). In addition to the disclosure in creation as a whole, God has written the moral law within the human person: "Indeed, when Gentiles, who do not have the law, do by nature things required by the law, they are a law for themselves, even though they do not have the law, since they show that the requirements of the law are written on their hearts, their consciences also bearing witness, and their thoughts now accusing, now even defending them" (Rom 2:14-15).

Texts such as these lead many evangelical ethicists to accept the validity of some type of natural ethics. Humans could come to at least a partial knowledge of truth—including ethical truth—they conclude, by observing the traces of God's self-disclosure in "the way things are."

If the presence of divine revelation in creation makes the discernment of ethical truth universally possible, then the naturalistic impulse to derive an "ought" from an "is" is not misguided per se. Yet it carries a grave liability. Being a philosophical approach to ethics, naturalism shares with all such systems a debilitating anthropocentricity. For this reason it too requires a redemptive transformation.

The Christian transformation of naturalism involves a shift in tense—from the past to the future. Like naturalism, the Christian ethic has an indicative character.[31] It also moves from an "is" to an "ought." But the "is" to which the Christian ethic appeals for the justification of ethical assertions is not the "is" of the present tense, as in naturalism. Seen from our perspective in the present, this "is" is a future tense. The "is" of the Christian ethic is a "will be." Our focus does not rest exclusively on what God has placed in creation "in the beginning," although that remains an important vantage point. More importantly, we look to what God sets as the goal for creation. Hence the Christian ethic appeals to what ultimately will be, and thus to God's intention for creation.

Trutz Rendtorff alludes to this implication of the fundamental eschatological orientation of the Christian ethic when he declares, "When we regard ethics as dealing with the challenge to place our lives in the service of the good, we take it for granted that the good has not yet fully become reality. This 'not yet' expresses the time element in the ethical reality of life as an orientation to the future. This orientation is present whenever the question is raised of how to solve the ethical task, and the path is specified on which the good is to become reality."[32]

Why should our ethic give primacy to the future? The answer is actually quite obvious. In the eschatological new creation, "ought" and "is" are no longer two separate moments. Rather, "ought" and "is" coalesce, because in God's eternal community what "ought" to be "is," and what "is" is what "ought" to be.

Eschatologically, then, "ought" and "is" merge. However, they do not find their unity in themselves. Rather their true unity resides in what encompasses them both, namely, the divine will. Looking at ethics from the vantage point of the eschatological renewal, we discover that what "ought to be" is in fact what "is." As God effects the divine will for creation, God's will both defines the "ought" and accomplishes it. Thereby the divine will makes what "ought" to be also what "is."

This eschatological convergence of "ought" and "is" carries ethical implications. The merging of the two in the divine will means that we are called to live out in the present what will be, so that as far as possible "ought" and "is" can likewise converge in the present. The task of actualizing God's eschatological purposes—God's future "is"—comprises the "ought" of our present. Ethical living entails that we continually inquire about how our purpose as designed by God should affect, motivate and even determine the present and the present situation. Although this "ought" is not yet completely an "is" in our experience, we live in the confident hope that the "ought" we hear now will fully become an "is" in the glorious eschatological consummation. In this manner "the future good has ontological precedence over the present life," to borrow Rendtorff's words.[33]

In this way the Christian ethic reveals itself to be a "deontology of the future."[34] Certain actions are right and certain traits are good because they belong to the "is," which although now may be hidden is in fact already present in God's future. At the same time the eschatological orientation of the Christian ethic brings about a unification of "being" with "doing." Ethical actions arise as we come to understand our true identity; they flow out of our identity as the redeemed, Christlike persons we will be and hence ontologically now are.

The universality of the Christian ethic. The eschatological "naturalism" I have sketched here offers a bridge between the Christian ethic and the general systems devised by the philosophical ethicists. But one problem remains. The Christian ethic is based in the revelation of God in Christ, which draws together a specific community, the fellowship of disciples who gather around Jesus. The philosophical tradition, in contrast, desires to establish a universal ethic, an ethic for all humankind. Given this distinction, how can we claim that the Christian vision is not merely a tribal ethic but in fact is for everyone? How can we say that the Christian ethic is universal?

Our deliberations suggest two connecting points. First, a connection between the revealed ethic of the Christian community and the ethical quest of all humankind lies in the universality of the divine intent. God's eschatological goal is not designed for only a select few but for all humans. Regardless of whether all will in fact eventually participate in God's eternal community, the God who wants all "to be saved and to come to a knowledge of the truth" (1 Tim 2:4) desires that all participate in the divine goal for creation.

The universal intent of God's purposes lies at the heart of the Bible. Although Jesus came primarily as Israel's Messiah, our Lord's mission encompassed the Gentiles as well, and therefore the early community spoke of Jesus as "the Savior of the world" (e.g., 1 Jn 4:14). Similarly, even though those who actually come to Christ in repentance and faith may be the direct focus of divine salvation, in Christ God acted for the reconciliation of all humankind (2 Cor 5:19; 1 Jn 2:2).

The universal intent of the divine work (1 Tim 2:3-4) forms an important foundation for the biblical idea of election. God elected Abraham so that through him the electing God might bless the nations (Gen 12:3). Similar to Israel in the Old Testament, the church is the elect people of

God for the sake of the world. This realization provides an important motivation for Christian living. We seek to be a people who embody God's intention for all humankind. Thus we view the ethic we proclaim as more than merely the way of life of a specific religious tradition. Rather than huddling together as the "chosen few" who live unto themselves, our desire is to live according to God's will in the midst of, and for the sake of, the many. We long that the many might join with us—become part of "the few" as it were—so as to actualize God's intentions for all humankind. In this manner we can correctly claim that the Christian ethic is nothing less than God's desire for all people everywhere.

The second connection between the revealed Christian ethic and all humankind arises from the link the Bible forges between creation and new creation. Although God's intention is not derived completely from creation, it nevertheless is closely connected with original creation, because it marks the completion of creation. The same universe that God called into existence "in the beginning" God will transform into the eschatological new creation. In the same way the very people who now exist in this world God will make perfect through the resurrection after the pattern of the resurrected Lord Jesus Christ (for through faith they are united to Christ).

In so far as this is God's intention, we can rightly say that the eschatological new creation is present in embryonic form in creation. More important for ethics, however, the renewed inhabitant of the eternal community is present within our human nature as created by God "in the beginning." And this is a design or purpose which all humans share. This universal divine purpose for humankind means that in so far as it arises from an understanding of God's intent for us, the Christian ethic is for all.

The Christian ethic, however, offers an even more concrete bridge between creation and new creation. This bridge is Christ. The New Testament writers boldly assert that God created the world through Christ (Col 1:15-16), who is the divine Word (Jn 1:3). Christ's role in creation is cosmic in extent, for he is the one in whom all things find their center (Col 1:17). But Christ is also the one through whom God reconciled the world (2 Cor 5:18-19). It is through connection with Jesus that we—and the entire cosmos—can participate in God's new creation.[35] This eschatological reality is not a new divine act of creation ex nihilo, but the transformation of *this* universe which God called into existence out of nothing "in the beginning."

The ethical dimension of this christological focus is vividly portrayed in Paul's typology between the First Adam and the Second Adam (Rom 5:12-21; 1 Cor 15:21, 45). In this manner the apostle asserts that the goal of our very existence as the children of Adam is that we might experience eschatological transformation after the pattern of the resurrected Christ. For this reason all human beings meet at the foot of the cross and at the door into the empty tomb. Through his death and resurrection Christ is the "lifegiving Spirit" (1 Cor 15:45) who seeks the transformation of what was begun in the creation of the First Adam.[36]

The ultimate basis for the Christian claim to universality, therefore, rests in the fact that the goal it announces is in reality nothing else than the goal of all creation.[37] The Christian ethic is the exploration of the implications of our anticipated eschatological renewal for life in the present context. Because God desires that all humankind participate in the coming transformation, this exploration is for all and the Christian desire to live out the biblical ethic is on behalf of all.

The connection we have outlined here provides the foundation for a Christian affirmation of general ethics. In its own way the human moral quest embodies our common, albeit often unconscious and unexpressed, desire to live according to our true identity as those whom God has created for an eschatological purpose. Yet unless it is redeemed from its anthropocentricity through the transformative role of Christian ethics, general ethics leaves us wandering within a cul-de-sac. As Christian participants in the philosophical ethical discussion, our task is to set forth the transcendent vision of God's eschatological new creation. And as Christians living in the world our task is to embody that transcendent vision, which we believe is nothing less than God's intention for all humankind.

Christian Ethics as a Community-Based Ethic of Being

In the preceding paragraphs I have given a theoretical response to the perennial question of the relation between the Christian ethic and the human ethical quest, especially as that quest is the focus of what is often called "general ethics." The conclusions I drew should predispose us to give a sympathetic ear to the public ethical discussions that seem to be mushrooming in our society today.

As noted earlier in this chapter, these contemporary discussions seem to be taking a specific direction, namely, toward the goal of constructing a community-based ethic of being. Consequently our pursuit of the larger goal of understanding the Christian ethic within the contemporary situation requires a journey through this discussion. I will offer a preliminary appraisal of the contemporary development, seeking to discover its implications for articulating the Christian ethic today. Hence, I must ask, is the Christian vision compatible with the quest for a community-based ethic of being? Or to push the matter further, is the Christian moral vision itself a community-based ethic? The answer to this question will add the final aspect of the foundation for my comprehensive statement of a Christian ethic.

The Christian vision of integrity. At first glance, we might be tempted to reject categorically the new emphasis on constructing an ethic of being. After all, isn't the Bible concerned with our conduct? Do we not find in Scripture a host of ethical imperatives? And will not the eschatological judgment be a divine appraisal of our works—that is, our conduct (Jer 17:10; 32:19; Mt 16:27; Rom 2:6; 2 Cor 5:10; Gal 6:7-8; Rev 22:12)?

Further, the interest in traits seems to move the focus of ethics away from the biblical emphasis on being concerned for the needs of others to a seemingly selfish desire for growth in personal character. Gilbert Meilaender capsulized this difficulty: "The focus of one who trusts in God's pardoning grace must, especially in the exceptional moment, be not his own character but the neighbor's need; for, otherwise, his character cannot be fully shaped by the virtue of faith."[38]

While acknowledging the apparent biblical foundation for the interest in formulating an ethic of doing that dominated the modern era, we must place it in a broader scriptural context. Seen from the perspective of the whole, the biblical viewpoint does not lead to a concern solely for acts in themselves and hence for a pure ethic of doing. In addition to an obvious interest in right actions, the biblical authors display a great concern for what motivates conduct. This is evident in the repeated admonitions in Scripture that Christians seek God's glory. As Paul instructed the Corinthians, "So . . . whatever you do, do it all for the glory of God (1 Cor

10:31). The important role of motivation likewise formed a central aspect of Jesus' critique of the religious leaders of his day. Outwardly they evidenced conformity to the Old Testament law. But their motives were wrong. They were seeking only their own benefit; they were motivated by selfishness. This biblical concern has led certain ethicists to focus on the motivational foundation of conduct. Helmut Thielicke, for example, declares, "The specifically 'Christian' element in ethics is rather to be sought explicitly and exclusively in the motivation of the action."[39]

Yet even the quest for right motives does not tap the central heartbeat of the New Testament conception of the ethical life. Motivation is itself related to something deeper. According to the New Testament writers the ultimate wellspring of action is our "heart," or what Jonathan Edwards referred to as our "affections."[40] Jesus himself declared that God's intention for us does not stop with mere outward conformity to laws, especially humanly devised legal strictures. A focus on outward obedience fails to acknowledge that the human "heart" is the source of evil actions (Mk 7:14-23; Mt 12:33-37). For this reason, Jesus—echoing the Old Testament prophets before him—decried the condition of the religious leaders of his day. They honored God with their lips, but their hearts were far from his heavenly Father (Mt 15:8).

His focus on the heart as the wellspring of action led Jesus—again following the Old Testament itself—to conclude that the two greatest commandments were to love God and neighbor (Mt 22:37-40). In so doing, he reunited the inward and the outward. For Jesus love meant an inward affection turned toward God and others, as well as the outward action such a godly affection produces.

This uniting of the inward and the outward which characterized Jesus' ethical teaching leads us to the concept of integrity. It suggests that a focus on integrity, and thus on character or virtue, must be central to our statement of the Christian ethic. For this reason we can readily find affinity with contemporary thinkers like Alasdair MacIntyre, who spoke about the ethical life as involving "singleness of purpose" or the virtue of integrity.[41]

But what is *integrity?* The common dictionary definition of the term characterizes it as "uprightness in character" and as involving traits such as honesty.[42] Although these are important aspects, Christian integrity goes deeper. Basically integrity has to do with authenticity. Persons of integrity are free from duplicity. With them, "what you see is what you get." You don't go away wondering whether they are motivated by "hidden agendas." Authenticity suggests that integrity means "acting in accordance with one's stated beliefs." People of integrity do what they say. To use the common parlance, they "walk" their "talk." And hence they are free from hypocrisy. There is in their lives a congruence between the *confessio fidei* and actual conduct.[43] Likewise, integrity has to do with the courage of conviction. Persons of integrity act on their beliefs even when this exacts a great personal cost.

The Wisdom literature of the Bible suggests that such integrity leads to a good reputation, and indeed consistent, authentic, courageous people do become known as persons of integrity. The book of Proverbs points out the exceedingly great value of such a reputation: "A good name is more desirable than great riches; to be esteemed is better than silver or gold" (Prov 22:1).

Even with this focus on integrity as defined above, we are not yet at our goal. The ethical life may be the life of integrity, the coherence of inner conviction with conduct and action. But what is the source of a person's inner convictions? Do they arise *sui generis* out of the individual moral agent?

Here again we can readily find ourselves in agreement with and can profitably draw from contemporary ethical thought. As I noted earlier, communitarians are alerting us to the foundational role of the communities in which we participate in the building of personal identity and moral sensitivities. Communities, they argue, transmit from generation to generation traditions of virtue, common good and ultimate meaning.[44]

In this way communities are crucial to the sustaining of character and values. Ultimately we derive our personal convictions from the community from which we gain our understanding of virtue and goodness. This suggests that the life of integrity entails living out the principles or worldview of that community of reference.

Viewed from this perspective, the ethical life is integrally linked to a communal vision, a shared worldview, or what we might even venture to call a *theology*. This constitutes the great methodological innovation of postmodern ethics. In the postmodern world we are becoming increasingly aware that every ethical proposal—even ethics itself—is embedded in an interpretive framework which in the end comprises the shared belief structure—the theology—of a community. In short, every understanding of the ethical life is ultimately derived from a community-based vision, which links the personal life with something beyond.[45]

A Christian communitarian virtue ethic. These conclusions suggest that the contemporary quest for a community-based ethic of being has much to offer our reflections on the Christian ethic. For this reason we must pursue this line of thought further. Can we draw from the idea of integrity to outline the shape of a Christian communitarian virtue ethic?

Foundational to our understanding of the ethical life is the realization that as Christians we constitute a particular community. We are a people who gather around our common confession that Jesus is the Christ. This suggests that the Christian ethic, in turn, is the call to live out the worldview of the community that gathers around Jesus the Christ. It entails acting according to the foundational belief structure or convictions of this community, especially as derived from the Bible, the foundational text of the community of Christ.

In the ethical task, therefore, we are guided by the Christian vision, a vision that arises from the biblical narrative. At the heart of this narrative is the story of the God who is active in the world. This story plays a central role in Christian ethics. One such aspect is the reference point it provides Christians from which to understand or define central ethical concepts. For example, the biblical narrative depicts God's steadfast resoluteness toward humankind. As we noted in chapter three, the Scriptures speak of the God who enters into a special relationship—a covenant—with God's creation. Even in the face of human rebellion, God remains steadfast. God continues to act in accordance with God's good intentions for us. The biblical word for God's resoluteness is *faithfulness.*

One foundation for Christian integrity, therefore, lies in the God who is faithful to the divine covenant despite human failure and sin. In the midst of his lament for the fall of Jerusalem at the hand of the invading Babylonian armies, the prophet Jeremiah reminded himself of God's faithfulness: "Because of the LORD's great love we are not consumed, for his compassions never fail. They are new every morning; great is your faithfulness" (Lam 3:22-23; see also Ps 94:14). As the One who is faithful to this covenant, God is trustworthy. We can entrust ourselves to God, knowing that God will fulfill the divine promises. And we know what true faithfulness is by our experience of God's own covenantal faithfulness.

The God who is faithful to this covenant is also just. The biblical authors narrate a divine justice that is impartial. Rather than showing favoritism, God treats all persons fairly. God extends grace to all, causing the sun "to rise on the evil and the good" and sending "rain on the righteous and the unrighteous" (Mt 5:45), to return to a text cited earlier. God's impartiality also means that salvation is intended for all people, regardless of ethnic origin (Acts 10:34-35), social status or gender (Gal 3:28-29). Divine justice also entails compassion. All persons are the recipients of God's goodness (Ps 145:8-9). Yet God cares especially for the less fortunate (Ps 146:7-8).

In setting forth a biblical ethic of integrity, Christians can appeal to the ways of the God of the biblical story for the foundation for understanding concepts such as faithfulness and justice. This provides a solution to a problem of general ethics to which we alluded earlier. In our postmodern context with its loss of moral consensus, such terms no longer carry any agreed-upon transcendent reference point. For the Christian, in contrast, ideals like faithfulness, justice and even integrity itself can only be defined in connection with God's own character as depicted in the biblical narrative of the divine Covenant-keeper.

Christians appeal to the example of the biblical God for another function as well. Perhaps even more important than serving as a transcendent reference point for ethical terms, God's way in the world forms a model for the Christian life in the world. For the Christian, integrity ultimately involves living in such a way that our lives mirror God's own nature and thereby show what God is like. In this task Christians appeal above all to the life of Jesus the Christ, who is Immanuel, "God with us" (Mt 1:23), and the incarnate Word of God (Jn 1:14). To be an ethical Christian means to live consistently as Jesus' followers.

The foundation for the life of integrity is our personal sense of identity as derived from the community of Christ. The New Testament authors, especially Paul, describe the essence of the Christian life as union with Christ, or Christ in us, which constitutes our person (e.g., Col 1:27). This means that we gain our foundational identity from the biblical narrative of Jesus. As we declare in baptism (Rom 6:1-8) and repeatedly reaffirm at the Lord's table (1 Cor 10:16), Christ's life *is* our life. Hence our goal is to be formed by his values and ideals, to live in accordance with what motivated him, and to love as he loved. We desire that our affections be set on things above, to allude to Paul's words (Rom 8:5)—that is, to be sincerely devoted to Christ and to the heavenly Father whom he loved and served. Thus in all of life we want to be conformed to his "image" both in our inward being and in our outward conduct (2 Cor 3:18).

On this basis the New Testament authors set forth a special concept of spirituality. The Christian life is "walking in the Spirit" (Gal 5:16), that is, being imbued with the same Spirit who guided our Lord Jesus himself. This indwelling Holy Spirit, the Spirit of Christ, forms Christlike character within the disciple and thereby becomes the author of the life of integrity.

In this task, however, the Christian community plays an essential role.[46] One dimension of that role is obvious. The narrative of Jesus is passed from generation to generation—and consequently to each disciple—by the historical community of which we are the contemporary expression. More importantly, however, the biblical narrative comes to be formed in us as the believing community becomes our primary social context, our ultimate community of reference. For the Christian the life of integrity is more than merely "Jesus and me for each tomorrow." It is living according to the ideals of the Lord as embodied in the life of the community that embodies and transmits his vision.

For this reason Christian integrity is never an isolated, purely personal ethic. Rather, the life of integrity begins as the Christian develops an awareness of personal identity within the context of the fellowship of believers. Indeed, integrity means living out a sense of foundational status (who I am as a child of God) and a sense of calling or vocation (who I am in the program of God). But even this identity cannot be isolated from that of the group. Each Christian participates in a particular people. And even when living "in the world" each carries a personal responsibility as a representative of that people, the community of faith.

The potential pitfall of a communitarian Christian ethic. The short sketch of a Christian ethic of integrity found in the previous paragraphs (and which will be elaborated in chapter seven) suggests that the move to a communitarian understanding holds promise as a way of articulating the Christian ethic in the emerging postmodern context. But one potentially devastating problem surfaces immediately. The community-based approach seems to undercut any claim to express a universal ethic.

The loss of universality appears to be inherent in any understanding that views the ethical life as integrally embedded in the life of the social group. Such a focus serves to highlight the multiplicity of communities and hence the diversity of ethical visions present in our world. This multiplicity, in turn, seems to lead us headlong into a communitarian pluralism. The multiplicity of community-based ethical visions appears to call into question any attempt to claim that one is somehow more correct than the others. Rather than promoting the search for the one, universal human ethic, the various interpretative frameworks or theological visions seem to offer equally valid foundations for ethics in the postmodern context.

For this reason embarking on the communitarian pathway may risk casting us into the murky waters of a new "conventionalism." In such a situation, as a community each social group determines its own rules of conduct in accordance with its own customs (or conventions) which in turn are based on its own unique vision of reality. Taken to the extreme, such a conventionalism leaves each community with the prerogative of requiring uncritical conformity to such social authority.[47]

Forming the intellectual foundation for this new situation is what Jean-François Lyotard elevates as the defining characteristic of the postmodern condition: "incredulity toward metanarratives."[48] By this Lyotard means that postmodernism involves the rejection of every all-encompassing interpretation of human life. Its ethos emerges as the claims to universality of the various overarching belief systems that attempt to encapsulate the story of all humankind, so indicative of the modern era, are discounted.

This situation is especially grave for Christianity, with its inherent tendency to universalize its own transcendent narrative of the divine-human drama. To the postmodern mind the Christian story is only one such imperialistic metanarrative. The categorical rejection of every metanarrative does not deny Christians the right to uphold the biblical story as the defining narrative for our specific community. But the postmodern ethos demands that we not "privilege" that story, that is, that we give up every ambition to bring all other communities under the umbrella of the biblical story of creation-Fall-new creation. In this context the Christian vision becomes merely one among the many.

By implication the postmodern critique demands that Christians also refrain from subsuming all other visions of the ethical life under the rubric of "Christian ethics." Any talk of the universality of the Christian conception of the ethical life is abhorrent to the postmodern mind. Like the Christian narrative, the Christian vision is thereby reduced to being merely one of a manifold number of "tribal" ethical systems found in our global village.

The move to a communitarian ethic, therefore, raises perplexing questions for Christians. If every conception of the ethical life is embedded in the belief structure of a community of reference, then which community? And whose theology should we "privilege"? In short, how do we deal with the seemingly unavoidable pluralistic conventionism of the postmodern ethos? Finding an adequate answer to this question forms one of the most difficult challenges of Christian ethics in the contemporary context. In the closing paragraphs of this chapter, I will indicate the direction in which I think the answer to this query lies. To frame the question properly, however, I must return to the conclusion of chapter one.

The Christian ethic and religious ethical traditions. The survey of general ethics in chapter one led to the conclusion that philosophical ethical systems leave us in an anthropocentric cul-de-sac, because they by necessity lack a transcendent point of reference. Such systems begin with human reason and consequently end where they began. But not all ethical traditions appeal solely to human reason. Present in our world are ethical systems that, like the Christian ethic, arise out of a transcendent, religious vision. In fact we are now learning that ultimately all ethical systems are the outworking of some type of purportedly transcendent vision.

Such discoveries raise the crucial issue we outlined above. Perhaps there are multiple routes out of the cul-de-sac, each represented by a different religious tradition or religious community. This would mean that the new conventionalism—the acknowledgment of the value of every transcendent vision within the sphere of the community that gathers around it—is indeed the solution to the ethical dilemma of the postmodern context. But if this is the case, how can we continue to promote the specifically Christian ethical vision as encompassing God's ideal for all humankind? In short, we must now tackle the question of the relation between the Christian ethic and the ethical systems of the multiplicity of religious communities present in our global village.

Ethics and the religions. Our beginning point in addressing this question lies in the connection between ethics and the religions.[49] The foundation for such a connection lies in the crucial role in human life played by culture, understood—to quote Clifford Geertz—as "an historically transmitted pattern of meanings embodied in symbols, a system of inherited conceptions expressed in symbolic forms by means of which men communicate, perpetuate, and develop their knowledge about and attitudes toward life."[50] Religion, in turn, is a central, formative dimension of culture.

Modern sociologists have pointed out that all religions provide a foundation for ethics, in that they mediate a sense of the transcendent both to the individual and to the social dimensions of life. Émile Durkheim, for example, theorized that religion creates and maintains social solidarity, for it provides the common symbols by means of which a specific people understand their world.[51] Further, it affords a sense of cosmic unity necessary for such solidarity.[52] By furnishing the foundation for the social community in which we live, a specific religious tradition mediates to us the framework for group and personal identity formation. As a result, religion undergirds morality by mediating a transcendent foundation for conceptions of the ethical life. In short, as Geertz succinctly stated, "Religion supports proper conduct by picturing a world in which such conduct is only common sense."[53]

The foundational role of religion to human society, and by extension to ethics, has led some thinkers to consider the possibility of developing a religiously based "global ethic."[54] This project would appear possible in so far as each of the many religions has a "community-producing" function. One could then hope to arrive at certain conclusions about a global ethic of community derived from the common vision of community the religions share.

Although it originally arose as the outworking of the modern pluralist ethos, this goal looms perhaps even more workable in the postmodern climate. Earlier in this chapter I noted how contemporary thinkers seem quite able to close ranks around communitarian ideals such as friendship or neighborliness. In fact, if there is one nearly universally accepted guiding principle for ethics in the postmodern context, it is that the ethical life consists of whatever builds community. Thus Douglas Todd spoke for many when he held out the hope that today's public ethical discussions would foster "neighbourliness" and promote "the common good."

The seemingly universal quest for community and the social role of religion in human life suggests a criterion by which all such visions can be appraised. The common goal of community implies that one could evaluate the transcendent vision of every community (including Christianity) in part by determining the extent to which the beliefs it inculcates and the practices it fosters promote social cohesion. And through such a process one could hope to construct a global ethic, a universally acknowledged understanding of the ethical life.

At first glance the appeal to a universal criterion such as the promotion of social cohesion appears to provide the way forward in the postmodern world. But one debilitating problem remains. As the postmodern focus on "difference" or multiplicity reminds us, despite their common quest for social cohesion, even "community," the various communities remain quite different from each other. They espouse differing transcendent visions, and consequently they embody differing understandings of what actually constitutes true community.

Such divergence reintroduces the "impolite" question of truth. Rather than settling for the promotion of some vague concept of community, it leads us to ask, Which religious vision carries within itself the foundation for the community-building role of a transcendent religious vision? Which vision provides the foundation for the construction of true community?

The uniqueness of the Christian ethical vision. At this point the Christian gospel provides a unique answer. As with other community-based visions, a central goal of the Christian ethic is the advancement of social cohesion. And in keeping with other community-based ethical proposals, it speaks of this goal as "community" (or fellowship).

To see that community is integral to the Christian ethical vision, we need only remind ourselves that foundational to the Christian message is the declaration that the goal of life is community—fellowship with God, with others and with creation, and in this manner with oneself. Taken as a whole, the biblical narrative speaks of God at work establishing community. God's *telos* is nothing less than gathering a reconciled people, nurtured in a renewed creation and enjoying fellowship with the eternal God (Rev 21:1-5).

This biblical theme suggests one dimension in which Christians can cautiously affirm all religious traditions. By mediating a transcendent vision, all such traditions do contribute to the building of society and offer some semblance of "community." But the Christian message does not stop here. We firmly believe that the Christian vision sets forth more completely the nature both of community and the good life that all human ethical systems seek to foster. We humbly declare that other "visions," including the visions of other religious traditions, cannot provide community in its ultimate sense. And why not? Because they do not embody the highest understanding of who God actually is! Consequently their understanding of what true community is falls short of the fullness of fellowship God desires for us.

Foundational to the specifically Christian theological vision is the acknowledgment of God in God's triune fullness. We declare that the only true God is none other than the social Trinity, the eternal community of Father, Son and Spirit. The Christian vision speaks of humankind, in turn, as "created in God's image." The divine design is that we mirror within creation what God is like in God's own eternal reality. The goal of human existence has been revealed most completely in Jesus Christ, who in his life, death and resurrection modeled the divine principle of life, namely, life in intimate fellowship with his heavenly Father by the Holy Spirit who indwelt him.

In this manner the Christian vision of God as the social Trinity and our creation to be the *imago Dei* provides the transcendent basis for the human ethical ideal as life-in-community. Consequently the reciprocal, perichoric dynamic of the Triune God is the cosmic reference point for the idea of society itself. Just as God is a plurality-in-unity, so also to be human means to be persons-in-community. This glorious vision leads us to realize that the task of human society is to bring together the multiplicity of individuals into a higher unity (as is reflected so well in the motto of the United States—*e pluribus unum,* "out of the many, one"). This vision carries with it a universalizing tendency as well. It informs us that in the process of community building all persons—together with the gifts each brings—are important, valuable and contributive to the whole.

In short, the biblical vision of God at work establishing community is not merely a great idea that God devised in all eternity. Instead it is an outworking of God's own eternal reality. As a result, the human quest for community—which is often expressed today as "neighborliness" or "the common good," to use these somewhat pale and vacuous terms—is not misguided. At its heart it is nothing less than the quest to mirror in the midst of all creation the eternal reality of God and thereby to be the image of God.

Ultimately, this vision lies at the heart of the Christian ethic of integrity. The vision of the human community living together in the midst of the new creation in full integrity—that is, humankind showing forth the eternal fellowship of the triune God disclosed in the biblical narrative—is what Christians have to offer as the foundation of a truly constructive ethic in the postmodern context. And it is this vision of the fullness of community that we must seek to embody as the community we call "the church of Jesus Christ." For God has called this particular community out of the world to incarnate within its own life and to proclaim to the entire world God's universal intent for all humankind. For this reason we must continue to invite others to share with us the life within Christ's fellowship until that day when God brings history to completion in the eternal divine community, the new creation.

Chapter 7

FOUNDATIONS OF A CHRISTIAN ETHIC

God . . . has made us competent as ministers of a new covenant
—not of the letter but of the Spirit;
for the letter kills, but the Spirit gives life.
(2 CORINTHIANS 3:6)

The Reverend Henry Maxwell, pastor of the First Church of Raymond, had just ended his Sunday-morning sermon, and the church quartet was preparing to sing the closing selection. Suddenly the carefully planned flow of the worship service was interrupted by a stranger hurrying down the center aisle. Standing immediately below the pulpit, the man recounted how he, a recently widowed printer, had seen his job fall victim to the new technology. He wondered how the congregation could speak so glibly about following Christ in the face of the plight of people caught in such circumstances. As he ended his soliloquy, the forlorn figure crumpled on the floor next to the Communion table. Visibly moved by the event, the minister directed that the unconscious man be carried to the parsonage.

Early the next Sunday morning the visitor died. In his sermon Pastor Maxwell explained to the congregation how the words the deceased man had spoken on the previous Lord's Day, followed by his death in the parsonage, had compelled him to ask as he had never done before, "What does following Jesus mean?" The clergyman then offered a challenge to his hearers:

What I am going to propose now is something which ought not to

> appear unusual or at all impossible of execution. Yet I am aware that it will be so regarded by a large number, perhaps, of the members of the church. But in order that we may have a thorough understanding of what we are considering, I will put my proposition very plainly, perhaps bluntly. I want volunteers from the First Church who will pledge themselves, earnestly and honestly for an entire year, not to do anything without first asking the question, "What would Jesus do?" And after asking that question, each one will follow Jesus as exactly as he knows how, no matter what the results may be.[1]

This opening incident in Charles Sheldon's novel *In His Steps* set the stage for the ensuing story of a group of Christians who dared to take Christian discipleship seriously. The gripping tale became the primer for an entire generation as to what the Christian ethical life entails.

* * *

The first six chapters have led from general ethics to the specifically Christian ethic, understood in its connection to the disclosure of God's universal intention for human existence. In this chapter I want to develop more clearly the specifically Christian vision of the ethical life, first raising one additional foundational question: How does the Christian ethic arise from its primary source in revelation? Within the context of the answer I will set forth the core theological themes arising from the biblical narrative that shape, mold and propel that ethic.

The Revelational Source of Christian Ethics

Christians are often described as "people of the Book." This description is appropriate in that we acknowledge the Bible as embodying divine revelation and for this reason continually look to Scripture for instruction as to what we should believe and what we should do. We desire to be informed by the Bible so that we might live faithfully before God as followers of Jesus Christ. Hence Stephen Fowl and L. Gregory Jones rightly remind us that the goal Christians share "is to shape our common life in the situations in which we find ourselves according to the characters, convictions, and practices related in Scripture."[2]

But how does this basic commitment to being a people who live according to divine revelation work its way out in the quest for being an ethical people? How does divine revelation provide direction for living as God's people?[3] And what is the relationship between Scripture and the Spirit in the construction of a Christian ethic?

Christian ethicists differ with each other as to the manner in which divine revelation is to inform ethical living. Nor are they in agreement as to the connection between Spirit and Word. Two basic and seemingly mutually exclusive positions repeatedly find expression among Christian thinkers. Some ethicists propose a fundamentally "heteronomous" approach focusing almost exclusively on the written deposit of revelation in Scripture, whereas others uphold what is often referred to as a type of "autonomous" understanding, because it elevates the individual believer who possesses the internal light of revelation mediated by the indwelling Spirit.[4]

Heteronomy: revelation focused on the Word. Many Christian ethicists look primarily, if not exclusively, to an external source for ethical direction. God has disclosed to us how we should live, they argue; our task is to listen to what he has said and then obey his directives. Because this view assumes that the vehicle of God's revelational activity—and hence the source that determines the nature of the ethical life—is external to the acting moral agent, we might label it the heteronomous approach.[5]

Protestants have traditionally looked to the Bible as the ultimate source of divine guidance. In their conflict with the Roman Catholic Church, the Reformers set forth the principle of *sola Scriptura.* Because the primary repository of God's special revelation is the Bible, they argued, Scripture alone is the final court of appeal not only in matters of Christian belief but also for insight into Christian living.[6] Standing in the Reformation tradition, John Murray offered this definitional statement: "In the biblical ethic we are concerned with the norms, or canons, or standards of behaviour which are enunciated in the Bible for the creation, direction, and regulation of thought, life, and behaviour consonant with the will of God."[7] But what form does biblical revelation take? And how do we move from the Bible to the practicalities of life? Here heteronomists disagree with each other.

One prominent view asserts that the divine revelation comes to us in the form of commands or laws. Whatever else it may be, proponents suggest, the Bible is a book of rules or precepts designed to regulate human conduct. The ethical life, in turn, involves obedience to the divine laws as inscripturated in the Bible.[8] From this understanding of Scripture flows a seemingly obvious ethical method. The task of the Christian ethicist is to systematize the various divinely revealed exhortations given in the Bible for the sake of ordering human actions.

John Calvin may have been suggesting this approach[9] in his remark "It will be useful to collect from various places in Scripture a rule for the reformation of the life."[10] In any case, the nineteenth-century Princeton theologian A. A. Hodge encapsulated such an understanding when he described the goal of practical theology as "to deduce, from the doctrines and precepts of the Bible, rules for the organization and administration of the Christian Church in all her functions, and for the guidance of the individual Christian in all the relations of life."[11]

Many Christians follow in the footsteps of Calvin and Hodge when they seek to resolve ethical questions by appeal to specific verses in Scripture they believe address the issues at stake. In this manner ethical reflection becomes the search for biblical exhortations or commands that can instruct the believer as to how to respond in each problematic situation.

Evangelical legalists,[12] those who look primarily to the laws found in Scripture for the foundation of the ethical life, are generally careful to avoid two perennial pitfalls. One trap is to view obedience to divine law as the way of salvation or the means by which we can gain God's favor.[13] Eschewing this as the mistake of the Pharisees of Jesus' day,[14] evangelicals regularly sound the biblical theme that as humans we are unable to keep the law, or they appeal to the Pauline emphasis on the inability of the law to produce godly conduct, due to the pervasive power of sin. For the Christian the goal of scriptural injunctions, then, is not to attain salvation (which is God's gracious gift to all who believe) but to guide us in the quest for holy living.[15]

Most evangelical legalists likewise seek to avoid placing all biblical laws on the same level. More specifically, they are generally careful to differentiate between dimensions of the Old Testament law designed for ancient Israel alone and those which remain binding on the people of God (or on all humankind) in every era. These ethicists often argue that the ceremonial and national aspects of the law given to Israel have been superseded, in contrast to the moral law, itself encoded in the Ten

Commandments, which remains in force even in the church age.

It is not without cause that Christian legalism remains a perennially popular ethical method. It stands as a reminder that the Bible presents certain prescriptions that are not optional for the people of God.[16] Nevertheless, as an ethical system, legalism is beset with certain debilitating problems. The "law-book" approach raises the question as to how we should respond to the great variety of situations people face today that the Bible itself does not address. Hence the legalistic method leaves us with a seemingly truncated ethic that cannot speak to many of the social realities of contemporary life.[17]

The law-book approach also raises the question of the applicability of the manifold scriptural injunctions to life in the present. Nearly all biblical scholars agree that many commandments inscripturated in the Bible are not universal or universally binding. Consequently they deny that we can simply lift every biblical injunction out of its historical setting and apply it to today. At the very least we must seek to determine which precepts were specifically intended for the ancient peoples and which are designed to govern life in every era.

Whenever Christians eat pork (Lev. 11:7-8), refrain from stoning sexual offenders (Deut 22:13-24) or no longer require women to wear veils when they pray (1 Cor 11:5, 13), they bear silent witness to the apparent inadequacy of a simple rule-book ethic. This phenomenon suggests that some deeper principle must be at work providing the criterion by means of which to differentiate between the universally applicable and the situationally conditioned laws of Scripture. Admitting the existence of such a principle moves us beyond treating the Bible simply as a book of precepts for ethical living.

Considerations such as these often lead Christian ethicists to propose a somewhat different though still decidedly heteronomous approach. Rather than following the legalists in viewing the Bible as a book of rules, they see it primarily as a book of principles. These thinkers (whom we may speak of as Christian principlists) look to scriptural principles rather than specific laws as the primary source of guidance for the ethical life.[18]

Christian principalists acknowledge that the precepts and laws are significant. But their importance lies in their status as expressions in particular contexts or in particular situations of deeper, underlying, universal moral axioms. And the appropriate principles are not limited to biblical legislation, for they may emerge from other genres of Scripture as well. Consequently the goal of the Christian principalist is to discern the universal axioms revealed in Scripture and apply them to parallel situations today.

Whether the search be for the appropriate laws or for the appropriate principles, taken by itself the heteronomous approach suffers from a debilitating shortcoming, which mitigates against its ability to offer an adequate foundation for Christian ethics.[19] All heteronomous ethical methods build from the assumption that divine revelation is an objective given. Proponents assume that revelation exists "out there"—specifically, in the pages of Scripture—and is waiting to be discovered and appropriated for living ethically today. All that is needed for this to occur is the proper ethical method which will excavate the meaning of the Bible and apply it to the appropriate situations of life.[20]

This understanding evidences a problem endemic to the heteronomous pattern in general. Whatever the exact method, this approach draws from a truncated understanding of the nature of revelation and consequently a mistaken view of the significance of biblical commandments and biblical principles. Thereby it misses the true intention of God's self-disclosure[21] and hence of Scripture itself.

Viewing the Bible primarily as the repository of timeless rules or timeless principles for human conduct risks overlooking the actual goal of revelation. The ultimate purpose of God's self-disclosure is to bring us not into a relationship with either a body of timeless laws or universal moral axioms, but into relationship with the self-revealing God, and as a consequence with one another and with all creation. The precepts and moral principles found within the pages of Scripture serve the Bible's central purpose, namely, to facilitate fellowship or community.

By defining the ethical life as living according to an objectively given set of laws or axioms, the heteronomous approach likewise leads to a misunderstanding of the nature of the human response to God's initiative.[22] This method encourages us to assume that what God desires is our obedience to externally imposed rules or principles of conduct. Although some Christian heteronomists would vehemently object to such a characterization of their position, others readily acknowledge this conclusion. Hence, writing in the *Evangelical Dictionary of Theology,* J. A. Motyer asserted quite forthrightly, "In the OT as in the NT (e.g., Acts 5:32), obedience is a means of grace."[23] In this manner the heteronomous method risks transforming Christian discipleship into blind compliance with the divine commands that confront us in Scripture. And unless we are willing to sidestep the problem by introducing a questionable idea of natural law,[24] we end up depicting the divine will as being external and even alien to our true being.

Similar to Christian ethicists in every age, the biblical writers themselves raised the fundamental question, What does God require of us? However, the basic answer of Scripture to this question is quite different than that to which heteronomous ethics points. Rather than outward compliance, what God actually desires is "a renewed spirit" or "a right heart."

Not only is this an obvious theme of the New Testament, the focus on inward piety is also prevalent in the Old Testament. The prophets repeatedly declare that the response God desires lies at a deeper level than the various sacrifices stipulated in the law. Thus, through Hosea, God declared, "For I desire mercy, not sacrifice, and acknowledgment of God rather than burnt offerings" (Hos 6:6). Yet the classic statement of this distinction comes from Micah. This prophet raised the question as to whether strict obedience to revealed precepts is in fact the focus of the proper response to God: "With what shall I come before the LORD and bow down before the exalted God? Shall I come before him with burnt offerings, with calves a year old?" (Mic 6:3). Micah's conclusion is striking: "He has shown you, O man, what is the good. And what does the LORD require of you? To act justly and to love mercy and to walk humbly with your God" (v. 8).

The difficulty with any focus on mere compliance with external commandments or even the careful appeal to universal moral principles is that such a method can readily miss the heartfelt response which alone is pleasing to God. As we acknowledged earlier, precepts and principles do have a place in Christian ethical reflection. But we dare never allow them to direct our attention away from the transformed relationship God truly desires for us and which in turn becomes the wellspring for true obedience. For this reason, in his prayer of contrition after his adultery with Bathsheba and his complicity in the murder of her husband, David moved beyond the transgression of explicit commandments to focus on the heart. "Surely you desire truth in the inner parts" (Ps 51:6), he concludes. "Create in me a pure heart, O God, and renew a steadfast spirit within me" (Ps 51:10).

David's plea points us toward the basic difficulty posed by the heteronomous approach to the ethical life. In focusing so definitively on the written word, this ethical method readily results in a truncated pneumatology. It risks either misunderstanding or overlooking completely the role of the internally resident Holy Spirit. A heteronomous ethic either collapses the life-giving Spirit into the deposit of laws or links the Spirit solely with our ability to discern the implications of universal principles in each particular situation we face.

Autonomy: revelation present within the moral agent. If the problem with the heteronomous approach is its loss of the Spirit through an emphasis on the objective givenness of the Word, perhaps the way forward is to move the Spirit to center stage in our ethical method. But how? One repeatedly suggested way is to link the Holy Spirit with the regenerated spirit of the believing individual.

Christians who advocate this second alternative actually are expressing affinity with a broader approach in ethics, which historians often characterize with the potentially misleading label "autonomy."[25] At the heart of the autonomous proposal is the elevation of the individual moral agent and the rejection of all claims to moral authority external to the self. Moral direction is internal; it arises through the operation of some principle resident within the individual.[26]

Contrary to what we might at first assume, autonomists are not necessarily antinomian. They do not advocate lawlessness. These ethicists are convinced that the individual moral agent is able to attain direct access to moral truth apart from the imposition of some externally determined set of laws or principles. Nevertheless, they argue strongly that the individual remains subject to that moral truth.

The classic example of an autonomous ethic understood in this manner is the proposal of Immanuel Kant.[27] According to the German philosopher, ethics is rooted in the goodwill of the moral agent, the person who does one's duty for its own sake. As we noted in chapter one, for Kant the will determines what ought to be done in any given situation by appeal to the categorical imperative.

We may classify Kant's ethic as autonomous in that the moral agent can appeal to no externally imposed criteria in determining the rightness or wrongness of moral actions. Instead the light of reason within leads the will to determine the universal law. Hence, after setting forth as his third practical principle "the will of every rational being as a will which makes universal law," Kant added: "By this principle all maxims are repudiated which cannot accord with the will's own enactment of universal law. The will is therefore not merely subject to the law, but is so subject that it must be considered as also *making the law* for itself and precisely on this account as first of all subject to the law (of which it can regard itself as the author)."[28]

His elevation of reason marks Kant's as basically a general or "secular" autonomous ethic. Consequently, major differences separate his from the proposal of Christians who are concerned to follow the dictates of the Spirit. At the same time the philosophical attempts to carve out an autonomous ethic provide a context in which we can understand the proposals of those Christians, including many evangelicals,[29] who draw from the biblical theme of the indwelling Spirit.[30]

Proponents of the theological variety of the autonomous approach argue that Christians are the recipients of God's Spirit. Not only is God's law written on the human heart, but, more important, the indwelling Spirit mediates divine revelation directly to each believer. As a consequence of the Spirit's internal presence, advocates add, the ethical life flows quite naturally out of our inner being, which is the location of the Spirit. The indwelling Spirit renews and sanctifies our moral consciousness, mediating to us an intuitive sense of the right and the good.

The implication for determining ethical action follows quite readily: rather than concerning ourselves with externally imposed commandments, we ought to listen to the Spirit's voice within and follow the promptings of the indwelling Spirit speaking to and through our spirit. Indeed, as the Spirit within transforms the human spirit, the individual believer comes both to know how to act and to will that he or she act according to God's good pleasure. In this sense, we might correctly characterize the ethic of many Christians as "autonomous" or perhaps "individualist."

In the twentieth century, the neo-orthodox theologian Emil Brunner offered an interesting twist on the basic autonomous or individualist approach.[31] Brunner agreed with the heteronomous tradition that the ethical life involves obedience to divine command. In fact obedience lies at the heart of his ethic. In his words, "we are confronted by a Command which must be taken in dead earnest."[32]

While walking thus far with the heteronomists, Brunner then broke with what he saw as the sheer legalism of his opponents: "Whatever can be defined in accordance with a principle . . . is legalistic. This means that it is possible—by the use of this principle—to pre-determine 'the right' down to the smallest detail of conduct. . . . This legalistic spirit corrupts the true conception of the Good from its very roots. . . . There is no Good save obedient behaviour, save the obedient will. But this obedience is rendered not to a law or a principle which can be known beforehand, but only to the free, sovereign will of God. The Good consists in always doing what God wills at any particular moment."[33]

At this point Brunner showed his autonomous colors. According to the neo-orthodox theologian, the presence of admonitions in Scripture serves as a reminder that "every believer can indeed know the will of God for himself, through his faith in Christ."[34] In fact, rather than confirming the heteronomous approach to ethics, Brunner claimed that the apostles' use of exhortation actually "sweeps away all legalistic heteronomy." He said, "Not even an Apostle can tell you what you ought to do; God Himself is the only One who can tell you this. There is to be no intermediary between ourselves and the Divine Will. God wishes to deal with us 'personally,' not through any medium."[35]

For Brunner the key to the ethical life rests with the indwelling Spirit. The life of obedience emerges as in each situation the believer is obedient to God's Command. The agent of this encounter with the divine imperative is the indwelling Spirit. Although God's free and sovereign encounter may likely occur through the reading of Scripture, it is not the biblical commands or principles themselves that are crucial, but the Spirit confronting the believer who in the end is the divine Command.

Perhaps a more widely known expression of Christian autonomy is the situation ethics popularized by Joseph Fletcher in the 1960s, which I outlined in chapter five. This view suggests that rather than looking to a set of universal laws or principles to determine in advance what would be the right act, in any particular situation the believer must determine what is the most loving thing. While acknowledging the one moral principle (love), situation ethics is an autonomous method because it will allow no preconceived conceptions to dictate what love must mean in any specific context. The "law of love" cannot be defined according to any external criteria, nor can the nature of love be determined by appeal to any other universal principles. Biblical exhortations may be helpful as rules of thumb, but they cannot claim to be prescriptive norms. In essence the situationist argues that in seeking to determine the right course of action the moral agent must harken solely to the internal voice of the Spirit speaking in each situation.

Although heteronomy may be the more widely advocated theory among evangelical ethicists, the autonomous method has its following in the church. Christians talk about having been "led" to do something, or they defend their behavior by asserting that a course of action simply "seemed right." Such talk is not categorically different from the illuminating line from the award-winning popular song of the 1970s, "It can't be wrong if it feels so right." The appeal to an inner sense of rightness quickly silences all protestations, for how can we argue with a person's inner sense that an act was "right"? To be fair to Christian autonomists, however, we must add that they are not suggesting that believers base their conduct on mere human desire. Instead, the "feeling" which they elevate as the proper court of appeal is what they perceive to be the inner pressure that comes from the indwelling Spirit or the sanctified moral consciousness of the redeemed believer.

Viewed from this perspective, the autonomous or individualist approach seems to hold great potential. It offers the confidence that we can trust the promptings we sense within ourselves, believing that they arise from the indwelling Spirit or the human spirit purified according to the divine image. This assumption, however, marks the Achilles' heel of this approach. Autonomy fails to take seriously the evil impulse that remains present within the regenerate individual.

As noted in chapter three, Paul spoke of the Christian ethical life as a struggle, a war of the Spirit against the flesh (Gal 5:17). Hence even

"Spirit-filled" Christians do not necessarily do what is right, and even the good deeds believers do are regularly tainted by mixed motives. Part of the problem lies in the cloudiness of our moral vision. Until the eschaton even the most sanctified Christian still sees and knows only "in part" (1 Cor 13:12). Consequently we dare not simply assume that we will be able to discern clearly, let alone act decisively upon, the Spirit's voice, or that our sanctified moral consciousness will always carry the day. Nor can we possibly determine the "right act" in any situation simply by seeking to do the "most loving thing." Rather, we must be instructed as to the parameters within which the loving response is found. To live as we should, therefore, we require ongoing instruction, especially instruction from Scripture (2 Tim 3:14-17).

In short, autonomists run into the opposite danger to that of their heteronomist opponents. Whereas the heteronomous approach collapses the Spirit into the Word, the autonomous alternative all too readily separates the Spirit from the Word. It assumes that the voice of the Spirit can be heard apart from the parameters set forth in Scripture. Consequently the autonomist rejects the givenness of revelation as inscripturated in the Bible in the name of the indwelling Spirit.

Word and Spirit: the theonomous way. Our characterization of heteronomists as collapsing the Spirit into the Word and autonomists as abandoning the Word in favor of the Spirit suggests that the proper ethical method lies somewhere between these two alternatives. The correct approach draws the inscripturated Word and the internally active Spirit together. Borrowing again from Tillich's terminology, we might speak of this as the "theonomous" way.[36]

Lying at the basis of the theonomous alternative is a foundational theme outlined in chapter six. In my appraisal of natural ethics I observed that to be human means to be morally conditioned. I then suggested that our sense of moral conditionedness points to a deeper reality, namely, the impact of the divine will on our human existence. There is another implication of the acknowledgment that our experience of being moral agents indicates that we are God's creatures: our sense of moral conditionedness reminds us that we stand continually before God. We live every moment in the very presence of God.

Living before God means that the omniscient God is continually cognizant of how we respond to the moral conditionedness that presses upon us in each moment. It means as well that in each moment we remain responsible to a holy God who has preferences and therefore challenges us to live in accordance with the divine purpose for our existence. In short, as the Reformers emphasized, to be human means to exist constantly in a special relationship with God, a relationship that we might seek to deny, but that we can never escape.

The foundational assumption that we live in constant, inescapable relationship with a holy God marks the theonomous alternative as unabashedly theocentric and relational. As noted earlier, the anthropocentric approach of the philosophical tradition begins with the human person, often with some specific endowment (such as reason or will) humans naturally possess. The ethical task, in turn, is to use that endowment so as to reach what the philosopher perceives to be the goal of human existence (e.g., the contemplation of eternal truth).

The theonomous approach, in contrast, begins with humans-in-relationship. Above all it views us as persons who continually live before the Creator and with whom God has chosen to enter into covenant. As those who stand in a moral relationship with God, we are also called to cultivate proper relationships with each other and even with all creation. For this reason the ethical life is always life-in-relationship. And the goal of ethical reflection is to draw from God's purposes for our relationships as revealed in Scripture—especially our standing before God as God's covenant partners—so as to discern the implications of our being-in-relationship for living in the contexts in which we find ourselves.

The awareness of the relational character of the ethical life indicates a crucial shortcoming that the heteronomous and autonomous approaches often share. Proponents of both methods readily presume that ethics is primarily an individual task and that the ethical life is a quest on which we embark primarily as independent individuals. In keeping with this tendency, proponents from both perspectives often view divine revelation as addressed to individual believers. This is obviously the orientation of the autonomous ethical method, with its focus on the individual person indwelt by the Spirit. But it is likewise the case among those heteronomists who simply assume that the Bible was written for the instruction of individuals rather than to communities God has called into being.[37] But if the ethical life is ultimately life-in-relationship, then this orientation toward the isolated individual is simply unwarranted.[38]

The relational, covenantal orientation of theonomous ethics also carries important implications for our view of the imperatives in Scripture. The theonomous approach suggests that we can properly understand the law only within the relational context in which the ethical life occurs. God did not give us the law in order that we might thereby produce the ethical life. Indeed, even if we could live in perfect conformity to the law (which we cannot), our lives would not thereby correspond to God's intention for us (cf. Mt 19:16-26). Because God's intent is that we develop person-to-person relationships which reflect God's own relationality, true obedience is not marked by outward compliance to a set of laws but by inward piety (e.g., Mk 7:1-23). Indeed in itself the law is simply powerless to create the kind of godly relationships God wants us to enjoy.[39]

Scripture clearly teaches that the task of bringing about the ethical life falls solely to the indwelling Spirit. This divine Spirit, who is the Spirit of Jesus, brings us into right relationships with God, each other and all creation. Paul summed up the biblical view when he asserted, "For what the law was powerless to do in that it was weakened by the sinful nature, God did by sending his own Son in the likeness of sinful man to be a sin offering. And so he condemned sin in sinful man, in order that the righteous requirements of the law might be fully met in us, who do not live according to the sinful nature but according to the Spirit" (Rom 8:3-4, cf. Gal 5:16-25).

If the purpose of the law cannot be that of producing ethical people, its intent must lie elsewhere. Primarily the various biblical imperatives fulfill a somewhat negative function. Scriptural prohibitions and injunctions serve to indicate the parameters within which the relationships God desires for us can flourish. Such imperatives, therefore, work hand in hand with the Spirit. As we seek to live within the realm toward which the law points, the indwelling Spirit creates the kind of relationships that honor God.

* * *

The husband-wife relationship offers a helpful example. The biblical law of marriage stipulates that husbands and wives should be careful to maintain sexual fidelity. In the Ten Commandments we read, "You shall not commit adultery" (Ex 20:14), a law that our Lord strengthened (Mt 5:27-28) and the New Testament writers reaffirmed (1 Cor 6:18; Heb 13:4). But is sexual fidelity all that it takes to have a godly marriage? Hardly. God's real intention is that a man and a woman develop a relationship of holy love. This means that as a husband I am to love my wife "just as Christ loved the church and gave himself up for her" (Eph 5:25). How does the law prohibiting adultery relate to the divine intention that I be a loving husband?

We must admit that the Seventh Commandment is powerless to create the kind of marriage relationship God desires. The fact that I slavishly conform to this law, that is, that I refrain from committing adultery, does not itself mark me as a loving husband nor does it mean that ours is a model marriage. In fact I may with all due care remain sexually faithful to my wife and yet be a mean, abusive and despicable spouse. And despite all outward appearances to the contrary, our marriage may be in fact deplorable.

Taken by itself, the law of marriage cannot produce a God-honoring marital relationship. My growth in becoming a truly loving Christian husband is dependent on the presence of the life-giving Spirit within my heart and within our marriage. Only the Spirit can accomplish the radical transformation that releases me to love my wife as God desires. And only the Spirit can create the kind of community within our relationship that fulfills God's intention.

But does this mean that I can simply throw out the biblical injunction? By no means. What the negative command, the prohibition of adultery, does is delineate a boundary within which the kind of relationship God desires can develop. Only within the context of obedience to the adultery law can my relationship to my wife flourish. Consequently, if I transgress this boundary (by committing adultery), I have evacuated the realm in which a truly godly marriage can arise. This act places me outside the realm in which by the power of the Spirit the loving relationship God desires that I have with my wife can emerge.

Therefore, while the indwelling Spirit takes me beyond the dictates of the law of marriage, this transforming Spirit would never lead me to transgress the Seventh Commandment. The connection between Spirit and Word indicates that any impulse I may feel to commit adultery, regardless of what I think are my true motivations, is not the prompting of the indwelling Spirit. It is the impulse of the as-of-yet not eradicated sinful nature.

* * *

We have noted that the foundational focus of a theonomous ethic is relationships. In this manner the theonomous approach coheres with our earlier conclusion that the goal of divine revelation is to bring us into relationship with the living God and consequently with each other and all creation. We have seen as well that the theonomous method leads us to understand the law within the context of its role of pointing out the boundaries in the midst of which the Spirit seeks to produce godly relationships. Rather than looking to biblical commandments alone for the pattern for ethical living, we must place them in the context of the biblical teaching about the God before whom we live and our calling to live before this God.[40] Now we must note one further implication of this insight.

By drawing our attention back to the God in whose presence we live, the theonomous approach leads us squarely into the realm of theology. Consequently ethics becomes "theology in action," and theology—"the whole counsel of God"—becomes the fundamental intellectual resource for ethical living.[41] This means that, as many Christian thinkers have concluded,[42] there is a close kinship between Christian theology and Christian living.[43] Doctrine has a specifically moral function.[44] As Robin Gill rightly asserted about the discipline of ethics, "Christian beliefs . . . form the parameters of the discipline, parameters that give it a degree of unity—a unity of general attitude rather than specific content."[45]

The ethical life arises as we live out our fundamental theological convictions in the midst of the situations of life, so that we may enjoy Spirit-filled relationships that reflect the love that characterizes the triune God. These commitments, in turn, must be thoroughly Christian. That is, they must be informed by the Scriptures—by the biblical vision of God and of a creation under God. At the same time these commitments are not ends in themselves. Instead, as Philip Edgcumbe Hughes correctly remarked,

"The end of theology is practice. Doctrine is for doing, not just for hearing and learning, and that is why in Scripture it is always presented as bearing ethical consequences."[46] Our doctrinal commitments form the "web of belief" through which the Spirit gives shape to our life-in-relationship. As the Spirit fulfills this task in us, we come to be characterized by the true Christian integrity we spoke about in the previous chapter.

This brings us back to our discussion of revelation and the Christian ethic. The theonomous approach opens the way for an integration of the active Spirit with the written Word. Rather than following either the dead legalism of heteronomy or the vacuous, free-floating, formless contextualism of autonomy, a truly theonomous ethic views Word and Spirit as the unified voice of God speaking into the specific situations of moment-by-moment living. Through the pages of the Bible, the Spirit leads us to capture the biblical vision of a world in relationship to God. And through the inscripturated Word, the living Spirit directs us to discern what it means to live as God's covenant people in the contemporary world.

By speaking through the pages of Scripture, the Spirit shapes our identity as Christians.[47] As the vehicle through which the Spirit speaks, the Bible serves as the primary source for our shared understanding of the God who enters into covenant with us and therefore of ourselves as those God has called to be his covenant people. To this end the Bible narrates the story of the covenant-making God who has displayed divine faithfulness to us despite our failure, a narrative that climaxes in the coming of Jesus and the outpouring of the Spirit.[48] Through this narrative and the attendant teaching the biblical writers draw from it, the Spirit endows us with a special identity. As participants in the covenant community, we become a people imbued with the Spirit of Jesus who transforms us into Christ's image—a people whom the Spirit draws into living in accordance with the beliefs, ideals, values and character our Lord revealed in his own life among us.

Although not using the specific term, Harmon Smith summarized well the nature of the theonomous ethic: "What the Gospel offers is not a self-validating rational standard, but a community of loyalty. Christian ethics has to do with the *ethos* of Christians, with a style of life which reflects the character of a new people who are shaped by living now in the new age. It is a community ethics, because it is the story of a people's journey; it is a religious ethics, because it is the story of a people's journey with their God."[49]

The Theological Foundations of the Christian Ethic

Throughout the Bible the ethical life is rooted in a theological context.[50] The biblical writers do not approach ethics as a philosophical discipline nor treat ethical discussions as a universally human concern. For them ethics is not a subtopic under anthropology. Instead, as noted earlier, the writers of Scripture understand ethics always and only as life under God and before God. Consequently for them religious conviction and morality are intertwined, and the claim to know the true God and correct personal conduct form a single, seamless garment.[51]

The ethical life emerges as God's people seek to understand the implications of the biblical vision of life under God for existence in the concrete moment. The Christian ethic is fundamentally the life of integrity—theology in action—as in our relationships we seek to live out the implications of our Christian theological commitments as derived from the narrative of the biblical God, climaxing in the story of Jesus the Christ.[52] This biblical vision speaks about who God is, who we are as God's creatures, and where God is taking all creation. Our goal in the remainder of this chapter, therefore, is to look at these basic themes of our Christian commitment with an eye toward their relevance as providing a theological foundation for ethics.[53]

The God before whom we live. The central subject of the biblical narrative is the God who has called us into covenant.[54] Foundational to the biblical understanding is God's status as Creator. Just as the Bible opens with the ringing statement "In the beginning God created the heavens and the earth" (Gen 1:1), so also the Apostles' Creed rightly commences with the words "I believe in God the Father Almighty, the Creator of the heavens and the earth." "Creator" delineates the fundamental relationship between God and the world.[55] To confess God as Creator is to acknowledge that everything in the universe owes its existence and being to, and derives its existence and being from, the God of the Bible: "For in him we live and move and have our being" (Acts 17:28). This confession carries important implications for the Christian ethic.

The declaration "God is Creator" provides the ultimate answer to the ethical question of value. As noted in chapter one, philosophical ethics is concerned with what humans ought to value and what forms the basis for valid value judgments. The answers philosophers generally offer indicate the basically anthropocentric character of the philosophical approach. In the end the final court of appeal can only be the human person and human conceptions of the good life. Humans value whatever they perceive contributes to that life.

To acknowledge God as Creator, however, is to raise the discussion to the theocentric level and offer a theological foundation for value. The Christian ethic approaches questions of value from the scriptural account of the divine Valuer. All value is ultimately determined solely by the Creator God of the biblical narrative. As the one who values truly, God is the standard for value, and this God calls us to value after the manner our Creator values.

This understanding has direct application to our understanding of the value of human beings. Contrary to the anthropocentric method found in natural or philosophical ethics, as well as in certain theological proposals which appeal to our being created in the divine image as the source of our value,[56] we cannot view the human person per se, but only in relation to God. As a result we are driven to deny the idea of humans possessing intrinsic value. The basis of our value does not lie in ourselves or in anything we might possess. Rather, our creation by God indicates that our value is *derived.* It arises solely from our relationship to the divine Valuer who values us.[57] As a result we can never dictate the value of any human life but are to value one another and ourselves as God does.

The realization that we "possess" derived value ought to foster true humility in us. None of us can extol his or her own value. Nor can we appeal to any value we claim to possess as the foundation for making demands on God or others. At the same time God's valuation should foster in us a true sense of worth. Rather than looking to others to determine our value, we can lift our heads high and boldly declare, "I am valuable, because God values me." In the same way the awareness that each is someone whom God values ought to lead us to treat everyone with the dignity which God affords us all.

* * *

One of the crucial issues surrounding the contemporary abortion debate is the question, Does the fetus have value? This debate, however, raises a deeper question, namely, Whose valuation of the fetus is most important—that of the pregnant woman, of the father, of society? Couched in these terms, the ensuing discussion often resorts to catch phrases such as "every child a wanted child."

The biblical understanding of value suggests that the question must be approached from a different perspective. More important than the opinion of mother, father or society is God's valuation of the fetus: What does God say about the one who is developing in the womb? In the end, Christians dare speak to the abortion question only from this perspective.[58]

* * *

The narrative of the Creator God declares likewise that all creation, including every human being, belongs ultimately to God alone. The Psalmist wrote, "The earth is the LORD's, and everything in it, the world and all who live in it; for he founded it upon the seas and established it upon the waters" (Ps 24:1-2). Cognizant of this, the Christian ethic involves looking at life in its entirety as a stewardship. Our calling is not to view ourselves as owners, but as administrators under God of whatever he has entrusted to us.

Being a steward means administering our personal lives, including all that we have and are—our physical being, intellectual acumen, abilities and even the years God entrusts to us—for the glory of our Creator (e.g., Mk 12:30).

* * *

Sometimes the Lord uses experiences to remind us of the need to be continually conscious that we are stewards of our lives. January 6, 1988, marked the beginning of the homeward leg of a Christmas holiday trip to Portugal and Spain. After saying our goodbys, I included in my prayer for the continued well-being of our friends the customary request for divine protection on our trip. In the mountains of southern Spain the "national highway" we followed became a narrow, winding, crudely paved trail. The adverse road conditions were made worse by the drizzle. Then came the one curve that the car simply refused to negotiate. I watched in disbelief as our automobile headed over the embankment to face an uncertain fate. The car's left rear wheel bore the initial impact of the fall, but our momentum caused us to continue to roll. We hit ground again on the front right corner of the roof before coming to a stop on all four wheels in a soft, rain-soaked meadow some twenty feet below the roadway. Yet we were alive; we were uninjured; we had even landed on "all fours."

The accident occurred one day before my thirty-eighth birthday. Later as I reflected on this incident, it was as if the Lord were speaking: "What is your life expectancy—some seventy-six years? You and your family could have died at the midpoint of your life. But I protected you. Now here is the second half of your life. What are you going to do with it?"

* * *

Stewardship extends to our relationships with others as well. Husband and wife do not own each other, parents do not own their children, and employers do not own their employees. Instead in these and all our relationships we are to act as stewards who bring glory to God. Similarly as stewards we take seriously our presence in society. Realizing that residency in a local community, citizenship in a nation and even participation in the "global village" entail responsibilities, we work with others to promote social structures that honor the biblical God.

God likewise calls us to live as stewards within the world around us. According to the biblical narrative, God's universe is "good" (Gen 1:31). As God's good creation the universe displays the divine glory (Rom 1:19-20) and fulfills its purpose of glorifying God (Ps 19:1; 148; 150:6).[59] The hymn writer states this theological conviction in poetic form: "All nature sings, and 'round me rings the music of the spheres."[60] Consequently, "nature" does not exist primarily as a resource for human use and consumption, nor simply to serve as the backdrop for the drama of human history,[61] but for God's own delight (Ps 104:31). For this reason we should approach creation with an appropriate sense of wonder and appreciation, open to see the spiritual truths God's creatures portray, after the example of the Old Testament Wisdom literature and Jesus' parables.

Although the acknowledgment that "God is Creator" is foundational to the biblical narrative, it does not take us to the heart of the Christian understanding of God. As noted in chapter six, the doctrine of the Trinity is the central theological contribution of the Christian faith and consequently the foundational conviction for Christian ethics.[62] We confess that the one God is the trinitarian persons in an eternal relationship of mutual love, and hence that God is love (e.g., 1 Jn 4:16).[63] Creation, in turn, exists by the divine love, for it is the product of the overflowing of the mutual love of the Father and the Son, that is, the personal Holy Spirit.[64]

Ultimately the divine goal in creating the universe is to bring creation to share in the eternal love within the heart of the trinitarian God and to evoke a loving response from God's creatures, especially human beings. This divine intention defines as our fundamental ethical task to respond properly to God's love by reciprocating the divine love and loving one another after the pattern exemplified by God.

The doctrine of the Trinity likewise provides the theological foundation for the way of the biblical God in the world. The entire scriptural narrative portrays God acting toward creation with the resolute love that reveals the divine character. Creation experiences God's love in many ways, but especially through God's care for all creatures (e.g., Gen 9:8-17; Jon 4:11; Mt 6:26, 30). God's glorious love is visible in a special manner in the focus of the biblical narrative: "For God so loved the world that he gave his one and only Son" (Jn 3:16).

As this text from the Fourth Gospel indicates, although God entered into covenant with all creation, humans are God's special covenant partners. We alone are called to be the *imago Dei,* a term which, contrary to the dominant tradition in both Western philosophy and theology, does not refer primarily to our rationality[65] but to our calling to mirror the character of God.[66] As God's image-bearers we are to reflect God's character to each other and to all creation by aligning ourselves with the divine cause in the world. Hence we continually ask, What are God's intentions, and how can we best be God's instruments in fostering the divine will in the present situation?

Living as God's image-bearers involves expressing God's loving concern for all of creation. Above all, however, this mandate includes seeking to develop loving relationships with others, so that in our attitudes and actions toward all people we reflect God's love. We will look more closely at this central dimension of the Christian ethic in the next chapter.

The desire to mirror God's love mandates Christian involvement in social issues, including the quest for justice in its many forms. We are attentive to justice issues simply because we share God's loving concern for all creation, and therefore we desire to be the vehicles through which God expresses that love to all. Our desire to be vehicles of God's love leads to attempts to transform social structures that work against God's loving purposes. To this end we become God's advocates in confronting evil, and we champion the cause of the weak, the marginalized and the downtrodden, just as Jesus has shown us by his own example.

This discussion carries a grave implication for how we approach human rights. Specifically it alerts us to the often unacknowledged sharp chasm that exists between the theocentric Christian vision of human rights and the generally anthropocentric foundation offered by the contractarianism that has dominated the Enlightenment political tradition.[67] Some ethicists suggest that originally the concept of human rights emerged from a theological basis.[68] Whether or not that is the case, the Enlightenment tradition of rights language builds from the assumption that the autonomous individual endowed with certain natural rights is the fundamental building block of society. By an act of the will, free, independent, autonomous individuals enter into what Jean-Jacques Rousseau (1712-1778), following John Locke (1632-1704), termed a "social contract," for the purpose of preserving the person and property of each.[69] Although entrance into the social contract entails the giving up of one's natural rights, as a citizen the individual gains a set of civil rights. According to modern interpreters of this tradition, the possession of rights means that the self has a claim against others.[70] And because others have certain obligations toward the self, the self can demand their fulfillment.[71]

In contrast to this tradition, the Christian ethic, following the model of the social Trinity, speaks only of persons-in-relationships. Thereby the biblical vision seeks to bring together the self and the community in which the self is embedded. And hence in a certain sense it places communal relations on the same ontological level as the self. Consequently a truly Christian ethic cannot follow the sharp bias toward individualism found in the architects of the Western political tradition, who view the precepts of the law of nature as concerned mostly with individual rights rather than with individual responsibilities within society.[72] Christians simply cannot be content to argue the language of the rights of autonomous individuals in isolation, but must balance the appeal to any presumed inherent rights with an equal appeal to the responsibilities bound up with the relational embeddedness of the self.[73]

Paul Ramsey noted this already in 1950: "Human rights cannot be fully analyzed as if they pertained to the individual apart from society. They are not claims which a man makes the conditions of his reluctant participation in societal concerns. . . . Rights do not inhere in the isolated, 'natural' individual. They pertain to the individual insofar as there are certain powers which he must be allowed to exercise in order that maximum general welfare may be obtained."[74]

The paradigm for truly Christian relationships can only be the Lord Jesus Christ. He willingly laid aside whatever prerogatives his exalted position entailed so that he might live and die for our sake and thereby glorify his heavenly Father. The "Christian way" involves exemplifying in all our relationships the same mindset (2 Cor 8:9; Phil 2:5). Again to cite Ramsey, "A person's primary relationship to the various communities of which he is a member is one of service, and not first of all one of making demands upon them."[75] For this reason, rather than arising from the inherent rights we or any other individuals have, ethical obligations emerge from the character of the community of Christ in which we are members.[76]

Humans as living before God. As the above discussion indicates, we cannot talk about the triune God as our Creator without also speaking about humans as the creation of the triune God. We have already pursued several of the implications of this foundational Christian commitment.

In addition to declaring that we are the divine image-bearers, Christian anthropology teaches that God created us as a unity and consequently that God's design for us is holistic.[77] This means that God's intention for each person extends to the totality of his or her being. From beginning to end the biblical narrative assumes the unity of the human person. After forming him from the material elements of the earth, God breathed into Adam the breath of life, and he became a living being (Gen 2:7). The fundamental personal unity we find in the creation narrative is confirmed by our future resurrection. On that great eschatological day we will be transformed in our entirety after the pattern of the resurrected Lord Jesus Christ (Rom 8:11, 23). Because we are whole beings, God's concern and purposes for us are not limited to any one aspect of our existence, such as the "immortal soul" to the exclusion of the physical body. Instead each of us is the recipient of God's love and is responsible before God in the totality of our embodied existence.

Our creation as a unity means as well that in the divine intention humankind forms a corporate whole. God's purposes are for all humans, and for all together. Paul, for example, repeatedly spoke of the unifying impulse of God's reconciliation of humankind in Christ. He declared that God's reconciling activity overcomes racial, socioeconomic and gender barriers (Eph 2:15; Gal 3:28). Indeed, just as our solidarity in Adam leads to death, so also God intends that we all participate in life through Jesus Christ (Rom 5:12-21; 1 Cor 15:22).

Similarly, God's goal for us is social. Rather than a realm of isolated individuals each inhabiting his or her own special cubicle, the Bible pictures our eternal home as a city, the new Jerusalem, which symbolizes community on the highest plane—a redeemed people dwelling in a renewed creation and enjoying the presence of the triune God (Rev 21:1-3; 22:1-5).[78] Within the church, this glorious purpose is already a partial reality. The redeemed people of God form one body (1 Cor 12:12-26), a social reality constituted by individuals whom the Holy Spirit unites into a single whole, which we graphically symbolize whenever we eat from the one loaf at the Lord's supper celebration (1 Cor 10:17).

The communal nature of the divine intention indicates that the ethical life encompasses our fundamental existence as persons-in-relationship. There is, of course, an intensely individual dimension of the ethical teaching of Scripture. We live as individuals before a holy God, and we are individually responsible to this God. But the biblical ethic does not address the individual in isolation. Instead, knowing that we constantly live in social contexts, we can only speak to persons-in-relationship.[79] The biblical writers call us to live as God's people in all our relationships, and as a result, the Christian ethic is never merely a "personal" but always also a "social" ethic.[80]

In addition to drawing us to view the ethical life as living in relationships, the fundamental awareness that we are a created unity ought to lead us to seek holistic responses to ethical problems. Rather than focusing on only one aspect of human existence, we must always regard one another as the unitary beings we are. The human sciences are becoming increasingly aware of this necessity. For example, the older understanding of medical care tends to view the patient as analogous to a physical machine composed of "parts" to be "fixed" when they break or malfunction. Contemporary caregivers, in contrast, are more willing to acknowledge that sicknesses are more than merely malfunctions of the body. The human person is increasingly being viewed as a unity encompassing the physical, the psychological and even the spiritual. To the extent that it reflects a biblical anthropology, Christians can welcome this development (see, for example, Jas 5:14-15).

Our responses to ethical problems must also be holistic in that they are directed beyond the individual in isolation to humans in their social context, and they take into consideration the social dynamics at work in the various situations of our life together. Likewise the Christian ethic is holistic in that it moves us beyond the myopic focus on ourselves and those in our immediate circle[81] to a global perspective that fosters concern for all persons without exception and without prejudice. The Christian outlook ought to lead us to view everyone as valuable in God's sight and as a potential participant in God's eternal community, and then to gauge our attitudes and actions according to this awareness. Christian holism also encompasses all creation, as we lift our eyes to consider the wider connectedness we share with the earth that nourishes us and even with the entire universe in which God has placed us.

Christian anthropology moves from the "good news" that we are God's handiwork to the "bad news." Humans are fallen, sinful creatures.[82] Ultimately sin is failure—our failure to live in accordance with our God-given design or purpose. This failure lies at the very core of who we are, so that at the depth of our being we are alienated from God, from others, from creation and even from ourselves.[83]

Our creation as a unity implies a unitary understanding of sin. If we are created as unitary persons, then no one "part" of our being, such as the body, can be viewed as the source of sin. Instead, the person as a whole is a sinner.

Similarly the unity of humankind means that sin cannot be relegated solely to the individual in isolation. Sin also has a corporate or social aspect. We do not only sin as individuals, we also sin as groups and against groups. The Old Testament prophets reflected this reality when they called the rich in Israel to act justly toward the poor and the privileged to defend the cause of the less fortunate. Not only do we sin corporately, sin is also transmitted corporately. Through the process of socialization we teach others, including our children, to sin. And our involvement in social structures transmits sin within society. In keeping with this understanding, the prophets knew the importance of confessing corporate sin. For example, his vision of God's holiness led Isaiah not only to declare "I am a man of unclean lips," but then to add, "and I live among a people of unclean lips" (Is 6:5; see also Dan 9:4-11). So strong is the social dimension of sin that the New Testament speaks about a kingdom of evil.

The biblical writers use the word *enslavement* to characterize our situation: We are held captive by a foreign, evil power. The pervasive presence of sin taints all our actions. Even in our most pious moments or most noble acts we can readily discover—if we are honest with ourselves—the presence of faulty, self-serving motivations.

* * *

When I was a seminary student, my church history professor described to the class one day an incident that illustrates the pervasive presence of sin, even in the lives of Christians. This godly man was present at a gathering of evangelicals. At one of the sessions the leader singled him out to pray. The professor offered a sincere, heartfelt, eloquent prayer. But as he sat down, his first thought was self-congratulatory: "My, but you did a good job!"

* * *

Our acknowledgment of the pervasive presence of sin leads us to reject "contextual absolutism," which holds that, in the words of one proponent, "in each and every ethical situation, no matter how extreme, there is a course of action that is morally right and free of sin."[84] It also leads us to realize that all human responses to grave ethical dilemmas can in the end offer only partial solutions. For this reason we must approach all ethical problems with a strong dose of what Reinhold Niebuhr called "Christian realism."[85] Try as we will, we can never bring the final resolution to any difficulty. In fact we may discover to our dismay that our "final solutions" often generate new problems.

This realization ought to be a sobering reminder that *we* are not the answer to the world's problems. The solution does not lie simply in the expansion of the church in the world, as important as this is. Our role is not to *be* the answer, but to be a sign pointing toward the only ultimate answer, namely, God's gracious provision in Christ. In this manner the Christian teaching about human sin leads to the acknowledgment that we stand in need of divine grace and that the ethical life emerges as the result of God's faithfulness to the covenant in spite of our failure.

The center of the Christian life. This basic scriptural teaching leads us to the heart of the Christian faith. In contrast to the Greek philosophers, with their concern for determining the good life and delineating ethical principles through rational reflection, the biblical writers begin with a story about a God who acts in human history and in so doing models the ethical ideal. This narrative focuses on one specific, historical life, Jesus of Nazareth, whom Christians acknowledge as God's glorious provision for our human situation. Building on this conviction, Christian ethicists throughout the ages have declared that the focus of the ethical life is Jesus, and that ultimately the Christian ethic *is* Jesus Christ.[86]

R. E. O. White encapsulated the entire tradition when he concluded, "This is Christianity's unique contribution to ethics: the identification of the moral ideal with a historical person; the translation of ethical theory into concrete terms in a real human life; the expression of moral obligation in the language of personal loyalty; and the linking of the highest moral aspiration with the most powerful motives of personal admiration, devotion, gratitude, and love. In thus uniting the only hope of eternal salvation with the highest expression of the moral ideal in one historic person, lies the unique power of the Christian gospel."[87]

But in exactly what sense is Jesus the center of the Christian ethic? Traditionally Christians have answered this question by speaking of our

Lord as God's disclosure of both the divine essence and the divine intention for human existence. Or, to draw from the great christological confession of the church, Jesus is both divine and human. As a result we may speak of the ethical life as "christopraxis," to borrow Edmund Arens's term.[88]

To say that Jesus is divine is to acknowledge that he is the revelation of God, for in this historical person we see what God is like.[89] Above all Jesus reveals to us the divine principle of life, which arises from the very heart of God, namely, that the foundation for true living is love. In so doing, Jesus has disclosed God's way in the world—a manner that is radically different from the practice of the world itself. According to Jesus God does not effect the divine program through the strength of coercion but by the power of self-sacrificial love. God's way involves vulnerability, suffering and even death. However, self-sacrificial love is not sentimentality. On the contrary it involves steadfast, tenacious fortitude for the sake of others.

In declaring that Jesus is truly human we acknowledge that he is the revelation of what we are to be.[90] Above all, our Lord demonstrates that true humanness entails loving God and living on behalf of others so that God may be glorified. Because Jesus reveals true humanness, the ethical life is the imitation of Christ. Herein lies the truth of Charles Sheldon's call to Christians to ask in each situation, What would Jesus do?

But the imitation of Christ moves beyond mere deeds. It is neither possible nor desirable to try to determine how Jesus would act in every context. The life of imitation involves being motivated by the ideals, goals and purposes that moved Jesus. It entails living in acknowledgment of God's lordship and on behalf of others, after Jesus' own pattern of life. Its focus, as Jesus' example indicates, must be on humble servanthood for the sake of God's glory. Hence in each situation we desire that the character and ideals of Jesus be manifested through our lives.

Because Jesus is the revelation of God, the imitation of Christ is simultaneously the imitation of God. Consequently as we live in conformity with Christ we become the *imago Dei*, for we thereby reflect the character of the God who is love.

Insofar as the focal point of the Christian ethic is a historical life, the ethical ideal cannot be reduced to a list of laws, principles or axioms. As Paul Lehmann wrote, "Christian ethics . . . is oriented toward revelation and not toward morality."[91] The ethical life is constituted by a relationship. It emerges as we become true disciples of Jesus and thereby honor the One he called "Father." We live out the biblical ethic when our devotion to the One who loved us motivates us to reflect through our lives the ethical ideal we have personally experienced, which ideal characterizes the life of the eternal God.

Its christological focus does not leave Christian ethics merely in the past or even the present; it also mediates to the ethical life a decidedly eschatological perspective.[92] From the Old Testament prophets to the seer of the Apocalypse, the writers of Scripture appeal to the vision of God's future in calling for ethical living in the present. The biblical ethic is directed toward something that lies beyond the present, namely, God's final purpose, the new creation Christ has revealed.

This eschatological direction is evident in Paul's extended discussion of the future resurrection. After forcefully presenting the good news that one day God will transform us into immortal spiritual bodies that bear the likeness of Christ, the apostle concluded with a resounding "therefore": "Therefore, my dear brothers, stand firm. Let nothing move you. Always give yourselves fully to the work of the Lord, because you know that your labor in the Lord is not in vain" (1 Cor 15:56). Paul's point is obvious: because God is going to do this, you must do that!

Participation in the resurrection is not merely a hope for our physical existence, however. We will likewise be morally transformed after the likeness of Christ. John stated this succinctly: "Dear friends, now we are children of God, and what we will be has not yet been made known. But we know that when he appears, we shall be like him, for we shall see him as he is" (1 Jn 3:2). He then moved from the future hope to the present: "Everyone who has this hope in him purifies himself, just as he is pure" (v. 3).

According to the viewpoint of the biblical writers, therefore, our true identity lies in God's future, and not in either our past or our present as some given essential nature that we already possess as humans.[93] We are the glorified saints who we one day will be, as Paul declared: "And God raised us up with Christ and seated us with him in the heavenly realms in Christ Jesus" (Eph 2:6). If this is who we are, the ethical imperative follows, an imperative which in reality is closely connected to an indicative:[94] Be/become who you are! Live in the present in accordance with the perfect conformity to Christ which one day you will enjoy, because in fact you are the glorified saints who you will one day be. This eschatological focus of the Christian ethic led Paul Lehmann to exclaim, "The Christian lives neither by his 'Adamic' past nor by his 'Christian' past, but by the future, of which his present is an exhilarating foretaste."[95]

This dimension of the biblical imperative brings us to the scriptural truth that God's provision for our situation goes beyond revealing what it means to live ethically. This provision also creates in us what God wills for us. For this reason the biblical narrative presents Jesus as the one who reconciles us to God, frees us from sin and pours out his Spirit upon us.[96] As a result of Christ's work on our behalf we enjoy a new identity: we are God's children.[97] Our new status or identity forms the starting point of the ethical life. This life entails living according to the identity the Father so freely bestows on us in the Son and thereby becoming the very persons God has declared us to be in Christ.

In this manner the biblical ethic flows out of the transformed life God creates in us. David recognized this when he entreated, "Create in me a pure heart, O God, and renew a steadfast spirit within me" (Ps 51:10). And Paul reiterated the point: "Through Christ Jesus the law of the Spirit of life set me free from the law of sin and death" (Rom 8:2). With good reason, then, Donald Bloesch concluded, "Ethics in this theological perspective is no longer a submission to law but instead a response to divine grace."[98] And on this basis Helmut Thielicke drew an appropriate distinction between Christian and philosophical ethics: "In philosophical ethics the ethical acts are determined by the 'task' to be performed. In evangelical ethics they are determined by the 'gift' already given."[99]

As these texts indicate, the biblical writers pinpoint the identity of the one who renews the human heart. The author of the new, eschatological life is the Holy Spirit.[100] And this "eschatological Spirit"[101] is none other than the Spirit of the Lord Jesus, for the goal of his transforming work is to bring us to a full maturity[102] marked by nothing less than "the whole measure of the fullness of Christ" (Eph 5:13).

Ethical living, therefore, flows out of the new life given us by the Holy Spirit through our relationship to Jesus Christ. Hence, rather than reason controlling the will, as the Greek philosophers with their elevated faith in human reason proposed, the Christian ethic envisions a life directed by the

Spirit. It speaks about believers who are filled—that is, empowered, guided and controlled—by the Spirit of God. And consequently, as Thielicke exclaimed, "Theological ethics is eschatological or it is nothing."[103]

The link to the Holy Spirit is what gives the biblical ethic its capacity for continual application throughout history. It allows this ethic to remain a living tradition, which continues to meet the challenges of life despite the changing contexts in which we find ourselves. The ethical life does not focus on rote obedience to a set of axioms, principles or laws set forth in some bygone era and which therefore may not provide guidance for living today. Instead the Christian ethic envisions life guided by a living person, the Holy Spirit, who speaks through the Scriptures to the community of faith in every generation. In every age the ethical life emerges as believers seek to follow the Spirit's lead in guiding them to respond to the challenges they face. As we listen to the Spirit's voice speaking through the Scriptures and appropriate the divine power he mediates, we receive the grace we need to live as the people of God in the contemporary context.

The direction of the ethical life. Grounded in the triune God and focused on the living Lord Jesus Christ present among God's people through the Holy Spirit, the Christian ethic flows out of the vision of God's goal for creation which marks the climax of the biblical narrative. As noted earlier, this goal is nothing less than the establishment of community on the highest plane, namely, a redeemed people inhabiting a renewed creation and enjoying fellowship with the triune God.

The eschatological goal of the divine program in the world leads us to the biblical theme of the reign of God, which the authors of Scripture present as both a future hope and a present reality.[104] The kingdom refers ultimately to the eschatological consummation of history in the eternal community in which God's will is fully actualized throughout all creation. Yet even in the present, the power of the future remains continually active. As a consequence the kingdom is present to the extent that God's will—God's purpose, goal or design—is actualized in the situations of life. Wherever and whenever community emerges in our fallen world, God comes to reign. Above all, however, God's purposes are accomplished as we commit our lives to Christ, and as a result the Spirit brings us into fellowship with God, one another and God's creation.

The biblical vision of community provides Christian ethics with its specific direction. The ethical life entails living each moment eagerly anticipating and diligently advancing the reconciled fellowship God wills for us and for all creation. This life emerges as we seek to allow the vision of God's intention shape the way we live in the here and now. Being the people of God in the present involves "incarnating" the divine principle of life within all our relationships. To this end we continually ask, How could God's goal for creation best be fostered in this situation? What would the present look like if it were to reflect God's purpose, namely, the creation of true community? What needs to happen for the current situation to conform to the divine ideal?

The eschatological vision of God's purposes for creation provides the context in which to understand the church as an ethical community. The church functions in this manner through its role as a shaper of moral identity.[105] As we noted already, we do not construct our personal identity (or personhood) as isolated individuals but through our participation in communities of reference. Being a Christian involves participation in a particular community, the fellowship of those who draw their fundamental identity from the biblical narrative of God's provision in Jesus. The ethical life, in turn, flows out of this specific self-identity, together with a unique vision that the Spirit mediates to us as participants in the believing community.

The church also functions as an ethical community as it becomes the vehicle through which we learn to live according to the divine pattern of life as revealed by Jesus.[106] Perhaps the most formative events surround our life together as a worshiping community.[107] As we join together in the symbolic acts within our worshiping life (including baptism and the Lord's Supper), as well as in the public reading of Scripture and prayer, we are reminded of who we are. At the same time through these acts we invite the Holy Spirit to mold us into the particular kind of people whom God has already constituted us through Christ, and we petition the Spirit to guide and empower us for the task of living as that people in the contemporary context.[108]

Through the fulfillment of its edification mandate, the church likewise serves as the vehicle through which we learn how to live. This mandate includes the many ways that we instruct one another in the ways of the

Lord. It extends also to what we might properly call "church discipline." In extreme situations such discipline may take the form of excommunicating an unrepentant immoral member (1 Cor 5:1-5). More commonly, however, it entails simply walking together as a covenant people. At each step of our journey together we encourage—even admonish—one another, and we hold one another accountable as fellow pilgrims en route to the glorious fellowship we will share in God's eternal community.

This reference to our final goal suggests another dimension of the Christian vision of the church. We are to be even now the eschatological community of Christ. Indeed, this—and not some universal ideal arising out of human nature—is the direction toward which the entire Christian ethic points.[109] God's intention for our life together as Jesus' disciples is to bring into the present, as far as possible, the future fullness of God's reign by being a community gathered around our Lord, who by his Spirit lives in our midst. Within the eschatological community which he draws together, the Spirit inaugurates the peaceable reign of God, which is the future of all creation.

Our fundamental commitment to be shaped by the Spirit into God's eschatological people provides the contours for our life together and hence of the ethical ideal. Our stalwart conviction that God has acted, is acting and will act to bring about the divine intention ought to lead us to live in such a way that we hasten the consummation of God's program. Speeding the day of God, to cite Peter's designation (2 Pet 3:12), demands that we not only live holy lives (v. 11), but above all that in all our relationships we embody the character of God, which is love.

This ideal includes modeling true community within our corporate life. As those who know God's gracious forgiveness and who enjoy the reconciliation Christ has effected, we are led to forgive one another (e.g., Col 3:13) and to be reconciled with each other. Similarly, as those who have been touched by Christ, we seek to be a people whose relationships with one another are infused with the healing power of our Lord. In this manner the church stands as a glaring contradiction to the alienation and mean-spiritedness so prevalent in the world.

The ideal of the church as an ethical contradiction to the world leads to yet a third dimension of our mandate.[110] Our calling does not end at the boundary of the church but includes an ethical mission to the world.

Foundational to our mandate to be the people of God in the world is our task of proclaiming God's intention for creation in general and humankind in particular, and of admonishing human society around us to respond properly to Christ's claim to lordship. Our very presence as a community of faith gathered within the wider context constitutes a partial fulfillment of this task.

Bound up with this admonishing function is a continually implicit and repeatedly explicitly voiced critical stance against every dimension of human social interaction that does not serve or conform to God's goal of establishing true community. But we do not merely point out the shortcomings or denounce the presence of evil in society. Instead we seek to be what Robert Webber and Rodney Clapp have called a "diacritical community,"[111] a people who model an alternative, as in our own communal life we point toward the future community that will come as God's eschatological gift. In so doing, the church becomes a "sacrament" in the world, or what Philip LeMasters spoke of as a " 'subculture' of 'sacramentality' that pursues and embodies the implications of the gospel for human interaction."[112] But our mission in the world requires one additional step as well. We must be willing to affirm the traces of community present by God's grace everywhere and even seek to assist society in the task of structuring itself according to the principles of God's eternal community.

The radically future orientation of the biblical vision stands as a reminder that the goal of history comes only as God's gracious gift to us. A proper awareness of this leaves no room for triumphalism. We readily acknowledge the fallenness of our world and the impossibility of truly being an eschatological people prior to God's final renewal of creation. We realize that all our attempts to be a holy people and to seek the transformation of society in accordance with God's purposes will at best be only partially successful. We know that in the end we can only trust God, wait for God and in faith beseech him, knowing that the Father of our Lord Jesus Christ will one day act decisively through the Holy Spirit to bring the divine plan to completion (Lk 18:1-8).

At the same time the ethical ideal continually confronts us in the present as "the impossible possibility," to borrow Reinhold Niebuhr's poignant term.[113] The biblical ethic admonishes God's people throughout the ages to live in the light of that future hope and to order life according to the vision of God's future, so far as it is possible within the parameters of existence in the here and now. Hence, the vision of God's glorious eschatological community remains our calling in every concrete present. God invites us to be partners in the divine work in the world. As a result of this gracious invitation and through the empowerment of the indwelling Holy Spirit, our cooperation—our "labor in the Lord"—is significant in the process of bringing God's purposes into being. Therefore, despite the limitations of our present existence, we diligently seek God's kingdom and God's righteousness in accordance with Jesus' admonition. And at each step we trust that the Holy Spirit is at work in and through us, whether we be involved in fervent prayer, diligent appropriation of the disciplines of character formation or concerted efforts toward social reform. Above all we anticipate the Spirit's work in us, forming us into the *imago Dei* so that we reflect the divine character, which is love, and thereby truly live as the disciples of Jesus our Lord.

Chapter 8

COMPREHENSIVE LOVE

The Content of the Christian Ethic

And now these three remain: faith, hope and love.
But the greatest of these is love.
(1 CORINTHIANS 13:13)

Don and Donna met three months ago at a divorced persons' support group. Both had gone through difficult marital breakups after some twenty years of marriage, which seriously wounded their self-esteem. These common elements of their stories initially drew the two together. One month ago Don asked Donna to join him for an evening of dinner and dancing. On the dance floor something happened: each found solace in the arms of the other. The last two weeks have been "heavenly" for both. In fact, they have seen each other daily, doing all those "fun" activities together that the day-to-day responsibilities of married life had crowded out of their schedules.

With the increased contact has come increased physical involvement as well. Both Don and Donna are Christians who were raised on the dictum that premarital sex is wrong. But both find themselves increasingly desiring to engage in sexual intercourse. As a result, each is struggling in silence with the same question: Could it be that the ethic of abstinence is only for adolescents? Could it be that the situation is different for mature adults who truly love each other?

* * *

George Russell lay in his hospital bed musing about his uncertain future. The prostate surgery had apparently gone without a hitch, thanks to Dr. Jonathan Rogers, who was the "best in the business." And in his postsurgical consultation the specialist had only chuckled when his worrywart of a patient had remarked that the operation had probably not entirely eliminated the problem. Yet George remained apprehensive. Dr. Rogers had seemed a bit too methodical and matter-of-fact in offering his crisp response to George's expression of anxiety. The patient wished he could feel confident that everything was indeed "going to be all right."

For his part, Rogers was oblivious to Russell's anxieties. For the specialist the operation had been just another part of the daily routine. And George Russell was just another name to be checked off the patient list now that his illness had been eliminated, thanks to the surgeon's skills and the wonders of modern medicine.

* * *

In chapter seven I outlined the vision that provides the theological foundation of the Christian ethic. This vision speaks of the ethical life as the actualization of the divinely given design or intention for us, namely, that we be the image of God. The God whose image we are called to be is none other than the social Trinity, the trinitarian persons in eternal fellowship. The biblical writers declare that the character and essential nature of this God is love. And the biblical narrative recounts how the triune God demonstrates this love toward all creation, but especially toward humankind.

The Christian vision declares that ultimately the task of fulfilling our purpose as the *imago Dei* involves our being transformed into conformity with Christ (2 Cor 3:18), who is the embodiment of the divine image (Col 1:15). This entails being imbued with Jesus' own character and being motivated with the ideals that he exemplified. Thereby we become the glorified saints that God has already declared us to be. The agent of our transformation is the Holy Spirit, who brings us into the fellowship of

Christ's community, the church. Hence, just as the God whose loving character we are designed to reflect is the social Trinity, so also the ethical life is relational. The biblical vision focuses on persons-in-relationship.

For this reason Christian ethicists throughout the ages, taking their cue from the conclusion to Paul's great hymn to love (1 Cor 13:13), have emphasized the foundational importance of love to the ethical life. Christians repeatedly elevate love as representing the heart of the biblical vision of the human ethical ideal, an ideal which arises out of the dynamic of the divine life. Gilbert Meilaender speaks for many in asserting, "Our task is nothing less than this: to achieve within human life the love that is a dim reflection of the life of God. In the Triune God—Father as initiating ground, Son as coequal respondent, and Spirit as the mutual bond which springs from their giving and receiving—we have a picture of love."[1]

My final goal in this overview of theological ethics is to look more closely at the theme of love that has so captivated the entire Christian ethical tradition. Specifically I want to pursue the course charted by the Old Testament, Jesus, the apostles and Christian thinkers from Augustine to Paul Ramsey in order to understand in what sense love leads us into the heart of the Christian ethic and at the same time determine what characterizes Christian love.

The Foundation for a Christian Understanding of Love

As anyone acquainted with the Christian tradition knows, love is enjoined throughout the Bible. Our Lord did not own the copyright to the answer he gave when the Jewish legal expert asked, "Teacher, which is the greatest commandment in the law?" In his response Jesus summarized the entire Old Testament law as love for God and one's neighbor:[2] "'Love the Lord your God with all your heart and with all your soul and with all your mind.' This is the first and greatest commandment. And the second is like it: 'Love your neighbor as yourself.' All the Law and the Prophets hang on these two commandments" (Mt 22:37-40; cf. Mk 12:28-34; Lk 10:25-28).

Many of our Lord's followers view this teaching as "the core and climax of the whole of moral doctrine," to cite Rudolf Schnackenburg's description.[3] Although the radical elevation of love may have been unique to Jesus' message,[4] the Teacher himself learned the double command from the Hebrew Scriptures (Deut 6:4-5; Lev 19:18). And as Paul's memorable words to the Corinthian believers indicate (1 Cor 13:13), the apostles passed on the admonition to love they had heard the Master reiterate.

The biblical focus on love requires that we pursue the ethical meaning of the concept. Hence we must ask, What actually is this quality that we find acclaimed throughout the Bible? And on what foundation can we build an understanding of love?

Love in the Greek language. Many scholars have pointed out that, in contrast to the impoverished situation of our mother tongue, the language of the New Testament has several words referring to dimensions of what we call "love." According to C. S. Lewis, the ancient Greek speaker/writer had available four possibilities: *storgē* (affection, especially within families), *philia* (friendship), *eros* (love between the sexes or being in love) and *agapē* (charity or self-giving love).[5]

In spite of the array of options that stood before them, the biblical authors are amazingly one-sided in their choice of terms. Two of the four words, *storgē* and *eros,* do not find their way into the New Testament at all.[6] The third, *philia,* ranks as the most commonly used term for love in Greek literature. William Barclay described the richness of the noun and its cognates: "There is a lovely warmth about these words. They mean to look on someone with affectionate regard. They can be used for the love of friendship and for the love of husband and of wife. *Philein* is best translated to *cherish:* it includes physical love, but it includes much else beside."[7]

At first glance we might anticipate that the richness of *philia* would have attracted the attention of the New Testament writers. In fact, however, they use the word only sparingly. The noun itself is found only in James 4:4, where it is put to negative use. In addition, it occasionally appears within related, compound terms, such as *philadelphia* (e.g., Heb 13:1). The verb *phileō* is slightly more prominent, occurring about two dozen times (e.g., Mt 10:37). Yet half of these are in the Fourth Gospel, leading Gustav Stählin to note in the *Theological Dictionary of the New Testament* that outside of John "there is no special liking for *phileō.*"[8] In short, although *philia* found its way into the canonical writings, the concept did not play a leading role in the thinking of the early church.

In contrast to the relatively meager presence of the other three terms, the repeated use of *agapē* indicates that it is the word of choice in the New Testament. Its prominence leads us to ask, What does this word mean? And how is it related to the other Greek terms for "love"?[9]

Although some observers caution against assuming too strict a demarcation between *agapē* and *philia,* a clear distinction does seem to have existed between the two. Stählin, for example, has pointed out that although in the New Testament *philia* may approach *agapē* in meaning, the Greeks sensed a distinction between the two terms similar to our differentiation between "to like" and "to love," especially when love was accompanied "with strong feeling, inwardness, devotion, and even passion."[10] More significantly, the biblical writers do not generally use *philia* to speak about either God's love for humans or our love for God.[11]

Christians have traditionally drawn an even greater disjunction between *agapē* and *eros.*[12] Derived directly from the name of the Greek god who "is compelled by none but compels all," *eros* may be defined as the "passionate love which desires the other for itself."[13] Whether taking the form of sensual intoxication (such as in the fertility rites and temple prostitution of the Greek religious cults) or the more sublime experience of ecstatic union with the One (articulated, as we saw in chapter two, by Plotinus), the underlying goal was the same. For the Greeks *eros* involved the experience of transcending one's own life.[14]

No wonder Christians from the patristic era into the present follow the example of the New Testament and elevate *agapē* to center stage.[15] This previously obscure word[16] of uncertain etymology, lacking both the power or magic of *eros* and the warmth of *philia,* was just what the early Christians needed to articulate their understanding of love.

In part the reason for the choice of *agapē* lay in the meaning of the term itself. In classical Greek, the verb form *agapaō* can carry the idea of "to prefer," "to set one good or aim above another," "to esteem one person more highly than another." As a result it could denote God's preference for a particular person and hence the one whom God blesses with particular gifts and possessions. Consequently, to the ancient Greek mind *agapē* spoke of a love that moved beyond emotion—beyond an experience which, in the words of Barclay, "comes to us unsought, and, in a way, inevitably."[17] Instead, *agapē* is "a principle by which we deliberately live."[18] This kind of love has to do with the mind and the will.

In keeping with this distinction, Ethelbert Stauffer drew an illuminating contrast between *agapē* and *eros*:

> *Eros* is a general love of the world seeking satisfaction wherever it can. *Agapan* is a love that makes distinctions, choosing and keeping to its object. *Eros* is determined by a more or less indefinite impulsion towards its object. *Agapan* is a free and decisive act determined by its subject. *Eros* in its highest sense is used of the upward impulsion of man, of his love for the divine. *Agapan* relates for the most part to the love of God, to the love of the higher lifting up the lower, elevating the lower above others. *Eros* seeks in others the fulfilment of its own life's hunger. *Agapan* must often be translated "to show love"; it is a giving, active love on the other's behalf.[19]

The narrative of the loving God. These distinctions in nomenclature lead us back to the biblical narrative. As we have seen, when the writers of Scripture offer ethical teachings, they do not base their statements on an appeal to philology but to a narrative. Hence the various dimensions of the biblical ethic arise out of a story line which focuses on the God who acts in the constancy of divine love.

Forming the backdrop to the story is an affirmation of the universal goodness of God borne out of love. The biblical writers proclaim the One who lovingly sustains all creatures. In love God provides water, food and shelter for the animals (Ps 104:10-28) and by the Spirit renews the face of the earth (v. 30). As a loving heavenly Father, God cares for even the most insignificant of creatures—the birds and the grass (Mt 6:26-30).

At the center of the biblical narrative, however, lies a particular object of divine love. While not discounting the importance of all creation, the central task of the Bible is to speak about God's steadfast, resolute disposition toward humankind.[20] The curtain rises on the drama with the creation of the first humans, followed by the shattering of their bliss through willful sin. The rest of the story recites how the loving God makes provision for fallen humankind. The Old Testament speaks about God's selection of Abraham to be the one through whom he would bless the nations and about God's entering into covenant with Israel. The New Testament, in turn, elevates the story of Jesus as the focal point of God's loving provision and the supreme expression of the divine love. Paul summarized the biblical narrative by pointing to Jesus' self-sacrifice on behalf of miserable human beings: "For you know the grace of our Lord Jesus Christ, that though he was rich, yet for your sakes he became poor, so that you through his poverty might become rich" (2 Cor 8:9).

The implication is obvious: As we come to see how God has acted toward us—that is, as we understand the biblical narrative—we discover what love truly is. Hence, Paul declared that it was "while we were still sinners" that God demonstrated his love for us by sending Jesus Christ to die (Rom 5:8; cf. 1 Jn 4:10). This grand narrative of the One who freely sacrificed for our sakes led the biblical writers to the previously obscure Greek word *agapē*, for this term expresses the self-giving attitude that characterizes the God of the salvation narrative.

The New Testament writers, following the path charted by the Hebrew Scriptures, take the grand biblical narrative one additional step. God's glorious love for us leads us to love also. John stated this truth with sublime simplicity: "We love because he first loved us" (1 Jn 4:19). This human response to the divine act entails loving the One who loved us. Hence in the early community Jesus' "first and greatest commandment" quickly became a self-evident assumption (e.g., Jas 1:12; 2:5; 1 Pet 1:8).

Love for God also quite naturally moves toward others. John, "the apostle of love," summarized the horizontal aspect of the New Testament agapaic ethic: "Since God so loved us, we also ought to love one another" (1 Jn 4:11). The same appeal to the divine narrative is evident in what Paul acknowledged about the Thessalonian believers: "Now about brotherly love *[philadelphia]* we do not need to write you, for you yourselves have been taught by God to love *[agapaō]* each other" (1 Thess 4:9). In whatever relational contexts we find ourselves—marriage (Eph 5:22-32), the Christian community (e.g., Rom 14:15) or even in a hostile world in which people mistreat or persecute us (1 Pet 2:20-24; 3:9)—believers are to draw from the narrative of the loving God and the self-giving example of Christ the model for living.

Following Jesus' own teaching—"All the law and the prophets hang on these two commandments"—the New Testament writers put forth this agapaic ethic as the fulfillment of the law. In Paul's words, "Let no debt remain outstanding, except the continuing debt to love one another, for whoever loves others has fulfilled the law. The commandments . . . are summed up in this one rule: 'Love your neighbor as yourself'" (Rom 13:8-9; cf. Gal 5:13-14). Hence *agapē* recapitulates the Old Testament law. And by being the bond that unites the individual commandments into a unified whole, it provides the perspective from which believers understand the law,[21] as we developed in chapter seven.

Why *agapē?* In chapter three I outlined the Pauline answer. In keeping with the ethical teaching of the Old Testament and of Jesus, Paul agrees that love is crucial because it characterizes God. The narrative of God's action on behalf of sinful humankind reveals the greatness of the divine love. As we love, we imitate God. Further, love is central because the community of faith is the primary context for living as believers.[22] The apostle did not conceive of Christ's followers living an isolated, solitary existence but as called *together* to form the one body of Christ (e.g., 1 Cor 12:12). Community life is the life of love, and *agapē* expresses well the idea of life in community.[23]

Above all, however, the agapaic focus arises out of love's eternal significance.[24] Whereas all other aspects of Christian existence will one day cease, love will carry over into the new aeon (1 Cor 13:8-13). Of the various dimensions of the moral life, love is central to the whole, for it alone provides insight into the coming age. Indeed, love is the actual quality of the age to come.[25] Where love exists the new aeon is present. And the moral life is eschatological living: It involves acting now as those who belong to the age to come.

The foundation for agapē in the divine life. This reminder of the Pauline focus on *agapē* as representative of the entire biblical vision of the ethical life leads us to inquire as to why the narrative of the *loving* God stands at the heart of the biblical drama and thereby forms the foundation for the Christian agapaic ethic. In other words, Why can we say with theological confidence that the God revealed in the biblical narrative is love? The search for an answer to this question leads us into the mystery of the eternal God, touched on in chapter six and again in chapter seven. Ultimately God's steadfast love for creation, and especially for wayward humankind, arises out of nothing less than the dynamic within the heart of the triune God.

The biblical witness suggests that the God of the salvation narrative is triune, the fellowship of Father, Son and Holy Spirit. Further, the ontological unity which the three constitute and therefore which comprises the divine essence is *agapē,* for as John carefully declared concerning the divine character and essence, "God is love" (1 Jn 4:8, 16). John's choice of *agapē*—the giving of oneself for the other—to describe God's essential nature is illuminating. As several Christian thinkers as early as Athanasius[26] have noted, the divine unity is comprised by reciprocal self-dedication among the trinitarian members. God is, therefore, indeed love, for the divine essence is the love that binds together the triune God.

To see this more clearly requires that we set forth an understanding of the dynamic that inheres within the divine life. According to the church fathers, this dynamic involves two movements. Theologians speak of the first movement as "generation." Throughout eternity the Father generates the Son, to use Origen's characterization. This movement does not only constitute the second member of the Trinity who draws his life from the Father. Rather, as Athanasius insightfully perceived, it also constitutes the first member, for without the Son he is not the Father.[27]

Although differentiated, the Father and the Son are also bound together. The bond between the two is the mutual love they share. Throughout all eternity the Father loves the Son, and the Son reciprocates this love. Augustine noted that the love between the Father and the Son is the Holy Spirit, the eternal Spirit of the relationship[28] or the bond[29] between the Father and the Son. Being the Spirit of the relationship between the first and second trinitarian members, the Spirit proceeds from the Father and the Son, according to the Western version of the creed. In this manner the movement of generation constituting the Father and the Son necessitates as well the procession of the Spirit as the Spirit of the Father and the Son.

God's triune nature as Father, Son and Spirit indicates how John can truly say "God is love." Love is a relational term, requiring both subject and object (someone loves someone else). Were God a solitary loving subject, God would require the world as the object of the divine love in order to be the Loving One. But because God is triune, the divine reality already comprehends both love's subject and object—both lover and beloved—as well as the love they share. Consequently the essence of God does indeed lie in the relationship between the Father and the Son (love), a relationship concretized as the personal Holy Spirit, who is the essence of the one God (Jn 4:24).

Through all eternity God is the social Trinity, the community of love. The God who is love cannot but respond to the world in accordance with God's own eternal essence—love. Hence *agapē* is not only the description of the eternal God in all eternity, it is likewise the fundamental characteristic of God in relationship with creation. With profound theological insight, therefore, John burst forth, "For God so loved the world that he gave" (Jn 3:16).

A Comprehensive Ethic of Love

This theological discussion reminds us that the ultimate foundation for the Christian agapaic ethic resides in the eternal dynamic of the triune God. We fulfill our purpose as those designed to be the *imago Dei* as we love after the manner of God, that is, as our relationships are likewise characterized by *agapē*. No wonder Christian ethicists have consistently spoken about the centrality of this kind of love.

But does this indicate that *agapē* alone comprises the fullness of the meaning of Christian love and hence that *agapē* determines completely the content of the biblical vision of the ethical life as the life of love? Or is there a comprehensive love ethic that encompasses more than may be ascribed solely through the equating of love with *agapē?*

Agapē and the other dimensions of love. Christian ethicists have repeatedly engaged with the implications of the biblical focus on *agapē* for the proper description of the ethical life. And they often articulate this question in terms of the implications of the biblical focus on *agapē* for the role of the other Greek concepts in the Christian ethical vision.

One widely held proposal depicts *agapē* as divine love in contrast to *storgē, philia* and *eros,* which are merely "natural loves." In *The Four Loves* C. S. Lewis contrasted the divine "Gift-love" (which God can impart to humans and which in us becomes images of himself) with what he called the "Need-loves," which "have no resemblance to the Love which God is."[30]

The contrast between *agapē* and the other types of love often leads to the elevation of the former over the latter. Paul Tillich, for example, found the others ambiguous unless they are infused by *agapē:* "In the holy community the *agapē* quality of love cuts into the *libido, eros,* and *philia* qualities of love and elevates them beyond the ambiguities of their self-centeredness."[31] Lewis himself offered a somewhat more optimistic appraisal. He argued that because affection, friendship and desire are natural loves, *agapē* can work through them and thereby bring them to participate in "the eternity of Charity."[32] He wrote, "The Divine Love does not *substitute* itself for the natural—as if we had to throw away our silver to make room for the gold. The natural loves are summoned to become modes of Charity while also remaining the natural loves they were."[33]

Lewis's proposal provides an ingenious way through which the human experiences of affection, friendship and even sexual desire gain access to the transcendent realm of eternity. But his suggestion (even more so than Tillich's)[34] denies that the natural loves enjoy any transcendent grounding, any foundation in the divine life.

Several thinkers today are questioning this traditional focus on *agapē* or selflessness as the apex of the ethical life.[35] Given its presence in the New Testament itself, *philia* (friendship) is the obvious choice for rehabilitation. To understand this we must remind ourselves of the classic critique of *philia.* Tillich, following Augustine's lead, articulated the standard appraisal: "The ambiguities of the *philia* quality of love appeared already in its first description as person-to-person love between equals. However large the group of equals may be, the *philia* quality of love establishes preferential love. Some are preferred, the majority are excluded. . . . *Agapē* does not deny the preferential love of the *philia* quality . . . it elevates the preferential love into universal love. . . . *Agapē* cuts through the separation of equals and unequals, of sympathy and antipathy, of friendship and indifference, of desire and disgust. It needs no sympathy in order to love; it loves what it has to reject in terms of *philia. Agapē* loves in everybody and through everybody love itself."[36]

Recently Gilbert Meilaender has called into question the traditional position exemplified by Tillich. Meilaender wondered if proponents of this view "purchase universal love at the cost (at least in this life) of all particular attachments." And he pointed out the dilemma of the pure agapaic ethic: "Once we have come to see the goal toward which philia calls us, how can we justify continuing to enjoy our preferential loves rather than pressing as best we can toward that goal of universal love even in this life?"[37]

Meilaender's desire to find a place for *philia* within the Christian ethic is laudable in the light of the New Testament use of the cognate word *philadelphia* in injunctions to the Christian community. Hence, Paul admonished the Romans, "Be devoted to one another in brotherly love" (Rom 12:1; cf. Heb 13:1), although Peter added the reminder that by itself such love is insufficient (1 Pet 1:22; 2 Pet 1:7). And Paul even used the cognate verb to speak about our love for Christ, for he warned the Corinthians, "If anyone does not love *[philei]* the Lord—a curse be on him" (1 Cor 16:22).

Even more importantly, the biblical materials suggest that like *agapē*, *philia* may find its foundation in the salvation narrative. After speaking about the great love that would lead him to lay down his life for his friends, our Lord called his disciples "friends" (Jn 15:13-15; cf. Lk 12:4). Thereby he revealed the heart of the God who spoke to Moses "as a man speaks with his friend" (Ex 33:11) and to whom the patriarch Abraham was "friend" (2 Chron 20:7; Is 41:8; Jas 2:23).

We might less directly connect the affection expressed in the word *storgē* with the biblical God in that the narrative repeatedly speaks about the divine compassion. At the center of the faith of the Hebrew community stood a declaration of God's compassion, which the book of Exodus describes as having its source in God himself. After revealing the divine name to Moses on Mount Sinai, Yahweh declared himself "the compassionate and gracious God, slow to anger, abounding in love and faithfulness" (Ex 34:6; cf. Neh 9:17; Ps 86:15; 103:8; 111:4; 116:5; 145:8; Joel 2:13; Jon 4:2; Is 54:10). This God is compassionate in spite of human rebellion (Dan 9:9) and apart from our merit (Ex 33:19; Dan 9:18; Rom 9:15-16, 18).[38]

Jesus appealed to God's ways to enjoin a similar compassion within the fellowship of his disciples: "You have heard that it was said, 'Love your neighbor and hate your enemy.' But I tell you: Love your enemies and pray for those who persecute you, that you may be sons of your Father in heaven. He causes his sun to rise on the evil and the good, and sends rain on the righteous and the unrighteous" (Mt 5:43-45; see also the parable of the good Samaritan, Lk 10:30-37). Our Lord's own life comprises a vivid illustration of this principle.

As Jesus' words suggest, in the biblical writings divine compassion draws from the familial imagery often connected with *storgē*. This is evident in the story that is perhaps the most moving illustration of God's compassion, the parable of the prodigal son. While the wayward son "was still a long way off," Jesus declared, the father saw him "and was filled with compassion for him" (Lk 15:20). In a similar manner Jeremiah described God as desiring to have compassion on Ephraim, "my dear son" (Jer 31:20). And although the Old Testament narrative foundation for divine compassion may actually have been in the idea of God's covenant faithfulness, the Hebrew term "compassion" *(raham)* also carries the idea of family relations. Because the word's linguistic stem means "womb," compassion could be seen as referring to "the feeling of those born from the same womb" or "the love of a mother for her child."[39]

Meanings associated with *storgē* and *philia* may claim a basis in the biblical narrative. But what about *eros?*[40] Here we step onto thinner ice. Christian thinkers readily admit the role of "desire" not only in human sexual relations but even in religious devotion. There is a long-standing tradition that draws from the experience of longing and desire as forming the foundation for the quest for God. But is there any sense in which we can predicate *eros* of God?

We must admit that any attempt to do so is fraught with theological danger. Linking God with *eros* risks undermining the great truth that God is complete within the eternal community of the triune life and hence that creation is a nonnecessary act. As a result any *eros* within God cannot be in the form of a desire for creation born from God's own insufficiency or need.[41]

Having said this, we must also acknowledge that one powerful motif in the biblical narrative of God's love for his people draws from marital love.[42] The Old Testament prophets illumined God's relationship to Israel through a three-act drama. Act one consists of the betrothal of Israel to Yahweh. The loving God intended that Israel respond to his love like a virgin bride who gives herself willingly, continually and exclusively to her husband (Jer 2:2) and thereby becomes his delight (Is 62:5). Hence, rather than the typical ancient understanding, which carried connotations of a contract between king and vassals, God's covenant with his people was to be a relationship of mutual love.

Act two speaks about Israel's unfaithfulness. Yahweh's bride showed herself to be an adulterous spouse, forsaking her husband for other lovers. As a consequence Yahweh "gave faithless Israel her certificate of divorce and sent her away because of all her adulteries" (Jer 3:8; cf. Hos 2:2, 4-5). Despite Israel's adultery, in the glorious third act the loving God proved his faithfulness.

The faithful love of Israel's husband formed the basis for the hope of a future restoration. God declared, "I will show my love to the one I called 'Not my loved one.' I will say to those called 'Not my people,' 'You are my people'; and they will say, 'You are my God'" (Hos 2:23).

New Testament writers such as Paul (Rom 9:25) and Peter (1 Pet 2:9-10) applied this dramatic motif of marital love to God's relationship with his new people. But they generally shifted the imagery to speak more specifically about Christ and the church. Through his self-sacrificial life and death, Christ, the loving bridegroom (Mk 2:18; Jn 3:29; Rev 21:9), demonstrated his love for the church (Eph 5:32). In this manner the New Testament brings the marital drama into the broader, overarching narrative of the loving God who sends Jesus Christ to die for sinful humans.

The marital narrative raises a critical theological question: How can we affirm the erotic aspect of the divine love it embodies without falling into the trap of making God dependent on creation? Although we did not note it earlier, the same potential difficulty arises—even if less obviously—from our discussion of *storgē* and *philia.* Our earlier treatment of the theological foundation for *agapē* points toward the answer. Together with *agapē,* we must lodge these concepts within, and bring them together in, the divine trinitarian life.

The love dynamic within the triune God is, of course, primarily *agapē,* self-giving love, as John declared. Throughout eternity the Father gives his life to the Son. And as Jesus' obedience to his heavenly Father reveals, the Son eternally reciprocates that love in an eternal act of self-giving. In this manner the divine essence is *agapē,* an essence concretized in the Holy Spirit.

Yet the eternal love is infused with the other dimensions as well. As a relationship between Father and Son (suggested by the traditional trinitarian language), the divine love includes the familial affection *(storgē).* And we can readily understand that it involves the friendship enjoyed by eternal Friends as well *(philia).* But does the inner-trinitarian relationship also involve *eros?* To this query we can answer yes if we understand *eros* in its deeper sense of a desire for communion with the beloved.[43]

Trinitarian *eros* is the reciprocal holy desire of the eternal Persons for communion within the divine life. Throughout his earthly sojourn, Jesus demonstrated that he shares a unique communion with the one he called "Abba." The evangelists linked Christ's communion with his Father, in turn, with his glorification by the Father. This is evident, for example, in what is often called Jesus' "high priestly" prayer: "Father, I want those you have given me to be with me where I am, and to see my glory, the glory you have given me because you loved me before the creation of the world" (Jn 17:24). Here Jesus indicated that the intimacy of love the Father showers upon the Son—the communion they share—is the Son's glory. And it is precisely this glorious communion with the Father that we will eternally enjoy through the Son on the day of our eschatological glorification.[44]

These considerations suggest that while retaining the primacy of *agapē*, our understanding of divine love must incorporate aspects of the other concepts too. In fact, when stripped of the dimensions of love expressed in *philia, storgē* and to some extent even *eros,* our conception of the God who is *agapē* can easily degenerate into a distant, austere, "Stoic" deity.

This mistaken theological conception often leads to a mistaken understanding of God's relationship to creation. The "Stoic" God rescues humans for no other reason than because it is his "job" to do so. Repeatedly theologians have been guilty of projecting a dispassionate God who is unmoved by his awareness of the human situation but is bound by duty to save. As we have already indicated, the biblical God, in contrast, is passionate, emotional and *com*passionate. This God *longs* to reconcile sinful humans who are at enmity with him, thereby transforming them into friends, and to bring them into glorious fellowship—even communion—as the reconciled members of his eternal family. (Note the tone of emotion in 2 Cor 5:20.)

Comprehensive Love and the Christian Ethic

Earlier we described the Christian ethical task as that of living out our destiny as the *imago Dei.* Above all, this task mandates that we reflect the divine love. Because God's love is comprehensive, encompassing the dimensions represented in the four Greek terms, our Christian ethic of love must likewise embody the various aspects of the one concept of love, albeit as ruled and guided by *agapē*. This means that all four dimensions must be present in all our relationships, yet in a form appropriate to each and always with *agapē* at the center.

James Nelson stated well the rationale for this conclusion: "If we define Christian love as agape or self-giving alone—without elements of desire, attraction, self-fulfillment, receiving—we are describing a love which is both impoverished and impoverishing. But the other elements of love without agape are ultimately self-destructive."[45] But what does such a comprehensive ethic of love entail? Two examples of the contexts in which we relate to one another offer insight.

One obvious example is marriage. We would naturally expect to find both *storgē* (familial affection and compassion) and *philia* (companionship) between husband and wife. But what about *eros?* Can *eros* find "redemption" within marriage through its interaction with *agapē?*

God's intention is clearly that *eros,* present in the form of sexual desire, play a central role in the joining together of man and woman to become "one flesh." Rather than deprecating the physical aspect of marital relations, as certain Christian thinkers have done, the biblical writers even celebrate the erotic dimension (e.g., Song of Songs; cf. 1 Cor 7:3-5; Heb 13:4).

Yet the erotic cannot serve as the sole—or even the central—foundation for a healthy marriage. The other aspects of love—friendship and affection—are equally important. But above all the controlling dimension must be *agapē,* expressed through the mutual submission Paul cited as the foundation for his discussion of the ideal marriage (Eph 5:21). Whenever *eros* triumphs over *agapē,* unethical relationships emerge. For example, when a married person commits adultery, personal desire for another *(eros)* has triumphed over self-sacrifice for the sake of faithfulness to the marriage covenant partner *(agapē).*[46]

Perhaps of even more consequence is the interaction of the four dimensions under the rulership of *agapē* in caregiving. I will illustrate this by looking at one area of immense interest today, namely, ethical reflection on medical caregiving.

Medical personnel have steadfastly defined themselves under the rubric of care. In the caregiving function medical ethicists have pinpointed the foundational principles of respect for patient autonomy and justice. In addition, health-care professionals have traditionally committed themselves to cultivate the virtues of beneficence ("do good") and nonmaleficence ("do no harm").[47] Medical personnel have repeatedly practiced these virtues at great personal cost. Their self-sacrificial actions in the pursuit of their vocation have led many in our society to revere health-care practitioners as examples of the kind of self-giving love the biblical writers speak of through the use of the term *agapē*.

Medical professionals dare not lose this focus on an agapaic ethic. Indeed *agapē* ought to remain the controlling understanding of love within any ethic of care. Yet the elevation of the twin principles of beneficence and nonmaleficence as the central virtues of health care ethics and as defining an agapaic ethic for caregivers risks allowing the patient-caregiver relationship to degenerate into a type of austere paternalism. Even the best actions motivated by a concern to uphold beneficence and nonmaleficence can all too readily become mechanical, and the professional caregiver can easily become "merely a professional." Whenever health-care practitioners fulfill their duties in an aloof or condescending manner, caregiving becomes devoid of "care" and health care is delivered in an "uncaring" manner.[48]

Certain contemporary ethicists have rightly pinpointed the problem. Uncaring health care stems from the total lack of emotional connection to the patient. Especially important to caregiving is one particular emotion, compassion, which means literally "to suffer with." Hence, the standard dictionary definition speaks of compassion as "a sympathetic emotion created by the misfortunes of another accompanied by a desire to help."[49]

The contemporary appeal to the concept of compassion to provide the foundation for an ethic of care links medical ethics to the biblical narrative. Human compassion can be measured only according to the compassionate God revealed in the biblical narrative. Indeed the Scriptures repeatedly present the divine compassion as the response of God's loving heart confronted with human need. Above all we find the divine compassion in the example of Jesus, who willingly offered his healing touch to the medical outcasts of his day (Mk 1:41). As the Evangelist points out, our Lord was not moved by a sense of duty but by a genuine "suffering with" the needy people he encountered. Consequently, care given from a sympathetic heart is in accordance with the biblical call to us to reflect the divine character in our relationships with all people (Job 30:25; Col 3:12; Heb 13:3; 1 Pet 3:8) and thereby to act as true neighbors to those in need (Lk 10:25-37).

This kind of compassion-filled medical care may not necessarily be triggered by a commitment to an agapaic ethic alone, especially if it is simply defined by beneficence and nonmaleficence. Even acts of *agapē*—acts in which a caregiver gives of himself or herself for the sake of the other—can all too readily be understood in a narrow, duty-bound, uncompassionate manner. Such "love" devoid of emotion may actually lead to the very paternalism that medical professionals need to avoid. As James Childress remarked, "Paternalism clearly rests on the principle of love for the neighbor in our religious traditions and on the duty to benefit the patient in the Hippocratic tradition of medicine."[50]

As a solution to this problem Childress calls for devising "practices and procedures that can indicate care and concern."[51] But from what springs the standard whereby we can pinpoint, as well as the motivation we need to apply, such "careful" medical practices? It is here that we must invoke a more comprehensive understanding of love than *agapē* alone can muster. Stating the point more directly, the genesis of true care lies in a love that goes beyond giving of oneself for the sake of the other as motivated by a sense of duty. It involves an *agapē* infused with the emotional tones represented in other dimensions of love.

Putting the matter in Christian theological terms, the kind of love that lies at the heart of the Christian agapaic ethic is an *agapē* informed by a "sensing with" others as those whom God has created with the goal of participating in an eternal community. As the Holy Spirit mixes the self-giving impulse *(agapē)* with a compassionate familial concern for *(storgē),* plus a sincere desire to enjoy the friendship of *(philia)* and true communion with *(eros)* each other in God's eternal fellowship, the Spirit of the relation between the Father and the Son leads us into the fullness of the Christian love ethic. It is this kind of comprehensive love that characterizes truly *Christian* caregiving relationships, not only in the medical realm but in every context.

The Ethic of Love and the Community of Christ

The focus on the triune God reflected in these sentences brings us back one more time to the community of faith.

The route we traversed in arriving at the conception of love we articulated here did not lead us to reflect philosophically on some supposedly essential nature innately present within each person. Instead our understanding arose from reflection on a specific narrative, the story of the way of the triune God in the world. The method we followed indicates that we cannot extract love—at least not in the manner we have described it—from the narrative in which our description is embedded. We cannot isolate the comprehensive understanding of love we outlined from the triune Life in which it is preeminently found. We cannot treat it as an entry in our "dictionary of the English language" to be trotted out whenever we need it to serve as a convenient descriptor for a virtue or an act which we supposedly have observed in ourselves or in another.

Similarly, in these paragraphs we have not espoused a universally human ethic. The way of love cannot be extolled without further qualifications as the ideal for humankind. Nor can love function as the content of our ethical admonition to all without distinction. Instead, what we have presented is the vision of the ethical life of a specific community, namely, the fellowship of those who gather around Jesus Christ, whom they acknowledge as the embodiment of the fullness of the divine love. In this sense the way of comprehensive love can only be the way of the Christian community, with its mandate to express through its corporate life and through its presence in the world the comprehensive love of the triune God, who has called the church into covenant.

The comprehensive ethic of love we have outlined, therefore, is embedded in a specific community that bears a specific self-identity. As we have noted repeatedly, the biblical narrative speaks about a God whose purpose is to bring humankind to reflect to all creation the eternal divine nature, that is, to be the image of God. This goal forms the cosmic context for the scriptural drama of salvation.

Although it includes the salvation of the individual, God's ultimate program is not directed toward the human person in solitary aloneness but toward persons-in-relationships. And it even moves beyond the isolated human realm to encompass all creation (Rom 8:18-22). This salvation climaxes in the eschatological establishment of a reconciled humankind (Eph 2:14-19) living in the renewed creation and enjoying fellowship with the triune God (Rev 21:1-5a). For this reason the biblical drama depicts how the Father sent the Son into the world and has poured out the Holy Spirit in order to overcome our failure and alienation, and thus to effect the healing of our relationships to God, to one another and to creation.

As a consequence God's gracious salvation extends to us in our social relations and to our interconnectedness with all creation. God's program is directed toward and is experienced in community. The church, in turn, is to be the community of salvation, the fellowship of those whose relationships are being transformed by the grace of God and power of the Spirit to reflect the divine love in its comprehensive glory.

Another path leads us to the same conclusion. God's salvation entails sending the Son and pouring out the Spirit so that we might become the children of God (Jn 1:12-13; Rom 8:15; Gal 4:6). But our filial status is exactly the relationship the Son enjoys with the Father. Through conversion the Spirit—who is the Spirit of the relationship between the Father and the Son—constitutes us the brothers and sisters of Christ. Thereby the Spirit brings us to share in the love the Son enjoys with the Father and hence which lies at the heart of the divine life.

Participation in the dynamic of trinitarian love, however, is not ours as isolated individuals. It is a privilege we share with all other believers. Because of Christ's work on our behalf and the Spirit's activity within us, we are co-adoptees into the family of God, coparticipants in the love the Father showers on the Son and through the Son on us as well. In mediating this relationship to us, the Spirit draws us together as one family. Only in our Spirit-produced corporateness do we truly reflect to all creation the grand dynamic that lies at the heart of the triune God. As we share together in the Holy Spirit, we truly are the community of love, a people bound together by the love present among us through the power of God's Spirit.

This glorious indicative forms the basis of the ethical imperative. The church is a people who covenant together to belong to God—that is, to be holy, to be set apart from the world for God's special use. Our calling as this holy people is to show forth the divine reality, that is, to be the image of God. The church reflects God's character in that it lives as a genuine community—as it lives in love—for only as the community of love can the church mirror the nature of the triune God.[52] The ethical mandate of the church, therefore, is to reflect as far as possible in the midst of the brokenness of the present that eschatological ideal community of love which models itself after the community of the triune God. This occurs as all our relationships embody the comprehensive reality of love revealed in the biblical narrative of God in Christ effecting the reconciliation of the world.

Ultimately, then, the Christian ethic of love is an ethic of salvation. It draws its meaning from, and leads the community which acknowledges it as its ideal into, the narrative of the God who acts for the salvation of all creation. In this manner the ethic of comprehensive love moves beyond all human definition to become the ethic of eternal life in the eschatological community of God.

As Paul Tillich noted in the concluding sentences to his short treatise on ethics, "I have given no definition of love. This is impossible because there is no higher principle by which it can be defined. It is life itself in its actual unity. The forms and structures in which love embodies itself are the forms and structures in which life is possible, in which life overcomes its self-destructive forces. And this is the meaning of ethics: the expression of the ways in which love embodies itself, and life is maintained and saved."[53]

* * *

Over dinner one evening Don and Donna engaged in an open discussion about their relationship. In the course of conversation the two concluded that they had been confusing their desire for friendship and true communion born out of compassionate affection for each other with sexual desire. While not wanting to eliminate all physical expressions, they committed themselves to enjoy the deeper aspects of their relationship uncluttered by the guilt and entanglement that engaging in sexual intercourse would introduce. They agreed that as believers they could best reflect God's love by abstaining from sex until such a time as before God they had committed themselves to each other in a lifelong partnership.

* * *

On his way home from the morning worship service, Russell's family physician dropped by to see him. During their brief conversation, Dr. Rogers sensed the anxiety in the voice of his patient. Carefully and slowly he explained to Russell the prognosis for his future and the steps they would take together to insure a full recovery. Obviously relieved, Russell abruptly asked Rogers about his golf game.

Epilogue

THE CELEBRATIVE NATURE OF THE CHRISTIAN ETHIC

Therefore, I urge you . . . in view of God's mercy, to offer your bodies as living sacrifices, holy and pleasing to God—this is your spiritual act of worship. Do not conform any longer to the pattern of this world, but be transformed by the renewing of your mind. Then you will be able to test and approve what God's will is—his good, pleasing and perfect will.
(ROMANS 12:1-2)

The goal of the preceding chapters has been to set forth a theological understanding of the Christian ethic. I have attempted to accomplish this task in the context of the traditional dialogue of Christian thinkers with the philosophical approach to ethics and with a view toward the contemporary revival of interest in a religiously oriented, community-based understanding of the ethical dynamic. Cognizant of this wider discussion, I have argued that the Christian ethic is fundamentally the exploration of the practical significance of the theological vision disclosed in and through the biblical narrative. This vision has implications for life, for sound Christian theological commitments provide the basic resources for living as the relational beings God intends us to be.

For this reason I explored certain central aspects of the Christian theological ethic. The foundation of the life of the believing community lies in the triune God, coupled with the biblical teaching that God's intention is that we be the *imago Dei*. The center of the ethical life is Jesus Christ, who is the revelation of the divine provision for human life after the divine image, and consequently the Holy Spirit, who is God's transforming presence within the community of those who gather around Christ. The direction of the Christian life then followed. To live ethically means to anticipate and actualize in the brokenness of the present the fellowship we will share in the new creation, the eschatological community of God. Finally this indicated the content of the Christian ethic. In all our relationships as Christ's people, we are to embody the comprehensive love that characterizes God's own life.

I must touch on one additional point, however, without which the entire discussion remains somewhat hollow. Many Christians view the biblical ethic primarily as a list of "do's and don'ts"—with a special focus on the "don'ts." This leads to the perception that the ethical life is a stern, austere and basically joyless journey across a bleak or even hostile earth. The journey of life is something we simply must endure so that we might one day reach the glorious heavenly city, where somberness will finally give way to joy.

But the biblical writers paint a different picture. While acknowledging the importance of living with all due diligence and seriousness, they present the Christian life as exhilarating and glorious. Being the believing community, they tell us, involves festivity. The ethical life is above all the life of celebration.[1]

The celebrative note is clearly sounded in Paul's exhortation to the Philippian believers, "Rejoice in the Lord always. I will say it again: Rejoice!" (Phil 4:4). Then follows what we might call an ethical connection, coupled with an encouraging promise: "Let your gentleness be evident to all. . . . Whatever you have learned or received or heard from me, or seen in me—put it into practice. And the God of peace will be with you" (Phil 4:5, 9).

What is the source of this celebrative emphasis? The basic biblical answer is: worship. The ethical life is celebrative because of its connection to worship.

The Bible repeatedly speaks about worship, presenting worship as a celebrative event. The scriptural authors enjoin us to extol God as the Holy One. In the words of the Psalmist, "Ascribe to the LORD the glory due his name; worship the LORD in the splendor of his holiness" (Ps 29:2;

see also 96:8; 1 Chron 16:29). In so doing we consciously join with the angelic hosts who continually proclaim, "Holy, holy, holy is the Lord God Almighty, who was, and is, and is to come" (Rev 4:6-8; see also Is 6:3). The Scriptures also urge us to worship God as Creator. In his vision of the heavenly court, John observed the twenty-four elders (who symbolize the whole people of God) declare, "You are worthy, our Lord and God, to receive glory and honor and power, for you created all things, and by your will they were created and have their being" (Rev 4:11). As the powerful Creator, God is worthy of awe and praise (Ps 29:3-10).

Rather than being somber, dark and fear-filled, all such worship is celebrative. We glory in the creative wonders God has accomplished. The hymn writer puts it well:

O Lord my God, when I in awesome wonder
Consider all the worlds Thy hands have made . . .
Then *sings* my soul . . .[2]

Above all we are to worship God the Savior. The Old Testament writers continually reminded Israel to extol God because the one who had graciously entered into covenant with them (1 Chron 16:15) had done great wonders (v. 12), especially in rescuing them from their enemies. According to the New Testament the focal point of God's saving work is Jesus. In our worship life as the community that gathers around his name, we commemorate the foundational events of our spiritual existence, at the center of which is God's deliverance of humankind from bondage to sin.

Here the celebrative character of worship is most pronounced. It is with glad hearts that we rejoice in the Rock of our salvation (Ps 95:1-3). In our joy we "declare the praises of him who called [us] out of darkness into his wonderful light" (1 Pet 2:9).

The biblical writers take this one step further, however. Rather than focusing only on our verbalized praise—whether in spoken word or song—they repeatedly speak of the way we live as worship. Thus they place ethics in the context of worship.[3] This is evident, for example, in the letter to the Hebrews. After the exhortation "Through Jesus, therefore, let us continually offer to God a sacrifice of praise—the fruit of lips that confess his name," the author adds, "And do not forget to do good and to share with others, for with such sacrifices God is pleased" (Heb

13:15-16). Living ethically and being a worshiping community are not two disjoined moments but are integrally related.

According to the biblical vision the ethical life is a dimension of our response to God and God's grace. The writers of Scripture characterize this response in its totality as worship. Hence for God's covenant people—whether Old Testament Israel (Ps 24:3-4) or the New Testament church (Heb 13:15-16)—ethical living throughout the week emerges out of and leads back into the gathering of the community in worship on the sabbath or the Lord's Day. In this sense Willi Marxsen's summarization of Paul is correct: "We can say that genuine Christian ethics is the worship of God in everyday life."[4] And as the apostle himself reminded the Romans, living ethically—that is, offering our very bodies as living sacrifices, holy and pleasing to God—is itself a dimension of true, spiritual worship. The ethical life, the apostle asserted, is worship. It comes as the fruit of offering our very lives to God in an act of worshipful celebration for the glorious mercy we have received through Jesus Christ our Lord. With good reason Ralph Martin defined worship as "the dramatic celebration of God in his supreme worth in such a manner that his 'worthiness' becomes the norm and inspiration of human living."[5]

Our worship goes beyond the praises of our lips to encompass our lives. We celebrate God's salvation as our lives bring glory to the triune One. In this manner the ethical life is celebration. But we have not yet pierced to the heart of this dynamic. Paul hinted toward this deeper aspect when he declared that the ethical life involves our inner transformation, the renewing of our minds (Rom 12:2). The agent of our ethical renewal and hence the one who authors true celebrative worship is none other than the Holy Spirit.

We noted that worship arises as our thankful response to God's gracious salvation. We know as well that the agent of salvation, the One who calls us out of the world into the community of Christ, is the Holy Spirit. This same Spirit is also the author of our response to God. The life-giving Holy Spirit whom God pours out within us not only releases us *from sin* but also releases us for true heartfelt love *for God*. Hence we willingly respond to God because the Spirit of life has freed us to serve our glorious Savior and to come to know the true liberty for which Christ has set us free (Jn 8:36). As this spiritual transformation occurs, we serve God joyously from hearts filled with gratitude and celebration for the grace God has lavished upon us. Because it is authored by the divine Spirit, living by the empowering, indwelling Spirit truly is the way of celebration.

Finally, Paul indicated the result of the Spirit's transforming work. Through the Spirit we come to discern and approve the divine will (Rom 12:2). This marks a stark contrast to the perception of many that the biblical ethic involves forced compliance with externally imposed laws. On the contrary, God's intention is that the law be written on our hearts (Jer 31:33), that is, that God's preferences become internalized as a part of who we are, so that we truly know the Lord (Jer 31:34). The One who accomplishes this is the Holy Spirit, and as we "walk in the Spirit" our lives are well-pleasing to God and hence truly celebrative of God's grace.

The ethical life arises as the life of liberty in service to God through Christ by the power of the Spirit. The Christian life is also the celebration of life, for as we live in the Spirit we celebrate the life of the triune God. Offering ourselves as a thanksgiving for God's love and mercy lavished on us in Christ is the pathway to true joy and fullness of life.

This returns us to the human ethical quest where we began. I noted in chapter one that well-being and peace of mind have repeatedly formed the object of philosophers' deliberations. The biblical writers declare that within the community of Christ we gain an even greater peace than the great ethical thinkers sought. Our Lord mediates to us peace with God (Rom 5:1), a peace "which transcends all understanding" (Phil 4:7). This greater peace is not ours because we have sought after it, but because the Holy Spirit showers it upon us as a byproduct of our ethical quest, the quest for God's kingdom and righteousness. Knowing such peace is the cause for great celebration. And it is in this context of celebration that we discover the fulfillment of Jesus' promise, for "all these things" are truly given to us as well (Mt 6:33).

Notes

Introduction

[1]Scott Steele, "Truth or Consequences," *Maclean's* 108, no. 1 (January 2, 1995): 14.

[2]Several years ago a team at the University of Alberta inaugurated a study of this question. See "Legal Ethics of Using DNA Samples Pondered," *The Vancouver Sun*, August 31, 1994, p. A10.

[3]For this phrase, see Vigen Guroian, *Ethics After Christendom: Toward an Ecclesial Christian Ethic* (Grand Rapids, Mich.: Eerdmans, 1995), p. 12.

[4]T. S. Eliot noted the presence of this phenomenon in English society in lectures delivered at Cambridge in 1939. He declared, "A society has ceased to be Christian when religious practices have been abandoned, when behaviour ceases to be regulated by reference to Christian principle, and when in effect prosperity in this world for the individual or for the group has become the sole conscious aim." *The Idea of a Christian Society and Other Writings* (London: Faber and Faber, 1982), p. 47.

Chapter 1: Christian Ethics & the Ethical Task

[1]Rex Warner, *The Greek Philosophers* (New York: Mentor, 1958), p. 56.

[2]Vernon J. Bourke, *History of Ethics* (Garden City, N.Y.: Doubleday, 1970), 1:20.

[3]Leander S. Keyser, *A System of General Ethics*, 4th ed. (Burlington, Iowa: Lutheran Literary Board, 1934), p. 25; Henry Sidgwick, *Outlines of the History of Ethics for English Readers* (Boston: Beacon, 1960), p. 1.

[4]Aristotle *Nicomachean Ethics* 2.1 [1103a].

[5]The major branches of philosophy include metaphysics, epistemology and ethics. Carl Wellman, *Morals and Ethics* (Glenview, Ill.: Scott, Foresman, 1975), p. xv.

[6]Keyser, *System of General Ethics*, p. 25. See also Peter A. Angeles, *Dictionary of Philosophy* (New York: Harper & Row/Barnes and Noble Books, 1981), s.v. "moral."

[7]William S. Sahakian, *Systems of Ethics and Value Theory* (New York: Philosophical Library, 1963), pp. 2-3; Wellman, *Morals and Ethics*, p. xvi.

[8]Wayne A. Meeks, *The Origins of Christian Morality: The First Two Centuries* (New

Haven, Conn.: Yale University Press, 1993), p. 4.

[9]Sidgwick observes that "the term 'moral' is commonly used as synonymous with 'ethical'" (*History of Ethics,* p. 11).

[10]Richard Taylor, *Good and Evil: A New Direction* (New York: Macmillan, 1970), p. 6.

[11]Jack Glickman, introduction to *Moral Philosophy: An Introduction,* ed. Jack Glickman (New York: St. Martin's, 1976), p. 1.

[12]At least since the Enlightenment this has been the case. Alasdair MacIntyre, *After Virtue: A Study in Moral Theory,* 2nd ed. (Notre Dame, Ind.: University of Notre Dame Press, 1984), p. 39.

[13]For the analogy between ethics and science, see Virginia Held, "The Validity of Moral Theories," *Zygon* 18, no. 2 (1983): 167-81.

[14]See, for example, Robert N. Beck and John B. Orr, *Ethical Choice: A Case Study Approach* (New York: Free Press, 1970), p. xvii; William Frankena, *Ethics,* 2nd ed. (Englewood Cliffs, N.J.: Prentice-Hall, 1973), p. 4.

[15]Fred Feldman, *Introductory Ethics* (Englewood Cliffs, N.J.: Prentice-Hall, 1978), p. 9.

[16]For a similar delineation, see, for example, Wellman, *Morals and Ethics,* p. xv.

[17]For a similar classification see R. M. Hare, *The Language of Morals* (London: Oxford University Press, 1969), p. 3.

[18]For an example of a treatise in analytical ethics, see Paul W. Taylor, *Normative Discourse* (Englewood Cliffs, N.J.: Prentice-Hall, 1961).

[19]An illustrative example is Hare, *Language of Morals.*

[20]For an example see Terrance C. McConnell, "Moral Blackmail," *Ethics* 91, no. 4 (1981): 544-67.

[21]This term actually carries several meanings. For a short but helpful discussion, see Geoffrey W. Bromiley, "Casuistry," in *Baker's Dictionary of Christian Ethics,* ed. Carl F. H. Henry (Grand Rapids, Mich.: Baker Book House, 1973), p. 85-86.

[22]Anne Colby and Lawrence Kohlberg, *The Measurement of Moral Judgment* (Cambridge: Cambridge University Press, 1987), 2:1.

[23]Borden P. Bowne, *Principles of Ethics* (New York: Harper & Brothers, 1893), p. 25. Bowne refers to these as the "two grand divisions of ethical philosophy."

[24]Hence neither the deontological nor teleological approach necessarily leads to either the "prolife" or the "prochoice" position, although deontological theorists may be more likely to favor stricter abortion laws. I framed the arguments in the manner I did merely for illustrative purposes.

[25]See, for example, Charles C. Miltner, *The Elements of Ethics* (New York: Macmillan, 1948), p. 94.

[26]For an example of this position, see E. F. Carritt, *The Theory of Morals* (Oxford: Clarendon, 1928).

[27]Hence Charles Pinches, "Principle Monism and Action Descriptions: Situationism and Its Critics Revisited," *Modern Theology* 7, no. 3 (1991): 255.

[28]P. H. Nowell-Smith, *Ethics* (Harmondsworth, U.K.: Penguin, 1954), p. 134.

[29]Immanuel Kant, *Groundwork of the Metaphysic of Morals,* trans. H. J. Paton (New York: Harper & Row, 1964), [414; 39] p. 82. Numbers in brackets are uniform academic citation numbers.

[30]Immanuel Kant, *Fundamental Principles of the Metaphysic of Morals,* trans. Thomas K. Abbott (Indianapolis: Bobbs-Merrill, 1949), p. 38.

[31]Wellman, *Morals and Ethics,* p. 43.

[32]Kant, *Groundwork of the Metaphysic of Morals,* [429; 66-67] p. 96.

[33]Ibid., [432; 72-73] p. 100.

[34]For this interpretation of Kant, see Feldman, *Introductory Ethics,* p. 128.

[35]For a similar criticism see Clifford L. Barrett, *Ethics: An Introduction to the Philosophy of Moral Values* (New York: Harper & Brothers, 1933), p. 171.

[36]Emil Brunner, for example, asserts that the entire law points toward the single command to love. *The Divine Imperative: A Study in Christian Ethics,* trans. Olive Wyon (London: Lutterworth, 1937), p. 112.

[37]See Joseph Fletcher, *Situation Ethics: The New Morality* (Philadelphia: Westminster Press, 1966).

[38]See, for example, W. D. Ross, *The Right and the Good* (Oxford: Clarendon, 1930).

[39]Philosophers sometimes refer to the position which asserts that the sole ultimate standard of right and wrong is the divine will or the law of God as "theological voluntarism" or the "divine command theory" (Frankena, *Ethics,* p. 28). For an exposition of this theory, see Carl F. H. Henry, *Christian Personal Ethics* (Grand Rapids, Mich.: Eerdmans, 1957).

[40]See, for example, William Luck, "Moral Conflicts and Evangelical Ethics: A Second Look at the Salvaging Operations," *Grace Theological Journal* 8, no. 1 (1987): 19-34. See also Robert V. Rakestraw, "Ethical Choices: A Case for Non-conflicting Absolutism," *Criswell Theological Review* 2, no. 2 (1988): 239-67.

[41]For a discussion of exceptions to moral rules, see Miroslav Kis, "Moral Rules and Exceptions," *Andrews University Seminary Studies* 30, no. 1 (1992): 15-33.

[42]Corrie ten Boom, *The Hiding Place* (Washington Depot, Conn.: Chosen Books, 1971).

[43]For examples, see Norman L. Geisler, *Ethics: Alternatives and Issues* (Grand Rapids, Mich.: Zondervan, 1971), pp. 114-36; Richard Higginson, *Dilemmas: A Christian Approach to Moral Decision Making* (Louisville, Ky.: Westminster John Knox, 1988).

[44]See Norman L. Geisler, "Graded Absolutism," in *Christian Ethics: Issues and Alternatives* (Grand Rapids, Mich.: Baker Book House, 1989), pp. 113-32.

[45]For a fuller development of this criticism, see my article "The Flight from God," in *Christian Freedom: Essays in Honor of Vernon Grounds,* ed. Kenneth W. M. Wozniak and Stanley J. Grenz (Lanham, Md.: University Press of America, 1986), pp. 69-85.

[46]Wellman, *Morals and Ethics,* p. 37.

[47]See, for instance, Epicurus, "Letter to Menoeceus," in *Letters, Principal Doctrines and Vatican Sayings,* trans. Russel M. Geer (n.p.: Bobbs-Merrill, 1964), pp. 127b-29a.

[48]For an assertion that people do indeed always act in their own self-interest, see Claude Adrien Helvetius, *Treatise on Man: His Intellectual Faculties and His Education* (New York: Burt Franklin, 1969), 1.4.1, pp. 277-79.

[49]See, for example, Norman E. Bowie, *Making Ethical Decisions* (New York: McGraw-Hill, 1985), p. 12.

[50]See, for example, Bruce C. Birch and Larry L. Rasmussen, *Bible and Ethics in the Christian Life* (Minneapolis: Augsburg, 1976), p. 115.

[51]Some ethicists suggest that the way out of the dilemma emerges as we draw a distinction between self-confined love and the true self-love that does not conflict with loving people and things for their own sake. See Arthur F. Holmes, *Ethics* (Downers Grove, Ill.: InterVarsity Press, 1984), p. 35.

[52]For a similar definition, see Frankena, *Ethics,* p. 34.

[53]John Stuart Mill, *Utilitarianism, Liberty and Representative Government* (London: J. M. Dent and Sons, 1910), p. 6.

[54]Wellman, *Morals and Ethics,* p. 39.

[55]For a helpful summary of these problems, see Feldman, *Introductory Ethics,* pp. 30-60.

[56]A. C. Ewing, *Ethics* (London: English Universities Press, 1953), p. 47.

[57]For a helpful statement of this shift, see Richard B. Brandt, "Toward a Credible Form of Utilitarianism," in *Morality and the Language of Conduct,* ed. Hector-Neri Castaneda Calderon and George Nakhnikian (Detroit: Wayne State University Press, 1963), pp. 107-43.

[58]Frankena, *Ethics,* p. 39.

[59]For a helpful discussion of rule utilitarianism, see Feldman, *Introductory Ethics,* pp. 61-79; Wellman, *Morals and Ethics,* pp. 40-42, 48. For a defense of rule utilitarianism, see Richard B. Brandt, "The Real and Alleged Problems of Utilitarianism," *Hastings Center Report* 13, no. 2 (1983): 37-43.

[60]For a helpful summary of several related problems of teleological theories, see Steve Wilkens, *Beyond Bumper Sticker Ethics* (Downers Grove, Ill.: InterVarsity Press, 1995), pp. 92-98.

[61]Wellman, *Morality and Ethics,* p. 81. For a quite different contrast, namely, between internal and external goods, see MacIntyre, *After Virtue,* pp. 190-91.

[62]For a statement of this view, see Mill, *Utilitarianism,* pp. 5-24, esp. 6-7 and 11-12.

[63]Taylor, *Good and Evil,* p. 95.

[64]John Piper, *Desiring God: Meditations of a Christian Hedonist* (Portland, Ore.: Multnomah Press, 1986).

[65]For examples of several theories of value, see Wellman, *Morals and Ethics,* pp. 84-94. Taylor, in contrast, suggests that traditionally only three answers to the question of the good have been proposed: virtue, pleasure and happiness (or well-being; Taylor, *Good and Evil,* p. 5). The following discussion parallels roughly Taylor's claim, while adding his own view as a fourth.

[66]This view is defended by Richard Taylor, who calls it "moral voluntarism" (Taylor, *Good and Evil,* p. 149).

[67]J. H. Muirhead, *The Elements of Ethics: An Introduction to Moral Philosophy* (New York: Charles Scribner's Sons, 1898), p. 97.

[68]Henry W. Wright, *Self-Realization* (New York: Henry Holt, 1913), p. 190.

[69]Ibid., p. 189.

[70]Wellman cites Francis Herbert Bradley as a proponent of this view (Wellman, *Morals and Ethics*, p. 91).

[71]Germain Grisez and Russell Shaw, *Beyond the New Morality: The Responsibilities of Freedom*, rev. ed. (Notre Dame, Ind.: University of Notre Dame Press, 1980), p. 90.

[72]Ibid., p. 93.

[73]John Wild, "Authentic Existence: A New Approach to 'Value Theory,'" in *Invitation to Phenomenology: Studies in the Philosophy of Experience*, ed. James M. Edie (Chicago: Quadrangle Books, 1965), pp. 59-77.

[74]For a succinct synopsis of the critique virtue theorists level at act-theorists, see Scott B. Rae, *Moral Choices: An Introduction to Ethics* (Grand Rapids, Mich.: Zondervan, 1995), pp. 92-93.

[75]MacIntyre, *After Virtue*, pp. 118-19.

[76]For a helpful statement of the distinction between these two approaches, see Bernard Mayo, *Ethics and the Moral Life* (London: Macmillan, 1958), pp. 200-218.

[77]See Aristotle *Nicomachean Ethics* 5.6 [1134a16-24].

[78]David Hume *A Treatise of Human Nature* 3.2.1.

[79]Nel Noddings, *Caring: A Feminine Approach to Ethics and Moral Education* (Berkeley: University of California Press, 1984), pp. 50-51.

[80]Noddings acknowledges that her position is a type of ethic of virtue (ibid., p. 80).

[81]Ibid., p. 103.

[82]MacIntyre, *After Virtue*, p. 219.

[83]Not all philosophers would agree, of course. For an argument that "right" and "good" are not opposing concepts, see Elizabeth M. Pybus, "False Dichotomies: Right and Good," *Philosophy* 58, no. 223 (January 1983): 19-27.

[84]For a classical "personalist" example, see the suggestion offered in Bowne, *Principles of Ethics*, pp. 22-40. For an intriguing discussion of how Kant's deontological focus and Sidgwick's utilitarianism did in fact drift together, see T. V. Smith and William Debbins, *Constructive Ethics* (Englewood Cliffs, N.J.: Prentice-Hall, 1948), pp. 105-13.

[85]For a positive characterization of Schleiermacher's position, see Bowne, *Principles of Ethics*, p. 22.

[86]Frankena subsumes the varieties of this approach unter the label "definist theories" (Frankena, *Ethics*, pp. 97-98).

[87]For a statement of this theory see Ralph Barton Perry, *Realms of Value: A Critique of Human Civilization* (Cambridge, Mass.: Harvard University Press, 1954), pp. 86-118.

[88]Adam Smith *An Inquiry into the Nature and Causes of the Wealth of Nations* 4.2.

[89]For a succinct presentation of this approach, see Paul B. Henry, "Natural Law,"

in *Baker's Dictionary of Christian Ethics,* ed. Carl F. H. Henry (Grand Rapids, Mich.: Baker Book House, 1973), pp. 448-50.

[90]Noddings, for example, speaks of "caring" as innate and hence as the foundation for "our inclination toward and interest in morality" (*Caring,* p. 83).

[91]Raziel Abelson, *Ethics and Metaethics: Readings in Ethical Philosophy* (New York: St. Martin's, 1963), p. 184.

[92]Abelson declares that Aristotle "initiated the naturalistic tradition in ethical philosophy" (ibid., p. 187). See Aristotle *Nicomachean Ethics* 1.7 [1097a15-1098b].

[93]For a succinct statement, see Jacques Maritain, *The Rights of Man and Natural Law* (London: Geoffrey Bles/Centenary, 1944), pp. 34-41.

[94]Miltner, *Elements of Ethics,* p. 149.

[95]Abelson, *Ethics and Metaethics,* p. 189.

[96]See, for example, the discussion in Rae, *Moral Choices,* pp. 35-41.

[97]This phrase may have originated with G. E. Moore. See his *Principia Ethica* (London: Cambridge University Press, 1959), p. 10. For a helpful critique of modern naturalism, see Hare, *Language of Morals,* pp. 79-93.

[98]This question was raised by Hume *Treatise of Human Nature* 3.1.1. See also Taylor, *Normative Discourse,* pp. 240-59.

[99]Gottfried Wilhelm Leibniz *Theodicy* 1.7-10.

[100]Philosophers readily tie certain theological groundings of morality to naturalism. William Frankena, for example, suggests that a theologian might claim that *right* means "commanded by God" (*Ethics,* p. 98). Hence the statement "It is right for you to honor your father and you mother" or the imperative "Honor your father and your mother!" actually means "God has commanded us to honor our parents." Ethical judgments, consequently, are disguised assertions of metaphysical facts. The difference between ethical naturalism and its theological cousin, metaphysical moralism, is the field to which we would appeal to confirm the objective truth of our ethical judgments. For the truth of ethical judgments metaphysical moralists seek to discover whether or not God has in fact either commanded or prohibited the actions or virtues our statements either extol or disavow.

[101]Plato proposed this dilemma in his dialogue *Euthyphro,* in *The Dialogues of Plato,* trans. Benjamin Jowett, ed. R. M. Hare and D. A. Russell (London: Sphere Books, 1970), 10a, p. 46.

[102]For an interesting twist on this problem, see Alasdair MacIntyre, "Which God Ought We to Obey and Why?" *Faith and Philosophy* 3, no. 4 (1986): 359-71.

[103]For a rebuttal of this argument, see Stephen R. L. Clark, "God's Law and Morality," *Philosophical Quarterly* 32, no. 129 (October 1982): 339-47.

[104]For a helpful argument against this sweeping rejection of a theistic ethic, see ibid.

[105]For a helpful, succinct summary of intuitionism, see Robert E. Dewey, Francis W. Gramlich and Donald Loftsgordon, eds., *Problems of Ethics* (New York: Macmillan, 1961), p. 326.

[106]Abelson, *Ethics and Metaethics,* p. 184.

[107]E. D. Cook, "Intuitionism," in *New Dictionary of Christian Ethics and Pastoral Theology,* ed. David J. Atkinson et al. (Downers Grove, Ill.: InterVarsity Press, 1995), p. 502.

[108]Ibid.

[109]Wellman, *Morals and Ethics,* pp. 299-302.

[110]For a portrayal of Plato as an early intuitionist, see Abelson, *Ethics and Metaethics,* p. 184.

[111]Ibid., p. 193.

[112]Moore, *Principia Ethica,* chap. 1, par. 7.

[113]Dewey, *Problems in Ethics,* p. 326.

[114]Moore, *Principia Ethica,* chap. 5, par. 88.

[115]William David Ross, *Right and the Good* (Oxford: Clarendon, 1950), pp. 16-64, esp. 39-41.

[116]For an elaboration of this difference, see Sahakian, *Systems of Ethics,* pp. 416-17.

[117]Perhaps the most prominent proponent of this view is the logical positivist A. J. Ayer. See *Language, Truth and Logic,* 2nd ed. (New York: Dover, 1952).

[118]Ayer comes close to this view. See ibid., pp. 107-8. While Ayer admits that our expressions of feeling are often intended to stimulate similar feelings in others, his main point is that such statements are expressions of feelings—and not assertions—and therefore they have no truth value. For him any intent to stimulate feelings in others lies as an addition to the main goal of ethical statements, namely, to express personal feelings.

[119]For example, Charles Leslie Stevenson, *Ethics and Language* (New Haven, Conn.: Yale University Press, 1944), pp. 22, 24-26, 81-110.

[120]Ibid., pp. 90-94.

[121]Sahakian, *Systems of Ethics,* p. 434.

[122]Stevenson, *Ethics and Language,* pp. 206-26.

[123]For the classic statement of the prescriptivist position, see Hare, *Language of Morals.*

[124]Ibid., pp. 196-97.

[125]Friedrich Nietzsche *On the Genealogy of Morality* preface 6.

[126]Barrett, *Ethics,* p. 400.

[127]See, for example, Nowell-Smith, *Ethics,* pp. 228-36.

[128]Thomas Hobbes *Leviathan* 2.28.

[129]See, for example, Kai Nielsen, "Why Should I Be Moral?" in *Moral Philosophy: An Introduction,* ed. Jack Glickman (New York: St. Martin's, 1976), pp. 191-204.

[130]Ibid., p. 194.

[131]Nowell-Smith forms a typical example. While extolling the importance of moral rules (and hence the deontological dimension of ethics), he links the necessity of moral rules to a greater good they produce, namely, social harmony (*Ethics,* pp. 228-29).

[132]For an example of the Christian alternative to this answer, see James M.

Gustafson, *Christian Ethics and the Community* (Atlanta: John Knox, 1979), p. 88.

[133]Frankena, *Ethics,* p. 116.

[134]Taylor, *Normative Discourse,* p. 188.

[135]Nowell-Smith, *Ethics,* pp. 313-14.

[136]Ibid., p. 320.

[137]For a rejection of this proposal, see Kai Nielsen, "God and the Basis of Morality," *Journal of Religious Ethics* 10, no. 2 (1982): 335-50. The proposal is defended from its critics in Axel D. Steuer, "The Religious Justification for Morality," *International Journal of the Philosophy of Religion* 13 (1982): 157-68.

[138]Franklin I. Gamwell, "Religion and the Justification of Moral Claims," *Journal of Religious Ethics* 11, no. 1 (1983): 35-61.

[139]See, for example, James F. Smurl, *Religious Ethics: A Systems Approach* (Englewood Cliffs, N.J.: Prentice-Hall, 1972), pp. 67-68.

Chapter 2: The Greek Ethical Tradition

[1]Vernon J. Bourke, *History of Ethics* (Garden City, N.Y.: Doubleday, 1970), 1:10.

[2]See, for example, Rex Warner, *The Greek Philosophers* (New York: Mentor, 1958), p. 9.

[3]William L. Reese, "Thales," in *Dictionary of Philosophy and Religion* (Atlantic Highlands, N.J.: Humanities, 1980), p. 573.

[4]Bourke, *History of Ethics,* 1:24.

[5]Warner, *Greek Philosophers,* p. 72.

[6]Ethel M. Albert, Theodore C. Denise and Sheldon P. Peterfreund, *Great Traditions in Ethics: An Introduction* (New York: American Book, 1953), p. 9.

[7]Quoted in Warner, *Greek Philosophers,* p. 68.

[8]Hence, Cecil De Boer, *The If's and Ought's of Ethics* (Grand Rapids, Mich.: Eerdmans, 1936), p. 77.

[9]Plato *Republic* 431-41; Plato *Phaedrus* 246-47c, 253c-54b.

[10]Henry Sidgwick, *Outlines of the History of Ethics for English Readers* (Boston: Beacon, 1960), p. 45.

[11]Plato puts this suggestion into the mouth of his mentor. See Plato *Protagoras* 357d-e. There is some debate, however, whether Socrates states the viewpoint to defend or to criticize it. For short discussions of this point, see Alasdair MacIntyre, *A Short History of Ethics* (New York: Macmillan, 1966), pp. 21-24; Raziel Abelson, *Ethics and Metaethics: Readings in Ethical Philosophy* (New York: St. Martin's, 1963), p. 387.

[12]Plato *Protagoras* 355-57.

[13]Warner, *Greek Philosophers,* p. 68.

[14]For a discussion of this proposal, see H. D. Rankin, *Plato and the Individual* (London: Methuen, 1964).

[15]MacIntyre, *Short History of Ethics,* p. 25.

[16]See, for example, Sidgwick, *Outlines of the History of Ethics,* pp. 49-50; Gordon H. Clark and T. V. Smith, eds., *Readings in Ethics,* 2nd ed. (New York: Appleton,

1963), pp. 21-23.

[17]This example is drawn from Albert, *Great Traditions in Ethics*, pp. 12-13.

[18]Plato *Republic* 517b-c.

[19]For this conclusion see MacIntyre, *Short History of Ethics*, p. 49.

[20]Ibid., p. 48.

[21]For a succinct summary of some of the major criticisms of Plato, see William S. Sahakian, *Ethics: An Introduction to Theories and Problems* (New York: Barnes & Noble Books, 1974), pp. 52-54.

[22]For this criticism and its provision of the door to Aristotle, see MacIntyre, *Short History of Ethics*, p. 50.

[23]Clifford L. Barrett, *Ethics: An Introduction to the Philosophy of Moral Values* (New York: Harper & Brothers, 1933), p. 140.

[24]Louise Ropes Loomis, introduction to *Aristotle: On Man and the Universe*, ed. Louise Ropes Loomis (Roslyn, N.Y.: Walter J. Black, 1943), p. xxxvi.

[25]See Richard McKeon, introduction to *Introduction to Aristotle*, ed. Richard McKeon, Modern Library (New York: Random House, 1947), p. ix. Nicomachus was also the name of Aristotle's son and the one for whom the *Nicomachean Ethics* is named. For a discussion of the question of the authorship of the *Nicomachean Ethics*, see William S. Sahakian, *Systems of Ethics and Value Theory* (New York: Philosophical Library, 1963), pp. 1-2.

[26]Warner, *Greek Philosophers*, pp. 69-70.

[27]Loomis, *Aristotle*, p. ix; McKeon, *Introduction to Aristotle*, p. ix.

[28]Hence Warner's designation (*Greek Philosophers*, p. 70). See also Sahakian, *Systems of Ethics*, p. 2.

[29]See McKeon, *Introduction to Aristotle*, p. x.

[30]For a succinct summary of the four causes, see Loomis, *Aristotle*, p. xvi.

[31]Albert, *Great Traditions in Ethics*, p. 38.

[32]Aristotle *Nicomachean Ethics* 1.8 [1099a24-25].

[33]MacIntyre, *Short History of Ethics*, p. 59.

[34]Sidgwick, *Outlines of the History of Ethics*, pp. 56-57.

[35]Aristotle *Nicomachean Ethics* 1.7 [1098a16-17].

[36]See Albert, *Great Traditions in Ethics*, p. 45.

[37]This point has been noted by Warner, *Greek Philosophers*, p. 114. Cf. the delineation of the virtues in Sahakian, *Ethics*, pp. 57-58.

[38]Aristotle *Nicomachean Ethics* 3.1 [1110b27-29].

[39]This has been observed by Abelson, *Ethics and Metaethics*, p. 387.

[40]Sahakian, *Ethics*, p. 56.

[41]Bourke, *History of Ethics*, p. 41. Aristotle *Nicomachean Ethics* 3.1 [1109b35-1111b1].

[42]Aristotle *Nicomachean Ethics* 3.5 [1113b].

[43]Ibid. 2.9 [1109a].

[44]See R. W. Browne, "Analytical Introduction," in *The Nicomachean Ethics of Aristotle*, trans. R. W. Browne (London: George Bell and Sons, 1901), p. vii.

[45]Sahakian, *Ethics*, p. 56.

[46]Aristotle *Nicomachean Ethics* 2.6 [1106b36-1107a2].
[47]Ibid. 5.1 [1130a].
[48]Ibid. 5 [1129a1-1138b14].
[49]See Sahakian, *Ethics*, pp. 57-58; Bourke, *History of Ethics*, p. 39.
[50]Browne, "Analytical Introduction," p. v.
[51]See Warner, *Greek Philosophers*, p. 114; Sahakian, *Ethics*, pp. 58-59.
[52]Aristotle *Politics* 3.9 [1280b29-1281a2].
[53]For a summary of several crucial philosophical criticisms, see Sahakian, *Ethics*, pp. 59-61.
[54]Aristotle *Nicomachean Ethics* 1.7 [1097a-1098b]; 10.7 [1177a-1178a].
[55]See Warner, *Greek Philosophers*, p. 148.
[56]Clark, *Readings in Ethics*, p. 84.
[57]For a summary see Russel M. Geer, translator's introduction to Epicurus, *Letters, Principal Doctrines and Vatican Sayings*, trans. Russel M. Geer (n.p.: Bobbs-Merrill, 1964), pp. xxix-xxxi; Albert, *Great Traditions in Ethics*, pp. 60-61.
[58]According to Warner, Epicurus was the first teacher to welcome women as members of a school of philosophy (*Greek Philosophers*, p. 149).
[59]Clark, *Readings in Ethics*, p. 84.
[60]Taylor, *Good and Evil*, pp. 78-79.
[61]MacIntyre, *Short History of Ethics*, p. 107.
[62]Sidgwick, *Outlines of the History of Ethics*, p. 86.
[63]Epicurus, "Letter to Menoeceus," in *Letters, Principal Doctrines and Vatican Sayings*, trans. Russel M. Geer, Library of Liberal Arts (n.p.: Bobbs-Merrill, 1964), 132a.
[64]Albert, *Great Traditions in Ethics*, p. 63.
[65]Sidgwick, *Outlines of the History of Ethics*, p. 87.
[66]For a technical discussion of Democritus and his writings, see G. S. Kirk and J. E. Raven, *The Presocratic Philosophers* (Cambridge: Cambridge University Press, 1957), pp. 400-26.
[67]For a summary of this tradition see Geer, translator's introduction, pp. ix-xxix.
[68]For a summary of his position see Warner, *Greek Philosophers*, pp. 144-47.
[69]Epicurus, "Letter to Herodotus," in *Letters, Principal Doctrines and Vatican Sayings*, 39b-41a, 43-45a, 54-55a.
[70]But in contrast to Democritus, whose position leads to a replacing of providence with an absolute determinism of blind fate, Epicurus spoke of an indeterminate spontaneity in the flow of the atoms. For his theory of an atomic "swerve," see Warner, *Greek Philosophers*, pp. 150-51.
[71]MacIntyre, *Short History of Ethics*, p. 107.
[72]Bourke, *History of Ethics*, p. 57.
[73]Richard Taylor, *Good and Evil: A New Direction* (New York: Macmillan, 1970), p. 77.
[74]Epicurus "Letter to Herodotus" 63b-67.
[75]Epicurus "Letter to Menoeceus" 125.

[76]Lucretius *The Nature of Things* 1.62-71, trans. Frank O. Copley (New York: W. W. Norton, 1977), p. 3.
[77]Epicurus "Letter to Menoeceus" 131b-32b.
[78]Bourke, *History of Ethics,* p. 57.
[79]See Sidgwick, *Outlines of the History of Ethics,* p. 89.
[80]This statement is ascribed to W. W. Tarn. See Warner, *Greek Philosophers,* p. 165.
[81]Sidgwick, *Outlines of the History of Ethics,* p. 71.
[82]Zeno of Citium, regarded as the founder of the Stoic school of philosophy, ought not to be confused with an earlier Greek thinker, Zeno of Elea (490-430 B.C.).
[83]Clark, *Readings in Ethics,* p. 96.
[84]For example, Warner, *Greek Philosophers,* p. 166.
[85]The universe came into being out of divine fire. The early Stoics supposed that following an enormously long period of time, the universe would be reconsumed in a cosmic conflagration. This cycle would then repeat itself forever. See Warner, *Greek Philosophers,* p. 166.
[86]See Sidgwick, *Outlines of the History of Ethics,* p. 78.
[87]Hence MacIntyre, *Short History of Ethics,* p. 104.
[88]Bourke, *History of Ethics,* p. 49.
[89]Hence Sidgwick, *Outlines of the History of Ethics,* p. 75; Sahakian, *Ethics,* p. 14.
[90]MacIntyre, *Short History of Ethics,* pp. 105-6.
[91]See Warner, *Greek Philosophers,* p. 166.
[92]Bourke, *History of Ethics,* p. 51.
[93]Epictetus *Discourses* 2.5, 2.10.
[94]See Sidgwick, *Outlines of the History of Ethics,* p. 97.
[95]Ibid., p. 100.
[96]Bourke, *History of Ethics,* p. 53.
[97]For a summary see Albert, *Great Traditions in Ethics,* p. 84.
[98]Ibid., p. 87.
[99]Epictetus *Enchiridion* 1.
[100]Epictetus *Discourses* 1.6, 1.14, 2.14.11.
[101]Ibid. 1.18.11-12. Similarly, Marcus Aurelius wrote in his *Meditations* (4.7), "Take away your opinion, and then there is taken away the complaint, 'I have been harmed.' Take away the complaint, 'I have been harmed,' and the harm is taken away."
[102]Epictetus *Discourses* 2.18.12-13.
[103]Sidgwick, *Outlines of the History of Ethics,* p. 103.
[104]Warner, *Greek Philosophers,* p. 230.
[105]As cited in Elmer O'Brien, introduction to *The Essential Plotinus: Representative Treatises from the Enneads,* trans. Elmer O'Brien (New York: Mentor, 1964), p. 14 note 3.
[106]Warner, *Greek Philosophers,* p. 220.
[107]Bourke, *History of Ethics,* p. 60.
[108]Bourke declares that the Greek Neoplatonic school ends with Proclus

Diadochus (*History of Ethics,* p. 64).
[109]On this see Sidgwick, *Outlines of the History of Ethics,* pp. 105-6.
[110]For a concise statement of this transition, see ibid., p. 107.
[111]Some historians suggest that Plotinus derived his idea from Philo (O'Brien, introduction, pp. 15-16).
[112]Plotinus *Enneads* 6.9.2-3, 11.
[113]Ibid. 4.8.4, 4.8.8.
[114]O'Brien, introduction, p. 31.
[115]Plotinus *Enneads* 6.9.8.
[116]Ibid. 1.6.9.
[117]Ibid. 1.4.10.
[118]Ibid. 6.9.11, 6.7.17.
[119]Ibid. 6.9.4.
[120]Ibid. 6.7.36.
[121]Ibid. 5.1.3, 6.9.9.
[122]Ibid. 4.8.1.
[123]Ibid. 1.2.1.
[124]Ibid. 1.2.1.
[125]Ibid. 1.2.2.
[126]Ibid. 1.2.3.
[127]Ibid. 1.2.6.
[128]Ibid. 1.2.7.
[129]Warner, *Greek Philosophers,* p. 231.

Chapter 3: Ethics in the Bible

[1]See, for example, Christopher J. H. Wright, "The Use of the Bible in Social Ethics: Paradigms, Types and Eschatology," *Transformation* 1, no. 1 (1984): 11.
[2]See, for example, Waldemar Janzen, *Old Testament Ethics: A Paradigmatic Approach* (Louisville, Ky.: Westminster John Knox, 1994), pp. 1-2.
[3]R. E. O. White, *Biblical Ethics* (Atlanta: John Knox, 1979), p. 11.
[4]Robert J. Daly, *Christian Biblical Ethics* (New York: Paulist, 1984), p. 68.
[5]Walter C. Kaiser, *Toward Old Testament Ethics* (Grand Rapids, Mich.: Zondervan, 1983), p. 2.
[6]Bruce C. Birch, *Let Justice Roll Down: The Old Testament, Ethics and Christian Life* (Louisville, Ky.: Westminster John Knox, 1991), p. 40.
[7]For a helpful discussion of the importance of the covenant idea for Old Testament ethics, see ibid., pp. 146-57.
[8]Walther Eichrodt, preface to the English edition of *Theology of the Old Testament,* trans. J. A. Baker (Philadelphia: Westminster Press, 1961), 1:17.
[9]T. B. Maston, *Biblical Ethics* (Macon, Ga.: Mercer University Press, 1982), p. 17.
[10]See Gordon Wenham, "Grace and Law in the Old Testament," in *Law, Morality and the Bible,* ed. Bruce Kaye and Gordon Wenham (Downers Grove, Ill: InterVarsity Press, 1978), p. 10.

[11]Kaiser, *Toward Old Testament Ethics,* p. 2.

[12]Ibid., p. 3.

[13]Scholars are divided as to whether any one principle lies at the heart of the Old Testament and consequently whether there is a "center" to Old Testament ethics. See, for example, Christopher J. H. Wright, "The Ethical Authority of the Old Testament: A Survey of Approaches," *Tyndale Bulletin* 43, no. 1 (1992): 114-15.

[14]Kaiser goes so far as to declare that holiness is the central orgainizing feature of Old Testament ethics (*Toward Old Testament Ethics,* p. 139). For a critique of this position see Janzen, *Old Testament Ethics,* p. 115.

[15]For a succinct statement of the distinction between the Hebrew and the Greek approaches, see White, *Biblical Ethics,* pp. 16-17.

[16]See J. R. Williams, "Holiness," in *Evangelical Dictionary of Theology,* ed. Walter A. Elwell (Grand Rapids, Mich.: Baker Book House, 1984), p. 515.

[17]Bruce C. Birch, "Moral Agency, Community and the Character of God in the Hebrew Bible," *Semeia* 66 (1994): 34.

[18]Christopher J. H. Wright, "The Ethical Authority of the Old Testament: A Survey of Approaches, Part II," *Tyndale Bulletin* 43, no. 2 (1992): 227.

[19]Kaiser, *Toward Old Testament Ethics,* p. 77; cf. p. 32.

[20]See Gerhard von Rad, *Old Testament Theology,* trans. D. M. G. Stalker (New York: Harper & Row, 1962), 1:371.

[21]For a helpful explication of this idea, see Janzen, *Old Testament Ethics,* pp. 66-67.

[22]Birch, *Let Justice Roll Down,* p. 38.

[23]Even Kaiser acknowledges the foundational importance of the divine character (*Toward Old Testament Ethics,* p. 29).

[24]Edmond Jacob, *Theology of the Old Testament,* trans. Arthur W. Heathcote and Philip J. Allcock (New York: Harper & Row, 1958), p. 173.

[25]Birch, "Moral Agency," p. 31.

[26]See White, *Biblical Ethics,* p. 25; Maston, *Biblical Ethics,* pp. 52-58.

[27]Williston Walker, "Compassion," in *The International Standard Bible Encyclopedia* (Grand Rapids, Eerdmans, 1915), 2:695.

[28]See, for example, Kaiser, *Toward Old Testament Ethics,* p. 33.

[29]Maston, *Biblical Ethics,* p. 88.

[30]For a discussion of ethics in the wisdom literature, see Birch, *Let Justice Roll Down,* pp. 321-47.

[31]See, for example, W. S. Bruce, *The Ethics of the Old Testament,* 2nd ed. (Edinburgh: T & T Clark, 1909), p. 42.

[32]See Birch, *Let Justice Roll Down,* p. 164.

[33]See, for example, Kaiser, *Toward Old Testament Ethics,* pp. 7-10.

[34]Ibid., p. 69.

[35]Thomas W. Ogletree, *The Use of the Bible in Christian Ethics* (Philadelphia: Fortress, 1983), p. 80.

[36]H. L. Ellison states this perspective well: "The fact is that the popular conception of the individual is derived from Greek thought rather than from the Bible, and

may even be regarded as anti-Biblical. We tend to think of our bodies giving us our individuality and separating us, one from the other. In the Old Testament it is our flesh—a word for body hardly exists in Hebrew—that binds us to our fellow-men; it is our personal responsibility to God that gives us our individuality" (*Ezekiel: The Man and His Message* [London: Paternoster, 1956], p. 72).

[37]White writes, "In Ezekiel, neither the sins nor the merits of the fathers determine the destiny of the children—they answer for themselves." Although on the right track, White overstates the matter in declaring, "This is a milestone in biblical ethics" (*Biblical Ethics*, p. 27).

[38]Kaiser points out that the older consensus that group solidarity predominated until Ezekiel is now waning. However he mistakenly grounds the individual motif in the concept of the *imago Dei* (*Toward Old Testament Ethics*, p. 71).

[39]White, *Biblical Ethics*, p. 29.

[40]Birch, *Let Justice Roll Down*, pp. 297-300.

[41]Ibid., p. 271.

[42]Kaiser, *Toward Old Testament Ethics*, p. 10.

[43]Birch, *Let Justice Roll Down*, p. 272.

[44]Wolfgang Schrage, *The Ethics of the New Testament*, trans. David E. Green (Philadelphia: Fortress, 1988), p. 8.

[45]Ernst Käsemann, *Jesus Means Freedom*, trans. Frank Clarke (Philadelphia: Fortress, 1970), p. 40.

[46]See, for example, Rudolf Schnackenburg, *The Moral Teaching of the New Testament*, trans. J. Holland-Smith and W. J. O'Hara (New York: Seabury, 1965), pp. 60-65.

[47]Eduard Lohse, *Theological Ethics of the New Testament*, trans. M. Eugene Boring (Minneapolis: Fortress, 1991), p. 44.

[48]Maston, *Biblical Ethics*, p. 148.

[49]For a helpful discussion see White, *Biblical Ethics*, pp. 59-63.

[50]Willi Marxsen, *New Testament Foundations for Christian Ethics*, trans. O. C. Dean Jr. (Minneapolis: Fortress, 1993), pp. 125-26.

[51]See the interesting discussion in Marxsen, *New Testament Foundations*, pp. 95-97.

[52]See, for example, Schnackenburg, *Moral Teaching of the New Testament*, pp. 65-73.

[53]Ibid., pp. 158-59.

[54]See, for example, Schrage, *Ethics of the New Testament*, p. 18.

[55]For a helpful discussion of Jesus' kingdom ethic, see Ben Wiebe, *Messianic Ethics: Jesus' Proclamation of the Kingdom of God and the Church in Response* (Waterloo, Ont.: Herald, 1992).

[56]L. H. Marshall, *The Challenge of New Testament Ethics* (London: Macmillan, 1947), p. 31.

[57]White, *Biblical Ethics*, p. 108.

[58]Schrage, *Ethics of the New Testament*, pp. 42-43.

[59]One of the most contested questions in New Testament scholarship has been the significance of Jesus' ethical teaching for Christians in subsequent eras. For helpful summaries of this discussion, see Schnackenburg, *Moral Teaching of the New*

Testament, pp. 81-89; Schrage, *Ethics of the New Testament,* pp. 18-40. For a discussion of the implications of Jesus' eschatological ethic of the kingdom, see Jack T. Sanders, *Ethics in the New Testament: Change and Development* (Philadelphia: Fortress, 1974), pp. 1-29. For a summary and critique of several of the contemporary ways in which the reign of God has served as the basis of a social ethic, see Stephen Charles Mott, "The Use of the Bible in Social Ethics II: The Use of the New Testament, Part 1," *Transformation* 1, no. 2 (1984): 23-24.

[60]Marxsen, *New Testament Foundations,* p. 63.

[61]Schnackenburg, *Moral Teaching of the New Testament,* p. 25.

[62]Schrage rightly points out the deficiency of focusing exclusively on "an ethics of intention" (*Ethics of the New Testament,* pp. 43-44).

[63]White, *Biblical Ethics,* p. 81. For a helpful discussion of the double command, see Schnackenburg, *Moral Teaching of the New Testament,* pp. 90-109.

[64]Schnackenburg, *Moral Teaching of the New Testament,* p. 106.

[65]So claims Schrage, *Ethics of the New Testament,* p. 70.

[66]Wiebe, *Messianic Ethics,* pp. 123-24.

[67]See, for example, the discussion in Schrage, *Ethics in the New Testament,* pp. 91-98.

[68]For a discussion of Jesus' teaching in comparison with the Jewish background, see ibid., pp. 98-107.

[69]For the radical sharpness of this imperative, see Maston, *Biblical Ethics,* p. 148.

[70]Birger Gerhardsson, *The Ethos of the Bible,* trans. Stephen Westerholm (Philadelphia: Fortress, 1981), p. 41.

[71]White, *Biblical Ethics,* p. 74.

[72]See Wiebe, *Messianic Ethics,* pp. 131-32, 157-58.

[73]See, for example, Schnackenburg, *Moral Teaching of the New Testament,* pp. 161-67.

[74]White, *Biblical Ethics,* p. 109.

[75]Scholars readily point to John as the primary Gospel in which the idea of imitation emerges. But the theme is evident in the Synoptics as well. For a discussion of Jesus as model in Matthew's Gospel, see Gerhardsson, *Ethos of the Bible,* pp. 54-60.

[76]For a short discussion of Jesus as the example for the disciple, see Maston, *Biblical Ethics,* pp. 173-75.

[77]Hence Alister McGrath, "In What Way Can Jesus Be a Moral Example for Christians?" *Journal of the Evangelical Theological Society* 34, no. 3 (1991): 296-97.

[78]White, *Biblical Ethics,* pp. 112-13.

[79]For a similar idea see Gerhardsson, *Ethos of the Bible,* p. 126.

[80]White, *Biblical Ethics,* pp. 111-12.

[81]Ibid., p. 124.

[82]For the appropriateness of using the term *ethic* to speak about Paul's teaching on Christian conduct, see Victor Paul Furnish, *Theology and Ethics in Paul* (Nashville: Abingdon, 1968), pp. 208-12; Brian S. Rosner, " 'That Pattern of Teaching': Issues and Essays in Pauline Ethics," in *Understanding Paul's Ethics: Twentieth Century*

Approaches, ed. Brian S. Rosner (Grand Rapids, Mich.: Eerdmans, 1995), p. 4.

[83]Furnish, *Theology and Ethics in Paul,* pp. 144-47.

[84]J. Paul Sampley, *Walking Between the Times: Paul's Moral Reasoning* (Minneapolis: Fortress, 1991), p. 7.

[85]The theme of the indicative and the imperative is foundational for understanding Paul. Indeed, Furnish concludes his survey of modern interpretations of Paul's ethic by asserting that "it has become apparent that no interpretation of the Pauline ethic can be judged successful which does not grapple with the problem of the indicative and imperative in Paul's thought" (*Theology and Ethics in Paul,* p. 279). For helpful discussions of the Pauline indicative/imperative, see Michael Parsons, "Being Precedes Act: Indicative and Imperative in Paul's Writing," in *Understanding Paul's Ethics,* ed. Rosner, pp. 217-47; Lohse, *Theological Ethics of the New Testament,* pp. 108-12; Schrage, *Ethics of the New Testament,* pp. 167-72.

[86]Schrage, *Ethics of the New Testament,* p. 183.

[87]Sampley, *Walking Between the Times,* p. 17.

[88]For a helpful discussion of this theme, see Furnish, *Theology and Ethics in Paul,* pp. 218-23.

[89]Gordon D. Fee, *God's Empowering Presence: The Holy Spirit in the Letters of Paul* (Peabody, Mass.: Hendrickson, 1994), p. 882.

[90]R. J. Erickson, "Flesh," in *Dictionary of Paul and His Letters,* ed. Gerald F. Hawthorne, Ralph P. Martin and Daniel G. Reid (Downers Grove, Ill.: InterVarsity Press, 1993), pp. 303-4.

[91]D. L. Okholm, "Flesh," in *New Dictionary of Christian Ethics and Pastoral Theology,* ed. David J. Atkinson et al. (Downers Grove, Ill.: InterVarsity Press, 1995), p. 382.

[92]Fee, *God's Empowering Presence,* p. 137.

[93]Schnackenburg, *Moral Teaching of the New Testament,* p. 264.

[94]Herman Ridderbos, *Paul: An Outline of His Theology,* trans. John Richard De Witt (Grand Rapids, Mich.: Eerdmans, 1975), pp. 103, 116, 548.

[95]Fee, *God's Empowering Presence,* pp. 817-22.

[96]See Okholm, "Flesh," p. 383.

[97]Furnish, *Theology and Ethics in Paul,* pp. 137-38.

[98]Fee, *God's Empowering Presence,* p. 429.

[99]Ibid., pp. 425, 445-46, 883.

[100]See, for example, Schnackenburg, *Moral Teaching of the New Testament,* pp. 284-86.

[101]For a short discussion of Paul's use of the Old Testament, see Furnish, *Theology and Ethics in Paul,* pp. 28-34.

[102]Ibid., p. 160.

[103]Traugott Holtz, "The Question of the Content of Paul's Instructions," in *Understanding Paul's Ethics,* ed. Rosner, pp. 66-71.

[104]Eckhard J. Schnabel, "How Paul Developed His Ethics," in *Understanding Paul's Ethics,* ed. Rosner, pp. 294-95.

[105]See the helpful discussion in Fee, *God's Empowering Presence,* pp. 422-23.
[106]Schrage, *Ethics of the New Testament,* pp. 206-7.
[107]Fee, *God's Empowering Presence,* p. 816.
[108]Sampley, *Walking Between the Times,* pp. 37-43.
[109]John Knox concludes that for Paul, love "belongs essentially within the Christian community and has meaning there which it cannot have outside" (*The Ethic of Jesus in the Teaching of the Church* [Nashville: Abingdon, 1961], p. 92).
[110]Furnish, *Theology and Ethics in Paul,* p. 233.
[111]Waldo Beach and H. Richard Niebuhr, eds., *Christian Ethics: Sources of the Living Tradition,* 2nd ed. (New York: Ronald, 1973), p. 44. See also Fee, *God's Empowering Presence,* p. 883.
[112]See, for example, Sanders, *Ethics in the New Testament,* p. 56.
[113]Ibid., p. 63.
[114]Paul's understanding of the law is a much discussed and hotly debated topic in New Testament scholarship. For a helpful discussion of the apostle's view, see Lohse, *Theological Ethics of the New Testament,* pp. 157-65.
[115]Fee, *God's Empowering Presence,* p. 437.
[116]White, *Biblical Ethics,* p. 165.
[117]For an enlightening discussion of the distinction between the Pauline and the Pharisaic ethic, see Marxsen, *New Testament Foundations for Christian Ethics,* pp. 159-67.
[118]Parsons, "Being Precedes Act," p. 247.
[119]Schnabel, "How Paul Developed His Ethics," p. 296.
[120]H. Wheeler Robinson, *The Christian Doctrine of Man,* 3rd ed. (Edinburgh: T & T Clark, 1926), p. 125.
[121]This phrase is, of course, open to misunderstanding, as is indicated in Furnish, *Theology and Ethics in Paul,* p. 225. Yet the phrase does provide a helpful summary of the Pauline—and New Testament—ethic. Hence Fee, *God's Empowering Presence,* p. 130.
[122]Fee, *God's Empowering Presence,* p. 898.

Chapter 4: Model Christian Proposals

[1]Augustine *Confessions* 8.12.29.
[2]Augustine, Aquinas and Luther are likewise elevated for discussion in Robin Gill, *A Textbook of Christian Ethics* (Edinburgh: T & T Clark, 1985).
[3]Alasdair MacIntyre, *A Short History of Ethics* (New York: Macmillan, 1966), p. 115.
[4]Henry Sidgwick, *Outlines of the History of Ethics* (Boston: Beacon, 1960), p. 132.
[5]For this judgment, see Ethel M. Albert, Theodore C. Denise and Sheldon P. Peterfreund, *Great Traditions in Ethics: An Introduction* (New York: American Book, 1953), p. 108.
[6]Augustine himself recounts his life story in his famed *Confessions.* For a helpful biographical sketch see Roy W. Battenhouse, "The Life of St. Augustine," in *A Companion to the Study of St. Augustine,* ed. Roy W. Battenhouse (Grand Rapids,

Mich.: Baker Book House, 1979), pp. 15-56.

[7]W. H. C. Frend, "Augustinianism," in *Westminster Dictionary of Christian Theology,* ed. Alan Richardson and John Bowden (Philadelphia: Westminster Press, 1983), p. 55. See also L. H. Hackstaff, introduction to Augustine, *On Free Choice of the Will,* trans. Anna S. Benjamin and L. H. Hackstaff (Indianapolis: Bobbs-Merrill, 1964), pp. xi-xii.

[8]For a short summary of Manichaeism, see W. L. Reese, *Dictionary of Philosophy and Religion* (Atlantic Highlands, N.J.: Humanities, 1980), p. 329.

[9]For a helpful discussion see Hackstaff, introduction, pp. xiv-xxii.

[10]Ibid., p. xxii.

[11]Hans Schwarz, *Evil: A Historical and Theological Perspective,* trans. Mark W. Worthing (Minneapolis: Fortress, 1995), p. 101.

[12]Gordon H. Clark and T. V. Smith, eds., *Readings in Ethics* (New York: Appleton Century Crofts, 1935), p. 134.

[13]John A. Mourant, *Introduction to the Philosophy of Saint Augustine: Selected Readings and Commentaries* (University Park: University of Pennsylvania Press, 1964), pp. 14-15; Hackstaff, introduction, p. xxiii.

[14]Clark and Smith, eds., *Readings in Ethics,* p. 134.

[15]Mourant, *Introduction to Augustine,* p. 15.

[16]Frend, "Augustinianism," p. 55.

[17]Albert, *Great Traditions in Ethics,* p. 107. For a more detailed discussion of the question of Augustine's view of the idea of the natural divinity of the soul, see A. H. Armstrong, "St. Augustine and Christian Platonism," in *Augustine: A Collection of Critical Essays,* ed. R. A. Markus (New York: Doubleday, 1972), pp. 4-9.

[18]Clark and Smith, eds., *Readings in Ethics,* p. 135.

[19]For a helpful discussion of Augustine's involvement in this controversy, see Frederick W. Dillistone, "The Anti-Donatist Writings," in *Companion to the Study of Augustine,* ed. Battenhouse, pp. 175-202.

[20]Frend, "Augustinianism," p. 56.

[21]Victor L. Walter, "Donatism," in *Evangelical Dictionary of Theology,* ed. Walter A. Elwell (Grand Rapids, Mich.: Baker Book House, 1984), pp. 329-30.

[22]Ibid., p. 329.

[23]Frend, "Augustinianism," p. 56.

[24]For a helpful summary of this monumental work, see Edward R. Hardy Jr., "The City of God," in *Companion to the Study of Augustine,* ed. Battenhouse, pp. 257-83.

[25]For a helpful treatment of Augustine's controversy with the Pelagians, see Paul Lehmann, "The Anti-Pelagian Writings," in *Companion to the Study of Augustine,* ed. Battenhouse, pp. 203-34.

[26]Frend, "Augustinianism," p. 57.

[27]Schwarz, *Evil,* pp. 111-12.

[28]See, for example, Augustine *On the Merits and Remission of Sins, and on the Baptism of Infants;* see also Augustine *On Nature and Grace.*

[29]Hackstaff's comment is typical: "It is not too great an exaggeration to say that Neo-Platonism provided Augustine and the Christian Platonists who followed him with the theoretical substructure on which their theology was built" (introduction, p. xxvii).

[30]Thomas J. Bigham and Albert T. Mollegen, "The Christian Ethic," in *Companion to the Study of Augustine,* ed. Battenhouse, p. 371.

[31]Mourant, *Introduction to Augustine,* p. 7.

[32]MacIntyre offers a somewhat distinctive description of this indebtedness: "The Platonic dichotomy between the world of sense perception and the realm of Forms is Christianized by St. Augustine into a dichotomy between the world of the natural desires and the realm of divine order" (MacIntyre, *Short History of Ethics,* p. 117).

[33]Albert, *Great Traditions in Ethics,* p. 107.

[34]Augustine *Concerning the Nature of Good.*

[35]Augustine's ethic is often characterized as "eudaemonian." Hence Vernon J. Bourke, *History of Ethics* (New York: Doubleday, 1970), 1:84; R. E. O. White, *Christian Ethics* (Atlanta: John Knox, 1981), p. 100. For a more detailed discussion see Robert J. O'Connell, "Action and Contemplation," in *Augustine: A Collection of Critical Essays,* ed. R. A. Marks (New York: Doubleday, 1972), pp. 38-58.

[36]Augustine *City of God* 8.8.

[37]Augustine *On the Morals of the Catholic Church* 11.18.

[38]Augustine *Confessions* 1.1.1.

[39]Hence Frend comments, "Augustine ended his intellectual quest as he had begun, with the problem of evil" ("Augustinianism," p. 58).

[40]Augustine *Enchiridion on Faith, Hope and Love* 12.

[41]Ibid. 11.

[42]Augustine *City of God* 12.3.

[43]Augustine *Enchiridion* 11.

[44]See the discussion of this point in chapter two.

[45]Of course Augustine granted that ignorance was *a* problem. See, for example, *Enchiridion* 24.

[46]Augustine *The Problem of Free Choice (On Free Will)* 1.3.8.

[47]Augustine *On the Morals of the Manichaeans* 1.1.

[48]According to Augustine lust is the evil element in the specific acts people do (*On Free Choice of the Will* 1.3.20; see also *Enchiridion* 24).

[49]Augustine *City of God* 12.8.

[50]Augustine *On Free Choice of the Will* 3.1.8-9.

[51]"Love, and do what thou wilt" (Augustine "The Epistle of St. John" Homily 7.8).

[52]Augustine *On the Morals of the Catholic Church* 15.25.

[53]Arthur F. Holmes, *Ethics: Approaching Moral Decisions* (Downers Grove, Ill.: InterVarsity Press, 1984), p. 118.

[54]For a short discussion of this point, see William S. Sahakian, *Systems of Ethics and Value Theory* (New York: Philosophical Library, 1963), pp. 214-15.

[55]Augustine *On the Morals of the Catholic Church* 15.

[56]Hence Augustine concludes that "where there is no true religion there are no true virtues" (*City of God* 19.25). Sidgwick theorizes that Augustine's attempt to Christianize the Platonic list of virtues was due to the influence of Ambrose (*Outlines of the History of Ethics,* p. 133).

[57]Augustine *On the Morals of the Catholic Church* 26.50.

[58]Ibid. 25.51.

[59]Bigham and Mollegen, "Christian Ethic," pp. 376-82.

[60]Clark and Smith, *Readings in Ethics,* p. 136.

[61]For a concise summary of Aquinas's life, see Anton C. Pegis, *Introduction to Saint Thomas Aquinas* (New York: Modern Library, 1945), pp. xi-xii; Ralph McInerny, *St. Thomas Aquinas* (Notre Dame, Ind.: University of Notre Dame Press, 1977), pp. 13-29.

[62]Bourke, *History of Ethics,* 1:142.

[63]Roman Catholic thinkers often refer to the Dominican thinker by his given name, Thomas. See, for example, Timothy McDermott, editor's preface to St. Thomas Aquinas, *Summa Theologica: A Concise Translation,* ed. Timothy McDermott (Westminster, Md.: Christian Classics, 1989), p. xiii. Protestants tend to use the name drawn from his city of origin, Aquinas. Hence Norman L. Geisler, "Thomas Aquinas," in *Evangelical Dictionary of Theology,* 1091-92; Herbert McCabe, "Thomism," in *Westminster Dictionary of Christian Theology,* 568-71. In either case the theological program he fostered is consistently referred to as "Thomism."

[64]Timothy McDermott, "Preface: What the *Summa* Is About," in Thomas Aquinas, *Summa Theologica: A Concise Translation,* p. xviii; McInerny, *St. Thomas Aquinas,* p. 14.

[65]For a short comparison of the Dominicans and the Cistercians, see McDermott, preface, p. xix.

[66]See McInerny, *St. Thomas Aquinas,* pp. 15-16.

[67]Geisler states that Aquinas began studies under Albert in Paris and then started the school in Cologne with his teacher in 1248 (Geisler, "Thomas Aquinas," p. 1091). In this he follows McDermott, preface, p. xix.

[68]Pegis, introduction, p. xi.

[69]For Aquinas's short autobiographical remark about his ambition, see Thomas Aquinas *Summa Contra Gentiles* 1.2.2. This is available as Thomas Aquinas, *On the Truth of the Catholic Faith,* ed. Anton C. Pegis (Garden City, N.Y.: Doubleday/Image, 1955), 1:62.

[70]McDermott, preface, p. xx.

[71]McInerny, *St. Thomas Aquinas,* p. 21.

[72]William of Moerbeck may have engaged in this translation work at the request of Aquinas. See Anthony Meredith, "Aristotelianism," in *Westminster Dictionary of Christian Theology,* p. 42; McInerny, *St. Thomas Aquinas,* p. 22.

[73]McDermott, preface, p. xx; McInerny, *St. Thomas Aquinas,* p. 26.

[74]Meredith, "Aristotelianism," p. 42.

[75]For a helpful discussion of this point, see Pegis, introduction, pp. xv-xxvii.

[76]To this extent Augustine seemed to agree with the Platonic tradition. He too identified the person with the soul, spoke about the spiritual nature of the soul and suggested that the soul uses the body. For a discussion of these themes see Mourant, *Introduction to the Philosophy of Augustine,* pp. 12-14; Armstrong, "Augustine and Christian Platonism," pp. 9-12.

[77]Aquinas *Summa Theologica* 1.1.9; see also 1.85.3.

[78]Ibid. 1.75.4.

[79]Ibid. 1.76.1.

[80]Pegis, introduction, p. xxii.

[81]Ibid., p. xxiv.

[82]Sidgwick, *Outlines of the History of Ethics,* p. 141.

[83]Sahakian, *Systems of Ethics,* p. 220; Bourke, *History of Ethics,* 1:143, but see his altered conclusion on pp. 145-46.

[84]Aquinas *Summa Contra Gentiles* 3.2.

[85]See Jean Porter, *The Recovery of Virtue: The Relevance of Aquinas for Christian Ethics* (Louisville, Ky.: Westminster John Knox, 1990), p. 44.

[86]Aquinas *Summa Contra Gentiles* 3.17.

[87]For a discussion of the reason the contemplation of God is the end of the human person, see McInerny, *St. Thomas Aquinas,* p. 59.

[88]Aquinas *Summa Contra Gentiles* 3.25. See also 3.37.

[89]Ibid. 3.26.

[90]Ibid. 3.48.

[91]Aquinas *Summa Theologica* 3.51.

[92]Ibid. 1-2.109.5.

[93]On this distinction see McDermott, preface, p. xxx.

[94]See Bourke, *History of Ethics,* 1:145.

[95]For a concise summary of Aquinas's view, see Gordon R. Lewis and Bruce A. Demarest, *Integrative Theology* (Grand Rapids, Mich.: Zondervan, 1990), 2:125-26.

[96]Irenaeus *Against Heresies* 4.4.3, 4.37.1, 5.1.3.

[97]Aquinas *Summa Theologica* 1.93.4-8; 1.95.1.

[98]Ibid. 1-2.109.3.

[99]For this characterization of the Thomistic view, see Bourke, *History of Ethics,* 1:145.

[100]Aquinas *Summa Contra Gentiles* 1.3.2-3.

[101]Aquinas *Summa Theologica* 1.1.1.

[102]Hence Aquinas's contention that all persons by nature love God more fully than they love themselves (*Summa Theologica* 1.60.5).

[103]For this judgment see Porter, *Recovery of Virtue,* p. 104.

[104]Aquinas *Summa Theologica* 1-2.55.1.

[105]Ibid. 1-2.49.4.

[106]Ibid. 1-2.55.1.

[107]Porter, *Recovery of Virtue*, p. 110.
[108]Aquinas *Summa Theologica* 1-2.57.2.
[109]Ibid. 1-2.58.2.
[110]Ibid. 1-2.61.2.
[111]Ibid. 1-2.90.4.
[112]Ibid. 1-2.93.3.
[113]Ibid. 1-2.91.1.
[114]Ibid. 1-2.93.4.
[115]Ibid. 1-2.91.2. For a helpful treatment of this difficult topic, see McInerny, *St. Thomas Aquinas*, pp. 63-68.
[116]Aquinas *Summa Theologica* 1-2.94.2.
[117]Ibid. 1-2.91.3-4.
[118]Ibid. 1-2.62.1.
[119]Ibid. 1-2.62.2, 3.
[120]Ibid. 1-2.63.3, 109.2.
[121]Sidgwick, *Outlines of the History of Ethics*, p. 146.
[122]Holmes, *Ethics*, p. 119.
[123]For example, Bourke *(History of Ethics)* passes over Luther and Calvin, and Sidgwick *(Outlines of the History of Ethics)* speaks of the Reformation only in passing (pp. 154-55). MacIntyre's comment seems quite appropriate: "Machiavelli and Luther are morally influential authors about whom books on moral philosophy rarely contain discussions" (*Short History of Ethics*, p. 121).
[124]Thus R. E. O. White *(Christian Ethics)* treats both Luther and Calvin and then devotes a third chapter to ethics in the aftermath of the Reformation.
[125]Much has been written about the life of Luther. The classic work remains Roland H. Bainton, *Here I Stand: A Life of Martin Luther* (New York: New American Library/Mentor, 1950). For a short sketch of Luther's life, see John Dillenberger, introduction to *Martin Luther: Selections from His Writings*, ed. John Dillenberger (Garden City, N.Y.: Doubleday, 1961).
[126]Roland H. Bainton, *The Reformation of the Sixteenth Century* (Boston: Beacon, 1956), p. 23.
[127]Dillenberger, introduction, p. xiv.
[128]For a discussion of the importance of this problem in the context of the medieval church, see ibid., pp. xv-xvi.
[129]Bainton, *Here I Stand*, p. 144.
[130]Sidgwick offers the controversial conclusion that according to Duns Scotus, God's will lies beyond reason and consequently that God's ordering of the world is absolutely arbitrary (*Outlines of the History of Ethics*, p. 147).
[131]W. L. Reese, "William of Ockham," in *Dictionary of Philosophy and Religion*, p. 629.
[132]Bourke, *History of Ethics*, 1:155.
[133]Actually reason used as a means to attain to God, and not reason in service to God, was the target of Luther's attack. See George W. Forell, *Faith Active in Love:*

An Investigation of the Principles Underlying Luther's Social Ethics (Minneapolis: Augsburg, 1954), pp. 53-54.

[134]For this characterization of Luther's position, see Richard Klann, "Lutheran Ethics," in *Baker's Dictionary of Christian Ethics*, p. 400.

[135]For a discussion of this point and citations from appropriate sections of Luther's works, see Forell, *Faith Active in Love*, pp. 76-84.

[136]MacIntyre, *Short History of Ethics*, p. 121.

[137]Søren Kierkegaard, *Fear and Trembling*, trans. Alastair Hannay (London: Penguin Classics, 1985).

[138]Depravity does not mean that humans are completely evil or completely devoid of good. Rather it declares that no aspect of human existence and no natural human power is unaffected by sin. For a characterization of Luther's and Calvin's views, see Lewis and Demarest, *Integrative Theology*, 2:192-93.

[139]MacIntyre, *Short History of Ethics*, p. 122.

[140]See, for example, Martin Luther, "Treatise on Good Works," trans. W. A. Lambert, rev. James Atkinson, in *The Christian Society I*, ed. James Atkinson, vol. 44 of *Luther's Works*, ed. Helmut T. Lehmann (Philadelphia, Fortress, 1966), p. 97. Martin Luther, "Von den guten Werken, 1520," in *D. Martin Luthers Werke, kritische Gesammtausgabe*, ed. J. K. F. Knaake et al. (Weimar, Germany: Hermann Bohlau, 1888), 6:263.

[141]There is some discussion among historians as to whether Luther also added a third use of the law. For a characterization as to in what sense Luther divides the function of the law into three uses, see Paul M. Hoyer, "Law and Gospel: With Particular Attention to the Third Use of the Law," *Concordia Journal* 6, no. 5 (1980): 194-99.

Perhaps Long's conclusion is correct: "Luther hinted at a triple use of the law when he noted that the pious man and the impious man read the civil prescriptions of law very differently, but he never developed the fullblown conception which in Calvin provided the way of making the law a source of welcome and positive moral guidance for the believer" (Edward LeRoy Long Jr., *A Survey of Christian Ethics* [New York: Oxford University Press, 1967], p. 85).

[142]See, for example, Luther's poignant statement from 1523 in Martin Luther, "Temporal Authority: To What Extent Should It Be Obeyed?" trans. J. J. Schindel, rev. Walther I. Brandt, in *The Christian Society II*, ed. Walther I. Brandt, vol. 45 of *Luther's Works*, ed. Lehmann, pp. 75-129.

[143]Martin Luther, "In epistolam S. Pauli ad Galatas commentarius," in *D. Martin Luthers Werke*, 40/1:368. For the English translation, see Lehmann, ed., *Luther's Works*, 26:232.

[144]For a recent restatement of this fundamental Lutheran ethical principle, see Harmon L. Smith, *Where Two or Three Are Gathered: Liturgy and the Moral Life* (Cleveland: Pilgrim, 1995), p. 127.

[145]Forell, *Faith Active in Love*, p. 63.

[146]Paul Althaus, *The Ethics of Martin Luther*, trans. Robert C. Schultz (Philadelphia:

Fortress, 1972), p. 3.

[147]Luther, "In epistolam S. Pauli ad Galatas commentarius," p. 275. For the English translation, see Lehmann, ed., *Luther's Works,* 26:161.

[148]For this interpretation see Forell, *Faith Active in Love,* p. 100.

[149]White, *Christian Ethics,* p. 162.

[150]Martin Luther, "Letter to Philip Melanchthon: Wartburg 1 August 1521," letter 91, in *Letters I,* ed. and trans. Gottfried G. Krodel, vol. 48 of *Luther's Works,* ed. Lehmann, p. 282.

[151]Luther, "Treatise on Good Works," in *Luther's Works,* ed. Lehmann, 44:23-24, 54, 97; Luther, "Von den guten Werken," 6:204-5, 229, 263.

[152]MacIntyre, *Short History of Ethics,* p. 125.

[153]For a helpful discussion of the development of the two kingdoms teaching in Luther, see F. Edward Cranz, *An Essay on the Development of Luther's Thought on Justice, Law and Society* (Cambridge, Mass.: Harvard University Press, 1959), pp. 159-73.

[154]Martin Luther, "Whether Soldiers, Too, Can Be Saved," trans. Charles M. Jacobs, rev. Robert C. Schultz, in *The Christian Society III,* ed. Robert C. Schultz, vol. 46 of *Luther's Works,* ed. Lehmann, pp. 99-100.

[155]Martin Luther, "An Open Letter on the Harsh Book Against the Peasants," trans. Charles M. Jacobs, rev. Robert C. Schultz, in *The Christian Society II,* ed. Robert C. Schultz, vol. 46 of *Luther's Works,* ed. Lehmann, p. 70.

[156]Richard Klann, "Lutheran Ethics," in *Baker's Dictionary of Christian Ethics,* p. 400.

[157]Forell, *Faith Active in Love,* p. 155.

[158]MacIntyre, *Short History of Ethics,* p. 124.

[159]Althaus, *Ethics of Martin Luther,* pp. 149-51.

[160]Forell, *Faith Active in Love,* p. 149.

[161]See François Wendel, *Calvin: The Origins and Development of His Religious Thought,* trans. Philip Mairet (New York: Harper & Row, 1963), p. 200.

[162]John Calvin *Institutes of the Christian Religion* 2.7.12.

[163]William F. Keesecker, "The Law in John Calvin's Ethics," in *Calvin and Christian Ethics,* ed. Peter De Klerk (Grand Rapids, Mich.: Calvin Studies Society, 1987), p. 25.

[164]Gordon H. Clark, for example, declares that according to Calvinism "the Christian is sanctified by an ever more complete obedience to the Ten Commandments" ("Calvinistic Ethics," in *Baker's Dictionary of Christian Ethics,* p. 81).

[165]For a summary, see Wendel, *Calvin,* pp. 206-7.

[166]Calvin *Institutes* 2.8.1.

[167]R. H. Tawney, *Religion and the Rise of Capitalism* (London: John Murray, 1926), p. 109, cf. 93, 105.

[168]For a recent restatement of the disjuncture of philosophical and theological ethics along the lines of Reformation thought, see Donald G. Bloesch, *Freedom for Obedience: Evangelical Ethics for Contemporary Times* (San Francisco: Harper &

Row, 1987), pp. 19-42.

Chapter 5: Contemporary Christian Proposals

[1]Clyde A. Holbrook, "H. Richard Niebuhr," in *A Handbook of Christian Theologians,* ed. Martin E. Marty and Dean C. Peerman (Nashville: Abingdon, 1965), p. 375.

[2]H. Richard Niebuhr, *The Kingdom of God in America* (Chicago: Willett Clark, 1937), p. 193.

[3]Walter Rauschenbusch in *Cleveland's Young Men,* January 9, 1913, p. 2, as quoted in R. T. Handy, "Walter Rauschenbusch in Historical Perspective," *The Baptist Quarterly* [London] 20, no. 7 (July 1964): 315.

[4]Claude Welch, *Protestant Theology in the Nineteenth Century,* vol. 2, *1870-1914* (New Haven, Conn.: Yale University Press, 1985), p. 261.

[5]Walter Rauschenbusch, *Christianity and the Social Crisis* (New York: Macmillan, 1907), p. xi.

[6]Walter Rauschenbusch, *A Theology for the Social Gospel* (1917; reprint Nashville: Abingdon, 1978), p. 142.

[7]For a helpful summary of this see J. Philip Wogaman, *Christian Ethics: A Historical Introduction* (Louisville, Ky.: Westminster John Knox, 1993), pp. 257-68.

[8]On this see World Council of Churches, *Signs of the Spirit: Official Report, Seventh Assembly, Canberra Australia, 7-20 February 1991,* ed. Michael Kinnamon (Geneva: WCC; Grand Rapids, Mich.: Eerdmans, 1991), pp. 238-39.

[9]Edward LeRoy Long Jr., *A Survey of Christian Ethics* (New York: Oxford, 1967), p. 150.

[10]Karl Barth, *Epistle to the Romans,* trans. Edwyn C. Hoskyns (London: Oxford University Press, 1933), p. 28.

[11]Karl Barth, *Church Dogmatics,* ed. G. W. Bromiley and T. F. Torrance, trans. A. T. MacKay et al. (Edinburgh: T & T Clark, 1961), 3/4:4.

[12]Karl Barth, *Ethics,* ed. Dietrich Braun, trans. Geoffrey W. Bromiley (New York: Seabury, 1981), p. 18.

[13]Barth, *Church Dogmatics,* 2/2:509-51, 3/4:3-46.

[14]Ibid., 2/1:543.

[15]Ibid., 2/2:516-17.

[16]Barth, *Ethics,* p. 43.

[17]Barth, *Church Dogmatics,* 3/4:11-13.

[18]Barth, *Ethics,* pp. 80-83.

[19]Ibid., p. 87.

[20]Ibid., pp. 89, 92, 98, 106.

[21]For Barth's discussion of election see, for example, *Church Dogmatics,* 2/2:123, 163.

[22]Ibid., 3/4:4.

[23]Ibid., 2/2:520.

[24]Barth, *Ethics,* p. 77.

[25]Ibid., p. 16.

[26]Barth, *Church Dogmatics*, 3/1:97.
[27]For this appraisal see Wogaman, *Christian Ethics*, pp. 222-23.
[28]See, for example, Emil Brunner, *The Divine Imperative*, trans. Olive Wyon (Philadelphia: Westminster Press, 1947).
[29]James M. Gustafson, *Ethics from a Theocentric Perspective* (Chicago: University of Chicago Press, 1981), 1:83.
[30]Ibid., 1:84.
[31]Ibid., 1:163-64.
[32]Ibid., 1:185, 293-306.
[33]Ibid., 1:94.
[34]Ibid., 1:100.
[35]Ibid., 1:113.
[36]Ibid., 1:158.
[37]Ibid., 1:327, 342.
[38]Ibid., 1:120-24.
[39]For an example of this interest, see James M. Gustafson, *Christian Ethics and the Community* (New York: Pilgrim, 1979), pp. 153-63.
[40]For example, Gustafson, *Ethics*, p. 264.
[41]Ibid., pp. 235-51.
[42]Ibid., p. 311.
[43]Ibid., p. 316.
[44]Jean Porter notes that this has been a point emphasized by both Gustafson and his critics (*The Recovery of Virtue: The Relevance of Aquinas for Christian Ethics* [Louisville, Ky.: Westminster John Knox, 1990], pp. 26-27).
[45]Anders Nygren, *Agape and Eros*, trans. Philip S. Watson (Philadelphia: Westminster Press, 1953).
[46]For this interpretation see Warren A. Quanbeck, "Anders Nygren," in *Handbook of Christian Theologians*, p. 304.
[47]Paul Ramsey, *Basic Christian Ethics* (New York: Charles Scribner's Sons, 1950). For a clarification of his position in the light of the discussion that followed his earlier work, see Paul Ramsey, *Deeds and Rules in Christian Ethics*, Scottish Journal of Theology Occasional Papers 11 (Edinburgh: Oliver and Boyd, 1965).
[48]Ramsey, *Basic Christian Ethics*, p. 388.
[49]Ibid., p. 343.
[50]Ibid., p. xiv.
[51]Ibid., p. xi.
[52]Long, *Survey of Christian Ethics*, p. 65.
[53]For this label see Wogaman, *Christian Ethics*, p. 231.
[54]Ramsey, *Basic Christian Ethics*, p. 95.
[55]Ibid., p. 100.
[56]Ibid., p. 160.
[57]Ibid., p. xiii.
[58]Ibid., pp. 115-16.

[59]Ibid., pp. 112-13.
[60]Ibid., p. 78.
[61]See Wogaman, *Christian Ethics,* p. 231.
[62]Ramsey, *Basic Christian Ethics,* pp. 340, 343-44.
[63]See Long, *Survey of Christian Ethics,* p. 67.
[64]Ramsey, *Basic Christian Ethics,* p. 80.
[65]Ibid., p. 354.
[66]Ibid., p. 187.
[67]Ibid., p. 263.
[68]Ibid., p. 219.
[69]Ibid., pp. 219-26.
[70]Joseph Fletcher, *Situation Ethics: The New Morality* (Philadelphia: Westminster Press, 1966).
[71]Ibid., p. 55. See also Joseph Fletcher, "Contemporary Conscience: A Christian Method," *Kenyon Alumni Bulletin* 21, no. 3 (1963): 5-6.
[72]Fletcher, *Situation Ethics,* p. 134.
[73]Ibid., p. 28.
[74]Ibid., p. 153.
[75]Ibid., pp. 17-37.
[76]Ibid., p. 66.
[77]Ibid., p. 36.
[78]Ibid., pp. 28-29, 129-30.
[79]Ibid., p. 152.
[80]Ibid., pp. 87-99.
[81]Ibid., p. 119.
[82]Ibid., pp. 105, 117.
[83]Evangelicals have been among Fletcher's most strident critics. For examples of evangelical critiques see Millard J. Erickson, *Relativism in Contemporary Christian Ethics* (Grand Rapids, Mich.: Baker Book House, 1974); Erwin W. Lutzer, *The Necessity of Ethical Absolutes* (Grand Rapids, Mich.: Zondervan, 1981), pp. 27-39.
[84]Hence Wogaman, *Christian Ethics,* p. 230.
[85]Fletcher, *Situation Ethics,* pp. 154-57.
[86]Ibid., p. 34.
[87]Dietrich Bonhoeffer, *The Cost of Discipleship,* trans. R. H. Fuller, rev. ed. (New York: Macmillan, 1959).
[88]Dietrich Bonhoeffer, *Ethics,* trans. Neville Horton Smith (New York: Macmillan, 1965).
[89]Dietrich Bonhoeffer, *Letters and Papers from Prison,* trans. Eberhard Bethge (London: Collins/Fontana, 1953).
[90]Heinrich Ott concludes, "Christology was at all stages of his pilgrimage the inward law of his thinking, the definitive thought" (*Reality and Faith: The Theological Legacy of Dietrich Bonhoeffer,* trans. Alex. A. Morrison [Philadelphia: Fortress, 1972], p. 368). Many interpreters of Bonhoeffer agree with the assess-

ment that Christology is the key to Bonhoeffer's thought. See Edwin H. Robertson, "Bonhoeffer's Christology," in Dietrich Bonhoeffer, *Christ the Center,* trans. John Bowden (New York: Harper & Row, 1966), p. 12.

[91]Ott, *Reality and Faith,* 167. Bonhoeffer explicitly raised this question in his lectures on Christology. See *Christ the Center,* pp. 30-31.

[92]E.g., Dietrich Bonhoeffer, *No Rusty Swords: Letters, Lectures and Notes, 1928-1936,* trans. Edwin H. Robertson and John Bowden (New York: Harper & Row, 1965); *The Communion of the Saints: A Dogmatic Inquiry into the Sociology of the Church,* trans. R. Gregor Smith (New York: Harper & Row, 1961), p. 85; *Act and Being,* trans. Bernard Noble (New York: Harper & Row, 1961), p. 120; *Christ the Center,* pp. 59-61. John A. Phillips elevates this dimension to the center of Bonhoeffer's thinking, calling "Christ exists as the church" "the theme of Bonhoeffer's work." *Christ for Us in the Theology of Dietrich Bonhoeffer* (New York: Harper & Row, 1967), p. 48.

[93]Phillips sees in this move a dramatic step in Bonhoeffer's thinking: "In this manner he seeks to free his Christology from his ecclesiology in order to describe a Christ moving about freely in the world; no longer a Christ identified with a church fighting against the world for her existence" (*Christ for Us,* p. 137).

[94]Bonhoeffer, *Ethics,* pp. 244-45. For a discussion of this dimension of Bonhoeffer's ethic, see Long, *Survey of Christian Ethics,* pp. 153-55.

[95]Bonhoeffer, *Cost of Discipleship, p.* 36.

[96]Ibid., p. 40.

[97]Bonhoeffer, *Letters and Papers,* p. 93.

[98]Ibid., p. 112.

[99]Bonhoeffer declares, "If he pleases to grant us some overwhelming bliss, we ought not to try and be more religious than God himself. For then we should spoil that bliss by our presumption and arrogance" (*Letters and Papers,* p. 56).

[100]See Phillips's claim to this effect (*Christ for Us,* p. 236).

[101]Bonhoeffer, *Letters and Papers,* p. 166.

[102]See Bonhoeffer, *Ethics,* p. 142.

[103]Ibid., p. 133.

[104]Bonhoeffer, *Letters and Papers,* p. 125.

[105]In Bonhoeffer's words, "Christ does not only make men good: he makes them strong too" (ibid., p. 131).

[106]This tendency is evident in the influential book authored by the Mennonite scholar John Howard Yoder, *The Politics of Jesus* (Grand Rapids, Mich.: Eerdmans, 1972).

[107]For an example of Roman Catholic work in this area, see Stephen Happel and James J. Walter, *Conversion and Discipleship: A Christian Foundation for Ethics and Doctrine* (Philadelphia: Fortress, 1986).

[108]James William McClendon, *Ethics: Systematic Theology,* vol. 1 (Nashville: Abingdon, 1986).

[109]Ibid., p. 42.

[110]Ibid., p. 45.
[111]Ibid., p. 35.
[112]Ibid., pp. 47-48.
[113]Ibid., p. 66.
[114]Ibid., p. 273.
[115]Ibid., p. 210.
[116]Ibid., p. 239.
[117]Ibid., p. 212.
[118]Ibid., pp. 330-31.
[119]For a discussion of King's relationship to Rauschenbusch, see James P. Hanigan, *Martin Luther King Jr. and The Foundations of Nonviolence* (Lanham, Md.: University Press of America, 1984), pp. 143-48.
[120]This is the conclusion of Wogaman, *Christian Ethics*, p. 248.
[121]For this conclusion, see Hanigan, *Martin Luther King Jr.*, p. 118.
[122]Ibid., p. 116.
[123]For a helpful, concise summary of King's theology as it provides a foundation for his ethical theory, see ibid., pp. 69-102, 119-20.
[124]Martin Luther King Jr. Collection, Mugar Library, Boston University, Boston, Mass., file 14 (54); 14 (75); 14 (26); 14 (33); as cited in Hanigan, *Martin Luther King Jr.*, p. 121.
[125]Martin Luther King Jr., "Letter from Birmingham City Jail," in *A Testament of Hope: The Essential Writings of Martin Luther King Jr.*, ed. James Melvin Washington (1963; San Francisco: Harper & Row, 1986), p. 293.
[126]Martin Luther King Jr., *Where Do We Go from Here: Chaos or Community* (New York: Harper & Row, 1967), p. 48.
[127]King, BU Collection, 5, 177, as cited in Hanigan, *Martin Luther King Jr.*, p. 293.
[128]Ibid., p. 294.
[129]Martin Luther King Jr., *Stride Toward Freedom: The Montgomery Story* (New York: Harper & Row, 1964), pp. 78-79, 83-84.
[130]King viewed pragmatic nonviolence as an alternative form of violence (ibid., p. 83).
[131]For a discussion of this differentiation, see Hanigan, *Martin Luther King Jr.*, pp. 2-4.
[132]King, *Stride Toward Freedom*, p. 192.
[133]Ibid., p. 84.
[134]King, *Where Do We Go from Here*, p. 61.
[135]King, *Stride Toward Freedom*, pp. 85-87.
[136]Hanigan, *Martin Luther King Jr.*, pp. 193, 214.
[137]King, *Stride Toward Freedom*, p. 85.
[138]Ibid., p. 86.
[139]King's words as cited in Coretta Scott King, "Creative Suffering: The Ripple of Hope," *National Catholic Reporter*, April 2, 1969, p. 6.
[140]Robert McAfee Brown declared that this event "initiated a revolution in Latin

American church life that will finally mean a revolution in Latin American history" (*Gustavo Gutiérrez: An Introduction to Liberation Theology* [Maryknoll, N.Y.: Orbis, 1990], p. 11).

[141]Gustavo Gutiérrez, *A Theology of Liberation,* trans. and ed. Sister Caridad Inda and John Eagleson (Maryknoll, N.Y.: Orbis, 1988), p. xxix.

[142]In the words of Dermot A. Lane, "All knowledge tends to embody the social circumstances and conditions of its time" (*Foundations for a Social Theology: Praxis, Process and Salvation* [New York: Paulist, 1984], p. 77).

[143]For a basic overview of "critical theory" and its influence on liberation theology see Lane, *Foundations for a Social Theory,* pp. 43-56.

[144]Gustavo Gutiérrez, *The Power of the Poor in History* (London: SCM Press, 1983), p. 193.

[145]Ibid.

[146]Gutiérrez, *Theology of Liberation,* p. 151.

[147]Gutiérrez, *Power of the Poor,* p. 13.

[148]Gutiérrez, *Theology of Liberation,* p. xxxviii.

[149]Gutiérrez himself considered liberation theology to be a reconstruction of the doctrine of salvation (ibid., p. 83).

[150]Ibid., p. 18.

[151]Ibid., p. 104.

[152]Ibid., p. 116.

[153]Ibid., p. 118.

[154]Gutiérrez, *Power of the Poor,* p. 28.

[155]John Cobb Jr. may be cited as one influential Protestant theologian who at one point abandoned constructive theology in favor of offering a Christian theological perspective on the ecological crisis.

[156]Rosemary Radford Ruether, *Gaia and God: An Ecofeminist Theology of Earth Healing* (San Francisco: Harper & Row, 1992), p. 1.

[157]Ibid., p. 2.

[158]Ibid., p. 111.

[159]The propriety of the Gaia concept has been hotly debated in recent years. For an evangelical perspective on this issue, see Loren Wilkinson, "Gaia Spirituality: A Christian Critique," *Evangelical Review of Theology* 17 (April 1993): 176-89.

[160]Ruether, *Gaia and God,* p. 3.

[161]Ibid., p. 258.

[162]Ibid., pp. 2-3.

[163]Ibid., p. 201.

[164]Ibid., p. 48.

[165]Ibid., p. 57.

[166]Ibid., p. 139.

[167]Ibid., p. 256.

[168]Ibid., p. 141.

[169]Ibid., p. 142.

[170]Ibid., p. 254.
[171]Ibid., p. 227.
[172]Ibid., p. 253.
[173]Ibid., p. 255.
[174]Ibid., p. 273.
[175]For an example see Norman L. Geisler, *Christian Ethics: Issues and Alternatives* (Grand Rapids, Mich.: Baker Book House, 1989).
[176]For an example of this discussion see Mary Field Belenky et al., *Women's Ways of Knowing: The Development of Self, Voice and Mind* (New York: Basic Books, 1986).
[177]See Carol Gilligan, *In a Different Voice: Psychological Theory and Women's Development* (Cambridge, Mass.: Harvard University Press, 1982). See also Carol Gilligan, Janie Victoria Ward and Jill McLean Taylor, eds., *Mapping the Moral Domain: A Contribution of Women's Thinking to Psychological Theory and Education* (Cambridge, Mass.: Harvard University Press, 1988); Eva Feder Kittay and Diana T. Meyers, eds., *Women and Moral Theory* (Totowa, N.J.: Rowman & Littlefield, 1987).
[178]Nel Noddings, *Caring: A Feminine Approach to Ethics and Moral Education* (Berkeley: University of California Press, 1984).
[179]Ibid., p. 80.
[180]Ibid., p. 29.
[181]Ibid., pp. 50-51, 83.
[182]Ibid., p. 24.
[183]Ibid., p. 28.
[184]Ibid., pp. 28-29.
[185]Ibid., p. 29.
[186]Alasdair MacIntyre, *After Virtue: A Study in Moral Theory,* 2nd ed. (Notre Dame, Ind.: University of Notre Dame Press, 1984).
[187]Ibid., pp. 11-12.
[188]Ibid., p. 22.
[189]Ibid., pp. 118-19.
[190]Ibid., pp. 128-29.
[191]Ibid., p. 142.
[192]Ibid., pp. 216-19.
[193]Ibid., p. 219.
[194]Ibid.
[195]Ibid., p. 221.
[196]Stanley Hauerwas, *The Peaceable Kingdom: A Primer in Christian Ethics* (Notre Dame, Ind.: University of Notre Dame Press, 1983), p. 63.
[197]Ibid., p. 17.
[198]Ibid., p. 102.
[199]Ibid., p. 44.
[200]For an autobiographical description of the development of his approach, see

Stanley Hauerwas, "The Testament of Friends," *Christian Century* 107, no. 7 (1990): 212-16.

[201]Paul Nelson, *Narrative and Morality: A Theological Inquiry* (University Park: Pennsylvania State University Press, 1987), p. 109.

[202]Hauerwas, *Peaceable Kingdom*, pp. 16, 54.

[203]Stanley Hauerwas, *Truthfulness and Tragedy* (Notre Dame, Ind.: University of Notre Dame Press, 1977), p. 8.

[204]Ibid., pp. 75-77.

[205]Stanley Hauerwas, *The Community of Character* (Notre Dame, Ind.: Notre Dame University Press, 1981), p. 144.

[206]Stanley Hauerwas, *Vision and Virtue* (Notre Dame, Ind.: Fides, 1974), p. 67.

[207]Hauerwas, *Peaceable Kingdom*, p. 16. See also *Vision and Virtue*, pp. 2-3. The centrality of these concepts in Hauerwas's thought has been noted as well by Michael Goldberg, *Theology and Narrative* (Nashville: Abingdon, 1982), p. 174.

[208]Hauerwas, *Truthfulness and Tragedy*, p. 29.

[209]Hauerwas, *Vision and Virtue*, p. 59.

[210]Ibid., pp. 29, 36.

[211]Ibid., p. 74.

[212]Ibid., p. 73.

[213]Hauerwas, *Truthfulness and Tragedy*, p. 80.

[214]Hauerwas, *Peaceable Kingdom*, p. 100.

[215]Ibid., p. 97. Elsewhere Hauerwas states his goal as assisting Christians in rediscovering that their most important social task is "nothing less than to be a community capable of hearing the story of God we find in the scripture and living in a manner that is faithful to that story" (*Community of Character*, p. 1).

[216]Ibid., p. 3.

[217]Ibid., pp. 4, 95-96.

[218]Hauerwas, *Peaceable Kingdom*, p. 78.

[219]Hauerwas, *Community of Character*, p. 63.

[220]Ibid., p. 66.

[221]Hauerwas, *Peaceable Kingdom*, pp. 24-30.

[222]Carl F. H. Henry, *The Uneasy Conscience of Modern Fundamentalism* (Grand Rapids, Mich.: Eerdmans, 1947). For his later reflections on the problematic areas of fundamentalism and the need for evangelicals to move beyond it, see Carl F. H. Henry, *Evangelical Responsibility in Contemporary Theology* (Grand Rapids, Mich.: Eerdmans, 1957).

[223]Henry, *Uneasy Conscience of Modern Fundamentalism*, p. 16.

[224]Ibid., p. 68.

[225]Henry's most significant work is his general treatise on ethics, *Christian Personal Ethics* (Grand Rapids, Mich.: Eerdmans, 1957).

[226]Carl F. H. Henry, *God, Revelation and Authority*, 6 vols. (Waco, Tex.: Word, 1976-1983), 1:405; 2:136. The *imago Dei* means that humans can obtain a rational knowledge of ethics (Henry, *Christian Personal Ethics*, p. 151).

[227]Henry, *God, Revelation and Authority,* 1:244.

[228]Ibid., 3:457.

[229]Ibid., 3:248-487.

[230]Ibid., 4:426.

[231]Ibid., 3:173.

[232]Carl F. H. Henry, *The Protestant Dilemma* (Grand Rapids, Mich.: Eerdmans, 1949), p. 99.

[233]Henry, *God, Revelation and Authority,* 1:215.

[234]Indeed Henry declares, "The Christian doctrines of knowledge and ethics interpenetrate each other. The derivation of the whole of reality and life from a rational God means that any proposition gains its truth only from the Christian system" (*Christian Personal Ethics,* p. 160).

[235]Ibid., pp. 265, 327.

[236]For this interpretation of Henry's position, see Long, *Survey of Christian Ethics,* pp. 87-88.

[237]Henry, *Christian Personal Ethics,* p. 171.

[238]See, for example, ibid., p. 347.

[239]Ibid., pp. 201-3, 217.

[240]Ibid., p. 269.

[241]Ibid., p. 299.

[242]Ibid., p. 308.

[243]Ibid., p. 303.

[244]Ibid., p. 414.

[245]Ibid., p. 220.

[246]Ibid., p. 255.

[247]Ibid., pp. 529, 531.

[248]Henry writes, "Christian love is only half biblical when it deteriorates into a concern only for the souls of men and is indifferent to the needs of the body" (ibid., p. 230).

Henry repeatedly tackled questions of social ethics. His most pointed statement is the book *Aspects of Christian Social Ethics* (Grand Rapids, Mich.: Eerdmans, 1964). Important as well are the scattered discussions in *God, Revelation and Authority,* as well as essays in *A Plea for Evangelical Demonstration* (Grand Rapids, Mich.: Baker Book House, 1971), *The Christian Mindset in a Secular Society* (Portland, Ore.: Multnomah Press, 1984), and *The God Who Shows Himself* (Waco, Tex.: Word, 1966).

[249]Henry, *Plea for Evangelical Demonstration,* p. 107; *The God Who Shows Himself,* p. 31. For an extended discussion of justice, see *God, Revelation and Authority,* 6:402-54.

[250]Henry, *Plea for Evangelical Demonstration,* p. 115.

[251]See, for example, Henry, *God, Revelation and Authority,* 4:573-77.

[252]Henry, *Aspects of Christian Social Ethics,* p. 16.

[253]Henry, *Plea for Evangelical Demonstration,* pp. 46-47. For an extended discussion

of Christian political duty, see *God, Revelation and Authority,* 6:436-54.

[254]Oliver O'Donovan, *Resurrection and Moral Order: An Outline for Evangelical Ethics* (Grand Rapids, Mich.: Eerdmans, 1986).

[255]For a succinct summary of O'Donovan's argument, see ibid., pp. 26-27.

[256]Ibid., pp. 54-58.

[257]Ibid., p. 76.

[258]Ibid., pp. 14-15.

[259]Ibid., p. 101.

[260]Ibid., p. 102.

[261]Ibid., p. 106.

[262]Ibid., pp. 140-62.

[263]Ibid., p. 183.

[264]Ibid., p. 226.

[265]Ibid., p. 246.

[266]Ibid., p. 205.

[267]Ibid., p. 200.

[268]Ibid., p. 204.

[269]Ibid., p. 200.

[270]Ibid., p. 201.

[271]Ibid., p. 222.

[272]Thus O'Donovan speaks of "the epistemological priority of act" (ibid., p. 211).

[273]Ibid., p. 215.

[274]Ibid., p. 224.

Chapter 6: Christian Ethics & the Contemporary Context

[1]See Robert F. O'Neil and Darlene A. Pienta, "Economic Criteria Versus Ethical Criteria: Toward Resolving a Basic Dilemma in Business," *Journal of Business Ethics* 13 (1994): 73.

[2]Douglas Todd, "What on Earth Happens Next," *The Vancouver Sun,* December 31, 1994, p. D11.

[3]For examples of the turn-of-the-century focus on duty, see Henry E. Robins, *The Ethics of the Christian Life: The Science of Right Living* (Philadelphia: Griffith & Rowland, 1904); Newman Smyth, *Christian Ethics* (New York: Charles Scribner's Sons, 1906). Even some older works that speak of virtue in fact focus on duty. See, for example, A. D. Mattson, *Christian Ethics: The Basis and Content of the Christian Life,* rev. ed. (Rock Island, Ill.: Augustana, 1947).

[4]J. Philip Wogaman, *Christian Moral Judgment* (Louisville, Ky.: Westminster John Knox, 1989), pp. 13, 15.

[5]Immanuel Kant, *Critique of Pure Reason,* trans. Norman Kemp Smith (London: Macmillan, 1933), A805/B833, p. 635.

[6]Robert Kane, *Through the Moral Maze: Searching for Absolute Values in a Pluralistic World* (New York: Paragon, 1994), p. 97.

[7]Ibid., p. 98.

[8]Ibid.

[9]Wayne A. Meeks, *The Origins of Christian Morality: The First Two Centuries* (New Haven, Conn.: Yale University Press, 1993), p. 5.

[10]Ibid., p. 8.

[11]Harry Huebner and David Schroeder, *Church as Parable: Whatever Happened to Ethics?* (Winnipeg, Man.: CMBC Publications, 1993), p. 79.

[12]Ibid., p. 82.

[13]Of course this presupposes a specific answer to a prior question, namely, Is there a distictively *Christian* ethic? For a helpful study of this logically prior question, see *Readings in Moral Theology 2: The Distinctiveness of Christian Ethics,* ed. Charles E. Curran and Richard A. McCormick (New York: Paulist, 1980).

[14]So pervasive has this question been that Emil Brunner can introduce without fanfare "the question concerning the presence of a 'universal moral sense'" (*The Divine Imperative,* trans. Olive Wyon [Philadelphia: Westminster Press, 1947], p. 32).

[15]This may have been in part what William Shakespeare had in mind when he penned the famous line "All the world's a stage, and all the men and women merely players" (*As You Like It* 2.7.139-40).

[16]This conclusion runs counter to what some Christian thinkers have argued. See C. S. Lewis, *Mere Christianity* (New York: Macmillan, 1960), pp. 17-21.

[17]N. H. G. Robinson, *The Groundwork of Christian Ethics* (Grand Rapids, Mich.: Eerdmans, 1971), p. 261.

[18]Georgia Harkness sees in the Christian tradition a somewhat different set of three alternatives, namely incorporation/amalgamation, repudiation and critical appropriation (*Christian Ethics* [New York: Abingdon, 1957], pp. 17-18).

[19]See the discussion under the doctrine of creation in Stanley J. Grenz, *Theology for the Community of God* (Nashville: Broadman and Holman, 1994).

[20]On this distinction and its implications, see Robinson, *Groundwork of Christian Ethics,* p. 137.

[21]James M. Gustafson, *Ethics from a Theocentric Perspective* (Chicago: University of Chicago Press, 1981), 1:88.

[22]For the judgment that Kant's ethic is anthropocentric rather than theocentric, see Theodore M. Greene, "The Historical Context and Religious Significance of Kant's *Religion,*" in Immanuel Kant, *Religion Within the Limits of Reason Alone,* trans. Theodore M. Greene and Hoyt H. Hudson (New York: Harper & Row/Torchbooks, 1960), p. lxxvii.

[23]In late eighteenth-century American Calvinism, a position developed known as "disinterested benevolence." This view was somewhat reminiscent of a viewpoint suggested in Daniel Rogers, *Naaman the Syrian: His Disease and Cure* (London: Th. Harper, 1642; reprint Ann Arbor, Mich.: University Microfilms International, 1983 [R1799]), p. 18. More significant, however, it formed a response to the focus on self-love that had arisen in Calvinist philosophical and theological circles in the eighteenth century.

According to disinterested benevolence, true Christian spirituality includes even the willingness to be damned for the glory of God. This means that personal salvation cannot rank as one's primary or ultimate concern. Not even the quest for salvation should displace concern for the well-being—both eternal and temporal—of others and above all for God's glory.

Representing this position, Samuel Hopkins wrote in "A Dialogue Between a Calvinist and a Semi-Calvinist," "He [a regenerate person] cannot know that he loves God and shall be saved until he knows he has that disposition which implies a willingness to be damned, if it be not most for the glory of God that he should be saved." See Joseph A. Conforti, *Samuel Hopkins and the New Divinity Movement: Calvinism, the Congregational Ministry and Reform in New England Between the Great Awakenings* (Washington, D.C.: Christian University Press, 1981), p. 120.

[24]Gustafson, *Ethics from a Theocentric Perspective,* p. 99.

[25]For this term I am indebted to Robinson, *Groundwork of Christian Ethics,* pp. 100, 121-24.

[26]Alvah Hovey, *Commentary on the Epistle to the Galatians,* in *An American Commentary on the New Testament,* ed. Alvah Hovey (Philadelphia: American Baptist Publication Society, 1890), 5:70.

[27]F. F. Bruce, *The Epistle to the Galatians: A Commentary on the Greek Text,* New International Greek Testament Commentary (Grand Rapids, Mich.: Eerdmans, 1982), p. 251.

[28]Many Christian ethicists gravitate to naturalism. See, for example, Arthur F. Holmes, *Ethics* (Downers Grove, Ill.: InterVarsity Press, 1984), p. 62.

[29]For a short but helpful discussion of natural law and its connection with evangelical ethics, see Scott B. Rae, *Moral Choices: An Introduction to Ethics* (Grand Rapids, Mich.: Zondervan, 1995), pp. 35-41.

[30]For a succinct discussion of the common evangelical view of general revelation, see Bruce A. Demarest, "Revelation, General," in *Evangelical Dictionary of Theology,* ed. Walter A. Elwell (Grand Rapids, Mich.: Baker Book House, 1984), pp. 944-45.

[31]See, for example, Paul L. Lehmann, *Ethics in a Christian Context* (New York: Harper & Row, 1963), pp. 131, 159, 161.

[32]Trutz Rendtorff, *Ethics,* trans. Keith Crim (Philadelphia: Fortress, 1986), 1:80-81.

[33]Ibid., 1:81.

[34]For a similar idea see James M. Childs Jr., *Christian Anthropology and Ethics* (Philadelphia: Fortress, 1978), p. 154.

[35]See Helmut Thielicke, *Theological Ethics,* trans. John W. Doberstein, ed. William H. Lazareth (Philadelphia: Fortress, 1966), 1:383-451; Dietrich Bonhoeffer, *Ethics,* trans. Neville Horton Smith (New York: Macmillan, 1965), pp. 120-213.

[36]For a similar attempt to connect believers and nonbelievers together through the Adam-Christ typology, see Paul L. Lehmann, *Ethics in a Christian Context* (New York: Harper & Row, 1963), pp. 154-55.

[37]For a similar conclusion, see Brian Hebblethwaite, *Christian Ethics in the Modern Age* (Philadelphia: Westminster Press, 1982), p. 136.

[38]Gilbert C. Meilaender, *Faith and Faithfulness: Basic Themes in Christian Ethics* (Notre Dame, Ind.: University of Notre Dame Press, 1991), p. 106.

[39]Thielicke, *Theological Ethics,* 1:20.

[40]Jonathan Edwards, *Religious Affections: How Man's Will Affects His Character Before God* (reprint Portland, Ore.: Multnomah Press, 1984).

[41]Alasdair MacIntyre, *After Virtue: A Study in Moral Theory,* 2nd ed. (Notre Dame, Ind.: University of Notre Dame Press, 1984), p. 203.

[42]See, for example, Sidney I. Landau and Ronald J. Bogus, eds., *The Doubleday Dictionary for Home, School and Office* (Garden City, N.Y.: Doubleday, 1975), p. 374.

[43]See Harmon L. Smith, *Where Two or Three Are Gathered: Liturgy and the Moral Life* (Cleveland: Pilgrim, 1995), p. 86.

[44]For example, George A. Lindbeck, "Confession and Community: An Israel-like View of the Church," *The Christian Century* 107 (May 9, 1990): 495.

[45]The idea of an ethic of community has developed in the twentieth century. For example, already in the 1940s the British ethicist Sydney Cave spoke of ethics as "life in community." Yet for him the term *community* was merely a way of speaking about the older concept of the "orders of creation," which he divided into family, industry and the state (Sydney Cave, *The Christian Way: A Study of New Testament Ethics in Relation to Present Problems* [New York: Philosophical Library, 1949], p. 175).

[46]For a recent philosophical discussion of this, see Alistair I. McFayden, *The Call to Personhood: A Christian Theory of the Individual in Social Relationships* (Cambridge: Cambridge University Press, 1990), pp. 61-63.

[47]For a succinct summary of conventionalism, see Raziel Abelson, *Ethics and Metaethics: Readings in Ethical Philosophy* (New York: St. Martin's, 1963), pp. 303-4. See also Rae, *Moral Choices,* pp. 86-87.

[48]Jean-François Lyotard, *The Postmodern Condition: A Report on Knowledge,* trans. Geoff Bennington and Brian Massumi (Minneapolis: University of Minnesota Press, 1984), p. iv.

[49]For a discussion of this topic from the perspective of philosophy of religion, see James F. Smurl, *Religious Ethics: A Systems Approach* (Englewood Cliffs, N.J.: Prentice-Hall, 1972).

[50]Clifford Geertz, *The Interpretation of Cultures: Selected Essays* (New York: Basic Books, 1973), p. 89.

[51]See for example, Émile Durkheim, *The Elementary Forms of the Religious Life,* trans. Joseph Ward Swain (New York: Collier, 1961), pp. 463-87. For a helpful summary of Durkheim's view of religion, see Robert N. Bellah, introduction to Émile Durkheim, *On Morality and Society: Selected Writings,* ed. Robert N. Bellah (Chicago: University of Chicago Press, 1973), pp. xlv-lii.

[52]This is most obviously the case with monotheistic religions, which look to the

one God as the foundation of cosmic, and hence social, unity. But polytheistic religions can likewise offer a unified cosmic vision insofar as they elevate one god above the others.

[53]Geertz, *Interpretation of Cultures,* p. 129. See also Geertz's classic definition of religion, p. 90.

[54]This possibility was discussed at the Parliament of the World's Religions which met in Chicago in 1993.

Chapter 7: Foundations of a Christian Ethic

[1]Charles M. Sheldon, *In His Steps: What Would Jesus Do?* (1896; reprint New York: Grosset and Dunlap, 1935), pp. 13, 15.

[2]Stephen E. Fowl and L. Gregory Jones, *Reading in Communion: Scripture and Ethics in Christian Life* (Grand Rapids, Mich.: Eerdmans, 1991), p. 20.

[3]For an example of recent Roman Catholic thinking about the use of the Bible in Christian ethics, see Robert J. Daly et al., *Christian Biblical Ethics* (New York: Paulist, 1984).

[4]This nomenclature borrows the categories popularized by Paul Tillich. For another example of the use of this terminology in ethics, see James M. Childs Jr., *Christian Anthropology and Ethics* (Philadelphia: Fortress, 1978), p. 156.

[5]For a similar definition see Clark H. Pinnock, "Heteronomy," in *Baker's Dictionary of Christian Ethics,* ed. Carl F. H. Henry (Grand Rapids, Mich.: Baker Book House, 1973), p. 288.

[6]For a concise statement of this position, see Richard A. Muller, *Dictionary of Latin and Greek Theological Terms: Drawn Principally from Protestant Scholastic Theology* (Grand Rapids, Mich.: Baker Book House, 1985), p. 284.

[7]John Murray, *Principles of Conduct: Aspects of Biblical Ethics* (Grand Rapids, Mich.: Eerdmans, 1957), p. 14.

[8]En route to his articulation of a Christian ethic, for example, Arthur F. Holmes invokes the words of the Westminster Shorter Catechism: "Because God is the Lord, and our God and Redeemer, therefore we are bound to keep all his commandments" (*Ethics* [Downers Grove, Ill.: InterVarsity Press, 1984], p. 76).

[9]For this judgment see N. H. G. Robinson, *The Groundwork of Christian Ethics* (Grand Rapids, Mich.: Eerdmans, 1971), p. 152.

[10]John Calvin *Institutes of the Christian Religion* 1.3.6.1.

[11]A. A. Hodge, *The Outlines of Theology,* ed. William H. Goold (London: T. Nelson and Sons, 1870), p. 51.

[12]For a helpful statement of evangelical legalism, see Robertson McQuilkin, *An Introduction to Biblical Ethics* (Wheaton, Ill.: Tyndale House, 1989), pp. 45-74.

[13]Ibid., p. 67.

[14]Newer scholarship questions the older view that the Pharisees were legalists in the sense of relying on personal obedience to the law so as to earn divine acceptance. Instead, first-century Jewish leaders followed "nomism," the belief that having been accepted by God, the people were now required to obey the law. See

C. G. Kruse, "Law," in *New Dictionary of Christian Ethics and Pastoral Theology*, ed. David J. Atkinson et al. (Downers Grove, Ill.: InterVarsity Press, 1995), p. 539.

[15]McQuilkin, *Biblical Ethics*, p. 51.

[16]Nonlegalists Bruce C. Birch and Larry L. Rasmussen acknowledge this and criticise the modern tendency to discount the prescriptive dimension of biblical revelation (*Bible and Ethics in the Christian Life* [Minneapolis: Augsburg, 1976], pp. 186-87).

[17]For an example of this criticism, see Richard N. Longenecker, "New Testament Social Ethics for Today," in *Understanding Paul's Ethics: Twentieth Century Approaches*, ed. Brian S. Rosner (Grand Rapids, Mich.: Eerdmans, 1995), p. 339.

[18]In his book with the revealing title *Principles of Conduct*, Murray, for example, offers such principles as marriage and procreation, labor and the sanctity of life.

[19]For a recent defense of the heteronomous "divine command theory," see Jochem Douma, "The Use of Scripture in Ethics," *European Journal of Theology* 1, no. 2 (1992): 105-21.

[20]For this conclusion see Fowl and Jones, *Reading in Communion*, p. 4. These authors actually add a third task of the heteronomous method, namely, to identify how the meaning found in the Bible ought to be understood in relation to other possible sources of guidance.

[21]For an example of the employment of a critique that focuses on this problem, see David A. Sherwood, "Doing the Right Thing: Ethical Practice in Contemporary Society," *Social Work and Christianity* 20, no. 2 (1993): 147-48.

[22]Robinson, *Groundwork of Christian Ethics*, p. 154. See also Longenecker, "New Testament Social Ethics for Today," p. 339.

[23]J. A. Motyer, "Law, Biblical Conception of," in *Evangelical Dictionary of Theology*, ed. Walter A. Elwell (Grand Rapids, Mich.: Baker Book House, 1984), p. 625.

[24]Paul Tillich forms one example of such an appeal. He concludes that "a moral act is not an act in obedience to an external law, human or divine. It is the inner law of our true being, of our essential or created nature, which demands that we actualize what follows from it" (*Morality and Beyond* [New York: Harper & Row, 1963], p. 20). For an example of an evangelical writer making such an appeal, see Motyer, "Law," in *Evangelical Dictionary of Theology*, p. 624. For an extended critique of the natural law tradition, see Helmut Thielicke, *Theological Ethics*, ed. William H. Lazareth (Grand Rapids, Mich.: Eerdmans, 1979), 1:383-451. A helpful discussion of the entire problematic of natural law in Protestant circles is Carl E. Braaten, "Protestants and Natural Law," *First Things* no. 19 (January 1992): 20-26.

[25]See, for example, R. E. O. White, *Christian Ethics* (Atlanta: John Knox, 1981), pp. 225-40.

[26]Clark H. Pinnock, "Autonomy," in *Baker's Dictionary of Christian Ethics*, p. 48.

[27]Ibid., p. 48. See also R. E. O. White, *Christian Ethics* (Atlanta: John Knox, 1981), p. 240.

[28]Immanuel Kant, *Groundwork of the Metaphysic of Morals*, trans. H. J. Paton (New

York: Harper & Row, 1964), pp. 98-99.

[29]White cites the Puritans and especially the early Quakers as examples (*Christian Ethics,* pp. 248-53).

[30]For a succinct statement of this position, although written by an opponent, see Murray, *Principles of Conduct,* p. 19.

[31]For a slightly different interpretation of Brunner's ethic, see Longenecker, "New Testament Social Ethics for Today," pp. 341-42.

[32]Emil Brunner, *The Divine Imperative,* trans. Olive Wyon (Philadelphia: Westminster Press, 1947), p. 118.

[33]Ibid., pp. 82-83.

[34]Ibid., p. 118.

[35]Ibid.

[36]Birger Gerhardsson pinpoints the need for such an orientation: "From the biblical point of view, people themselves cannot create adequate norms for life; the Bible's ethos is not *autonomous.* But nor are the proper norms *heteronomous;* they are not imposed on men from without by an arbitrary, foreign will. According to biblical faith, the right norms for human life are *theonomous.* They come from the one who has created humankind and who is humankind's only true Lord. The demands which he makes are thus adequate and proper. When they are internalized in a person's heart, that person functions as the Creator intended, in relation both to other people and to the whole of existence" (*The Ethos of the Bible,* trans. Stephen Westerholm [Philadelphia: Fortress, 1981], p. 118).

[37]This problem is noted by Fowl and Jones, *Reading in Communion,* pp. 7-8.

[38]For a survey of recent developments pointing in this direction, see Lisa Sowle Cahill, "The New Testament and Ethics: Communities of Social Change," *Interpretation* 44, no. 4 (1990): 383-95.

[39]This Reformation emphasis remains a central emphasis even among nonevangelical Protestant ethicists. See, for example, Tillich's statement of this principle in *Morality and Beyond,* p. 49.

[40]Even many proponents of a more heteronomous approach acknowledge this point. McQuilkin, for example, declares that the "standard for the Christian is God himself." The standards codified in the law, in turn, flow out of the nature of God (*Biblical Ethics,* pp. 50-51).

[41]For a similar close connection between theology and ethics, see Thielicke, *Theological Ethics,* 1:36-38.

[42]See, for example, James M. Gustafson, *Christian Ethics and the Community* (New York: Pilgrim, 1979), pp. 136-38.

[43]For an extended statement of this thesis, see Stanley J. Grenz, *Created for Community: Connecting Christian Belief with Christian Living* (Wheaton, Ill.: Victor/BridgePoint, 1996).

[44]For a helpful statement of this thesis, see Ellen T. Charry, "The Moral Function of Doctrine," *Theology Today* 49, no. 1 (1992): 31-45.

[45]Robin Gill, *A Textbook in Christian Ethics* (Edinburgh: T & T Clark, 1985), p. 22.

[46]Philip Edgcumbe Hughes, *Christian Ethics in Secular Society* (Grand Rapids, Mich.: Baker Book House, 1983), p. 15.

[47]This point has been repeatedly made in our day. See, for example, Birch and Rasmussen, *Bible and Ethics in the Christian Life,* p. 184.

[48]The importance of story to the construction of a biblical ethic is likewise a common contemporary emphasis. See, for example, W. H. Bellinger Jr., "The Old Testament: Sourcebook for Christian Ethics," in *Understanding Christian Ethics,* ed. William M. Tillman Jr. (Nashville: Broadman, 1988), p. 41.

[49]Smith, *Where Two or Three are Gathered,* p. 175.

[50]Gerhardsson, *Ethics of the Bible,* pp. 117-18.

[51]R. E. O. White offers this summary of "the main thrust of the Biblical message: the touchstone of religion is morality, the proof of faith is obedience, while the spring and vindication of morality is always ultimately religious, and hope for the immoral lies not in self-reform but in divine salvation" (*Biblical Ethics* [Atlanta: John Knox, 1979], p. 228).

[52]The connection between foundational theological concepts and ethical orientation is widely acknowledged. Eduard Lohse declares, "Because the crucified and risen Christ is proclaimed as the Lord of all the world and of all realms of life, the ethical instruction of the church does not ask for this or that deed or performance, but rather addresses the whole person and summons him to follow Christ and place himself in the service of love. In the whole body of theology, therefore, the general human phenomenon of ethics receives an essential deepening" ("The Church in Everyday Life," in *Understanding Paul's Ethics: Twentieth Century Approaches,* trans. George S. Rosner and Brian S. Rosner, ed. Brian S. Rosner [Grand Rapids, Mich.: Eerdmans, 1995], pp. 264-65). For a helpful summary of the connection between theology and ethics in the Orthodox tradition, see Vigen Guroian, "The Shape of Orthodox Ethics," *Epiphany Journal* 12, no. 1 (1991): 8-21.

[53]For similar attempts to set forth a foundation for Christian ethics in Christian theological commitments, see Waldo Beach, *Christian Ethics in the Protestant Tradition* (Atlanta: John Knox, 1988), pp. 22-31; J. Philip Wogaman, *Christian Moral Judgment* (Louisville, Ky.: Westminster John Knox, 1989), pp. 17-26, 31-35. The importance of doctrine as a foundation for ethics has been argued in Alister E. McGrath, "Doctrine and Ethics," *Journal of the Evangelical Theological Society* 34, no. 2 (1991): 145-56.

[54]For an example of a presentation of the Christian ethic that seeks to pattern that ethic after the being and action of God and God's covenant love, see Joseph L. Allen, *Love and Conflict: A Covenantal Model of Christian Ethics* (Nashville: Abingdon, 1984), pp. 53-81.

[55]Wogaman suggests that "the doctrine of creation may finally prove decisive as the foundation for ethics" because through it "we express our understanding of how it is that God is concretely related to the actual events and structures of this world" (*Christian Moral Judgment,* p. 25).

[56]This position is effectively critiqued in Jeffery Gibbs, "The Grace of God as the Foundation for Ethics," *Concordia Theological Quarterly* 48, nos. 2-3 (1984): 185-201.

[57]Paul Ramsey, *Basic Christian Ethics* (New York: Charles Scribner's Sons, 1950), p. 277. For a lengthier discussion of God as creating our human worth, see Allen, *Love and Conflict*, pp. 62-67.

[58]See Stanley J. Grenz, "Abortion—A Christian Response," *Conrad Grebel Review* 2, no. 1 (1984): 21-30.

[59]This is also symbolized by the living creatures who in the vision of the seer surround the divine throne (Rev 4:6-8).

[60]Maltbie D. Babcock, "This Is My Father's World."

[61]It is not without significance that in the story of Noah God commands his servant to take into the ark both clean and unclean animals, both animals which could be eaten and those which were forbidden as food.

[62]See Paul Lehmann, *Ethics in a Christian Context* (New York: Harper & Row, 1963), p. 111.

[63]For a fuller discussion see Stanley J. Grenz, *Theology for the Community of God* (Nashville: Broadman and Holman, 1994), pp. 92-93.

[64]Ibid., pp. 132-33.

[65]In an interesting twist Ramsey declares that, far from being the *imago Dei*, reason and intelligence are capacities gained only through sin and the Fall (*Basic Christian Ethics*, p. 263).

[66]See Grenz, *Theology for the Community of God*, pp. 229-33. For an extended treatment of the *imago Dei* as a foundational concept in theological ethics, see Thielicke, *Theological Ethics*, 1:150-278.

[67]Perhaps the most well-known contemporary exposition of the contractarian tradition is John Rawls, *A Theory of Justice* (Cambridge, Mass.: Belknap, 1971).

[68]For an attempt by an evangelical thinker to reestablish a theologically grounded rights orientation, see John Warwick Montgomery, *Human Rights and Human Dignity* (Grand Rapids, Mich.: Zondervan/Probe Books, 1986).

[69]Jean-Jacques Rousseau, *The Social Contract*, 1.6, trans. Willmoore Kendall (Chicago: Henry Regnery, 1954), p. 18. See also John Locke, *The Second Treatise of Government*, 8.95-99, ed. Thomas P. Peardon (Indianapolis: Bobbs-Merrill, 1952), pp. 54-56.

[70]For an articulation and defense of this position, see Joel Feinberg, "The Nature and Value of Rights," *The Journal of Value Inquiry* 4 (Winter 1970): 243-57.

[71]David L. Schindler, "Introduction: Grace and the Form of Nature and Culture," in *Catholicism and Secularization in America*, ed. David L. Schindler (Notre Dame, Ind.: Communio, 1990), p. 18.

[72]For the conclusion that this was the position of Locke, see Thomas P. Peardon, introduction to Locke, *Second Treatise of Government*, p. xiii.

[73]For a critical appropriation of the rights tradition into a Christian ethic, see Terence R. Anderson, *Walking the Way: Christian Ethics as a Guide* (Toronto:

United Church Publishing House, 1993), pp. 88-103.

[74]Ramsey, *Basic Christian Ethics*, p. 358.

[75]Ibid.

[76]Harry Huebner and David Schroeder, *Church as Parable: Whatever Happened to Ethics?* (Winnipeg: CMBC Publications, 1993), p. 82.

[77]For a discussion of this theological point, see Grenz, *Theology for the Community of God*, pp. 202-12.

[78]Ibid., pp. 842-44.

[79]In a somewhat similar manner Tillich speaks of the ethical task as becoming "a *person* within a community of persons" (*Morality and Beyond*, p. 19). But he offers an alternative foundation for this understanding based on the personalism of Martin Buber (*Morality and Beyond*, pp. 36-37).

[80]Wogaman, *Christian Moral Judgment*, p. 38; Beach, *Christian Ethics*, p. 26.

[81]Albert Terrill Rasmussen summarizes the nature of this problem: "Selective love directed toward particular individuals with whom we have intimate relations, even though we should rise to sacrificial heights, does not meet the requirements of love. For such love will shower special privileges on these favoured few often at the expense of others. Selective love is one of the great moral problems of community. It is so tempting to squander all our love on those close at hand and have no concern left for those beyond our little horizon" (*Christian Social Ethics: Exerting Christian Influence* [Englewood Cliffs, N.J.: Prentice-Hall, 1956], p. 166).

[82]For a helpful discussion of the doctrine of sin and its implications for theological ethics, see Anderson, *Walking the Way*, pp. 173-86.

[83]For a more complete discussion of this topic, see Grenz, *Theology for the Community of God*, pp. 236-45.

[84]John Jefferson Davis, *Evangelical Ethics: Issues Facing the Church Today* (Phillipsburg, N.J.: Presbyterian and Reformed, 1985), p. 14.

[85]For an example of his thinking, see Reinhold Niebuhr, *Christian Realism and Political Problems* (New York: Charles Scribner's Sons, 1953).

[86]Hence Georgia Harkness asserts, "The term 'Christian ethics,' as I shall use it, means a systematic study of the way of life exemplified and taught by Jesus, applied to the manifold problems and decisions of human existence" (*Christian Ethics* [New York: Abingdon, 1957], p. 15).

[87]White, *Biblical Ethics*, p. 231.

[88]Edmund Arens, *Christopraxis: A Theology of Action*, trans. John F. Hoffmeyer (Minneapolis: Fortress, 1995), p. 121.

[89]See the discussion of this christological theme in Grenz, *Theology for the Community of God*, pp. 344-46.

[90]For this theme see ibid., pp. 367-70.

[91]Paul L. Lehmann, *Ethics in a Christian Context* (New York: Harper & Row, 1963), p. 45.

[92]According to Trutz Rendtorff the function of eschatology is that of "providing

critical distance for ethics." He then explains, "Eschatology cannot itself be ethics and cannot take the place of ethics. It makes ethics possible and demands that it be practiced. As doctrine of the 'highest good' it represents the completion of the ethical task, but it does so in a theological manner" (*Ethics,* trans. Keith Crim [Philadelphia: Fortress, 1986], 1:187).

[93]In this sense the biblical position differs radically with all ethical systems that focus on self-actualization, whether these be philosophical or theological. Theological systems of self-actualization tend to appeal to what is ours in creation. Hence Tillich writes, "The moral imperative is the demand to become actually what one is essentially and therefore potentially. It is the power of man's being, given to him by nature, which he shall actualize in time and space. His true being shall become his actual being—this is the moral imperative" (*Morality and Beyond,* p. 20).

[94]This point is repeatedly asserted by Protestant ethicists. See, for example, Lehmann, *Ethics in a Christian Context,* pp. 131, 159, 161; Donald G. Bloesch, *Freedom for Obedience: Evangelical Ethics for Contemporary Times* (San Francisco: Harper & Row, 1987), p. 21.

[95]Lehmann, *Ethics in a Christian Context,* p. 123.

[96]Tillich rightly points out that God's gracious provision includes forgiveness and fulfillment (*Morality and Beyond,* p. 63).

[97]Wogaman describes the foundation of the ethical life as our being "secure in the realization that we are valued at the center of our being by the source of all being" (*Christian Moral Judgment,* p. 34).

[98]Bloesch, *Freedom for Obedience,* p. 9.

[99]Thielicke, *Theological Ethics,* 1:52.

[100]Only in the last few decades have ethicists rediscovered the role of the Holy Spirit in ethics. Henlee H. Barnette, for example, views his work as a conscious attempt "to provide an introduction to Christian ethics which gives more attention to the biblical basis and the role of the Holy Spirit than is usually given in current texts on the subject" (*Introducing Christian Ethics* [Nashville: Broadman, 1961], p. viii).

[101]For the New Testament foundation of this designation, see Gerhard Lohfink, *Jesus and Community: The Social Dimension of Christian Faith,* trans. John P. Galvin (Philadelphia: Fortress, 1984), p. 82.

[102]Hence Lehmann rightly asserts, "Christian ethics aims, not at morality, but at maturity" (*Ethics in a Christian Context,* p. 54).

[103]Thielicke, *Theological Ethics,* p. 47.

[104]This topic is developed in Grenz, *Theology for the Community of God,* pp. 793-97.

[105]See, for example, Birch and Rasmussen, *Bible and Ethics in the Christian Life,* pp. 102-3, 129-41.

[106]L. Gregory Jones, *Transformed Judgment: Toward a Trinitarian Account of the Moral Life* (Notre Dame, Ind.: University of Notre Dame Press, 1990), pp. 94-95.

[107]For a discussion of this theme see Timothy F. Sedgwick, *Sacramental Ethics:*

Paschal Identity and the Christian Life (Philadelphia: Fortress, 1987).

[108]For a similar statement see Huebner and Schroeder, *Church as Parable,* pp. 192-93.

[109]Ben Wiebe declares, "The ethics of Jesus is aimed toward an eschatological people of God. This ethics is a religious and ecclesial teaching. It hinges not on human nature nor on natural law nor on philosophic foundations, but on the mission and destiny of the Jesus of history" (*Messianic Ethics: Jesus' Proclamation of the Kingdom of God and the Church in Response* [Waterloo, Ont.: Herald, 1992], p. 166).

[110]The three-dimensioned mandate of the church—worship, edification and outreach—is set forth in Grenz, *Theology for the Community of God,* pp. 637-64.

[111]Robert E. Webber and Rodney Clapp, *People of the Truth: The Power of the Worshipping Community in the Modern World* (San Francisco: Harper & Row, 1988), p. 56.

[112]Philip LeMasters, *Discipleship for All Believers: Christian Ethics and the Kingdom of God* (Scottdale, Penn.: Herald, 1992), p. 88.

[113]Reinhold Niebuhr, *An Interpretation of Christian Ethics* (New York: Meridian, 1956), pp. 97-123.

Chapter 8: Comprehensive Love

[1]Gilbert C. Meilaender, *Faith and Faithfulness: Basic Themes in Christian Ethics* (Notre Dame, Ind.: University of Notre Dame Press, 1991), p. 48.

[2]For a helpful discussion of the double command, see Rudolf Schnackenburg, *The Moral Teaching of the New Testament,* trans. J. Holland-Smith and W. J. O'Hara (New York: Seabury, 1965), pp. 90-109.

[3]Ibid., p. 106.

[4]So claims Wolfgang Schrage, *The Ethics of the New Testament,* trans. David E. Green (Philadelphia: Fortress, 1988), p. 70.

[5]C. S. Lewis, *The Four Loves* (London: Collins, 1963). William Barclay (*New Testament Words* [London: SCM Press, 1964], pp. 17-18) is in fundamental agreement with Lewis. However, Paul Tillich's love quadrilateral begins with *epithymia* ("desire") rather than *storgē* (*Love, Power and Justice: Ontological Analysis and Ethical Applications* [New York: Oxford University Press, 1960], p. 28). This may suggest that no one list is exhaustive.

[6]The adjective *philostorgos* does occur once (Rom 12:10). See Barclay, *New Testament Words,* p. 18.

[7]Ibid.

[8]Gustav Stählin, "φιλέω κτλ.," in *Theological Dictionary of the New Testament,* ed. Gerhard Kittel and Gerhard Friedrich, trans. Geoffrey W. Bromiley, 10 vols. (Grand Rapids, Mich.: Eerdmans, 1964-1978), 9:136.

[9]For an intriguing discussion of the relationship of Christian *agapē* love for neighbor to the other types of love, see Søren Kierkegaard, *Works of Love: Some Christian Reflections in the Form of Discourses,* trans. Howard and Edna Hong

(New York: Harper & Row, 1962), pp. 58-72.

[10]Stählin, "φιλέω κτλ.," 9:116.

[11]Ibid., 9:128, 134.

[12]Perhaps the most significant statement is Anders Nygren, *Agape and Eros,* trans. Philip S. Watson (Philadelphia: Westminster Press, 1953). For an interesting presentation of the distinction, see Kierkegaard, *Works of Love,* pp. 282-91.

[13]Ethelbert Stauffer, "ἀγαπάω κτλ.," in *Theological Dictionary of the New Testament,* ed. Gerhard Kittel and Gerhard Friedrich, trans. Geoffrey W. Bromiley, 10 vols. (Grand Rapids, Mich.: Eerdmans, 1964-1978), 1:35.

[14]Ibid., 1:35-36.

[15]See, for example, Paul Ramsey, *Basic Christian Ethics* (New York: Charles Scribner's Sons, 1950). For a short discussion of why Christian language chose *agapē* over the other terms, see Barclay, *New Testament Words,* pp. 20-21.

[16]Stauffer writes, "The examples of ἀγάπη thus far adduced are few in number, and in many cases doubtful or hard to date" ("ἀγαπάω κτλ.," 1:37).

[17]Barclay, *New Testament Words,* p. 20.

[18]Ibid., p. 21.

[19]Stauffer, "ἀγαπάω," 1:36-37.

[20]Hence, while the Bible focuses on humankind, it is not androcentric. God and not the human person is the acting agent of the biblical narrative. And God's purposes rather than human aspirations are the goal of biblical history.

[21]Schrage, *Ethics of the New Testament,* pp. 206-7.

[22]J. Paul Sampley, *Walking Between the Times: Paul's Moral Reasoning* (Minneapolis: Fortress, 1991), pp. 37-43.

[23]John Knox concludes that for Paul love "belongs essentially within the Christian community and has meaning there which it cannot have outside" (*The Ethic of Jesus in the Teaching of the Church* [Nashville: Abingdon, 1961], p. 92).

[24]See, for example, Jack T. Sanders, *Ethics in the New Testament: Change and Development* (Philadelphia: Fortress, 1974), p. 56.

[25]Ibid., p. 63.

[26]Athanasius wrote, "Since the Father has given all things to the Son, he possesses all things afresh in the Son" (*Apologia contra Arian* 3.36).

[27]Athanasius *Contra Arian* 3.6.

[28]Augustine *The Trinity* 6.5.7; see also 15.17.27; 5.11.12; 15.19.37. For the connection of this Augustinian idea to the Greek tradition, see Yves Congar, *I Believe in the Holy Spirit,* trans. David Smith (New York: Seabury, 1983), 3:88-89, 147-48. For a contemporary delineation of this position, see David Coffey, "The Holy Spirit as the Mutual Love of the Father and the Son," *Theological Studies* 51 (1990): 193-229.

[29]Augustine *The Trinity* 15.17.27-29, 31 [491-94, 495-96]; 15.19.37 [503-4].

[30]Lewis, *Four Loves,* p. 117.

[31]Tillich, *Love, Power and Justice,* p. 116.

[32]Lewis, *Four Loves,* p. 125.

[33]Ibid., p. 122.

[34]Tillich's critique of the "lower" forms of love moves from the acknowledgment that they are in fact "different qualities of the one nature of love" which he sees as an ontological category (*Love, Power and Justice,* pp. 24-28). At the same time Tillich does want to find a connection between *agapē* and the other qualities. See Paul Tillich, *Morality and Beyond* (New York: Harper & Row, 1963), p. 40.

[35]See, for example, Stephen G. Post, "The Inadequacy of Selflessness: God's Suffering and the Theory of Love," *Journal of the American Academy of Religion* 56, no. 2 (1988): 213-28. See also James B. Nelson, *Embodiment* (Minneapolis: Augsburg, 1978), pp. 110-14; James B. Nelson, *Body Theology* (Louisville, Ky.: Westminster John Knox, 1992), p. 22.

[36]Tillich, *Love, Power and Justice,* pp. 118-19.

[37]Gilbert C. Meilaender, *Friendship: A Study in Theological Ethics* (Notre Dame, Ind.: University of Notre Dame Press, 1981), p. 18.

[38]A fuller discussion of compassion is found in Stanley J. Grenz, *Theology for the Community of God* (Nashville: Broadman & Holman, 1994), pp. 122-27.

[39]Elizabeth R. Achtemeier, "Mercy, Merciful; Compassion; Pity," in *Interpreter's Dictionary of the Bible,* ed. George Arthur Buttrick (New York: Abingdon, 1962), 3:352.

[40]Nelson is among those contemporary voices who are offering an unconditional affirmative response to this question: "Of particular importance in our time is the reclaiming of the much-neglected, much-feared *erotic* dimensions of love" (*Body Theology,* p. 23).

[41]For a lengthier discussion of creation as God's free act, see Grenz, *Theology for the Community of God,* pp. 130-33.

[42]For a discussion of the implications of this dramatic narrative in the context of sexual ethics, see Stanley J. Grenz, *Sexual Ethics* (Dallas: Word, 1990), pp. 47-48.

[43]For a discussion of *eros* as communion, see Nelson, *Embodiment,* pp. 34-35, 110, 112.

[44]For a short discussion of this, see Grenz, *Theology for the Community of God,* pp. 844-45.

[45]Nelson, *Embodiment,* p. 113.

[46]For a fuller delineation of this point, see Grenz, *Sexual Ethics,* p. 93.

[47]Tom L. Beauchamp and James F. Childress, for example, declare that although these principles "do not provide a complete system for general normative ethics, they do provide a sufficiently comprehensive framework for biomedical ethics" (*Principles of Biomedical Ethics* [New York: Oxford University Press, 1989], p. 15).

[48]Paternalism does not always take the form generally discussed by medical ethicists, namely, actions in which medical personnel override the principle of respect for the patient's autonomy. The paternalism described here is also devastating to the professional-patient relationship. Our use of *uncaring* in this context reminds us that in colloquial speech the word *care* carries emotional overtones, as is also evidenced when we blurt out, "You don't care!" Such colloquial uses are not without consequence. They keep before us the widely held convic-

tion that true caregiving includes an emotional component.

[49]*New Webster's Dictionary of the English Language*, rev. ed. (1981), s.v. "compassion."

[50]James F. Childress, *Priorities in Biomedical Ethics* (Philadelphia: Westminster Press, 1981), p. 23.

[51]Ibid., pp. 32-33.

[52]This theme has been the subject of a few preliminary explorations. For an example of a discussion from a free church perspective, see Miroslav Volf, "Kirche als Gemeinschaft: Ekklesiologische Ueberlegungen aus freikirchlicher Perspective," *Evangelische Theologie* 49, no. 1 (1989): 70-76. For developments within Roman Catholic ecclesiology, see Kilian McDonnell, "Vatican II (1962-1964), Puebla (1979), Synod (1985): *Koinonia/Communio* as an Integral Ecclesiology," *Journal of Ecumenical Studies* 25, no. 3 (1988): 414.

[53]Tillich, *Morality and Beyond*, pp. 94-95.

Epilogue

[1]Waldo Beach writes, "A doxology of mind and heart, voiced or silent, is from first to last along the vertical plane the response from which spring all the other ethical norms of Christian living along the horizontal plane" (*Christian Ethics in the Protestant Tradition* [Atlanta: John Knox, 1988], p. 32).

[2]Stuart K. Hine, "How Great Thou Art," copyright 1953, renewed 1981 by Manna Music, Inc., 25510 Avenue Stanford, Suite 101, Valencia, CA 91355. Emphasis added.

[3]This theme is becoming increasingly important in contemporary ethical discussions. For an example of how an ethicist connects worship and social ethics, see John H. Yoder, "Sacrament as Social Process: Christ the Transformer of Culture," *Theology Today* 48, no. 1 (1991): 33-44.

[4]Willi Marxsen, *New Testament Foundations for Christian Ethics*, trans. O. C. Dean Jr. (Minneapolis: Fortress, 1993), p. 225.

[5]Ralph Martin, *The Worship of God* (Grand Rapids, Mich.: Eerdmans, 1982), p. 4.

Bibliography

Abelson, Raziel. *Ethics and Metaethics: Readings in Ethical Philosophy.* New York: St. Martin's, 1963.

Achtemeier, Elizabeth R. "Mercy, Merciful; Compassion; Pity." In *Interpreter's Dictionary of the Bible,* 3:352-54. 5 vols. Edited by George Arthur Buttrick. New York: Abingdon, 1962-1976.

Albert, Ethel M., Theodore C. Denise and Sheldon P. Peterfreund. *Great Traditions in Ethics: An Introduction.* New York: American Book, 1953.

Allen, Joseph L. *Love and Conflict: A Covenantal Model of Christian Ethics.* Nashville: Abingdon, 1984.

Althaus, Paul. *The Ethics of Martin Luther.* Translated by Robert C. Schultz. Philadelphia: Fortress, 1972.

Anderson, Terence R. *Walking the Way: Christian Ethics as a Guide.* Toronto: United Church Publishing House, 1993.

Angeles, Peter A. *Dictionary of Philosophy.* New York: Harper & Row, 1981.

Aquinas, Thomas. *On the Truth of the Catholic Faith.* Edited by Anton C. Pegis. Garden City, N.Y.: Doubleday/Image, 1955.

———. *Summa Theologica.* Translated by Fathers of the Dominican Province. 1911. Westminster, Md.: Christian Classics, 1981.

Arens, Edmund. *Christopraxis: A Theology of Action.* Translated by John F. Hoffmeyer. Minneapolis: Fortress, 1995.

Aristotle. *Nicomachean Ethics.* Translated by David Ross. Revised by J. L. Ackrill and J. O. Urmson. Oxford: Oxford University Press, 1980.

———.*The Politics.* Translated by T. A. Sinclair. Revised by Trevor J. Saunders. Rev. ed. London: Penguin, 1981.

Armstrong, A. H. "St. Augustine and Christian Platonism." In *Augustine: A Collection of Critical Essays,* pp. 3-37. Edited by R. A. Markus. New York: Doubleday, 1972.

Athanasius. *Apologia Contra Arian* 3.36. Translated by Atkinson. Edited by Archibald Robertson. In *A Select Library of Nicene and Post-Nicene Fathers of the Christian Church.* Vol. 4: *St. Athanasius: Select Works and Letters.* 2nd series. Grand Rapids, Mich.: Eerdmans, 1975.

Athanasius. *Contra Arian.* In *The Early Christian Fathers.* Edited and translated by Henry Bettenson. London: Oxford University Press, 1969.

Augustine. *City of God.* Translated by Marcus Dods. In *St. Augustin's City of God and Christian Doctrine.* Vol. 4 of *The Nicene and Post-Nicene Fathers.* 1886. Reprint ed. Grand Rapids, Mich.: Eerdmans, 1973.

———. *City of God: Books VIII-XVI.* Vol. 14 of *The Fathers of the Church.* Translated by Gerald G. Walsh and Grace Monahan. Washington, D.C.: Catholic University of America Press, 1952.

———. *Concerning the Nature of Good.* In *Basic Writings of Saint Augustine.* Translated by A. H. Newman. Edited by Whitney J. Oates. New York: Random House, 1948.

———. *The Confessions of St. Augustin.* Translated by J. G. Pilkington. In *The Nicene and Post-Nicene Fathers.* 1st series. Edited by Philip Schaff. Reprint ed. Peabody, Mass.: Hendrickson, 1994.

———. *The Enchiridion on Faith, Hope and Love.* Edited by Henry Paolucci. Chicago: Henry Regnery, 1961.

———. "The Epistle of St. John." Translated by H. Browne. Revised and edited by Joseph H. Myers. In *St. Augustin: Homilies on the Gospel of John, Homilies on the First Epistle of John, Soliloquies.* Vol. 7 of *The Nicene and Post-Nicene Fathers.* 1888. Reprint ed. Grand Rapids, Mich.: Eerdmans, 1974.

———. *On Nature and Grace.* Translated by John A. Mourant and William J. Collinge. In *Saint Augustine: Four Anti-Pelagian Writings.* Vol. 86 of *The Fathers of the Church.* Washington, D.C.: Catholic University of America Press, 1992.

———. *On the Merits and Remission of Sins, and on the Baptism of Infants.* Translated by Peter Holmes and Robert Ernest. Revised by Benjamin B. Warfield. In *Saint Augustine's Anti-Pelagian Works.* Vol. 5 of *The Nicene and Post-Nicene Fathers.* Edited by Philip Schaff. 1887. Reprint ed. Grand Rapids, Mich.: Eerdmans, 1971.

———. *On the Morals of the Catholic Church.* Translated by Richard Stothert and Albert H. Newman. In *St. Augustin: The Writings Against the Manichaeans and Against the Donatists.* Vol 4. of *The Nicene and Post-Nicene Fathers.* Edited by Philip Schaff. 1887. Reprint ed. Grand Rapids, Mich.: Eerdmans, 1974.

———. *On the Morals of the Manichaeans.* Translated by Richard Stothert and Albert H. Newman. In *St. Augustin: The Writings Against the Manichaeans and Against the Donatists.* Vol. 4 of *The Nicene and Post-Nicene Fathers.* Edited by Philip Schaff. 1887. Reprint ed. Grand Rapids, Mich.: Eerdmans, 1974.

———. *The Problem of Free Choice (On Free Will).* Translated by Dom Mark Pontifex. Vol. 22 of *Ancient Christian Writers.* Edited by Johannes Quasten and Joseph C. Plumpe. New York: Newman, 1955.

Aurelius, Marcus. *Marcus Aurelius and His Times.* Roslyn, N.Y.: Walter J. Black, 1945.

Ayer, A. J. *Language, Truth and Logic.* 2nd ed. New York: Dover, 1952.

Bainton, Roland H. *Here I Stand: A Life of Martin Luther.* New York: New American Library, 1950.

———. *The Reformation of the Sixteenth Century.* Boston: Beacon, 1956.

Barclay, William. *New Testament Words.* London: SCM Press, 1964.

Barnette, Henlee H. *Introducing Christian Ethics.* Nashville: Broadman, 1961.

Barrett, Clifford L. *Ethics: An Introduction to the Philosophy of Moral Values.* New York: Harper & Brothers, 1933.

Barth, Karl. *Church Dogmatics.* Edited by G. W. Bromiley and T. F. Torrance.

Translated by A. T. MacKay et al. Edinburgh: T & T Clark, 1961.

———. *Epistle to the Romans.* Translated by Edwyn C. Hoskyns. London: Oxford University Press, 1933.

———. *Ethics.* Edited by Dietrich Braun. Translated by Geoffrey W. Bromiley. New York: Seabury, 1981.

Battenhouse, Roy W. "The Life of St. Augustine." In *A Companion to the Study of St. Augustine.* Edited by Roy W. Battenhouse. Reprint ed. Grand Rapids, Mich.: Baker, 1979.

Beach, Waldo. *Christian Ethics in the Protestant Tradition.* Atlanta: John Knox, 1988.

Beach, Waldo, and H. Richard Niebuhr. *Christian Ethics.* New York: Ronald, 1955.

———, eds. *Christian Ethics: Sources of the Living Tradition.* 2nd ed. New York: Ronald, 1973.

Beauchamp, Tom L., and James F. Childress. *Principles of Biomedical Ethics.* New York: Oxford University Press, 1989.

Beck, Robert N., and John B. Orr. *Ethical Choice: A Case Study Approach.* New York: Free Press, 1970.

Belenky, Mary Field, et al. *Women's Ways of Knowing: The Development of Self, Voice and Mind.* New York: Basic Books, 1986.

Bellinger, W. H., Jr. "The Old Testament: Sourcebook for Christian Ethics." In *Understanding Christian Ethics,* pp. 35-58. Edited by William M. Tillman Jr. Nashville: Broadman, 1988.

Bigham, Thomas J., and Albert T. Mollegen. "The Christian Ethic." In *Companion to the Study of St. Augustine,* pp. 371-97. Edited by Roy W. Battenhouse. Reprint ed. Grand Rapids, Mich.: Baker, 1979.

Birch, Bruce C. *Let Justice Roll Down: The Old Testament, Ethics and Christian Life.* Louisville, Ky.: Westminster John Knox, 1991.

———. "Moral Agency, Community and the Character of God in the Hebrew Bible." *Semeia* 66 (1994): 23-41.

Birch, Bruce C., and Larry L. Rasmussen. *Bible and Ethics in the Christian Life.* Minneapolis: Augsburg, 1976.

Bloesch, Donald G. *Freedom for Obedience: Evangelical Ethics for Contemporary Times.* San Francisco: Harper & Row, 1987.

Bonhoeffer, Dietrich. *Act and Being.* Translated by Bernard Noble. New York: Harper & Row, 1961.

———. *Christ the Center.* Translated by John Bowden. New York: Harper & Row, 1966.

———. *The Communion of the Saints: A Dogmatic Inquiry into the Sociology of the Church.* Translated by R. Gregor Smith. New York: Harper & Row, 1961.

———. *The Cost of Discipleship,* Translated by R. H. Fuller. Rev. ed. New York: Macmillan, 1959.

———. *Ethics.* Translated by Neville Horton Smith. New York: Macmillan, 1965.

———. *Letters and Papers from Prison.* Translated by Eberhard Bethge. London: Collins/Fontana, 1953.

———. *No Rusty Swords: Letters, Lectures and Notes, 1928-1936.* Translated by Edwin H. Robertson and John Bowden. New York: Harper & Row, 1965.

Bourke, Vernon J. *History of Ethics.* Garden City, N.Y.: Doubleday/Image, 1970.

Bowie, Norman E. *Making Ethical Decisions.* New York: McGraw-Hill, 1985.

Bowne, Borden P. *Principles of Ethics.* New York: Harper & Brothers, 1893.
Braaten, Carl E. "Protestants and Natural Law." *First Things,* no. 19 (January 1992): 20-26.
Brandt, Richard B. "The Real and Alleged Problems of Utilitarianism." *Hastings Center Report* 13, no. 2 (April 1983): 37-43.
———. "Toward a Credible Form of Utilitarianism." In *Morality and the Language of Conduct,* pp. 107-43. Edited by Hector-Neri Castaneda and George Nakhikian. Ft. Wayne, Ind.: Wayne State University Press, 1963.
Bromiley, Geoffrey W. "Casuistry." In *Baker's Dictionary of Christian Ethics,* pp. 1185-86. Edited by Carl F. H. Henry. Grand Rapids, Mich.: Baker, 1973.
Brown, Robert McAfee. *Gustavo Gutiérrez: An Introduction to Liberation Theology.* Maryknoll, N.Y.: Orbis, 1990.
Browne, R. W. "Analytical Introduction." In *The Nicomachean Ethics of Aristotle,* pp. v-xii. Translated by R. W. Browne. London: George Bell and Sons, 1901.
Bruce, F. F. *The Epistle to the Galatians: A Commentary on the Greek Text.* New International Greek Testament Commentary. Edited by I. Howard Marshall and W. Ward Gasque. Grand Rapids, Mich.: Eerdmans, 1982.
Bruce, W. S. *The Ethics of the Old Testament.* 2nd ed. Edinburgh: T & T Clark, 1909.
Brunner, Emil. *The Divine Imperative.* Translated by Olive Wyon. Philadelphia: Westminster Press, 1947.
Cahill, Lisa Sowle. "The New Testament and Ethics: Communities of Social Change." *Interpretation* 44, no. 4 (October 1990): 383-95.
Calvin, John. *Institutes of the Christian Religion.* Vol. 1. Translated by Ford Lewis Battles. Edited by John T. McNeill. Vol. 20 of *Library of Christian Classics.* Philadelphia: Westminster Press, 1960.
Carritt, E. F. *The Theory of Morals.* Oxford: Clarendon, 1928.
Cave, Sydney. *The Christian Way: A Study of New Testament Ethics in Relation to Present Problems.* American ed. New York: Philosophical Library, 1949.
Charry, Ellen T. "The Moral Function of Doctrine." *Theology Today* 49, no. 1 (April 1992): 31-45.
Childress, James F. *Priorities in Biomedical Ethics.* Philadelphia: Westminster Press, 1981.
Childs, James M., Jr. *Christian Anthropology and Ethics.* Philadelphia: Fortress, 1978.
Clark, Gordon H. "Calvinistic Ethics." In *Baker's Dictionary of Christian Ethics,* pp. 80-81. Edited by Carl F. H. Henry. Grand Rapids, Mich.: Baker, 1973.
Clark, Gordon H., and T. V. Smith, eds. *Readings in Ethics.* New York: Appleton Century Crofts, 1935.
———. *Readings in Ethics.* 2nd ed. New York: Appleton, 1963.
Clark, Stephen R. L. "God's Law and Morality." *Philosophical Quarterly* 32, no. 129 (October 1982): 339-47.
Coffey, David. "The Holy Spirit as the Mutual Love of the Father and the Son." *Theological Studies* 51 (June 1990): 193-229.
Colby, Anne, and Lawrence Kohlberg. *The Measurement of Moral Judgment.* Cambridge: Cambridge University Press, 1987.
Conforti, Joseph A. *Samuel Hopkins and the New Divinity Movement: Calvinism, the Congregational Ministry and Reform in New England Between the Great Awakenings.*

Washington, D.C.: Christian University Press, 1981.

Congar, Yves. *I Believe in the Holy Spirit.* Translated by David Smith. 3 vols. New York: Seabury, 1983.

Cook, E. D. "Intuitionism." In *New Dictionary of Christian Ethics and Pastoral Theology,* pp. 502-3. Edited by David J. Atkinson and David F. Field. Downers Grove, Ill.: InterVarsity Press, 1995.

Cranz, F. Edward. *An Essay on the Development of Luther's Thought in Justice, Law and Society.* Cambridge, Mass.: Harvard University Press, 1959.

Curran, Charles E., and Richard A. McCormick, eds. *Readings in Moral Theology 2: The Distinctiveness of Christian Ethics.* New York: Paulist, 1980.

Daly, Robert J., et al. *Christian Biblical Ethics.* New York: Paulist, 1984.

Davis, John Jefferson. *Evangelical Ethics: Issues Facing the Church Today.* Phillipsburg, N.J.: Presbyterian and Reformed, 1985.

De Boer, Cecil. *The If's and Ought's of Ethics.* Grand Rapids, Mich.: Eerdmans, 1936.

Demarest, Bruce A. "Revelation, General." In *Evangelical Dictionary of Theology,* pp. 944-45. Edited by Walter A. Elwell. Grand Rapids, Mich.: Baker, 1984.

Dewey, Robert E., Francis W. Gramlich and Donald Loftsgordon, eds. *Problems of Ethics.* New York: Macmillan, 1961.

Dillenberger, John. "Introduction." In *Martin Luther: Selections from His Writings,* pp. xi-xxxiii. Edited by John Dillenberger. Garden City, N.Y.: Doubleday/Anchor, 1961.

Dillistone, Frederick W. "The Anti-Donatist Writings." In *Companion to the Study of St. Augustine,* pp. 175-202. Edited by Roy W. Battenhouse. Reprint ed. Grand Rapids, Mich.: Baker, 1979.

Douma, Jochem. "The Use of Scripture in Ethics." *European Journal of Theology* 1, no. 2 (1992): 105-21.

Durkheim, Émile. *The Elementary Forms of the Religious Life.* Translated by Joseph Ward Swain. New York: Collier, 1961.

———. *On Morality and Society: Selected Writings.* Edited by Robert N. Bellah. Chicago: University of Chicago Press, 1973.

Edwards, Jonathan. *Religious Affections: How Man's Will Affects His Character Before God.* Classics of Faith and Devotion. Portland, Ore.: Multnomah Press, 1984.

Eichrodt, Walther. *Theology of the Old Testament,* Translated by J. A. Baker. Philadelphia: Westminster Press, 1961.

Eliot, T. S. *The Idea of a Christian Society and Other Writings.* London: Faber and Faber, 1982.

Ellison, H. L. *Ezekiel: The Man and His Message.* London: Paternoster, 1956.

Epictetus. *The Discourses.* Translated by W. A. Oldfather. Loeb Classical Library. Cambridge, Mass.: Harvard University Press, 1925.

———. *Enchiridion.* Translated by George Long. Philadelphia: Altemus, 1908.

———. *Enchiridion.* Translated by Thomas Wentwork Higginson. In *The Works of Epictetus.* Rev. ed. Cambridge, Mass.: Little, Brown, 1890.

Epicurus. "Letter to Herodotus." In *Letters, Principal Doctrines and Vatican Sayings.* Translated by Russel M. Geer. Library of Liberal Arts. Indianapolis: Bobbs-Merrill, 1964.

———. "Letter to Menoecceus." In *Letters, Principal Doctrines and Vatican Sayings.* Translated by Russel M. Geer. Library of Liberal Arts. Indianapolis: Bobbs-

Merrill, 1964.
Erickson, Millard J. *Relativism in Contemporary Christian Ethics.* Grand Rapids, Mich.: Baker, 1974.
Erickson, R. J. "Flesh." In *Dictionary of Paul and His Letters,* pp. 303-6. Edited by Gerald F. Hawthorne, Ralph P. Martin and Daniel G. Reid. Downers Grove, Ill.: InterVarsity Press, 1993.
Ewing, A. C. *Ethics.* London: English Universities Press, 1953.
Fee, Gordon D. *God's Empowering Presence: The Holy Spirit in the Letters of Paul.* Peabody, Mass.: Hendrickson, 1994.
Feinberg, Joel. "The Nature and Value of Rights." *The Journal of Value Inquiry* 4 (Winter 1970): 243-57.
Feldman, Fred. *Introductory Ethics.* Englewood Cliffs, N.J.: Prentice-Hall, 1978.
Fletcher, Joseph. *Situation Ethics: The New Morality.* Philadelphia: Westminster Press, 1966.
Forell, George W. *Faith Active in Love: An Investigation of the Principles Underlying Luther's Social Ethics.* Minneapolis: Augsburg, 1954.
Fowl, Stephen E., and L. Gregory Jones. *Reading in Communion: Scripture and Ethics in Christian Life.* Grand Rapids, Mich.: Eerdmans, 1991.
Frankena, William. *Ethics.* 2nd ed. Englewood Cliffs, N.J.: Prentice-Hall, 1973.
Frend, W. H. C. "Augustinianism." In *Westminster Dictionary of Christian Theology,* pp. 55-58. Edited by Alan Richardson and John Bowden. Philadelphia: Westminster Press, 1983.
Furnish, Victor Paul. *Theology and Ethics in Paul.* Nashville: Abingdon, 1968.
Gamwell, Franklin I. "Religion and the Justification of Moral Claims." *Journal of Religious Ethics* 11, no. 1 (Spring 1983): 35-61.
Geertz, Clifford. *The Interpretation of Cultures: Selected Essays.* New York: Basic Books, 1973.
Geisler, Norman L. *Christian Ethics.* Grand Rapids, Mich.: Baker, 1989.
———. *Ethics: Alternatives and Issues.* Grand Rapids, Mich.: Zondervan, 1971.
———. "Thomas Aquinas." In *Evangelical Dictionary of Theology,* pp. 1091-92. Edited by Walter A. Elwell. Grand Rapids, Mich.: Baker, 1984.
Gerhardsson, Birger. *The Ethos of the Bible.* Translated by Stephen Westerholm. Philadelphia: Fortress, 1981.
Gibbs, Jeffery. "The Grace of God as the Foundation for Ethics." *Concordia Theological Quarterly* 48, nos. 2-3 (1984): 185-201.
Gill, Robin. *A Textbook of Christian Ethics.* Edinburgh: T & T Clark, 1985.
Gilligan, Carol. *In a Different Voice: Psychological Theory and Women's Development.* Cambridge, Mass.: Harvard University Press, 1982.
Gilligan, Carol, Janie Victoria Ward and Jill McLean Taylor, eds. *Mapping the Moral Domain: A Contribution of Women's Thinking to Psychological Theory and Education.* Cambridge, Mass.: Harvard University Press, 1988.
Glickman, Jack, ed. *Moral Philosophy: An Introduction.* New York: St. Martin's, 1976.
Goldberg, Michael. *Theology and Narrative.* Nashville: Abingdon, 1982.
Greene, Theodore M. "The Historical Context and Religious Significance of Kant's *Religion.*" In *Religion Within the Limits of Reason Alone* by Immanuel Kant, pp. ix-lxxviii. Translated by Theodore M. Greene and Hoyt H. Hudson. New

York: Harper & Row, 1960.
Grenz, Stanley J. "Abortion—A Christian Response." *Conrad Grebel Review* 2, no. 1 (Winter 1984): 21-30.
———. *Created for Community: Connecting Christian Belief with Christian Living.* Wheaton, Ill.: Victor/BridgePoint, 1996.
———. "The Flight from God." In *Christian Freedom: Essays in Honor of Vernon Grounds,* pp. 69-85. Edited by Kenneth W. M. Wozniak and Stanley J. Grenz. Lanham, Md.: University Press of America, 1986.
———. *Sexual Ethics.* Dallas: Word, 1990.
———. *Theology for the Community of God.* Nashville: Broadman and Holman, 1994.
Grisez, Germain, and Russell Shaw. *Beyond the New Morality: The Responsibilities of Freedom.* Rev. ed. Notre Dame, Ind.: University of Notre Dame Press, 1980.
Guroian, Vigen. *Ethics After Christendom: Toward an Ecclesial Christian Ethic.* Grand Rapids, Mich.: Eerdmans, 1995.
———. "The Shape of Orthodox Ethics." *Epiphany Journal* 12, no. 1 (Fall 1991): 8-21.
Gustafson, James M. *Christian Ethics and the Community.* New York: Pilgrim, 1979.
Gustafson, James M. *Ethics from a Theocentric Perspective.* 2 vols. Chicago: University of Chicago Press, 1981.
Gutiérrez, Gustavo. *The Power of the Poor in History.* London: SCM Press, 1983.
———. *A Theology of Liberation.* Translated and edited by Sister Caridad Inda and John Eagleson. Maryknoll, N.Y.: Orbis, 1988.
Hackstaff, L. H. "Introduction." In *Augustine: On Free Choice of the Will,* pp. ix-xxix. Translated by Anna S. Benjamin and L. H. Hackstaff. Indianapolis: Bobbs-Merrill, 1964.
Handy, R. T. "Walter Rauschenbusch in Historical Perspective." *The Baptist Quarterly* 20, no. 7 (July 1964): 313-21.
Hanigan, James P. *Martin Luther King Jr. and the Foundations of Nonviolence.* Lanham, Md.: University Press of America, 1984.
Happel, Stephen, and James J. Walter. *Conversion and Discipleship: A Christian Foundation for Ethics and Doctrine.* Philadelphia: Fortress, 1986.
Hardy, Edward R., Jr. "The City of God." In *Companion to the Study of St. Augustine,* pp. 257-83. Edited by Roy W. Battenhouse. Reprint ed. Grand Rapids, Mich.: Baker, 1979.
Hare, R. M. *The Language of Morals.* Reprint ed. London: Oxford University Press, 1969.
Harkness, Georgia. *Christian Ethics.* New York: Abingdon, 1957.
Hauerwas, Stanley. *The Community of Character.* Notre Dame, Ind.: Notre Dame University Press, 1981.
———. *The Peaceable Kingdom: A Primer in Christian Ethics.* Notre Dame, Ind.: University of Notre Dame Press, 1983.
———. "The Testament of Friends." *Christian Century* 107, no. 7 (February 28, 1990): 212-16.
———. *Truthfulness and Tragedy.* Notre Dame, Ind.: University of Notre Dame Press, 1977.
———. *Vision and Virtue.* Notre Dame, Ind.: Fides, 1974.

Hebblethwaite, Brian. *Christian Ethics in the Modern Age.* Philadelphia: Westminster Press, 1982.

Held, Virginia. "The Validity of Moral Theories." *Zygon* 18, no. 2 (June 1983): 167-81.

Helvetius, Claude Adrien. *Treatise on Man: His Intellectual Faculties and His Education.* New York: Burt Franklin, 1969.

Henry, Carl F. H. *Aspects of Christian Social Ethics.* Grand Rapids, Mich.: Eerdmans, 1964.

———. *The Christian Mindset in a Secular Society.* Portland, Ore.: Multnomah Press, 1984.

———. *Christian Personal Ethics.* Grand Rapids, Mich.: Eerdmans, 1957.

———. *Evangelical Responsibility in Contemporary Theology.* Grand Rapids, Mich.: Eerdmans, 1957.

———. *God, Revelation and Authority.* 6 vols. Waco, Tex.: Word, 1976-1983.

———. *The God Who Shows Himself.* Waco, Tex.: Word, 1966.

———. *A Plea for Evangelical Demonstration.* Grand Rapids, Mich.: Baker, 1971.

———. *The Protestant Dilemma.* Grand Rapids, Mich.: Eerdmans, 1949.

———. *The Uneasy Conscience of Modern Fundamentalism.* Grand Rapids, Mich.: Eerdmans, 1947.

Henry, Paul B. "Natural Law." In *Baker's Dictionary of Christian Ethics,* pp. 448-50. Edited by Carl F. H. Henry. Grand Rapids, Mich.: Baker, 1973.

Higginson, Richard. *Dilemmas: A Christian Approach to Moral Decision Making.* Louisville, Ky.: Westminister John Knox, 1988.

Hine, Stuart K. "How Great Thou Art." Copyright 1953, renewed 1981 by Manna Music Inc., 25510 Avenue Stanford, Suite 101, Valencia, CA 91355.

Hobbes, Thomas. *Leviathan.* 1651. Reprint ed. New York: Collier, 1962.

Hodge, A. A. *The Outlines of Theology.* Edited by William H. Goold. London: T. Nelson and Sons, 1870.

Holbrook, Clyde A. "H. Richard Niebuhr." In *A Handbook of Christian Theologians,* pp. 375-95. Edited by Martin E. Marty and Dean C. Peerman. Nashville: Abingdon, 1965.

Holmes, Arthur F. *Ethics: Approaching Moral Decisions.* Downers Grove, Ill.: InterVarsity Press, 1984.

Holtz, Traugott. "The Question of the Content of Paul's Instructions." In *Understanding Paul's Ethics: Twentieth Century Approaches,* pp. 51-71. Edited by Brian S. Rosner. Grand Rapids, Mich.: Eerdmans, 1995.

Hovey, Alvah. *Commentary on the Epistle to the Galatians.* In vol. 5 of *An American Commentary on the New Testament.* Edited by Alvah Hovey. Philadelphia: American Baptist Publication Society, 1890.

Hoyer, Paul M. "Law and Gospel: With Particular Attention to the Third Use of the Law." *Concordia Journal* 6, no. 5 (September 1980): 189-201.

Huebner, Harry, and David Schroeder. *Church as Parable: Whatever Happened to Ethics?* Winnipeg, Man.: CMBC Publications, 1993.

Hughes, Philip Edgcumbe. *Christian Ethics in Secular Society.* Grand Rapids, Mich.: Baker, 1983.

Hume, David. *Treatise of Human Nature.* 1739. Reprint ed. London: J. M. Dent and Sons, 1911.

Irenaeus. *Against Heresies.* Translated by Alexander Roberts and W. H. Rambaut. Edited by Alexander Roberts and James Donaldson. In *The Apostolic Fathers: Justin Martyr, Irenaeus.* Vol. 1 of *Ante-Nicene Fathers.* Edited by A. Cleveland Coxe. 1885. Reprint ed. Grand Rapids, Mich.: Eerdmans, 1975.

Jacob, Edmond. *Theology of the Old Testament.* Translated by Arthur W. Heathcote and Philip J. Allcock. New York: Harper & Row, 1958.

Janzen, Waldemar. *Old Testament Ethics: A Paradigmatic Approach.* Louisville, Ky.: Westminster John Knox, 1994.

Jones, L. Gregory. *Transformed Judgment: Toward a Trinitarian Account of the Moral Life.* Notre Dame, Ind.: University of Notre Dame Press, 1990.

Kaiser, Walter C. *Toward Old Testament Ethics.* Grand Rapids, Mich.: Zondervan, 1983.

Kane, Robert. *Through the Moral Maze: Searching for Absolute Values in a Pluralistic World.* New York: Paragon, 1994.

Kant, Immanuel. *Critique of Pure Reason.* Translated by Norman Kemp Smith. London: Macmillan, 1933.

———. *Fundamental Principles of the Metaphysic of Morals.* Translated by Thomas K. Abbott. Indianapolis: Bobbs-Merrill, 1949.

———. *Groundwork of the Metaphysic of Morals.* Translated by H. J. Paton. New York: Harper & Row, 1964.

Käsemann, Ernst. *Jesus Means Freedom.* Translated by Frank Clark. Philadelphia: Fortress, 1970.

Keesecker, William F. "The Law in John Calvin's Ethics." In *Calvin and Christian Ethics,* pp. 14-49. Edited by Peter De Klerk. Grand Rapids, Mich.: Calvin Studies Society, 1987.

Keyser, Leander S. *A System of General Ethics.* 4th ed. Burlington, Ia: Lutheran Literary Board, 1934.

Kierkegaard, Søren. *Fear and Trembling.* Translated by Alastair Hannay London: Penguin, 1985.

———. *Works of Love: Some Christian Reflections in the Form of Discourses.* Translated by Howard and Edna Hong. New York: Harper & Row, 1962.

King, Coretta Scott. "Creative Suffering: The Ripple of Hope." *National Catholic Reporter,* April 2, 1969, p. 6.

King, Martin Luther, Jr. "Letter from Birmingham City Jail." In *A Testament of Hope: The Essential Writings of Martin Luther King Jr.,* pp. 289-302. Edited by James Melvin Washington. 1963. Reprint ed. San Francisco: Harper & Row, 1986.

———. *Stride Toward Freedom: The Montgomery Story.* New York: Harper & Row, 1964.

———. *Where Do We Go from Here? Chaos or Community.* New York: Harper & Row, 1967.

Kirk, G. S., and J. E. Raven. *The Presocratic Philosophers.* Cambridge: Cambridge University Press, 1957.

Kis, Miroslav. "Moral Rules and Exceptions," *Andrews University Seminary Studies* 30, no. 1 (Spring 1992): 15-33.

Kittay, Eva Feder, and Diana T. Meyers, eds. *Women and Moral Theory.* Totowa, N.J.: Rowman & Littlefield, 1987.

Klann, Richard. "Lutheran Ethics." In *Baker's Dictionary of Christian Ethics,* pp. 398-400. Edited by Carl F. H. Henry. Grand Rapids, Mich.: Baker, 1973.

Knox, John. *The Ethic of Jesus in the Teaching of the Church.* Nashville: Abingdon, 1961.

Kruse, C. G. "Law." In *New Dictionary of Christian Ethics and Pastoral Theology,* pp. 539-40. Edited by David J. Atkinson et al. Downers Grove, Ill.: InterVarsity Press, 1995.

Landau, Sidney I., and Ronald J. Bogus, ed. *The Doubleday Dictionary for Home, School and Office.* Garden City, N.Y.: Doubleday, 1975.

Lane, Dermot A. *Foundations for a Social Theology: Praxis, Process and Salvation.* New York: Paulist, 1984.

"Legal Ethics of Using DNA Samples Pondered." *The Vancouver Sun,* August 31, 1994.

———. "The Anti-Pelagian Writings." In *Companion to the Study of St. Augustine,* pp. 203-34. Edited by Roy W. Battenhouse. Reprint ed. Grand Rapids, Mich.: Baker, 1979.

Lehmann, Paul L. *Ethics in a Christian Context.* New York: Harper & Row, 1963.

Leibniz, Gottfried Wilhelm. *Theodicy.* Translated by E. M. Huggard. Abridged by Diogenes Allen. Don Mills, Ont.: J. M. Dent, 1966.

LeMasters, Philip. *Discipleship for All Believers: Christian Ethics and the Kingdom of God.* Scottdale, Penn.: Herald, 1992.

Lewis, C. S. *The Four Loves.* London: Collins, 1963.

———. *Mere Christianity.* New York: Macmillan, 1960.

Lewis, Gordon R., and Bruce A. Demarest. *Integrative Theology.* Grand Rapids, Mich.: Zondervan, 1990.

Lindbeck, George A. "Confession and Community: An Israel-like View of the Church." *Christian Century* 107 (May 9, 1990): 492-96.

Locke, John. *The Second Treatise of Government.* Edited by Thomas P. Peardon. Library of Liberal Arts. Indianapolis: Bobbs-Merrill, 1953.

Lohfink, Gerhard. *Jesus and Community: The Social Dimension of Christian Faith.* Translated by John P. Galvin. Philadelphia: Fortress, 1984.

Lohse, Eduard. "The Church in Everyday Life." Translated by George S. Rosner and Brian S. Rosner. In *Understanding Paul's Ethics: Twentieth Century Approaches,* pp. 251-65. Edited by Brian S. Rosner. Grand Rapids, Mich.: Eerdmans, 1995.

———. *Theological Ethics of the New Testament.* Translated by M. Eugene Boring. Minneapolis: Fortress, 1991.

Long, Edward LeRoy, Jr. *A Survey of Christian Ethics.* New York: Oxford University Press, 1967.

Longenecker, Richard N. "New Testament Social Ethics for Today." In *Understanding Paul's Ethics: Twentieth Century Approaches,* pp. 337-50. Edited by Brian S. Rosner. Grand Rapids, Mich.: Eerdmans, 1995.

Loomis, Louise Ropes. "Introduction." In *Aristotle: On Man and the Universe,* pp. vii-xxxviii. Edited by Louise Ropes Loomis. Roslyn, N.Y.: Walter J. Black, 1943.

Luck, William. "Moral Conflicts and Evangelical Ethics: A Second Look at the Salvaging Operations." *Grace Theological Journal* 8, no. 1 (Spring 1987): 19-34.

Lucretius. *The Nature of Things.* Translated by Frank O. Copley. New York: W. W.

Norton, 1977.

Luther, Martin. *Lectures on Galatians Ch. 1-4* (1535). Vol. 26 of *Luther's Works.* Edited and translated by Jaroslav Pelikan. St. Louis, Mo.: Concordia Publishing House, 1963.

———. "Letter to Philip Melanchthon: Wartburg 1 August 1521." Letter 91. In *Letters I.* Edited and translated by Gottfried G. Krodel. Vol. 48 of *Luther's Works.* Edited by Helmut T. Lehmann. Philadelphia: Fortress, 1963.

———. "An Open Letter on the Harsh Book Against the Peasents." Translated by Charles M. Jacobs. In *The Christian Society III,* pp. 57-85. Edited by Robert C. Schultz. Vol 46 of *Luther's Works.* Edited by Helmut T. Lehmann. Philadelphia: Fortress, 1967.

———. "Temporal Authority: To What Extent Should It Be Obeyed?" Translated by J. J. Schindel. In *The Christian Society II,* pp. 75-129. Edited by Walther I. Brandt. Vol. 45 of *Luther's Works.* Edited by Helmut T. Lehmann. Philadelphia: Fortress, 1966.

———. "Treatise on Good Works." Translated by W. A. Lambert. In *The Christian Society I,* pp. 15-114. Edited by James Atkinson. Vol. 44 of *Luther's Works.* Edited by Helmut T. Lehmann. Philadelphia: Fortress, 1966.

———. "Von den Guten Werken" (1520). In *D. Martin Luthers Werke, kritische Gesammtausgabe,* 6:196-276. Edited by J. K. F. Knaake et al. Weimar, Germany: Hermann Boehlau, 1888.

Luther, Martin. "Whether Soldiers, Too, Can Be Saved." Translated by Charles M. Jacobs. In *The Christian Society III,* pp. 87-137. Edited by Robert C. Schultz. Vol. 46 of *Luther's Works.* Edited by Helmut T. Lehmann. Philadelphia: Fortress, 1967.

Lutzer, Erwin W. *The Necessity of Ethical Absolutes.* Grand Rapids, Mich.: Zondervan, 1981.

Lyotard, Jean-François. *The Postmodern Condition: A Report on Knowledge.* Translated by Geoff Bennington and Brian Massumi. Minneapolis: University of Minnesota Press, 1984.

MacIntyre, Alasdair. *After Virtue: A Study in Moral Theory.* 2nd ed. Notre Dame, Ind.: University of Notre Dame Press, 1984.

———. *A Short History of Ethics.* New York: Macmillan, 1966.

———. "Which God Ought We to Obey and Why?" *Faith and Philosophy* 3, no. 4 (October 1986): 359-71.

Maritain, Jacques. *The Rights of Man and Natural Law.* London: Geoffrey Bles/Centenary, 1944.

Marshall, L. H. *The Challenge of New Testament Ethics.* London: Macmillan, 1947.

Martin, Ralph. *The Worship of God.* Grand Rapids, Mich.: Eerdmans, 1982.

Marxsen, Willi. *New Testament Foundations for Christian Ethics.* Translated by O. C. Dean Jr. Minneapolis: Fortress, 1993.

Maston, T. B. *Biblical Ethics.* Macon, Ga.: Mercer University Press, 1982.

Mattson, A. D. *Christian Ethics: The Basis and Content of the Christian Life.* Revised ed. Rock Island, Ill.: Augustana Book Concern, 1947.

Mayo, Bernard. *Ethics and the Moral Life.* London: Macmillan, 1958.

McCabe, Herbert. "Thomism." In *Westminster Dictionary of Christian Theology,* pp. 568-71. Edited by Alan Richardson and John S. Bowden. Philadelphia:

Westminster Press, 1983.

McClendon, James William. *Ethics: Systematic Theology.* Vol. 1. Nashville: Abingdon, 1986.

McConnell, Terrance C. "Moral Blackmail." *Ethics* 91, no. 4 (July 1981): 544-67.

McDermott, Timothy. "Editor's Note." In *Summa Theologiae: A Concise Translation,* by Thomas Aquinas, pp. xiii-xv. Edited by Timothy McDermott. Westminster, Md.: Christian Classics, 1989.

———. "Preface: What the *Summa* Is About." In *Summa Theologiae: A Concise Translation* by Thomas Aquinas, pp. xvii-lviii. Westminster, Md.: Christian Classics, 1989.

McDonnell, Kilian. "Vatican II (1962-1964), Puebla (1979), Synod (1985): *Koinonia/Communio* as an Integral Ecclesiology." *Journal of Ecumenical Studies* 25, no. 3 (Summer 1988): 399-427.

McFayden, Alistair I. *The Call to Personhood: A Christian Theory of the Individual in Social Relationships.* Cambridge: Cambridge University Press, 1990.

McGrath, Alister E. "Doctrine and Ethics." *Journal of the Evangelical Theological Society* 34, no. 2 (June 1991): 145-56.

———. "In What Way Can Jesus Be a Moral Example for Christians?" *Journal of the Evangelical Theological Society* 34, no. 3 (September 1991): 289-98.

McInerny, Ralph. *St. Thomas Aquinas.* Notre Dame, Ind.: University of Notre Dame Press, 1977.

McKeon, Richard. "Introduction." In *Introduction to Aristotle,* pp. ix-xxix. Edited by Richard McKeon. New York: Random House/Modern Library, 1947.

McQuilkin, Robertson. *An Introduction to Biblical Ethics.* Wheaton, Ill.: Tyndale House, 1989.

Meeks, Wayne A. *The Origins of Christian Morality: The First Two Centuries.* New Haven, Conn.: Yale University Press, 1993.

Meilaender, Gilbert C. *Faith and Faithfulness: Basic Themes in Christian Ethics.* Notre Dame, Ind.: University of Notre Dame Press, 1991.

———. *Friendship: A Study in Theological Ethics.* Notre Dame, Ind.: University of Notre Dame Press, 1981.

Meredith, Anthony. "Aristotelianism." In *Westminster Dictionary of Christian Theology,* pp. 41-42. Edited by Alan Richardson and John S. Bowden. Philadelphia: Westminster Press, 1983.

Mill, John Stuart. *Utilitarianism, Liberty and Representative Government.* London: J. M. Dent and Sons, 1910.

Miltner, Charles C. *The Elements of Ethics.* New York: Macmillan, 1948.

Montgomery, John Warwick. *Human Rights and Human Dignity.* Grand Rapids, Mich.: Zondervan/Probe, 1986.

Moore, G. E. *Principia Ethica.* London: Cambridge University Press, 1959.

Mott, Stephen Charles. "The Use of the Bible in Social Ethics II: The Use of the New Testament, Part 1." *Transformation* 1, no. 2 (April-June 1984): 21-26.

Motyer, J. A. "Law, Biblical Concept of." In *Evangelical Dictionary of Theology,* pp. 623-25. Edited by Walter A. Elwell. Grand Rapids, Mich.: Baker, 1984.

Mourant, John A. *Introduction to the Philosophy of Saint Augustine: Selected Readings and Commentaries.* University Park: University of Pennsylvania Press, 1964.

Muirhead, J.H. *The Elements of Ethics: An Introduction to Moral Philosophy.* New

York: Charles Scribner's Sons, 1898.

Muller, Richard A. *Dictionary of Latin and Greek Theological Terms: Drawn Principally from Protestant Scholastic Theology.* Grand Rapids, Mich.: Baker, 1985.

Murray, John. *Principles of Conduct: Aspects of Biblical Ethics.* Grand Rapids, Mich.: Eerdmans, 1957.

Nelson, James B. *Body Theology.* Louisville, Ky.: Westminster John Knox, 1992.

———. *Embodiment.* Minneapolis: Augsburg, 1978.

Nelson, Paul. *Narrative and Morality: A Theological Inquiry.* University Park: Pennsylvania State University Press, 1987.

Niebuhr, Reinhold. *Christian Realism and Political Problems.* New York: Charles Scribner's Sons, 1953.

———. *An Interpretation of Christian Ethics.* New York: Meridian, 1956.

Niebuhr, H. Richard. *The Kingdom of God in America.* Chicago: Willett Clark, 1937.

Nielsen, Kai. "God and the Basis of Morality." *Journal of Religious Ethics* 10, no. 2 (1982): 335-50.

———. "Why Should I Be Moral?" Reprinted in *Moral Philosophy: An Introduction,* pp. 191-204. Edited by Jack Glickman. New York: St. Martin's, 1976.

Nietzsche, Friedrich. *On the Genealogy of Morality.* Translated by Carol Diethe. Edited by Keith Ansell-Pearson. Cambridge: Cambridge University Press, 1994.

Noddings, Nel. *Caring: A Feminine Aproach to Ethics and Moral Education.* Berkeley: Universtity of California Press, 1984.

Nowell-Smith, P. H. *Ethics.* Harmondsworth, Middlesex, England: Penguin, 1954.

Nygren, Anders. *Agape and Eros.* Translated by Philip S. Watson. Philadelphia: Westminster Press, 1953.

O'Brien, Elmer. "Introduction." In *The Essential Plotinus: Representative Treatises from the Enneads,* pp. 13-32. Translated by Elmer O'Brien. New York: Mentor, 1964.

O'Connell, Robert J. "Action and Contemplation." In *Augustine: A Collection of Critical Essays,* pp. 38-58. Edited by R. A. Marks. New York: Doubleday, 1972.

O'Donovan, Oliver. *Resurrection and Moral Order: An Outline for Evangelical Ethics.* Grand Rapids, Mich.: Eerdmans, 1986.

Ogletree, Thomas W. *The Use of the Bible in Christian Ethics.* Philadelphia: Fortress, 1983.

Okholm, D. L. "Flesh." In *New Dictionary of Christian Ethics and Pastoral Theology,* pp. 382-83. Edited by David J. Atkinson et al. Downers Grove, Ill.: InterVarsity Press, 1995.

O'Neil, Robert F., and Darlene A. Pienta. "Economic Criteria Versus Ethical Criteria: Toward Resolving a Basic Dilemma in Business." *Journal of Business Ethics* 13, no. 1 (1994): 71-78.

Ott, Heinrich. *Reality and Faith: The Theological Legacy of Dietrich Bonhoeffer.* Translated by Alex A. Morrison. Philadelphia: Fortress, 1972.

Parsons, Michael. "Being Precedes Act: Indicative and Imperative in Paul's Writing." In *Understanding Paul's Ethics: Twentieth Century Approaches,* pp. 217-247. Edited by Brian S. Rosner. Grand Rapids, Mich.: Eerdmans, 1995.

Pegis, Anton C. "Introduction." In *Introduction to Saint Thomas Aquinas,* pp. xi-xxx. Edited by Anton C. Pegis. New York: Modern Library, 1945.

Perry, Ralph Barton. *Realms of Value: A Critique of Human Civilization.* Cambridge, Mass.: Harvard University Press, 1954.

Phillips, John A. *Christ for Us in the Theology of Dietrich Bonhoeffer.* New York: Harper & Row, 1967.

Pinches, Charles. "Principle Monism and Action Descriptions: Situationism and Its Critics Revisited." *Modern Theology* 7, no. 3 (April 1991): 255.

Pinnock, Clark H. "Autonomy." In *Baker's Dictionary of Christian Ethics,* p. 48. Edited by Carl F. H. Henry. Grand Rapids, Mich.: Baker, 1973.

———. "Heteronomy." In *Baker's Dictionary of Christian Ethics,* p. 288. Edited by Carl F. H. Henry. Grand Rapids, Mich.: Baker, 1973.

Piper, John. *Desiring God: Meditations of a Christian Hedonist.* Portland, Ore.: Multnomah Press, 1986.

Plato. *Euthyphro.* In *The Dialogues of Plato.* Translated by Benjamin Jowett. Edited by R. M. Hare and D. A. Russell. London: Sphere, 1970.

———. *Phaedrus.* Translated by R. Hackforth. In *Plato: The Collected Dialogues.* Edited by Edith Hamilton and Huntington Cairns. Princeton, N.J.: Princeton University Press, 1963.

———. *Protagoras.* Translated by W. K. C. Guthrie. In *Plato: The Collected Dialogues.* Edited by Edith Hamilton and Huntington Cairns. Princeton, N.J.: Princeton University Press, 1963.

———. *The Republic.* Translated by Desmond Lee. 2nd ed. London: Penguin, 1987.

Plotinus. *Enneads.*

Porter, Jean. *The Recovery of Virtue: The Relevance of Aquinas for Christian Ethics.* Louisville, Ky.: Westminster John Knox, 1990.

Post, Stephen G. "The Inadequacy of Selflessness: God's Suffering and the Theory of Love." *Journal of the American Academy of Religion* 56, no. 2 (Summer 1988): 213-28.

Pybus, Elizabeth M. "False Dichotomies: Right and Good." *Philosophy* 58, no. 223 (January 1983): 19-27.

Quanbeck, Warren A. "Anders Nygren." In *A Handbook of Christian Theologians,* pp. 297-307. Edited by Martin E. Marty and Dean G. Peerman. Nashville: Abingdon, 1965.

Rae, Scott B. *Moral Choices: An Introduction to Ethics.* Grand Rapids, Mich.: Zondervan, 1995.

Rakestraw, Robert V. "Ethical Choices: A Case for Non-conflicting Absolutism." *Criswell Theological Review* 2, no. 2 (Spring 1988): 239-67.

Ramsey, Paul. *Basic Christian Ethics.* New York: Charles Scribner's Sons, 1950.

———. *Deeds and Rules in Christian Ethics.* Scottish Journal of Theology Occasional Papers 11. Edinburgh: Oliver and Boyd, 1965.

Rankin, H. D. *Plato and the Individual.* London: Methuen, 1964.

Rasmussen, Albert Terrill. *Christian Social Ethics: Exerting Christian Influence.* Englewood Cliffs, N.J.: Prentice-Hall, 1956.

Rauschenbusch, Walter. *Christianity and the Social Crisis.* New York: Macmillan, 1907.

———. *Theology for the Social Gospel.* Nashville: Abingdon, 1978.

Rawls, John. *A Theory of Justice.* Cambridge, Mass.: Belknap, 1971.

Reese, W. L. *Dictionary of Philosophy and Religion.* Atlantic Highlands, N.J.:

Humanities, 1980.
Rendtorff, Trutz. *Ethics.* Translated by Keith Crim. Philadelphia: Fortress, 1986.
Ridderbos, Herman. *Paul: An Outline of His Theology.* Translated by John Richard De Witt. Grand Rapids, Mich.: Eerdmans, 1975.
Robertson, Edwin H. "Bonhoeffer's Christology." In *Christ the Center,* by Dietrich Bonhoeffer. Translated by John Bowden. New York: Harper & Row, 1966.
Robins, Henry E. *The Ethics of the Christian Life: The Science of Right Living.* Philadelphia: Griffith & Rowland, 1904.
Robinson, H. Wheeler. *The Christian Doctrine of Man.* 3rd ed. Edinburgh: T & T Clark, 1926.
Robinson, N. H. G. *The Groundwork of Christian Ethics.* Grand Rapids, Mich.: Eerdmans, 1971.
Rogers, Daniel. *Naaman the Syrian, His Disease and Cure.* 1642. Reprint ed. Ann Arbor, Mich.: University Microfilms International, 1983 (R1799).
Rosner, Brian S. "`That Pattern of Teaching': Issues and Essays in Pauline Ethics." In *Understanding Paul's Ethics: Twentieth Century Approaches,* pp. 1-23. Edited by Brian S. Rosner. Grand Rapids, Mich.: Eerdmans, 1995.
Ross, W. D. *The Right and the Good.* Oxford: Clarendon, 1930.
Rousseau, Jean-Jacques. *The Social Contract.* Translated by Willmoore Kendall. Chicago: Henry Regnery, 1954.
Ruether, Rosemary Radford. *Gaia and God: An Ecofeminist Theology of Earth Healing.* San Francisco: Harper & Row, 1992.
Sahakian, William S. *Ethics: An Introduction to Theories and Problems.* New York: Barnes & Noble Books, 1974.
———. *Systems of Ethics and Value Theory.* New York: Philosophical Library, 1963.
Sampley, J. Paul. *Walking Between the Times: Paul's Moral Reasoning.* Minneapolis: Fortress, 1991.
Sanders, Jack T. *Ethics in the New Testament: Change and Development.* Philadelphia: Fortress, 1974.
Schindler, David L. "Introduction: Grace and the Form of Nature and Culture." In *Catholicism and Secularization in America,* pp. 10-30. Edited by David L. Schindler. Notre Dame, Ind.: Communio, 1990.
Schnabel, Eckhard J. "How Paul Developed His Ethics." In *Understanding Paul's Ethics: Twentieth Century Approaches,* pp. 267-97. Edited by Brian S. Rosner. Grand Rapids, Mich.: Eerdmans, 1995.
Schnackenburg, Rudolf. *The Moral Teaching of the New Testament.* Translated by J. Holland-Smith and W. J. O'Hara. New York: Seabury, 1965.
Schrage, Wolfgang. *The Ethics of the New Testament.* Translated by David E. Green. Philadelphia: Fortress, 1988.
Schwarz, Hans. *Evil: A Historical and Theological Perspective.* Translated by Mark W. Worthing. Minneapolis: Fortress, 1995.
Sedgwick, Timothy F. *Sacramental Ethics: Paschal Identity and the Christian Life.* Philadelphia: Fortress, 1987.
Shakespeare, William. *As You Like It.*
Sheldon, Charles M. *In His Steps: "What Would Jesus Do?"* 1896. Reprint ed. New York: Grosset and Dunlap, 1935.
Sherwood, David A. "Doing the Right Thing: Ethical Practice in Contemporary

Society." *Social Work and Christianity* 20, no. 2 (Fall 1993): 140-59.
Sidgwick, Henry. *Outlines of the History of Ethics.* Boston: Beacon, 1960.
Smith, Adam. *An Inquiry into the Nature and Causes of the Wealth of Nations.* Chicago: Encyclopedia Britannica, 1952.
Smith, Harmon L. *Where Two or Three Are Gathered: Liturgy and the Moral Life.* Cleveland: Pilgrim, 1995.
Smith, T. V., and William Debbins. *Constructive Ethics.* Englewood Clifs, N.J.: Prentice-Hall, 1948.
Smurl, James F. *Religious Ethics: A Systems Approach.* Englewood Cliffs, N.J.: Prentice-Hall, 1972.
Smyth, Newman. *Christian Ethics.* New York: Charles Scribner's Sons, 1906.
Stählin, Gustav. "φιλέω κτλ." In *Theological Dictionary of the New Testament,* 9:114-71. 10 vols. Edited by Gerhard Kittel and Gerhard Friedrich. Translated by Geoffrey W. Bromiley. Grand Rapids, Mich.: Eerdmans, 1964-1976.
Stauffer, Ethelbert. "ἀγαπάω κτλ." In *Theological Dictionary of the New Testament,* 1:21-55. 10 vols. Edited by Gerhard Kittel and Gerhard Friedrich, Translated by Geoffrey W. Bromiley. Grand Rapids, Mich.: Eerdmans, 1964-1976.
Steele, Scott. "Truth or Consequences." *Macleans* 108, no. 1 (1995): 14-17.
Steuer, Axel D. "The Relgious Justification for Morality." *International Journal of the Philosophy of Religion* 13, no. 3 (1982): 157-68.
Stevenson, Charles L. *Ethics and Language.* New Haven, Conn.: Yale University Press, 1944.
Tawney, R. H. *Religion and the Rise of Capitalism.* London: John Murray, 1926.
Taylor, Paul W. *Normative Discourse.* Englewood Cliffs, N.J.: Prentice-Hall, 1961.
Taylor, Richard. *Good and Evil: A New Direction.* New York: Macmillan, 1970.
ten Boom, Corrie. *The Hiding Place.* Washington Depot, Conn.: Chosen Books, 1971.
Thielicke, Helmut. *Theological Ethics.* Edited by William H. Lazareth. 3 vols. Grand Rapids, Mich.: Eerdmans, 1979.
———. *Theological Ethics.* Translated by John W. Doberstein. Edited by William H. Lazareth. Philadelphia: Fortress, 1966.
Tillich, Paul. *Love, Power and Justice: Ontological Analysis and Ethical Applications.* New York: Oxford University Press, 1960.
———. *Morality and Beyond.* New York: Harper & Row, 1963.
Todd, Douglas. "What on Earth Happens Next?" *The Vancouver Sun,* December 31, 1994.
Volf, Miroslav. "Kirche als Gemeinschaft: Ekklesiologische Ueberlegungen aus freikirchlicher Perspective." *Evangelische Theologie* 49, no. 1 (1989): 52-76.
von Rad, Gerhard. *Old Testament Theology.* Translated by D. M. G. Stalker. New York: Harper & Row, 1962.
Walker, Williston. "Compassion." In *The International Standard Bible Encyclopedia,* 2:695. 5 vols. Grand Rapids, Mich.: Eerdmans, 1915.
Walter, Victor L. "Donatism." In *Evangelical Dictionary of Theology,* pp. 329-30. Edited by Walter A. Elwell. Grand Rapids, Mich.: Baker, 1984.
Warner, Rex. *The Greek Philosophers.* New York: Mentor, 1958.

Webber, Robert E., and Rodney Clapp. *People of the Truth: The Power of the Worshipping Community in the Modern World.* San Francisco: Harper & Row, 1988.

Welch, Claude. *Protestant Theology in the Nineteenth Century: Volume 2, 1870-1914.* New Haven, Conn.: Yale University Press, 1985.

Wellman, Carl. *Morals and Ethics.* Glenview, Ill.: Scott, Foresman, 1975.

Wendel, François. *Calvin: The Origins and Development of His Religious Thought.* Translated by Philip Mairet. New York: Harper & Row, 1963.

Wenham, Gordon. "Grace and Law in the Old Testament." In *Law, Morality and the Bible,* pp. 3-23. Edited by Bruce Kaye and Gordon Wenham. Downers Grove, Ill.: InterVarsity Press, 1978.

White, R. E. O. *Biblical Ethics.* Atlanta: John Knox, 1979.

———. *Christian Ethics.* Atlanta: John Knox, 1981.

Wiebe, Ben. *Messianic Ethics: Jesus' Proclamation of the Kingdom of God and the Church in Response.* Waterloo, Ont.: Herald, 1992.

Wild, John. "Authentic Existence, A New Approach to Value Theory." In *An Invitation to Phenomenology,* pp. 59-77. Edited by James M. Edie. New York: Quadrangle/New York Times Book Co., 1965.

Wilkens, Steve. *Beyond Bumper Sticker Ethics.* Downers Grove, Ill.: InterVarsity Press, 1995.

Wilkinson, Loren. "Gaia Spirituality: A Christian Critique." *Evangelical Review of Theology* 17 (April 1993): 176-89.

Williams, J. R. "Holiness." In *Evangelical Dictionary of Theology,* pp. 514-16. Edited by Walter A. Elwell. Grand Rapids, Mich.: Baker, 1984.

Wogaman, J. Philip. *Christian Ethics: A Historical Introduction.* Louisville, Ky.: Westminster John Knox, 1993.

———. *Christian Moral Judgment.* Louisville, Ky.: Westminster John Knox, 1989.

World Council of Churches, *Signs of the Spirit: Official Report, Seventh Assembly, Canberra Australia, 7-20 February 1991.* Edited by Michael Kinnamon. Geneva: WCC Publications; Grand Rapids, Mich.: Eerdmans, 1991.

Wright, Christopher J. H. "The Ethical Authority of the Old Testament: A Survey of Approaches." *Tyndale Bulletin* 43, no. 1 (May 1992): 101-20.

———. "The Ethical Authority of the Old Testament: A Survey of Approaches. Part II." *Tyndale Bulletin* 43, no. 2 (November 1992): 203-21.

———. "The Use of the Bible in Social Ethics: Paradigms, Types and Eschatology." *Transformation* 1, no. 1 (January-March 1984): 11-20.

Wright, Henry W. *Self-Realization.* New York: Henry Holt, 1913.

Yoder, John Howard. *The Politics of Jesus.* Grand Rapids, Mich.: Eerdmans. 1972.

———. "Sacrament as Social Process: Christ the Transformer of Culture." *Theology Today* 48, no. 1 (April 1991): 33-44.

Author and Name Index

Subject Index

Scripture Index